Robert Jordan's

The Wheel of Time®

NEW SPRING

Robert Jordan's

The Wheel of Time®

NEW SPRING

TOR®

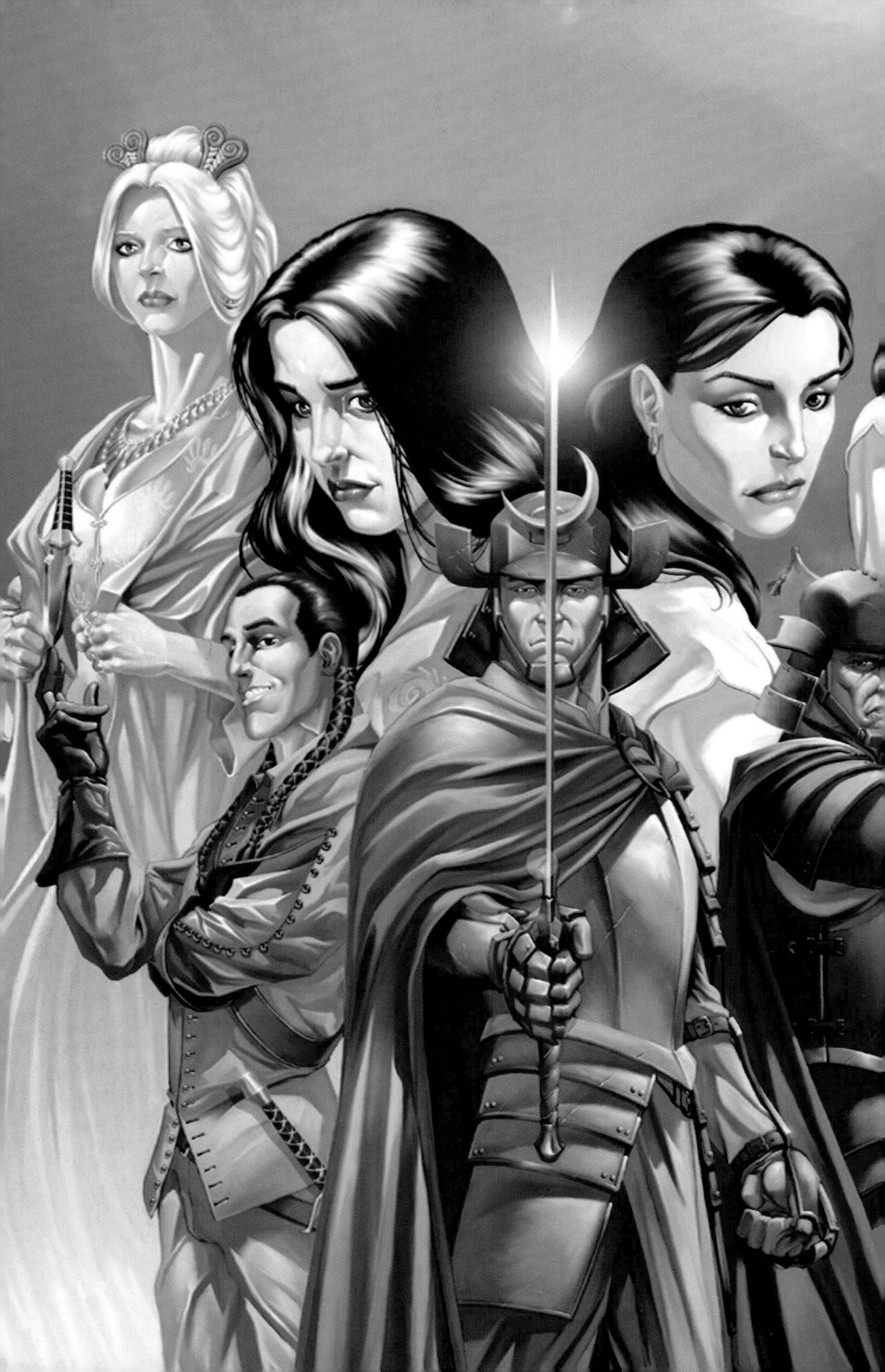

written by
ROBERT JORDAN

adapted by
CHUCK DIXON

artwork by
MIKE MILLER
HARVEY TOLIBAO
JOSEPH COOPER

colors by
ETIENNE ST. LAURENT
KIERAN OATES

lettered by
DAVE LANPHEAR
BILL TORTOLINI

original series edited by
ERNST DABEL
DEREK RUIZ

thematic consultants
MARIA SIMONS
and **BOB KLUTTZ**

consultation
ERNST DABEL
and **LES DABEL**

Collection edits by: DEREK RUIZ and DAVID LAWRENCE
Collection design by: BILL TORTOLINI

DYNAMITE
ENTERTAINMENT®

www.dynamiteentertainment.com
NICK BARRUCCI • PRESIDENT
JUAN COLLADO • CHIEF OPERATING OFFICER
JOSEPH RYBANDT • EDITOR
JOSH JOHNSON • CREATIVE DIRECTOR
JASON ULLMEYER • GRAPHIC DESIGNER

TOR®
A Tor Book
Published by Tom Doherty Associates, LLC
175 Fifth Avenue
New York, NY 10010
www.tor-forge.com

Tor® is a registered trademark of Tom Doherty Associates, LLC.

ISBN 978-0-7653-2380-4

First Edition: January 2011

Printed in the United States of America

Table of Contents

AN INTRODUCTION TO

THE WHEEL OF TIME

The world of THE WHEEL OF TIME lies in both our future
and our past, a world of kings and queens and Aes Sedai,
women who can wield saidar, the female half of the One Power,
which turns the Wheel and drives the universe. A world
where the war between the Light and the Shadow is fought every day.
At the moment of Creation, the Creator bound the Dark One
away from the world, but more than three thousand years ago
Aes Sedai, then both men and women, unknowingly bored
into that prison outside of time. The Dark One was only able
to touch the world lightly, and the hole was eventually sealed over,
but the Dark One's taint settled on saidin, the male half of the Power.
Every male Aes Sedai went mad, and in the Breaking of the
World they destroyed civilization and changed the very face of earth,
sinking mountains beneath the sea and bringing new seas where
land had been. Now only women bear the title Aes Sedai.
Commanded by their Amyrlin Seat and divided into seven Ajahs
named by color, they rule the great island city of Tar Valon,
where their White Tower is located.

Men still are born who can learn to channel the Power,
or worse, will channel one day whether they try to or not.
Doomed to madness, destruction, and death by the
taint on saidin, they are hunted down by Aes Sedai and
gentled, cut off forever from the Power for the safety of
the world. No man goes to this willingly. Even if they
survive the hunt, they seldom survive long after gentling.
For more than three thousand years, while nations and
empires rose and fell, nothing has been so feared as a man
who can channel. But for all those years there have been
the Prophecies of the Dragon, that the seals on the
Dark One's prison will weaken and he will touch the world
once more, that the Dragon, who sealed up that hole,
will be Reborn to face the Dark One again. A child,
born in sight of Tar Valon on the slopes of Dragonmount,
who will grow to be The Dragon Reborn.
The only hope of humanity in the Last Battle.

-- Robert Jordan

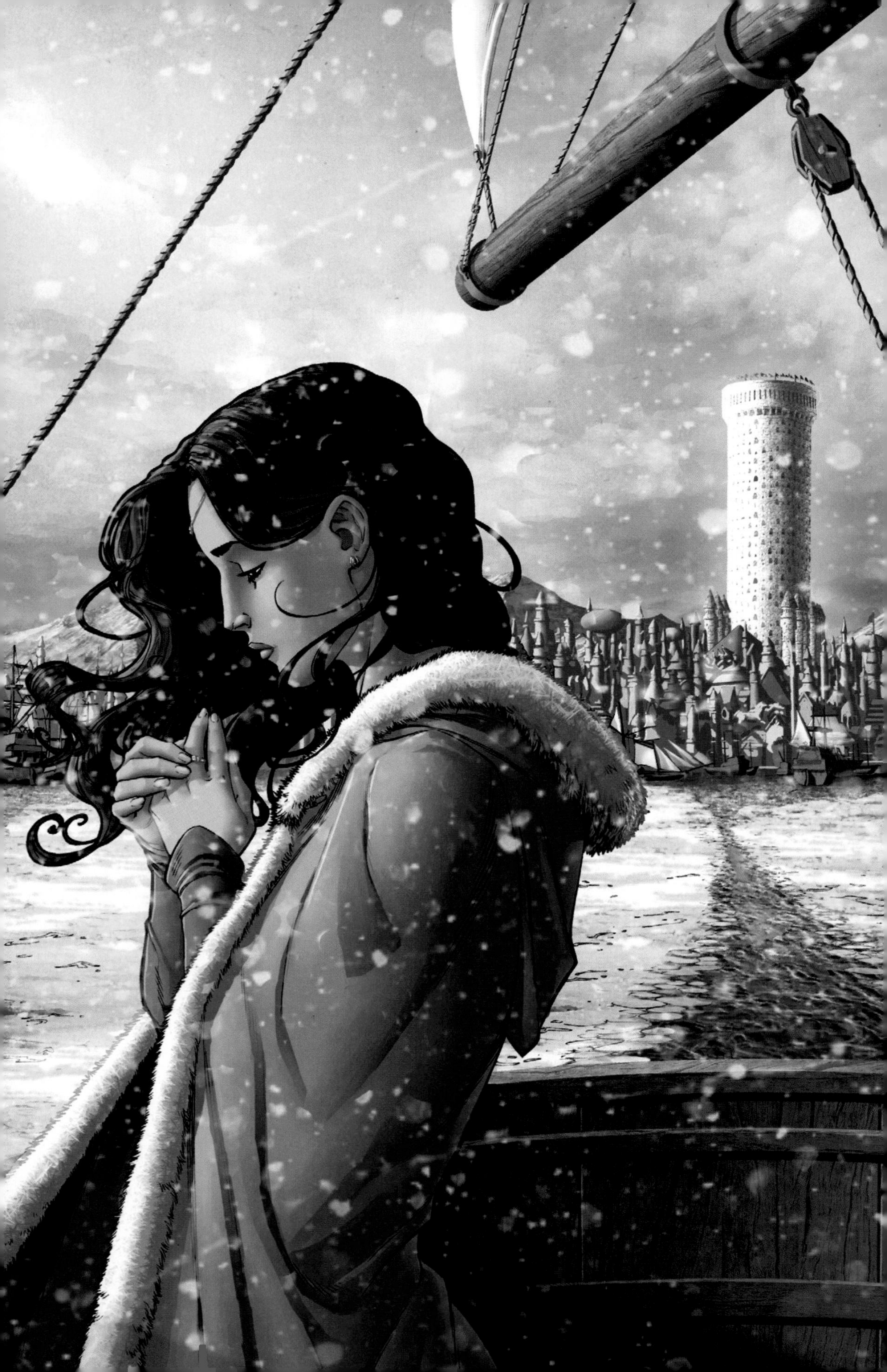

chapter one

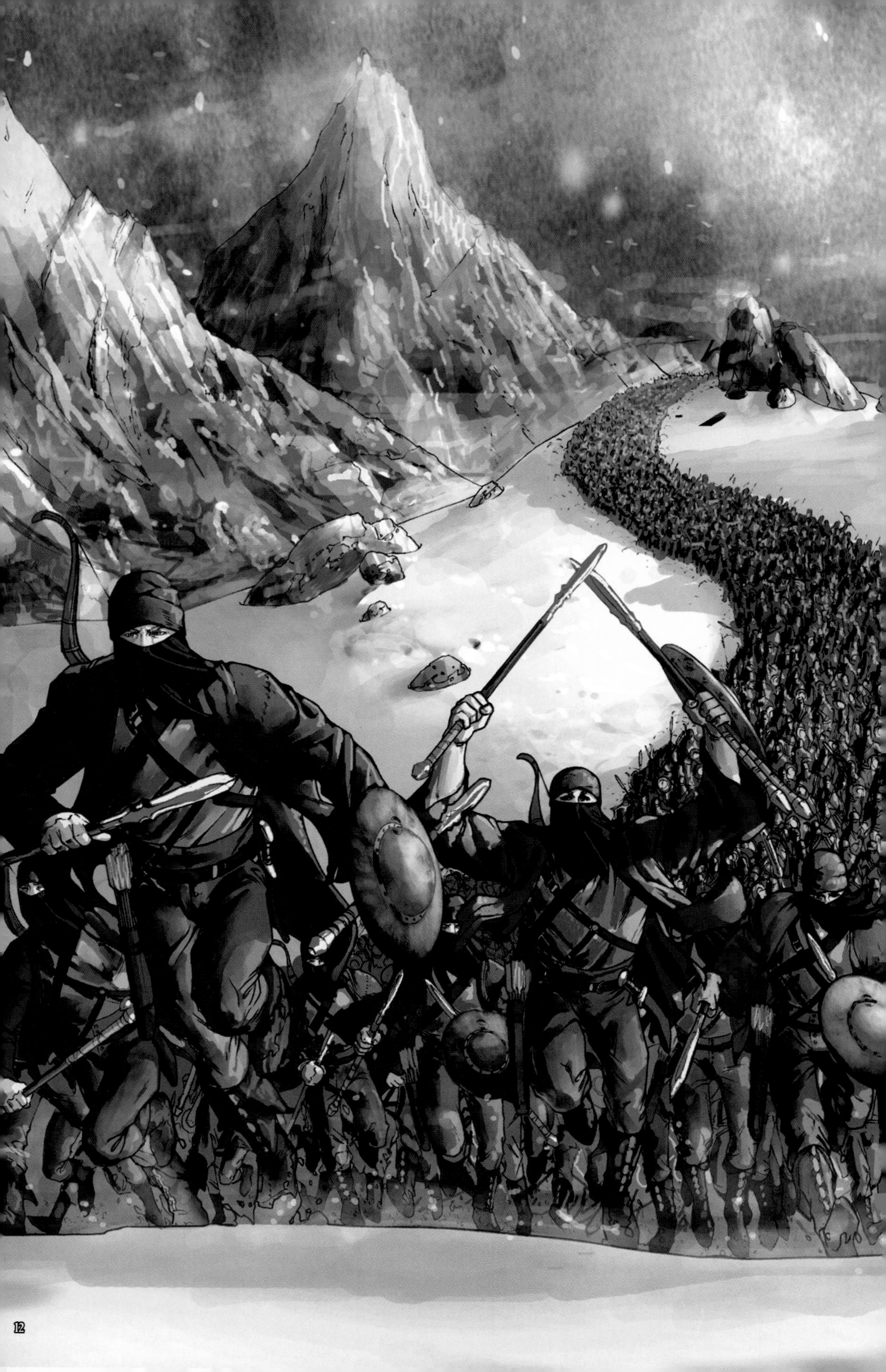

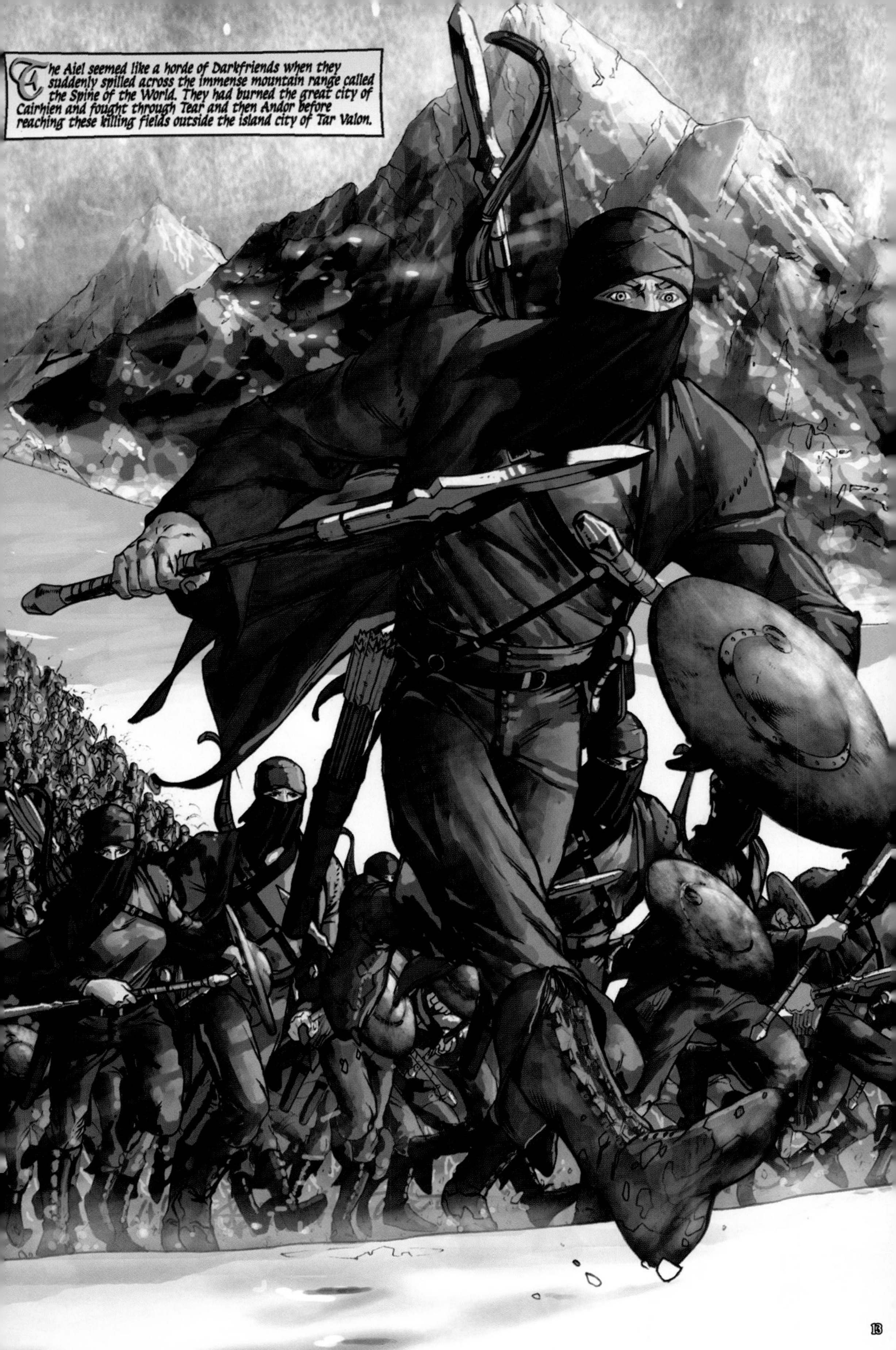
The Aiel seemed like a horde of Darkfriends when they suddenly spilled across the immense mountain range called the Spine of the World. They had burned the great city of Cairhien and fought through Tear and then Andor before reaching these killing fields outside the island city of Tar Valon.

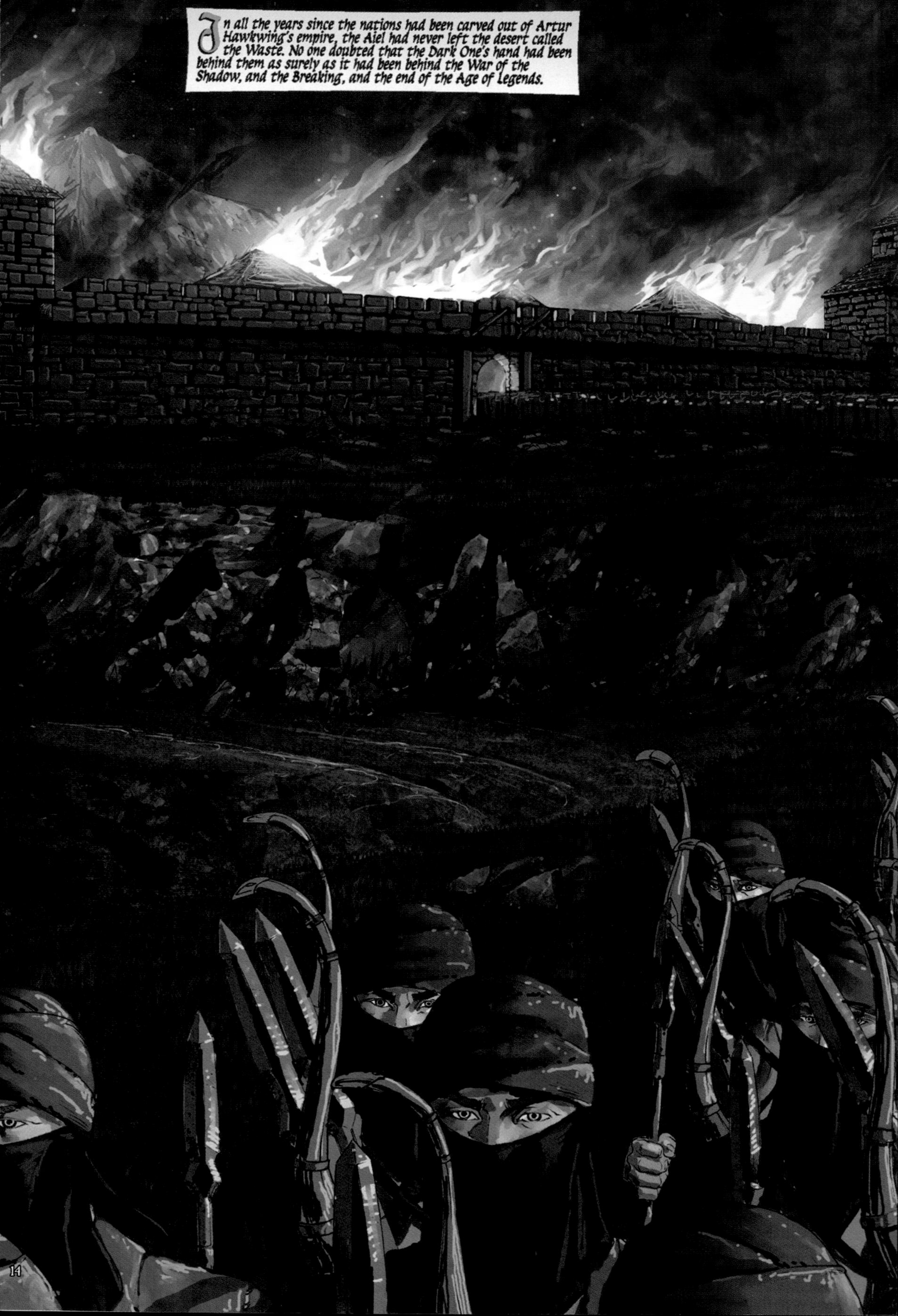
In all the years since the nations had been carved out of Artur Hawkwing's empire, the Aiel had never left the desert called the Waste. No one doubted that the Dark One's hand had been behind them as surely as it had been behind the War of the Shadow, and the Breaking, and the end of the Age of Legends.

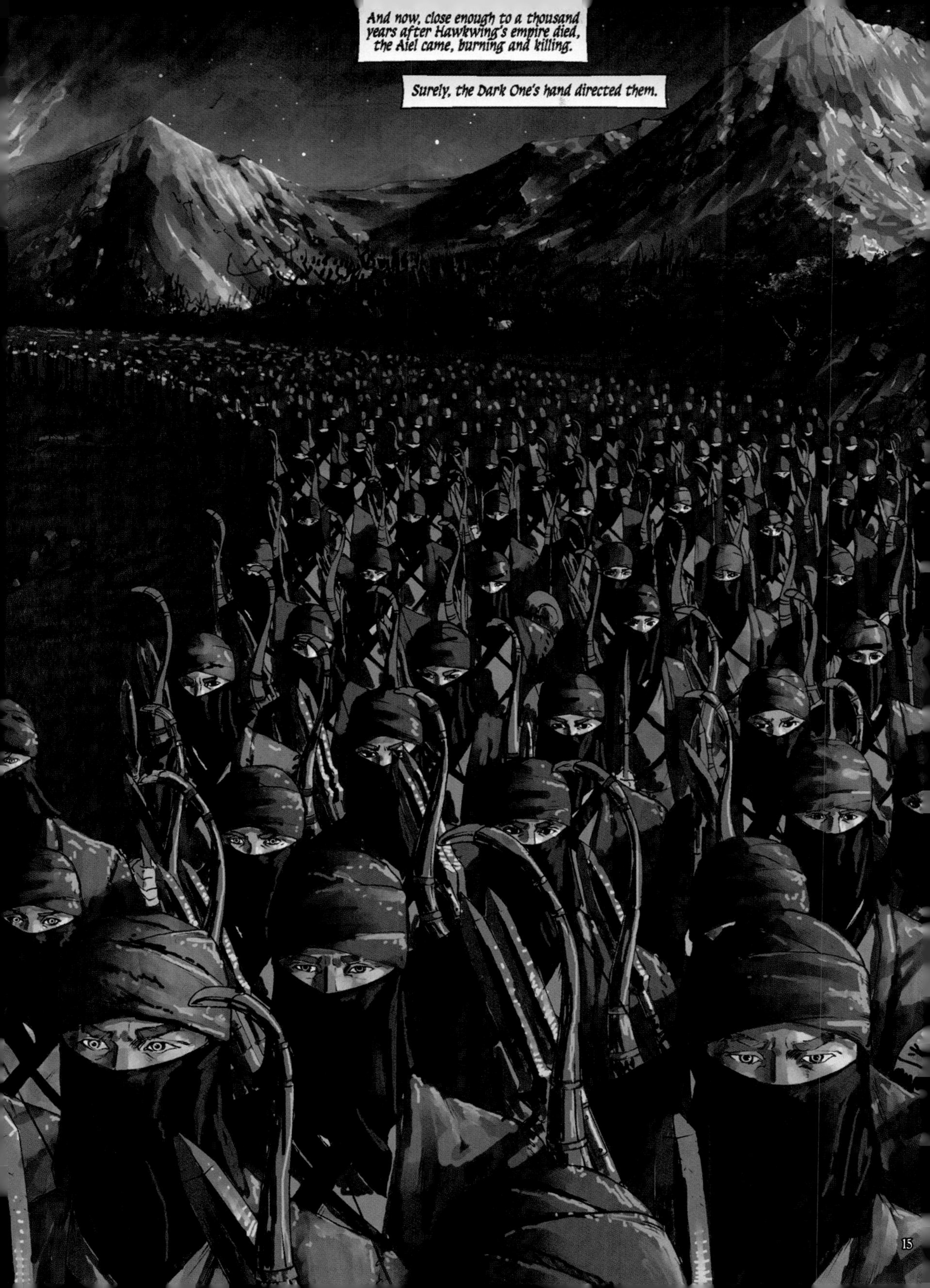
And now, close enough to a thousand years after Hawkwing's empire died, the Aiel came, burning and killing.
Surely, the Dark One's hand directed them.

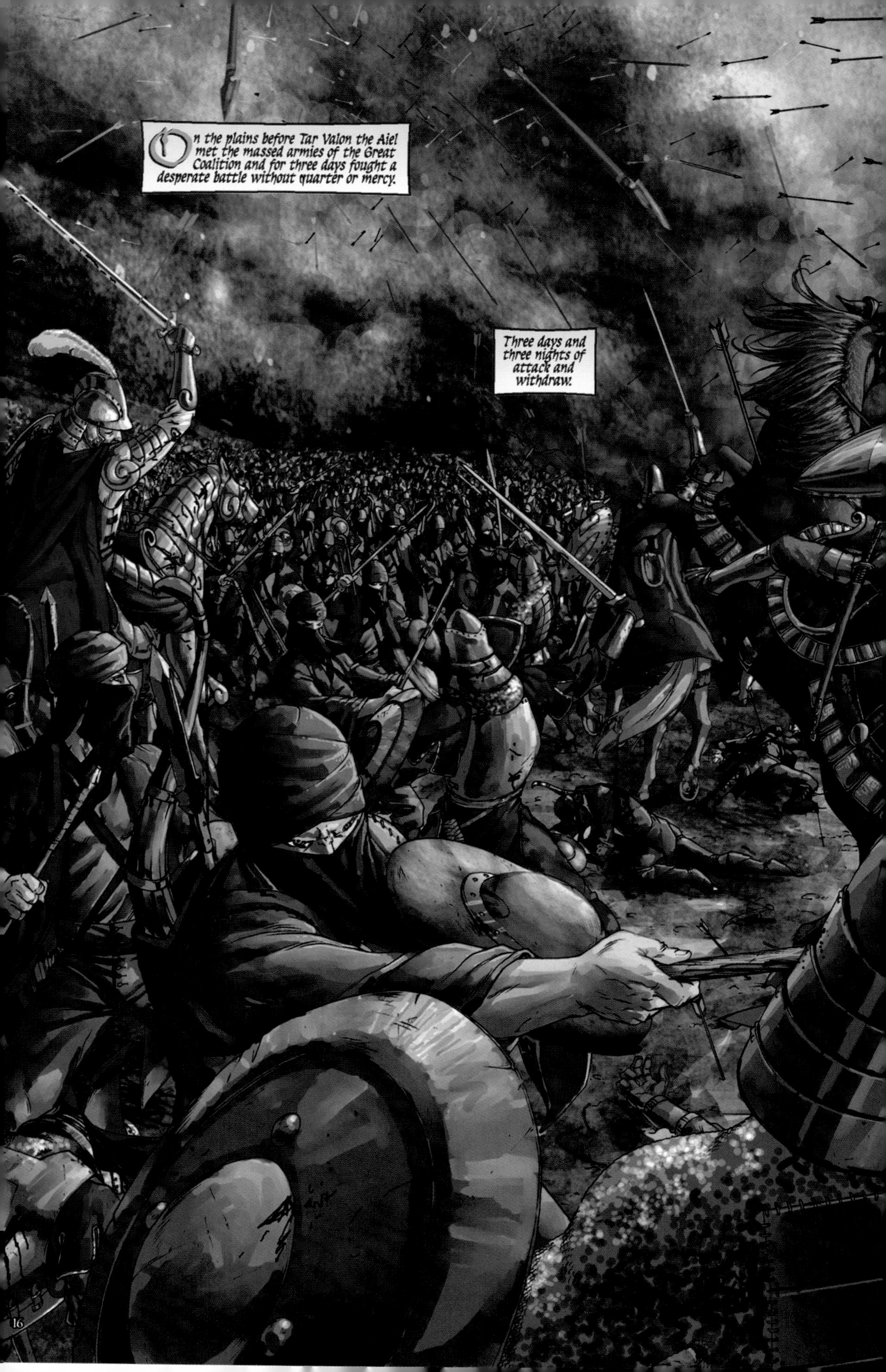
On the plains before Tar Valon the Aiel met the massed armies of the Great Coalition and for three days fought a desperate battle without quarter or mercy.
Three days and three nights of attack and withdraw.

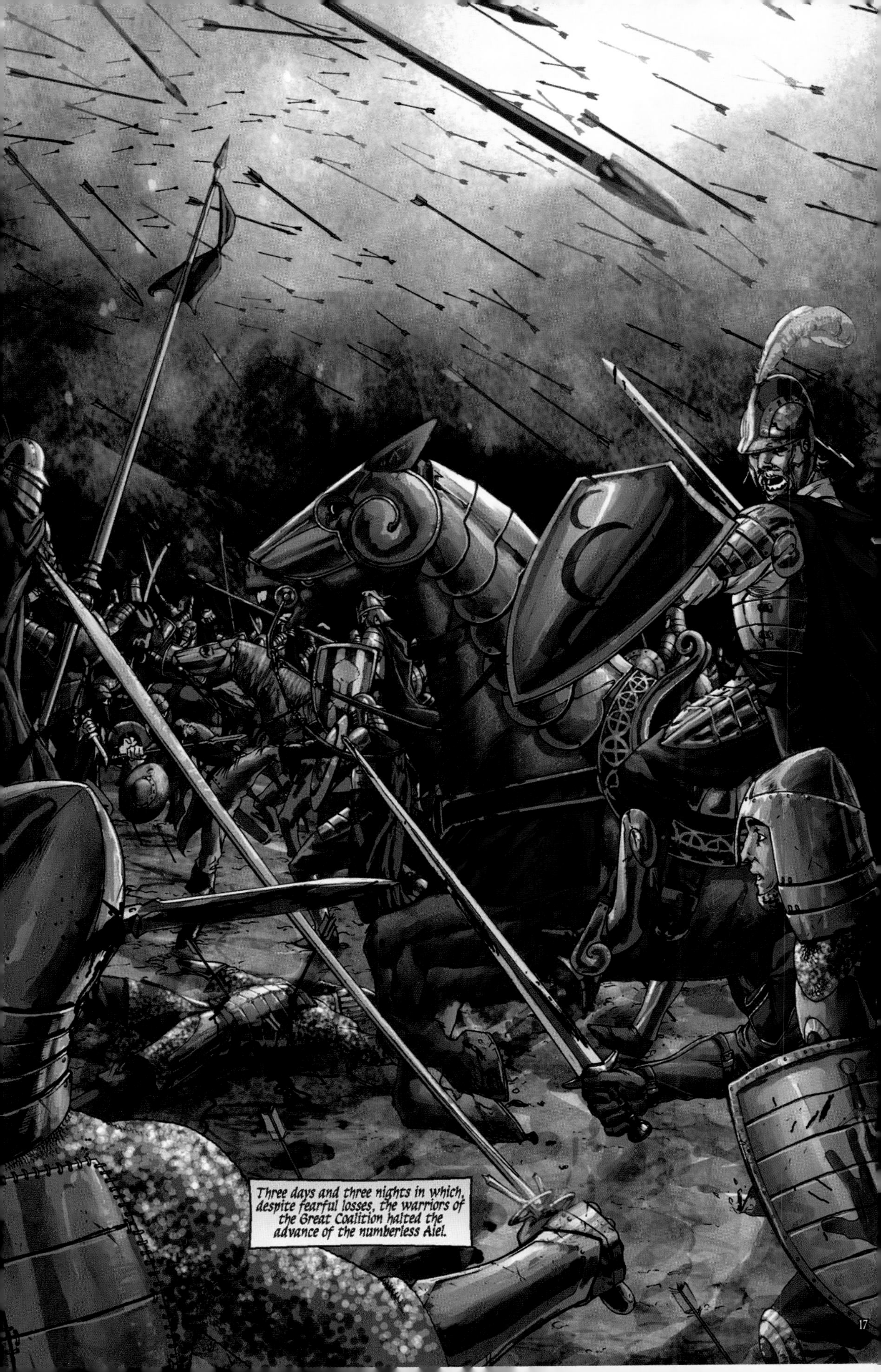
Three days and three nights in which, despite fearful losses, the warriors of the Great Coalition halted the advance of the numberless Aiel.

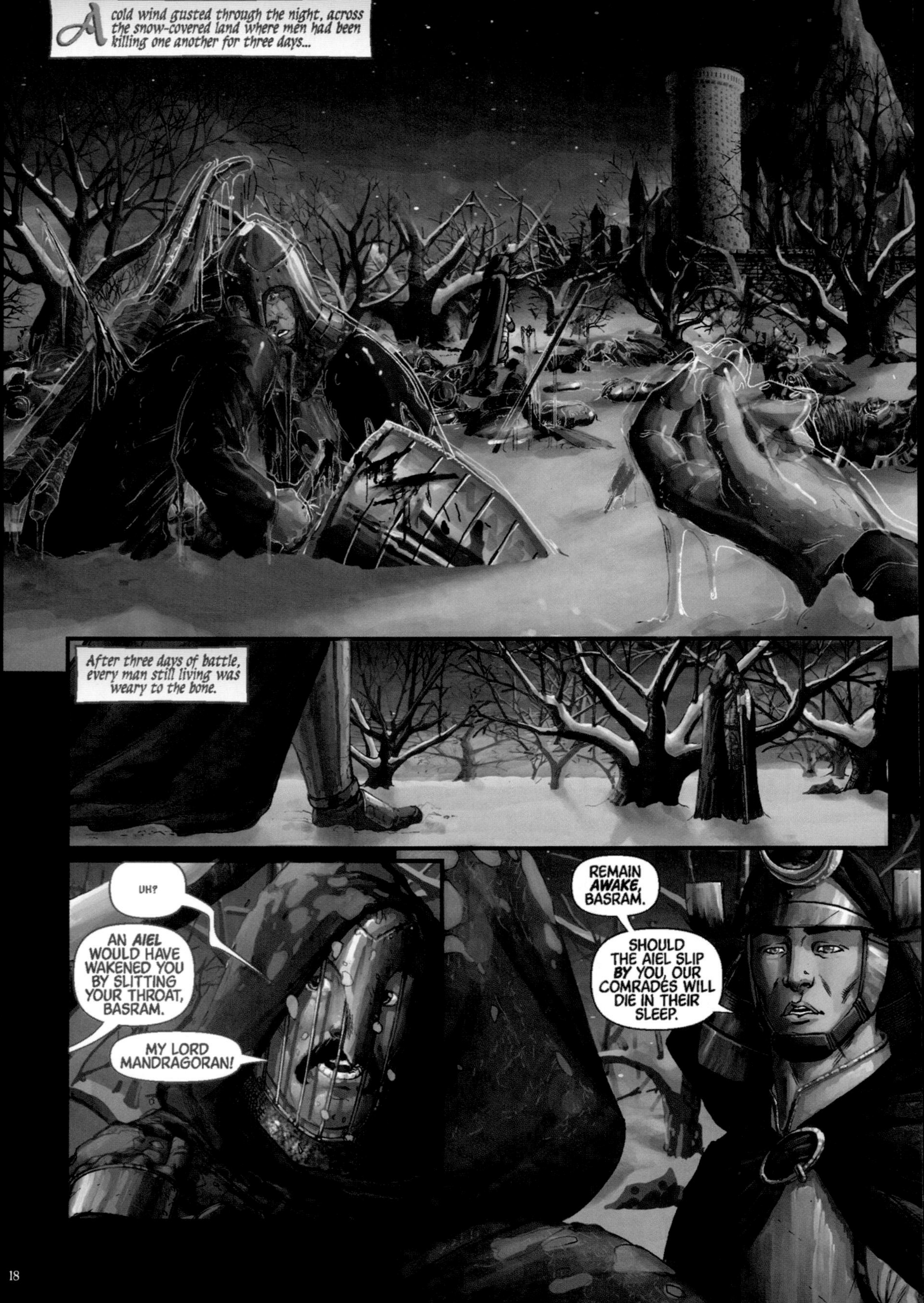
A cold wind gusted through the night, across the snow-covered land where men had been killing one another for three days...
After three days of battle, every man still living was weary to the bone.
UH?
AN AIEL WOULD HAVE WAKENED YOU BY SLITTING YOUR THROAT, BASRAM.
MY LORD MANDRAGORAN!
REMAIN AWAKE, BASRAM.
SHOULD THE AIEL SLIP BY YOU, OUR COMRADES WILL DIE IN THEIR SLEEP.

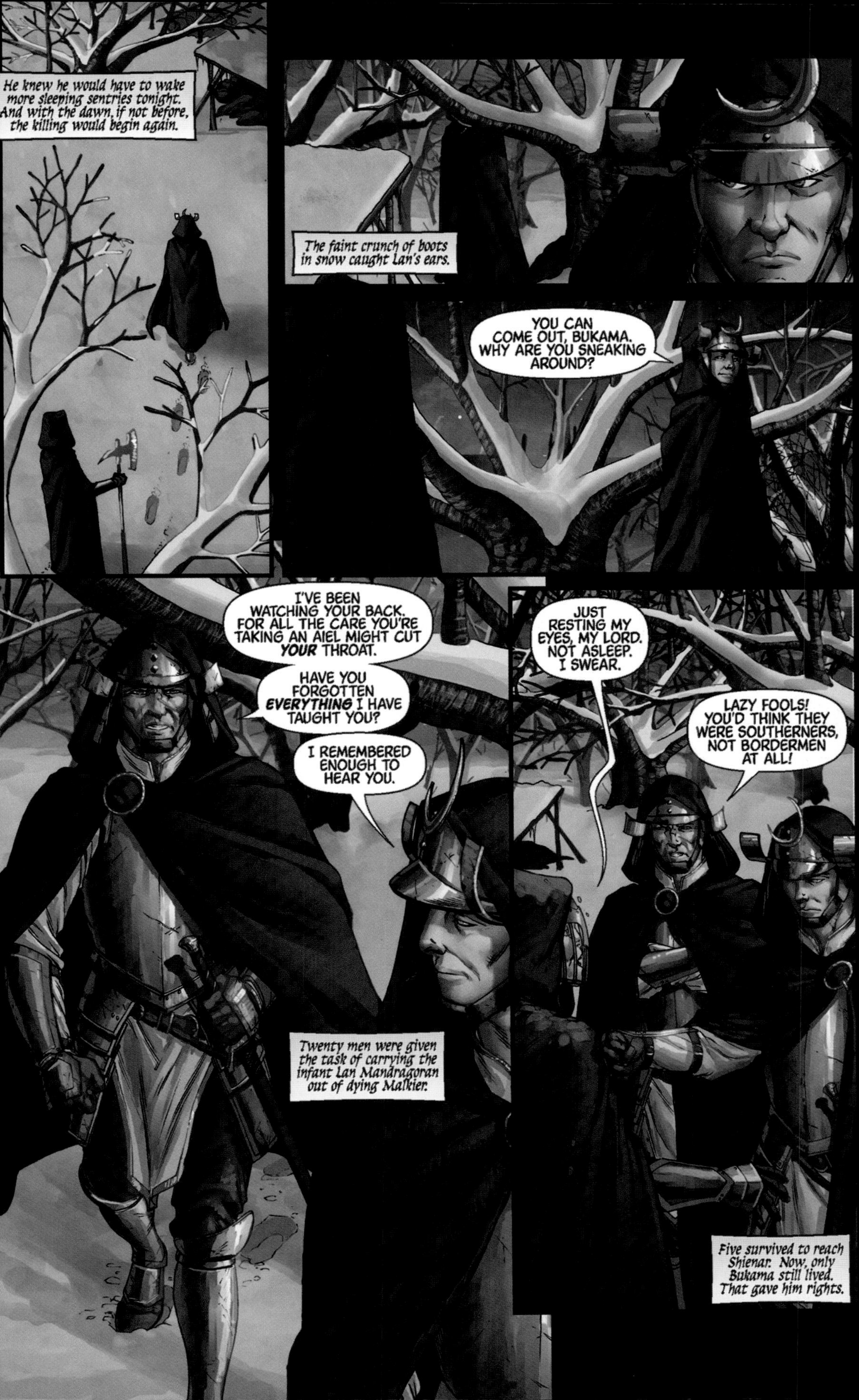
He knew he would have to wake more sleeping sentries tonight. And with the dawn, if not before, the killing would begin again.
The faint crunch of boots in snow caught Lan's ears.
YOU CAN COME OUT, BUKAMA. WHY ARE YOU SNEAKING AROUND?
I'VE BEEN WATCHING YOUR BACK. FOR ALL THE CARE YOU'RE TAKING AN AIEL MIGHT CUT YOUR THROAT.
HAVE YOU FORGOTTEN EVERYTHING I HAVE TAUGHT YOU?
I REMEMBERED ENOUGH TO HEAR YOU.
Twenty men were given the task of carrying the infant Lan Mandragoran out of dying Malkier.
JUST RESTING MY EYES, MY LORD. NOT ASLEEP. I SWEAR.
LAZY FOOLS! YOU'D THINK THEY WERE SOUTHERNERS, NOT BORDERMEN AT ALL!
Five survived to reach Shienar. Now, only Bukama still lived. That gave him rights.

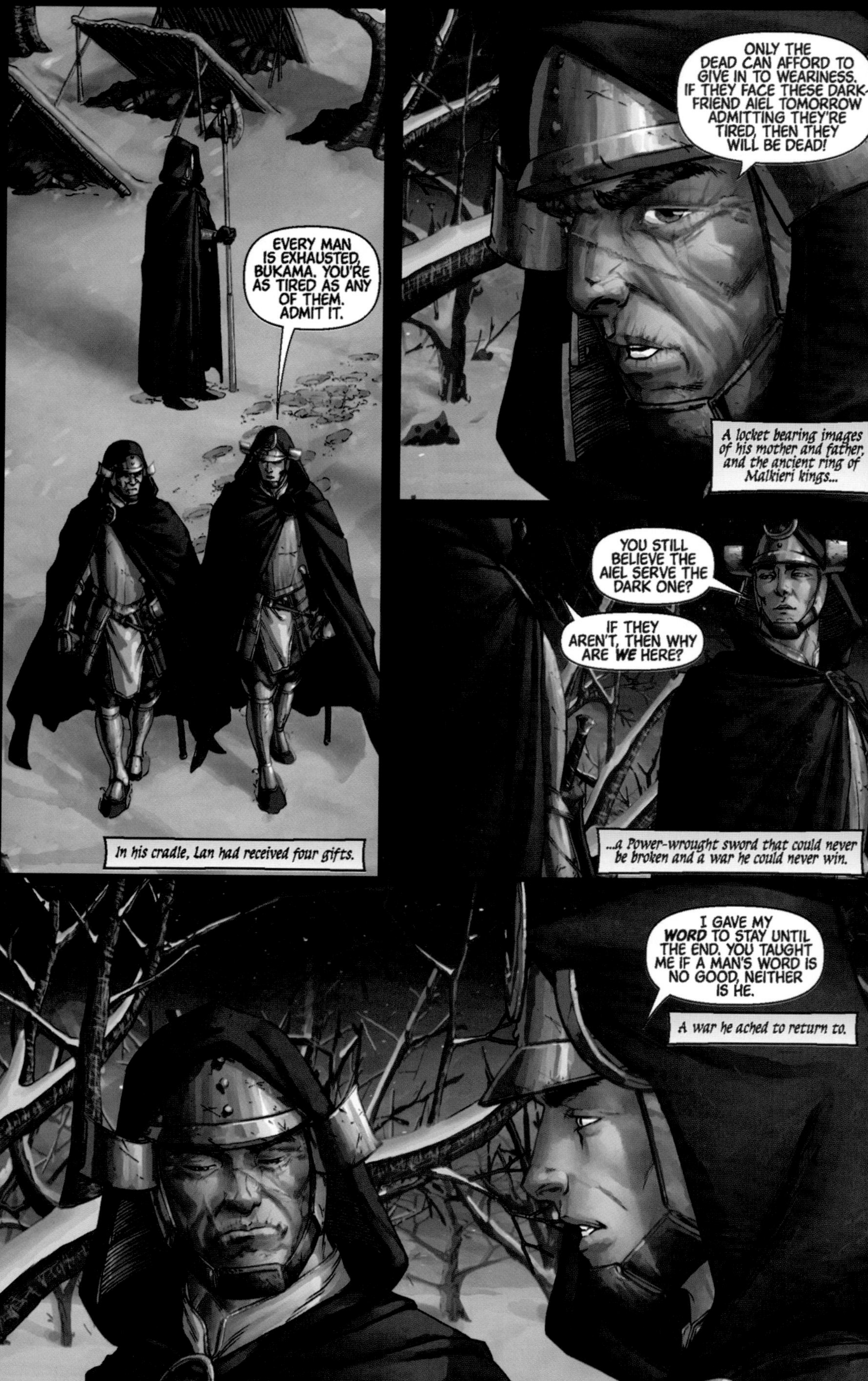
EVERY MAN IS EXHAUSTED, BUKAMA. YOU'RE AS TIRED AS ANY OF THEM. ADMIT IT.
In his cradle, Lan had received four gifts.
ONLY THE DEAD CAN AFFORD TO GIVE IN TO WEARINESS. IF THEY FACE THESE DARK-FRIEND AIEL TOMORROW ADMITTING THEY'RE TIRED, THEN THEY WILL BE DEAD!
A locket bearing images of his mother and father, and the ancient ring of Malkieri kings...
YOU STILL BELIEVE THE AIEL SERVE THE DARK ONE?
IF THEY AREN'T, THEN WHY ARE WE HERE?
...a Power-wrought sword that could never be broken and a war he could never win.
I GAVE MY WORD TO STAY UNTIL THE END. YOU TAUGHT ME IF A MAN'S WORD IS NO GOOD, NEITHER IS HE.
A war he ached to return to.

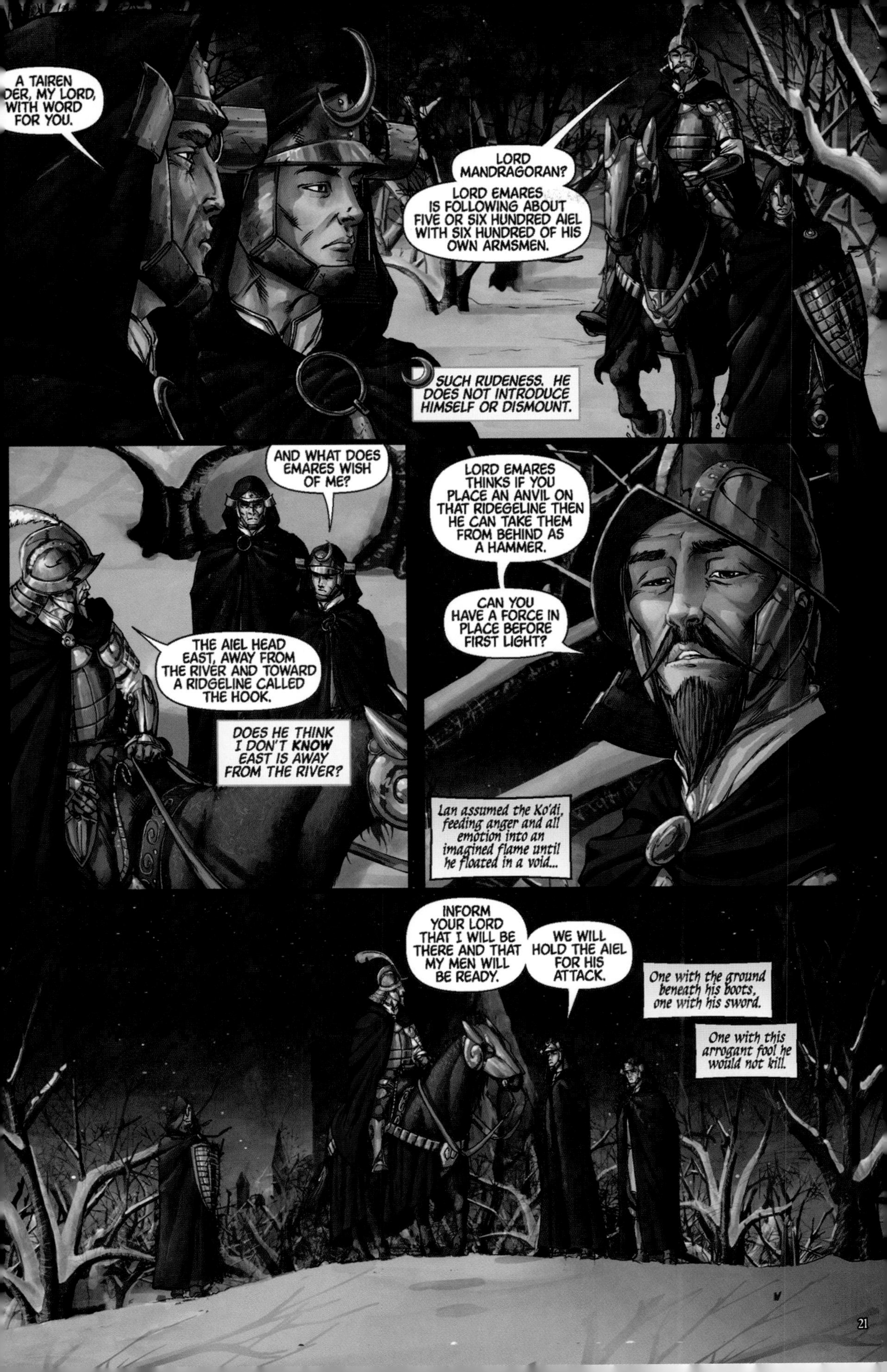
A TAIREN
DER, MY LORD,
WITH WORD
FOR YOU.
LORD MANDRAGORAN?
LORD EMARES IS FOLLOWING ABOUT FIVE OR SIX HUNDRED AIEL WITH SIX HUNDRED OF HIS OWN ARMSMEN.
SUCH RUDENESS. HE DOES NOT INTRODUCE HIMSELF OR DISMOUNT.
AND WHAT DOES EMARES WISH OF ME?
THE AIEL HEAD EAST, AWAY FROM THE RIVER AND TOWARD A RIDGELINE CALLED THE HOOK.
DOES HE THINK I DON'T **KNOW** EAST IS AWAY FROM THE RIVER?
LORD EMARES THINKS IF YOU PLACE AN ANVIL ON THAT RIDEGELINE THEN HE CAN TAKE THEM FROM BEHIND AS A HAMMER.
CAN YOU HAVE A FORCE IN PLACE BEFORE FIRST LIGHT?
Lan assumed the Ko'di, feeding anger and all emotion into an imagined flame until he floated in a void...
INFORM YOUR LORD THAT I WILL BE THERE AND THAT MY MEN WILL BE READY.
WE WILL HOLD THE AIEL FOR HIS ATTACK.
One with the ground beneath his boots, one with his sword.
One with this arrogant fool he would not kill.

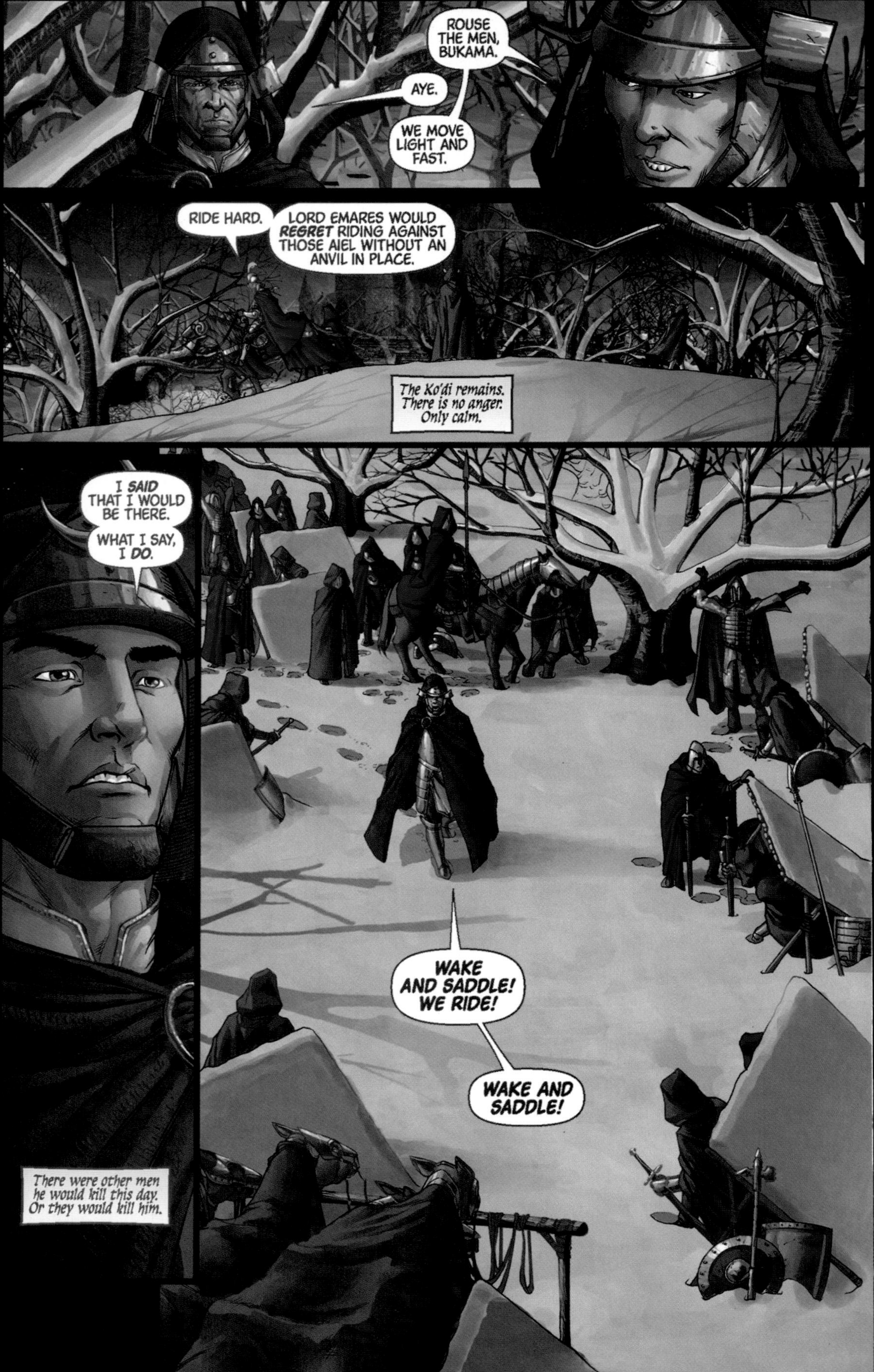
ROUSE THE MEN, BUKAMA.
AYE.
WE MOVE LIGHT AND FAST.
RIDE HARD.
LORD EMARES WOULD REGRET RIDING AGAINST THOSE AIEL WITHOUT AN ANVIL IN PLACE.
The Ko'di remains. There is no anger. Only calm.
I SAID THAT I WOULD BE THERE.
WHAT I SAY, I DO.
WAKE AND SADDLE! WE RIDE!
WAKE AND SADDLE!
There were other men he would kill this day. Or they would kill him.

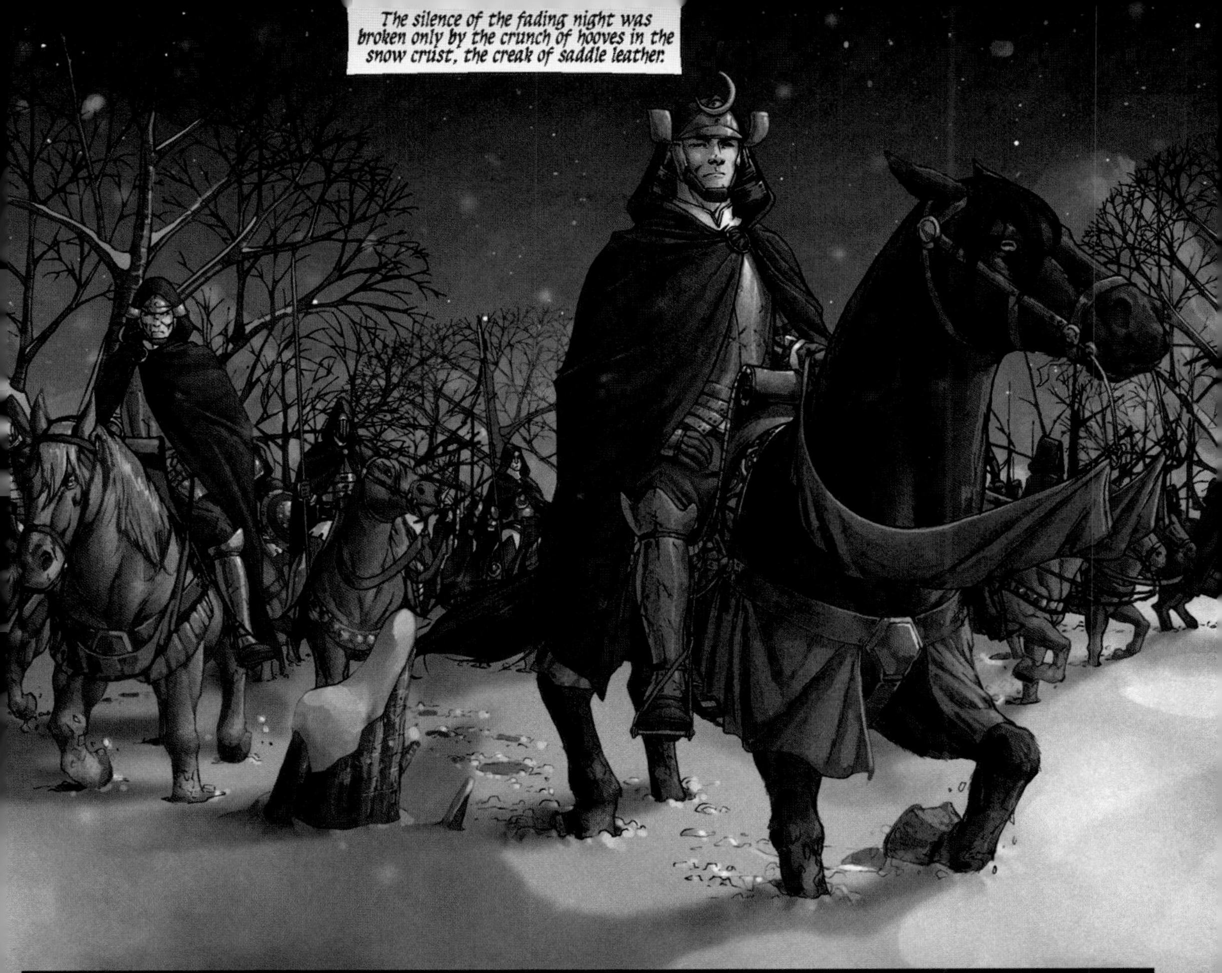
The silence of the fading night was broken only by the crunch of hooves in the snow crust, the creak of saddle leather.

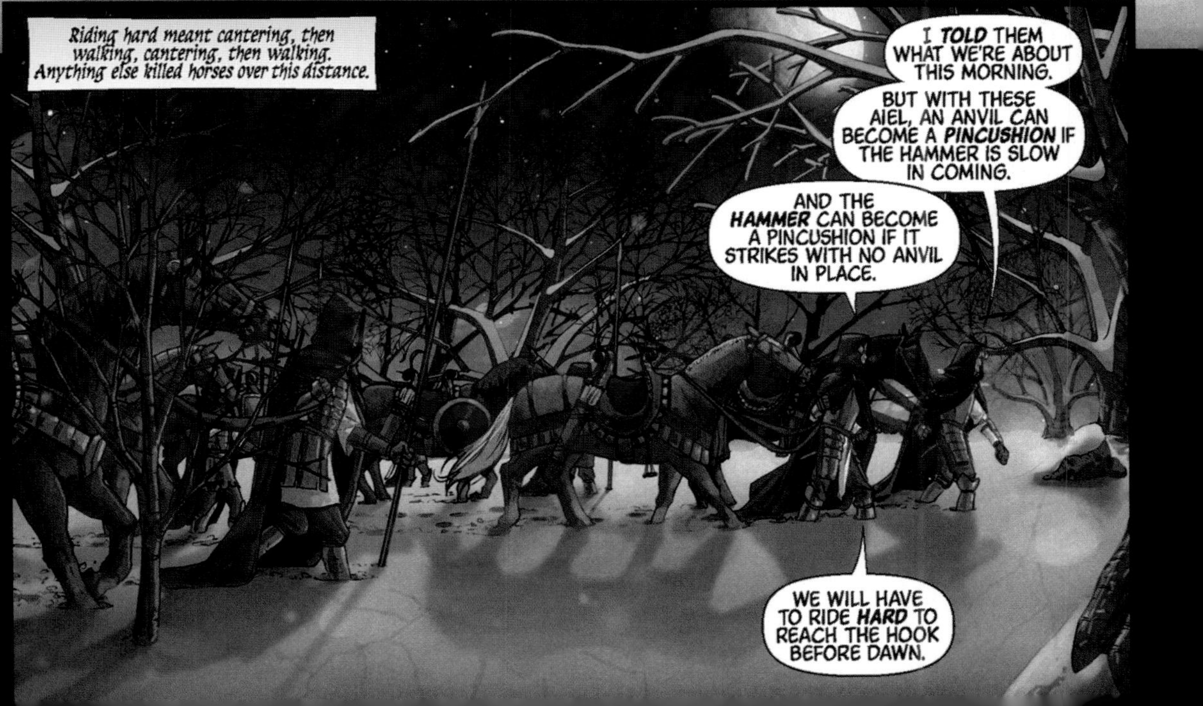
Riding hard meant cantering, then walking, cantering, then walking. Anything else killed horses over this distance.
WE WILL HAVE TO RIDE HARD TO REACH THE HOOK BEFORE DAWN.
I TOLD THEM WHAT WE'RE ABOUT THIS MORNING.
BUT WITH THESE AIEL, AN ANVIL CAN BECOME A PINCUSHION IF THE HAMMER IS SLOW IN COMING.
AND THE HAMMER CAN BECOME A PINCUSHION IF IT STRIKES WITH NO ANVIL IN PLACE.

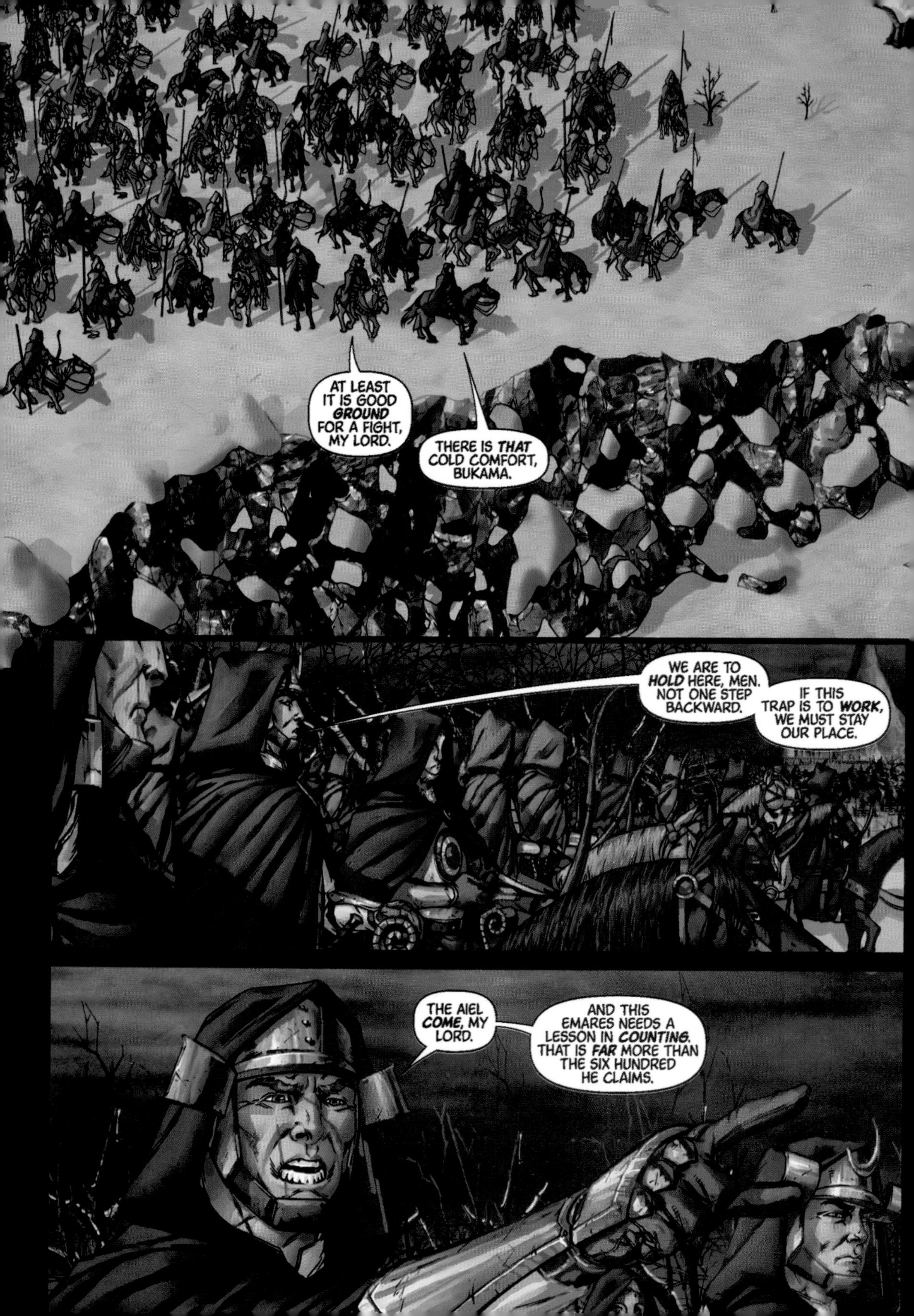
AT LEAST IT IS GOOD GROUND FOR A FIGHT, MY LORD.
THERE IS THAT COLD COMFORT, BUKAMA.
WE ARE TO HOLD HERE, MEN. NOT ONE STEP BACKWARD.
IF THIS TRAP IS TO WORK, WE MUST STAY OUR PLACE.
THE AIEL COME, MY LORD.
AND THIS EMARES NEEDS A LESSON IN COUNTING. THAT IS FAR MORE THAN THE SIX HUNDRED HE CLAIMS.

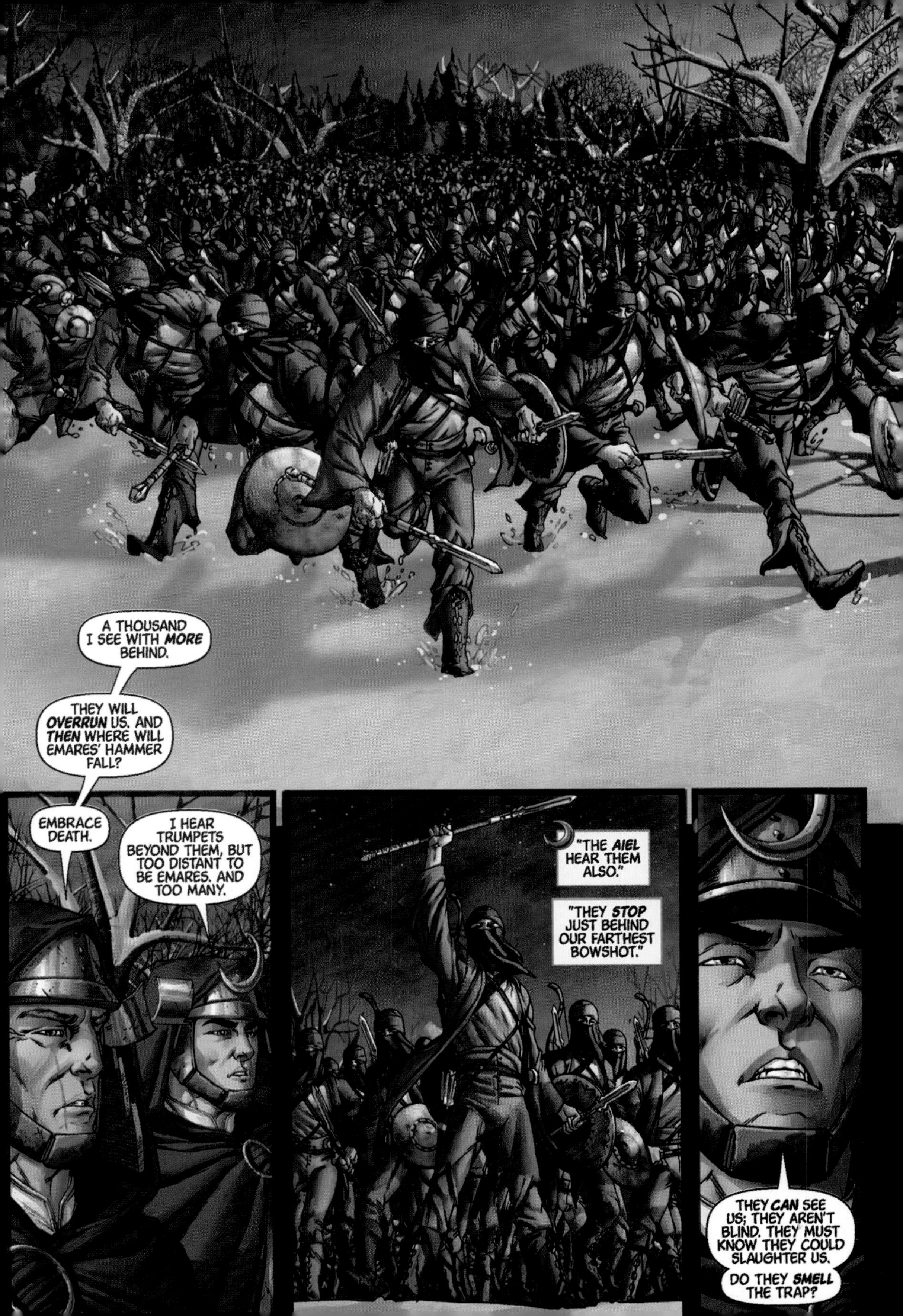
A THOUSAND I SEE WITH MORE BEHIND.
THEY WILL OVERRUN US. AND THEN WHERE WILL EMARES' HAMMER FALL?
EMBRACE DEATH.
I HEAR TRUMPETS BEYOND THEM, BUT TOO DISTANT TO BE EMARES. AND TOO MANY.
"THE AIEL HEAR THEM ALSO."
"THEY STOP JUST BEHIND OUR FARTHEST BOWSHOT."
THEY CAN SEE US; THEY AREN'T BLIND. THEY MUST KNOW THEY COULD SLAUGHTER US.
DO THEY SMELL THE TRAP?

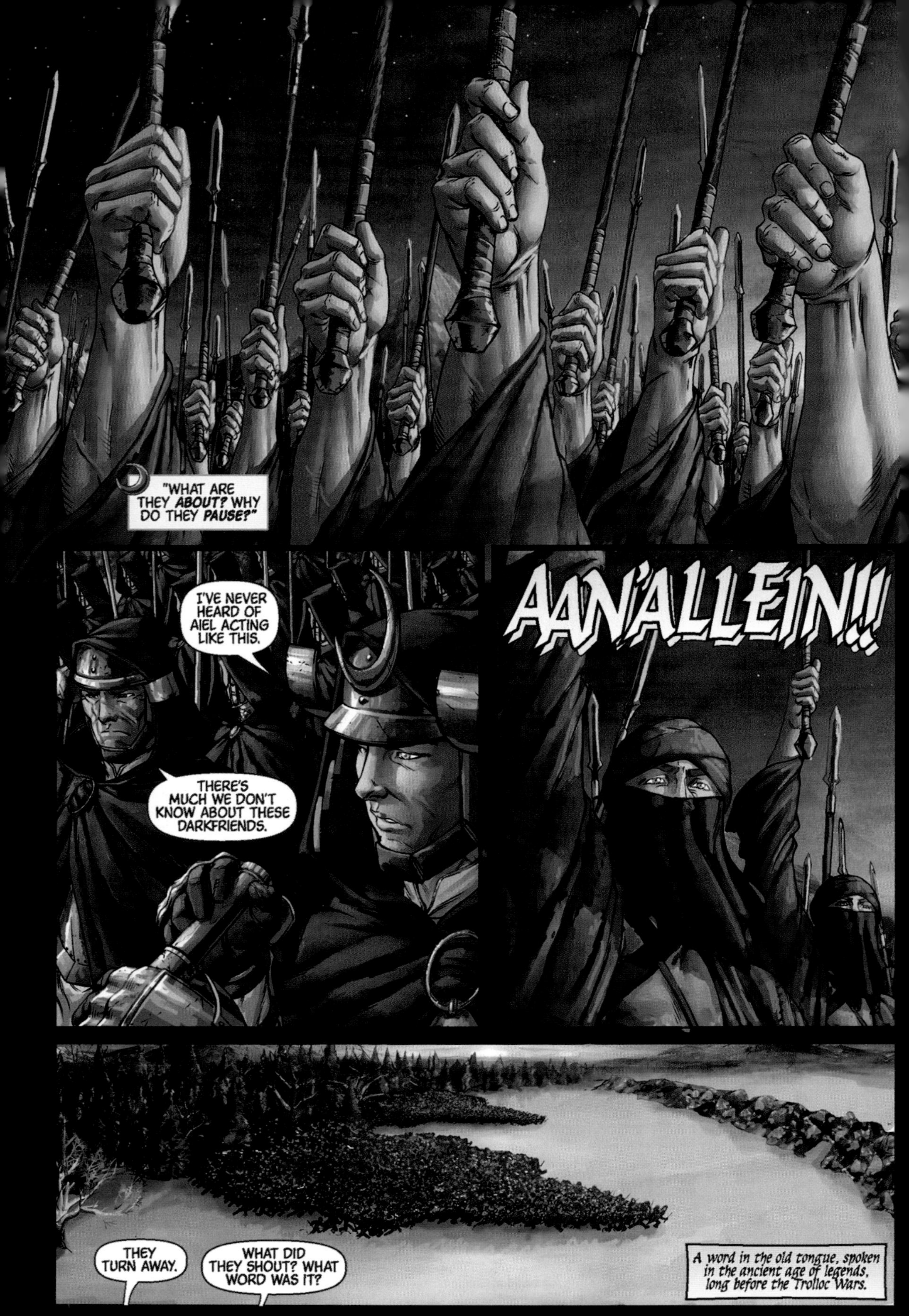
"WHAT ARE THEY *ABOUT?* WHY DO THEY *PAUSE?*"
I'VE NEVER HEARD OF AIEL ACTING LIKE THIS.
THERE'S MUCH WE DON'T KNOW ABOUT THESE DARKFRIENDS.
AAN'ALLEIN!!
THEY TURN AWAY.
WHAT DID THEY SHOUT? WHAT WORD WAS IT?
A word in the old tongue, spoken in the ancient age of legends, long before the Trolloc Wars.

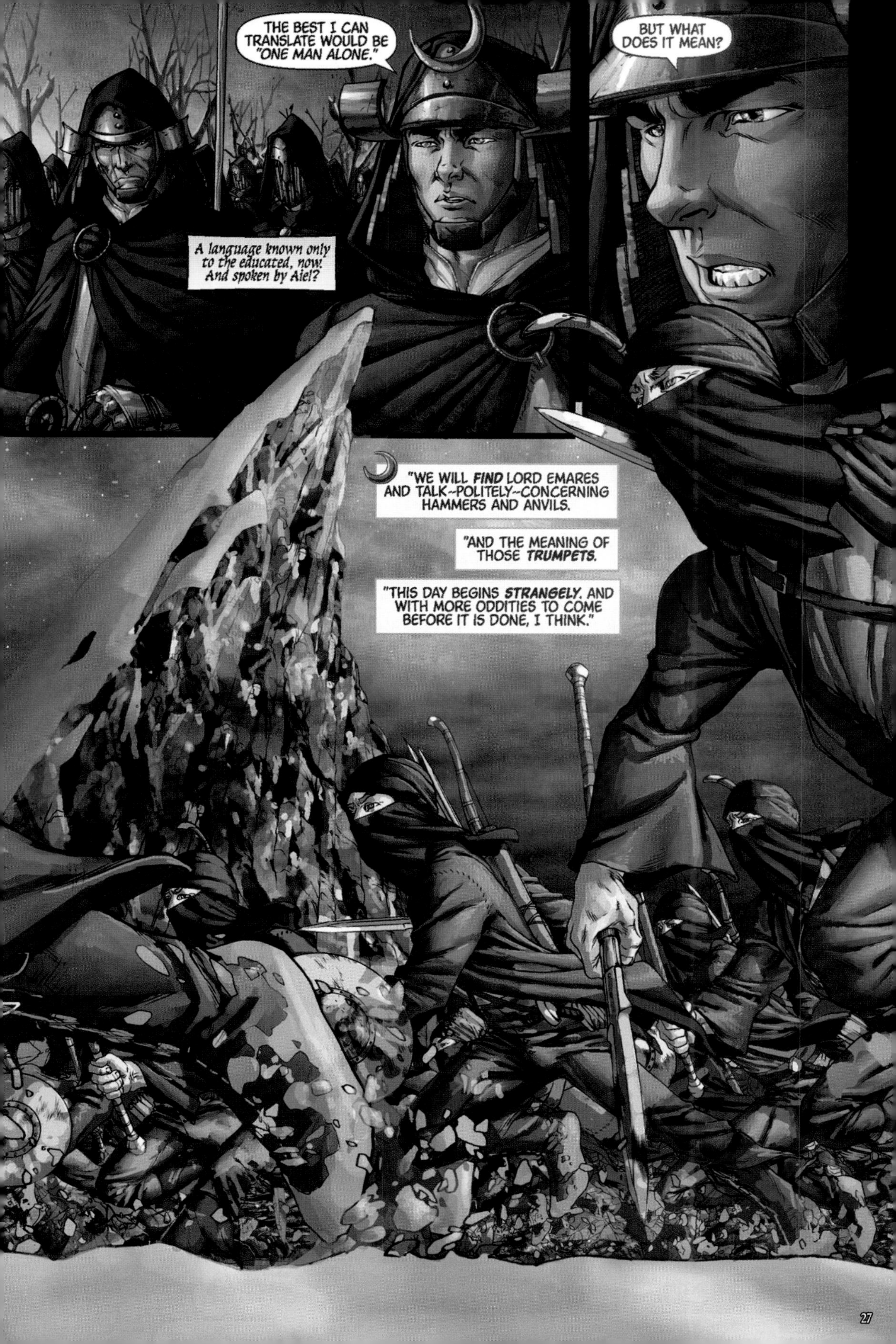
THE BEST I CAN TRANSLATE WOULD BE "ONE MAN ALONE."
A language known only to the educated, now. And spoken by Aiel?
BUT WHAT DOES IT MEAN?
"WE WILL FIND LORD EMARES AND TALK--POLITELY--CONCERNING HAMMERS AND ANVILS.
"AND THE MEANING OF THOSE TRUMPETS.
"THIS DAY BEGINS STRANGELY. AND WITH MORE ODDITIES TO COME BEFORE IT IS DONE, I THINK."

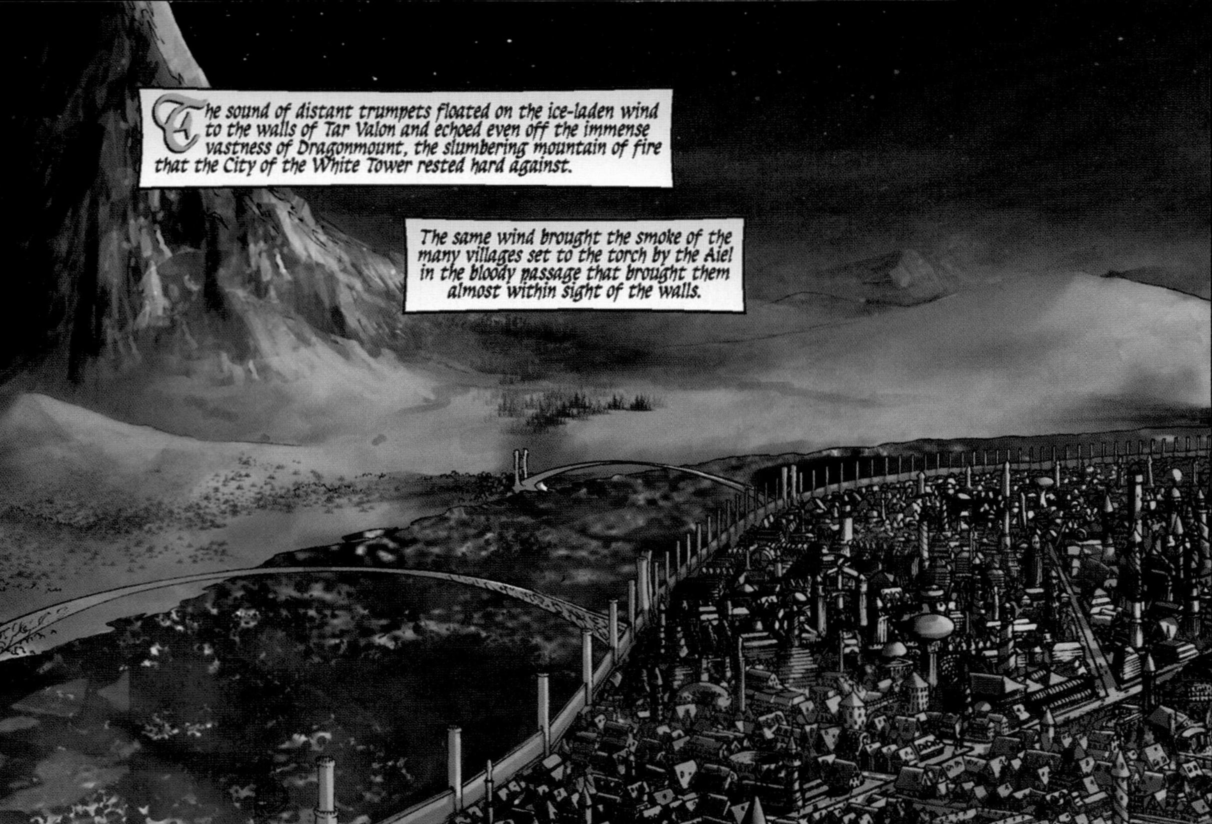
The sound of distant trumpets floated on the ice-laden wind to the walls of Tar Valon and echoed even off the immense vastness of Dragonmount, the slumbering mountain of fire that the City of the White Tower rested hard against.
The same wind brought the smoke of the many villages set to the torch by the Aiel in the bloody passage that brought them almost within sight of the walls.

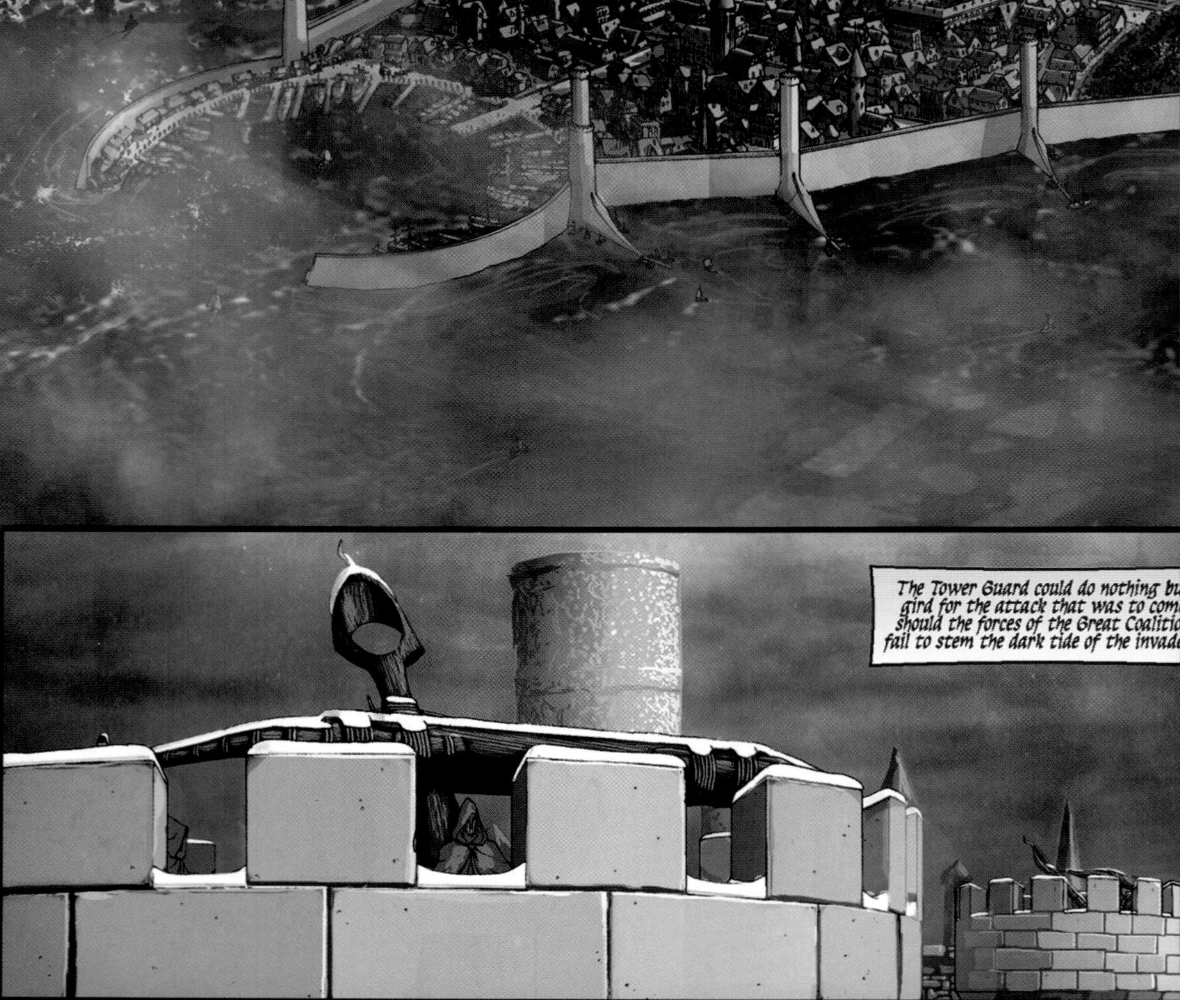
The Tower Guard could do nothing bu
gird for the attack that was to com
should the forces of the Great Coalitio
fail to stem the dark tide of the invade

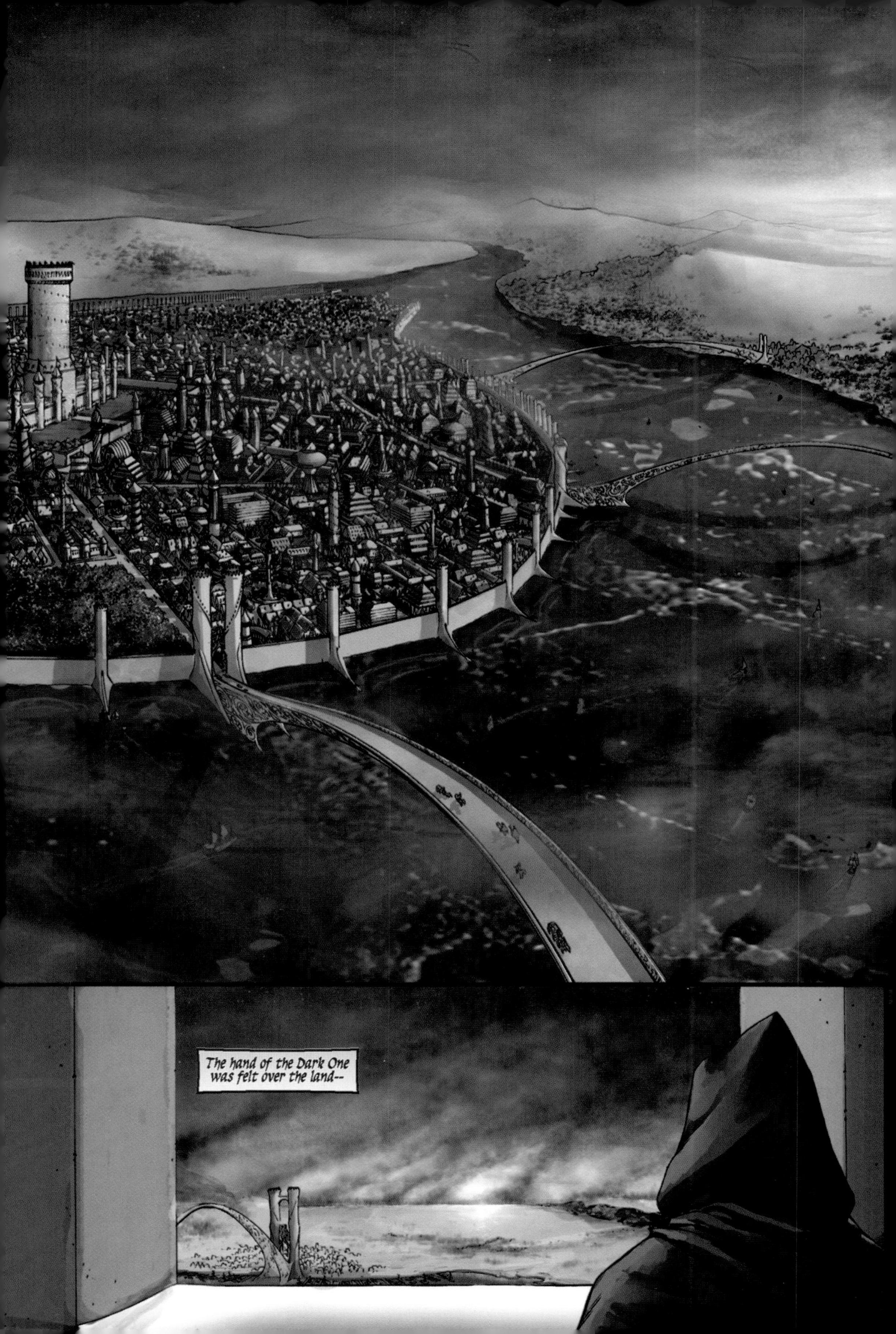
The hand of the Dark One was felt over the land--

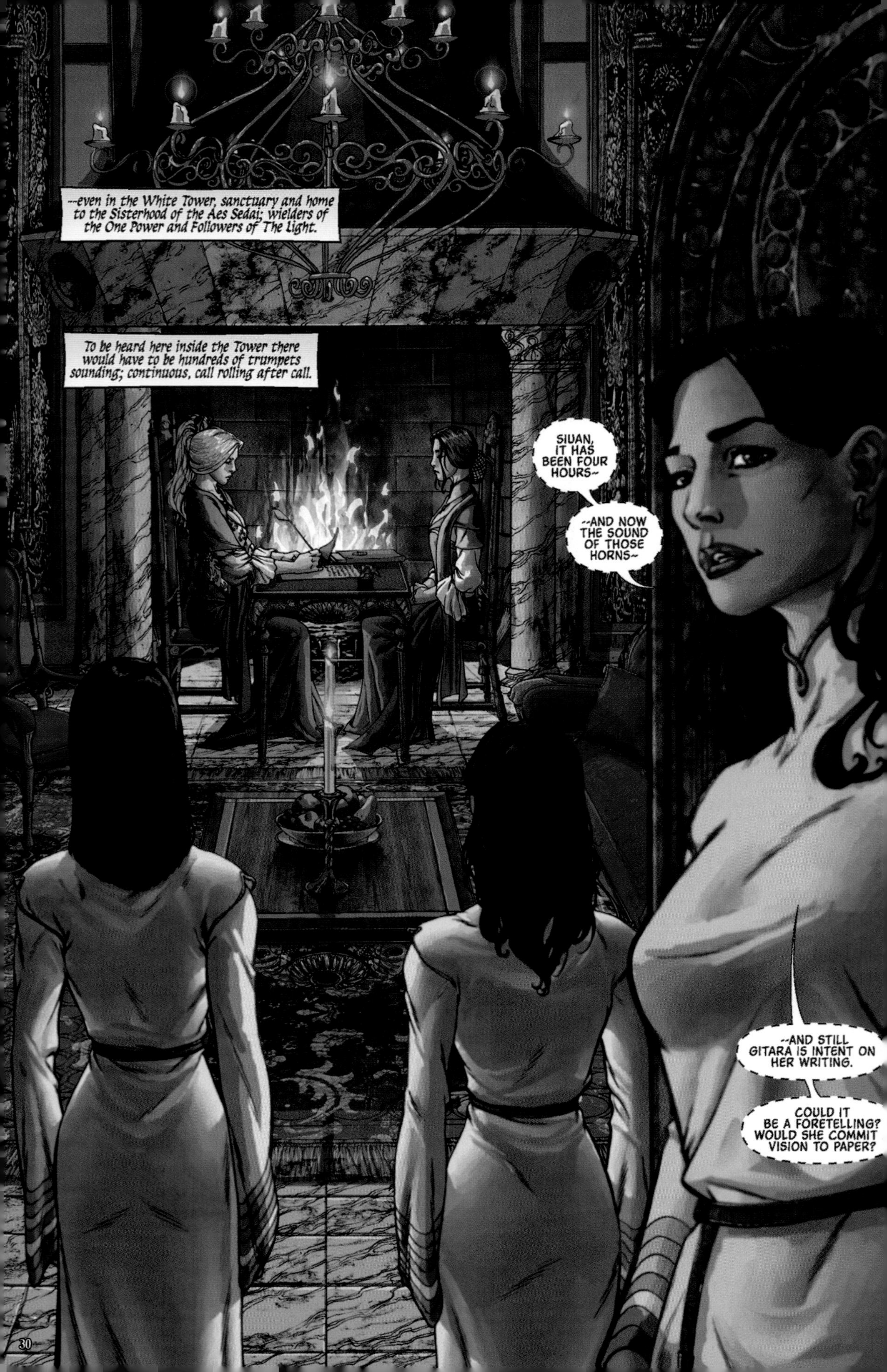
--even in the White Tower, sanctuary and home to the Sisterhood of the Aes Sedai; wielders of the One Power and Followers of The Light.
To be heard here inside the Tower there would have to be hundreds of trumpets sounding; continuous, call rolling after call.
SIUAN, IT HAS BEEN FOUR HOURS~
--AND NOW THE SOUND OF THOSE HORNS~
--AND STILL GITARA IS INTENT ON HER WRITING.
COULD IT BE A FORETELLING? WOULD SHE COMMIT VISION TO PAPER?

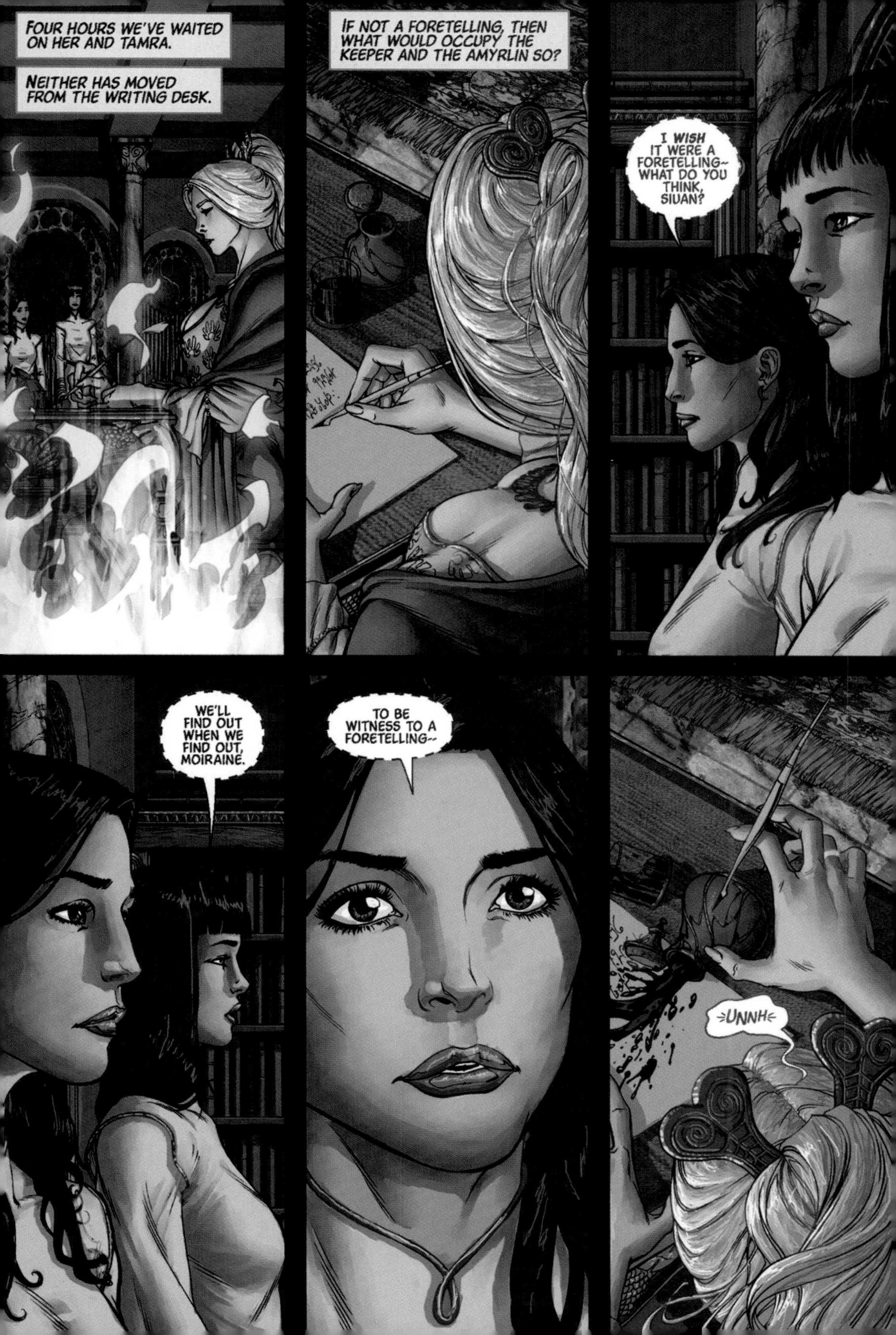
FOUR HOURS WE'VE WAITED ON HER AND TAMRA.
NEITHER HAS MOVED FROM THE WRITING DESK.
IF NOT A FORETELLING, THEN WHAT WOULD OCCUPY THE KEEPER AND THE AMYRLIN SO?
I WISH IT WERE A FORETELLING-- WHAT DO YOU THINK, SIUAN?
WE'LL FIND OUT WHEN WE FIND OUT, MOIRAINE.
TO BE WITNESS TO A FORETELLING--
UNNH

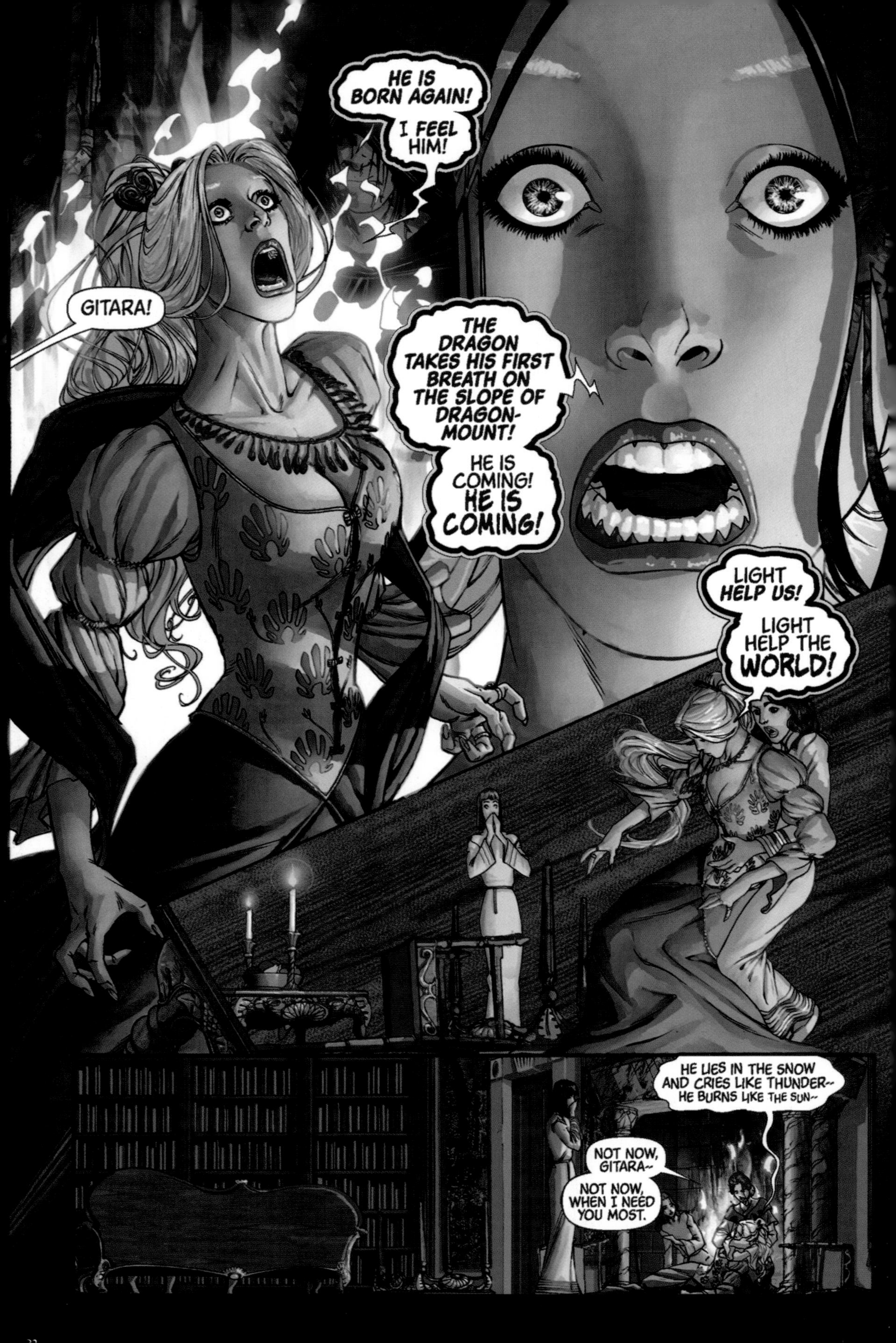
HE IS BORN AGAIN!
I FEEL HIM!
GITARA!
THE DRAGON TAKES HIS FIRST BREATH ON THE SLOPE OF DRAGON-MOUNT!
HE IS COMING! HE IS COMING!
LIGHT HELP US!
LIGHT HELP THE WORLD!
HE LIES IN THE SNOW AND CRIES LIKE THUNDER-- HE BURNS LIKE THE SUN--
NOT NOW, GITARA--
NOT NOW, WHEN I NEED YOU MOST.

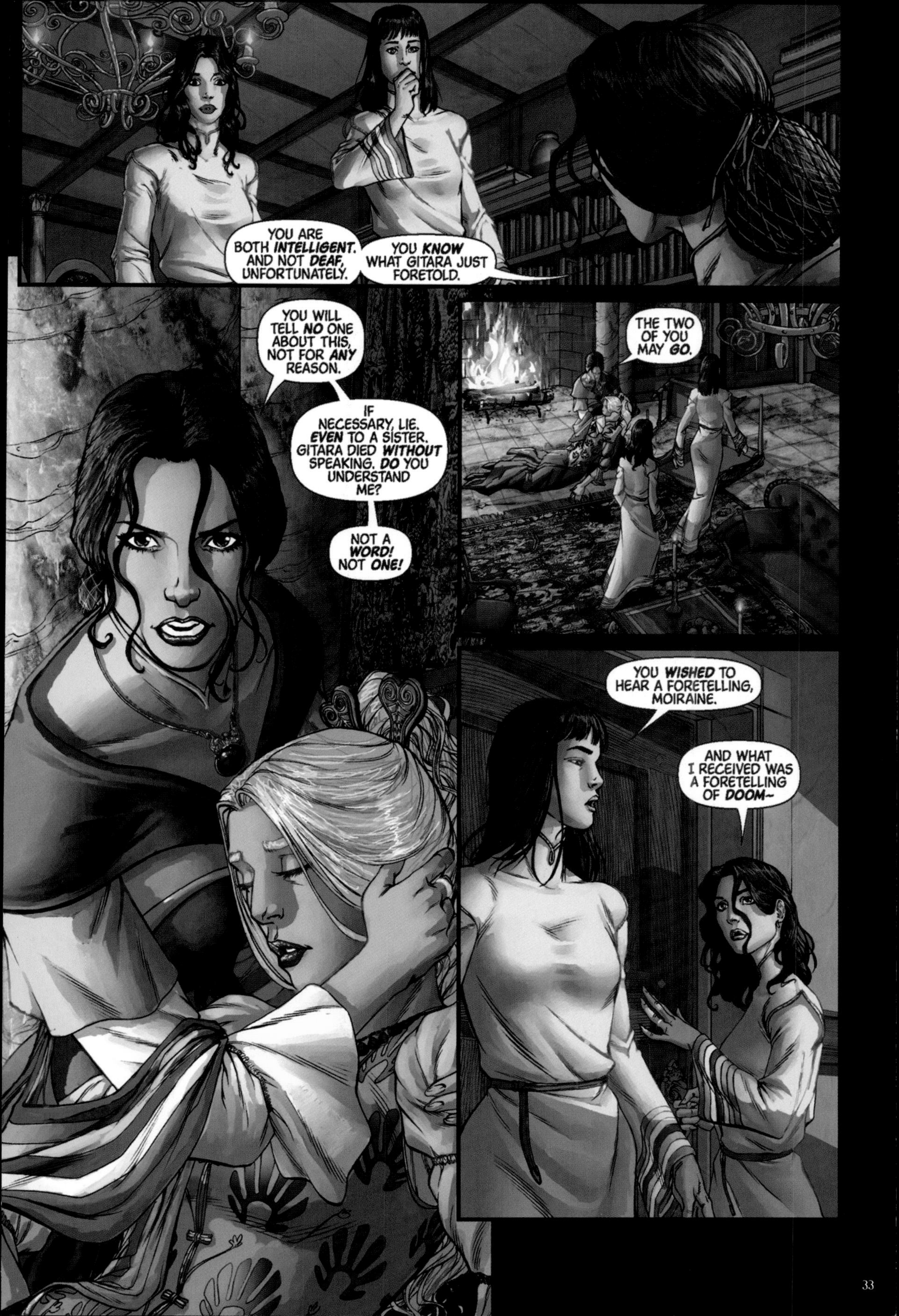
YOU ARE BOTH INTELLIGENT. AND NOT DEAF, UNFORTUNATELY.
YOU KNOW WHAT GITARA JUST FORETOLD.
YOU WILL TELL NO ONE ABOUT THIS, NOT FOR ANY REASON.
IF NECESSARY, LIE. EVEN TO A SISTER. GITARA DIED WITHOUT SPEAKING. DO YOU UNDERSTAND ME?
NOT A WORD! NOT ONE!
THE TWO OF YOU MAY GO.
YOU WISHED TO HEAR A FORETELLING, MOIRAINE.
AND WHAT I RECEIVED WAS A FORETELLING OF DOOM~

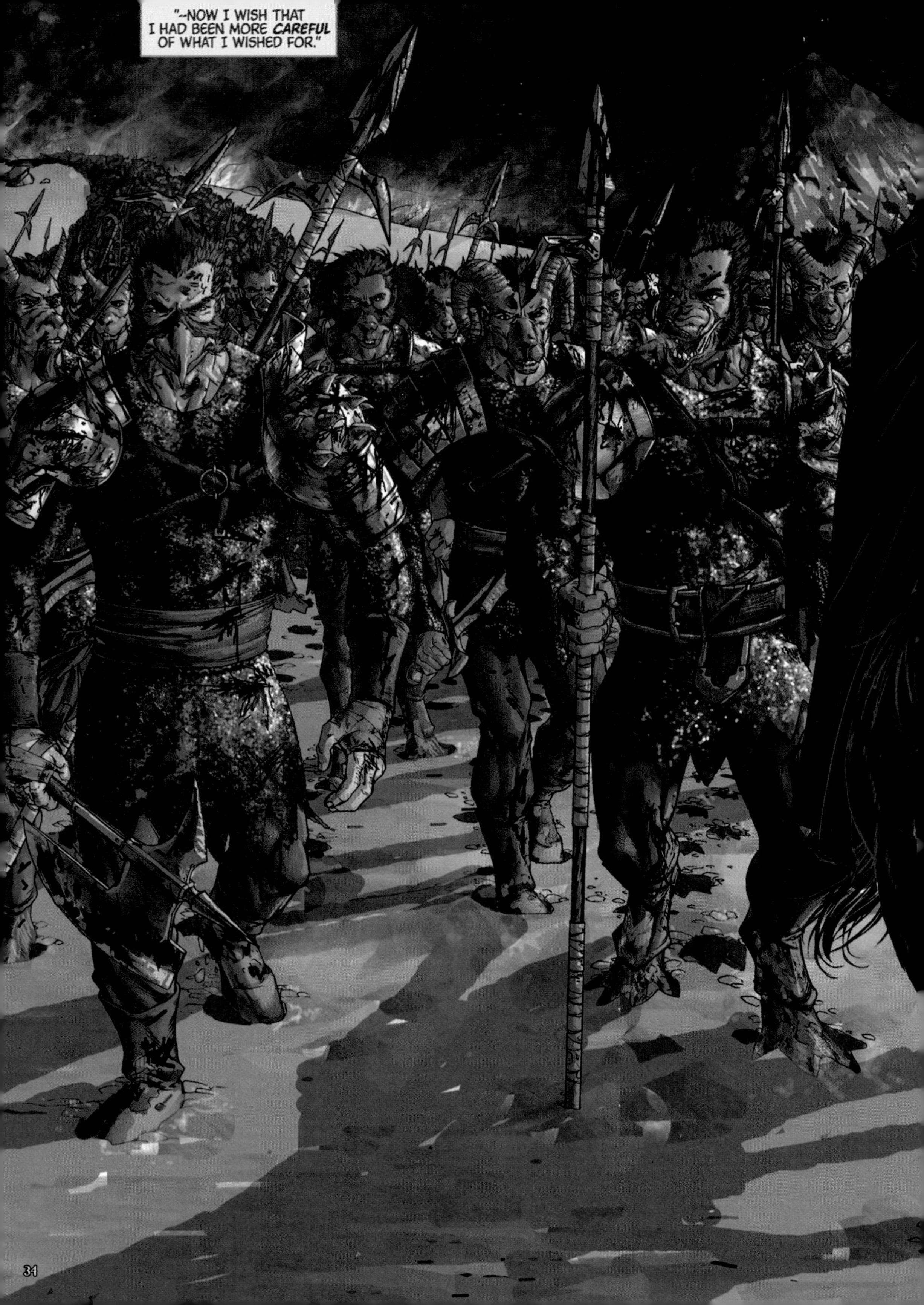
"--NOW I WISH THAT I HAD BEEN MORE *CAREFUL* OF WHAT I WISHED FOR."

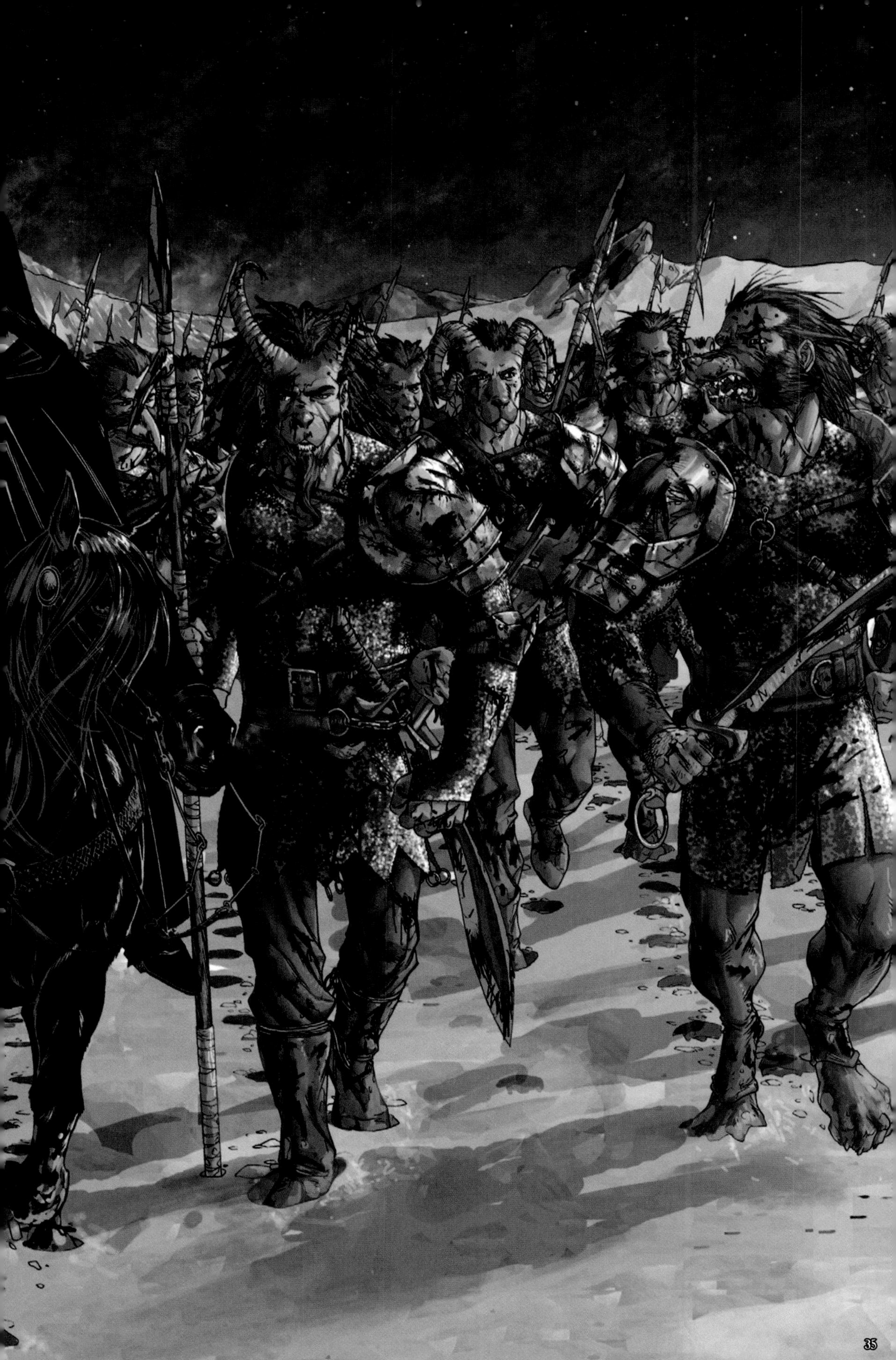

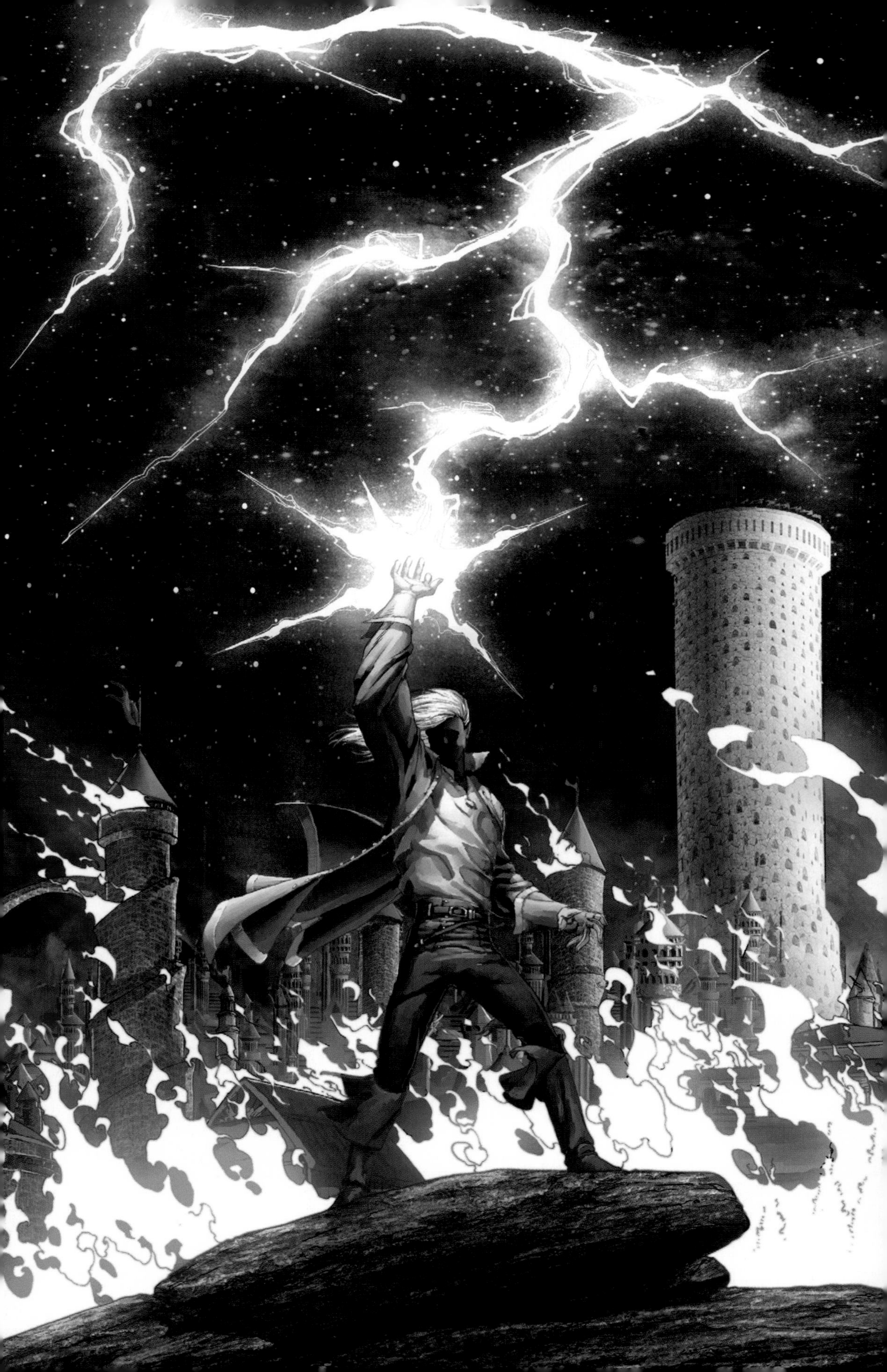

chapter two

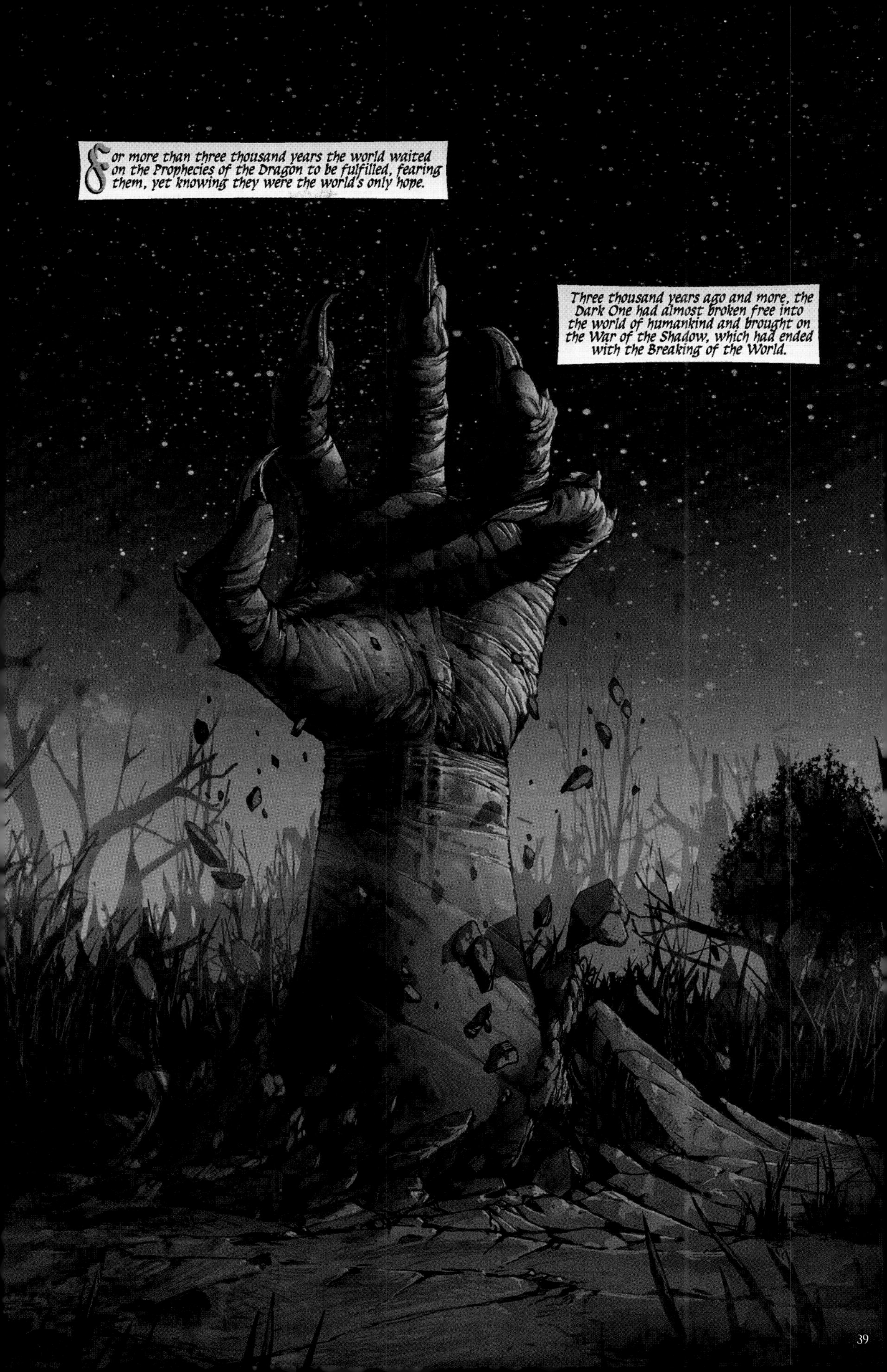
For more than three thousand years the world waited on the Prophecies of the Dragon to be fulfilled, fearing them, yet knowing they were the world's only hope.
Three thousand years ago and more, the Dark One had almost broken free into the world of humankind and brought on the War of the Shadow, which had ended with the Breaking of the World.

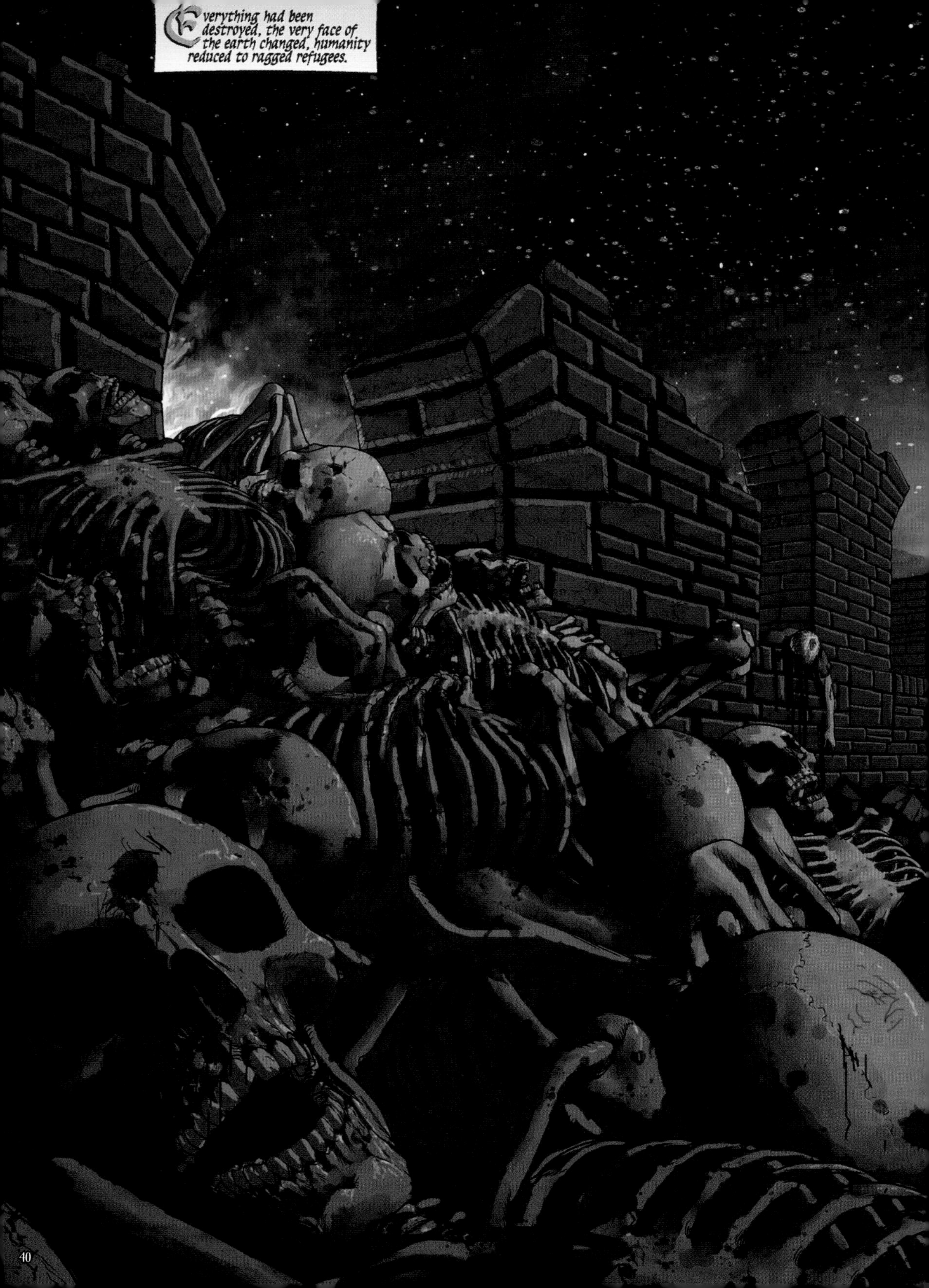
Everything had been destroyed, the very face of the earth changed, humanity reduced to ragged refugees.

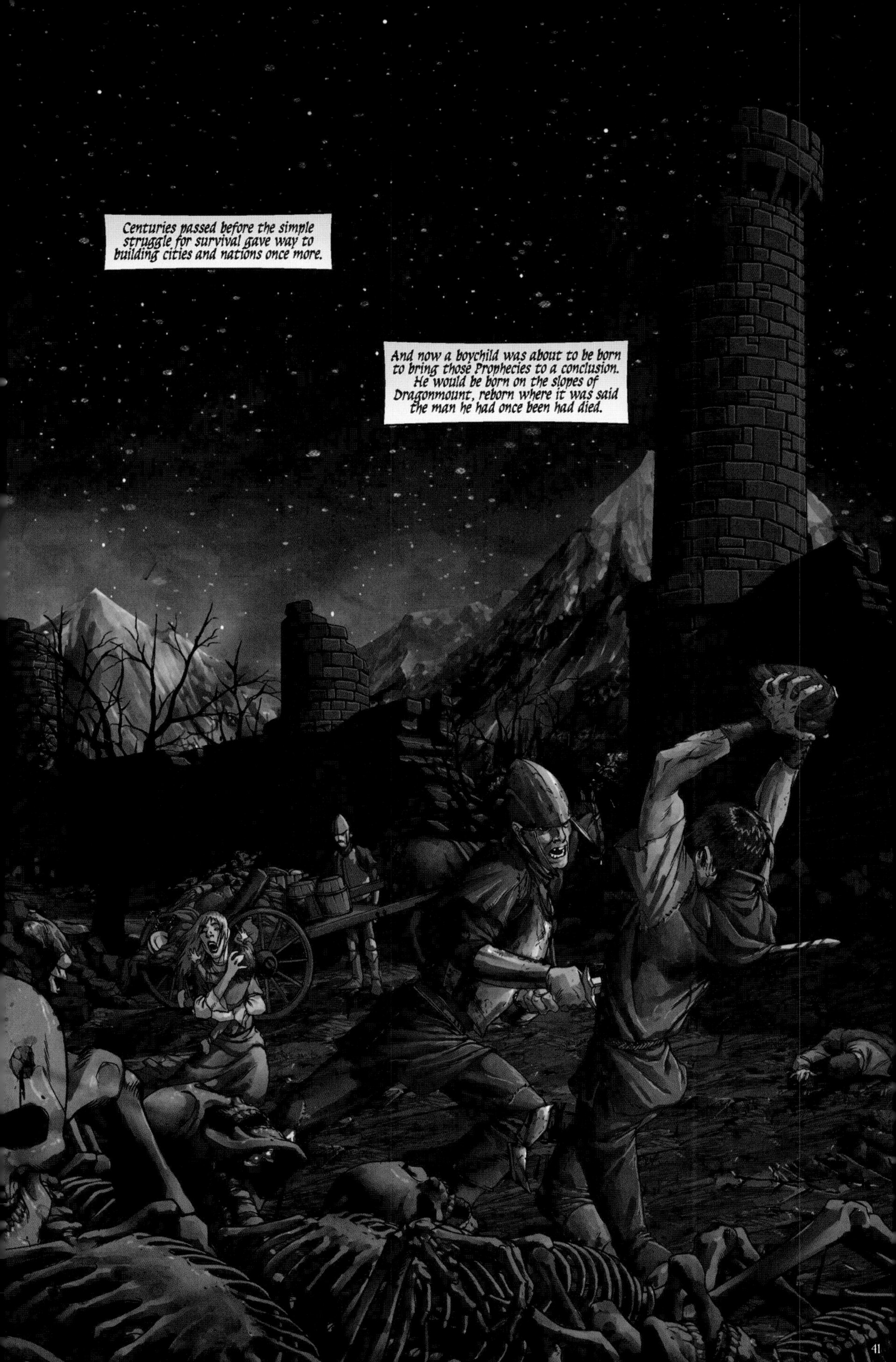
Centuries passed before the simple struggle for survival gave way to building cities and nations once more.
And now a boychild was about to be born to bring those Prophecies to a conclusion. He would be born on the slopes of Dragonmount, reborn where it was said the man he had once been had died.

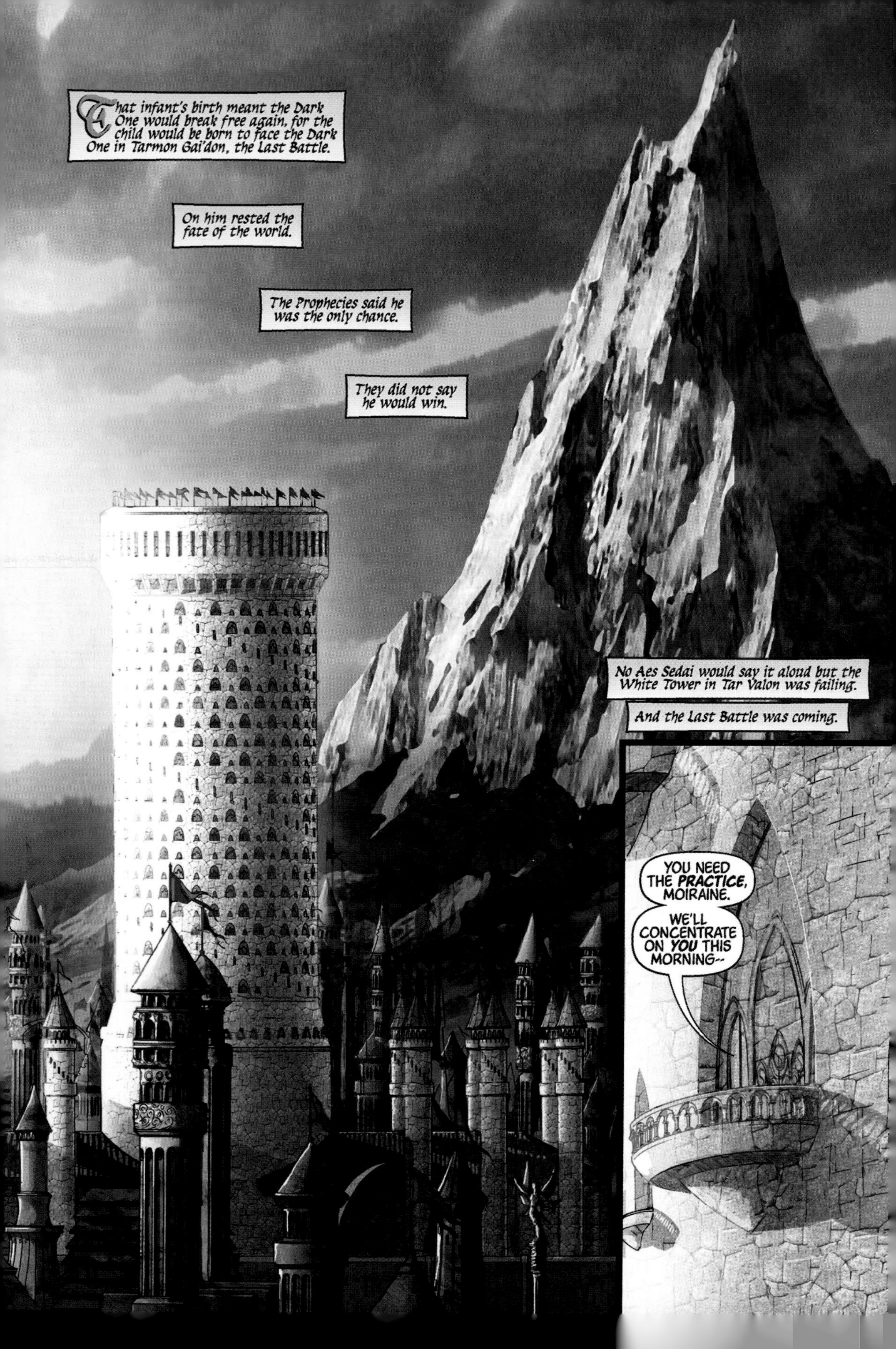
That infant's birth meant the Dark One would break free again, for the child would be born to face the Dark One in Tarmon Gai'don, the Last Battle.
On him rested the fate of the world.
The Prophecies said he was the only chance.
They did not say he would win.
No Aes Sedai would say it aloud but the White Tower in Tar Valon was failing.
And the Last Battle was coming.
YOU NEED THE PRACTICE, MOIRAINE.
WE'LL CONCENTRATE ON YOU THIS MORNING--

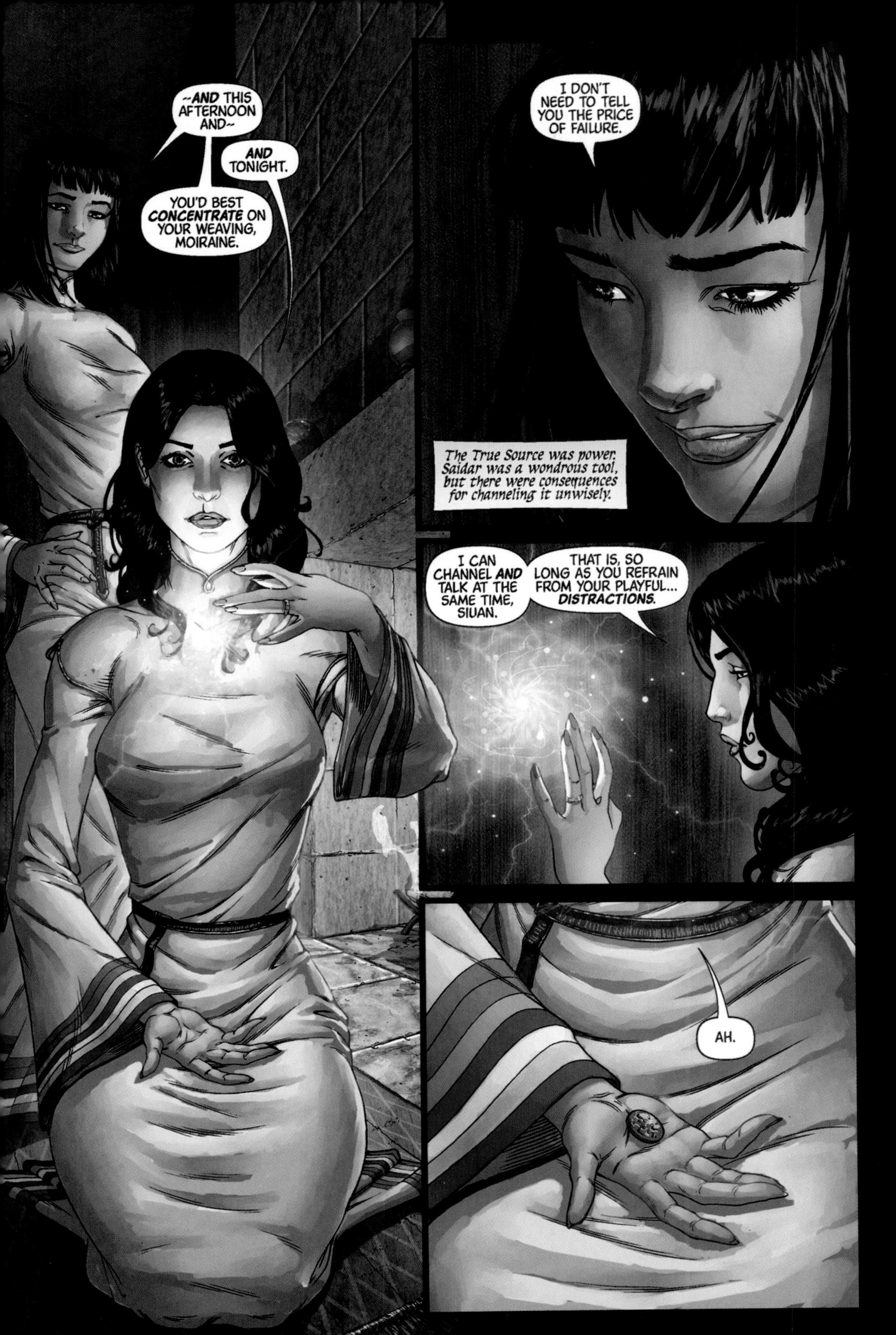
--AND THIS AFTERNOON AND--
YOU'D BEST CONCENTRATE ON YOUR WEAVING, MOIRAINE.
AND TONIGHT.
I DON'T NEED TO TELL YOU THE PRICE OF FAILURE.
The True Source was power. Saidar was a wondrous tool, but there were consequences for channeling it unwisely.
I CAN CHANNEL AND TALK AT THE SAME TIME, SIUAN.
THAT IS, SO LONG AS YOU REFRAIN FROM YOUR PLAYFUL... DISTRACTIONS.
AH.

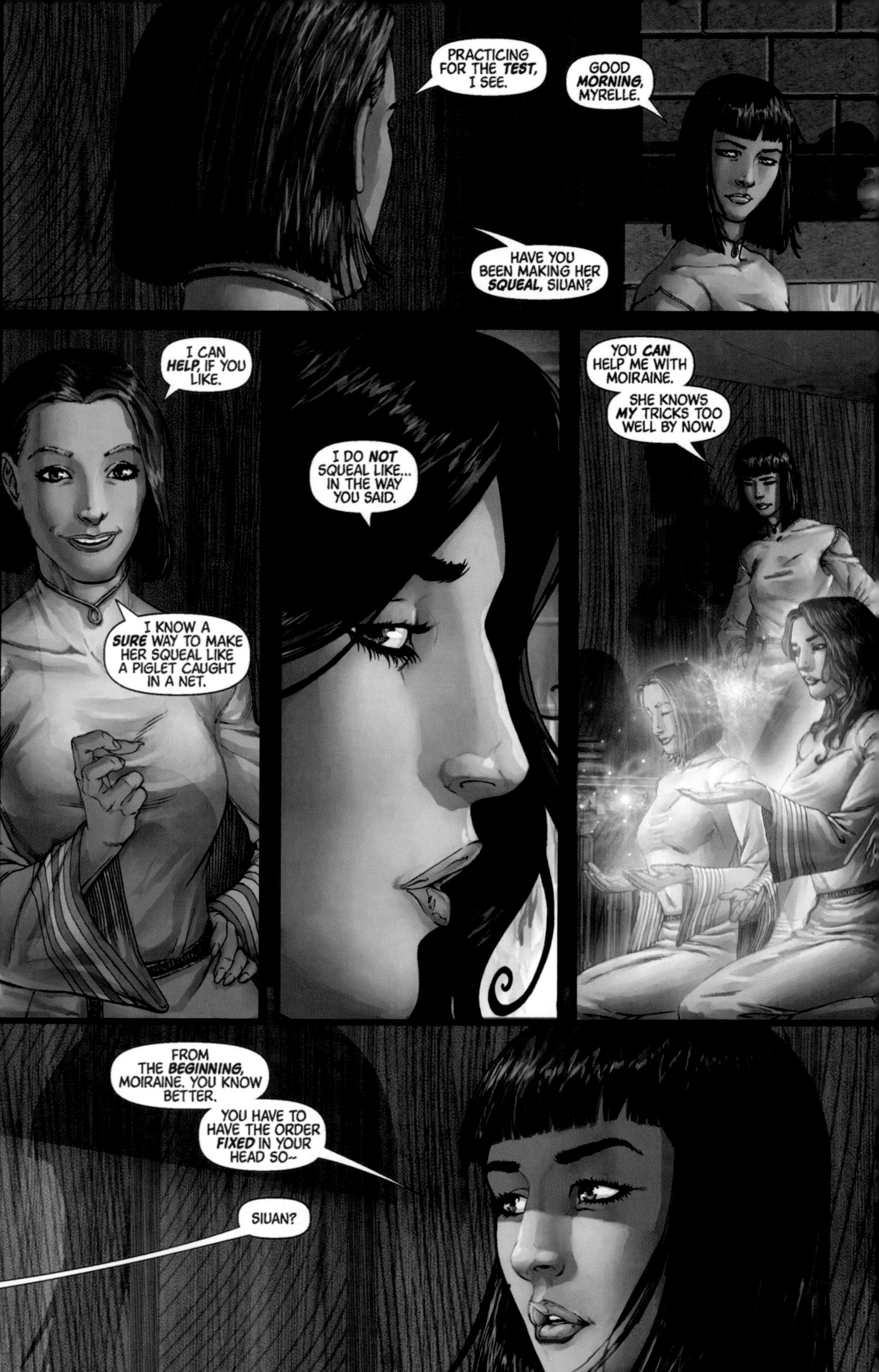
PRACTICING FOR THE TEST, I SEE.
GOOD MORNING, MYRELLE.
HAVE YOU BEEN MAKING HER SQUEAL, SIUAN?
I CAN HELP, IF YOU LIKE.
I KNOW A SURE WAY TO MAKE HER SQUEAL LIKE A PIGLET CAUGHT IN A NET.
I DO NOT SQUEAL LIKE... IN THE WAY YOU SAID.
YOU CAN HELP ME WITH MOIRAINE.
SHE KNOWS MY TRICKS TOO WELL BY NOW.
FROM THE BEGINNING, MOIRAINE. YOU KNOW BETTER.
YOU HAVE TO HAVE THE ORDER FIXED IN YOUR HEAD SO--
SIUAN?

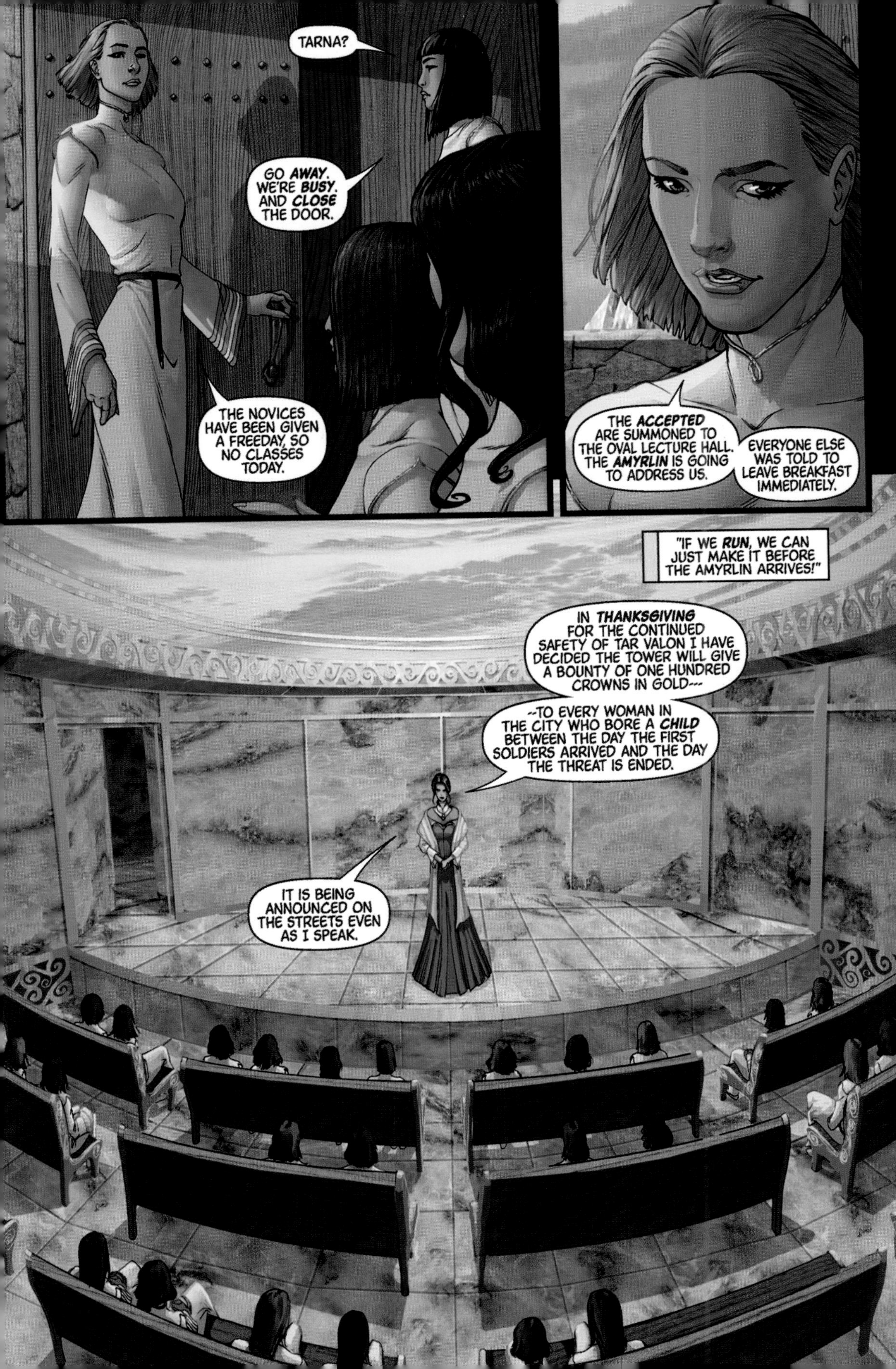
TARNA?
GO AWAY. WE'RE BUSY. AND CLOSE THE DOOR.
THE NOVICES HAVE BEEN GIVEN A FREEDAY, SO NO CLASSES TODAY.
THE ACCEPTED ARE SUMMONED TO THE OVAL LECTURE HALL. THE AMYRLIN IS GOING TO ADDRESS US.
EVERYONE ELSE WAS TOLD TO LEAVE BREAKFAST IMMEDIATELY.
"IF WE RUN, WE CAN JUST MAKE IT BEFORE THE AMYRLIN ARRIVES!"
IN THANKSGIVING FOR THE CONTINUED SAFETY OF TAR VALON I HAVE DECIDED THE TOWER WILL GIVE A BOUNTY OF ONE HUNDRED CROWNS IN GOLD---
--TO EVERY WOMAN IN THE CITY WHO BORE A CHILD BETWEEN THE DAY THE FIRST SOLDIERS ARRIVED AND THE DAY THE THREAT IS ENDED.
IT IS BEING ANNOUNCED ON THE STREETS EVEN AS I SPEAK.

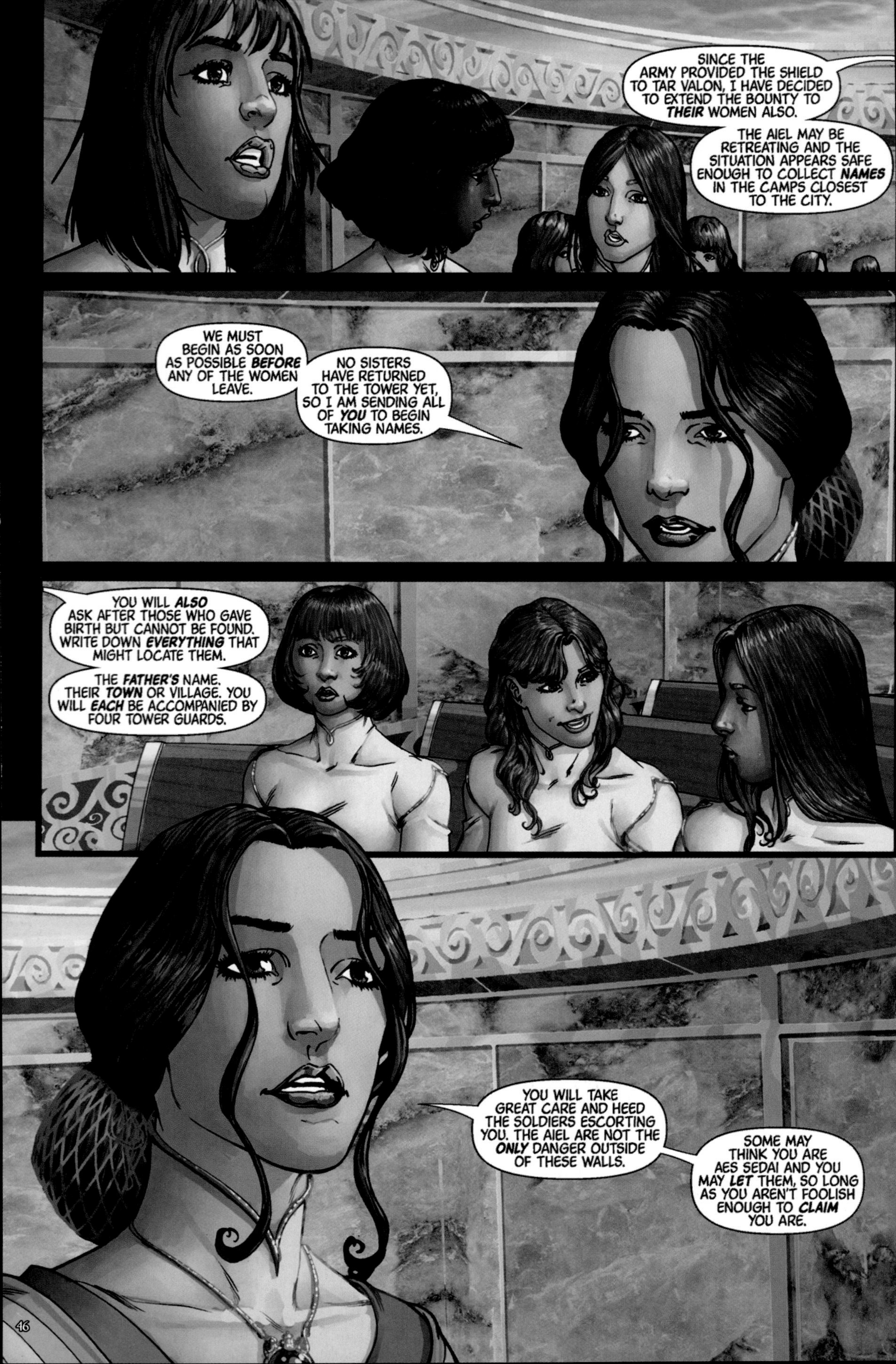
SINCE THE ARMY PROVIDED THE SHIELD TO TAR VALON, I HAVE DECIDED TO EXTEND THE BOUNTY TO *THEIR* WOMEN ALSO.
THE AIEL MAY BE RETREATING AND THE SITUATION APPEARS SAFE ENOUGH TO COLLECT *NAMES* IN THE CAMPS CLOSEST TO THE CITY.
WE MUST BEGIN AS SOON AS POSSIBLE *BEFORE* ANY OF THE WOMEN LEAVE.
NO SISTERS HAVE RETURNED TO THE TOWER YET, SO I AM SENDING ALL OF *YOU* TO BEGIN TAKING NAMES.
YOU WILL *ALSO* ASK AFTER THOSE WHO GAVE BIRTH BUT CANNOT BE FOUND. WRITE DOWN *EVERYTHING* THAT MIGHT LOCATE THEM.
THE *FATHER'S* NAME. THEIR *TOWN* OR VILLAGE. YOU WILL *EACH* BE ACCOMPANIED BY FOUR TOWER GUARDS.
YOU WILL TAKE GREAT CARE AND HEED THE SOLDIERS ESCORTING YOU. THE AIEL ARE NOT THE *ONLY* DANGER OUTSIDE OF THESE WALLS.
SOME MAY THINK YOU ARE AES SEDAI AND YOU MAY *LET* THEM, SO LONG AS YOU AREN'T FOOLISH ENOUGH TO *CLAIM* YOU ARE.

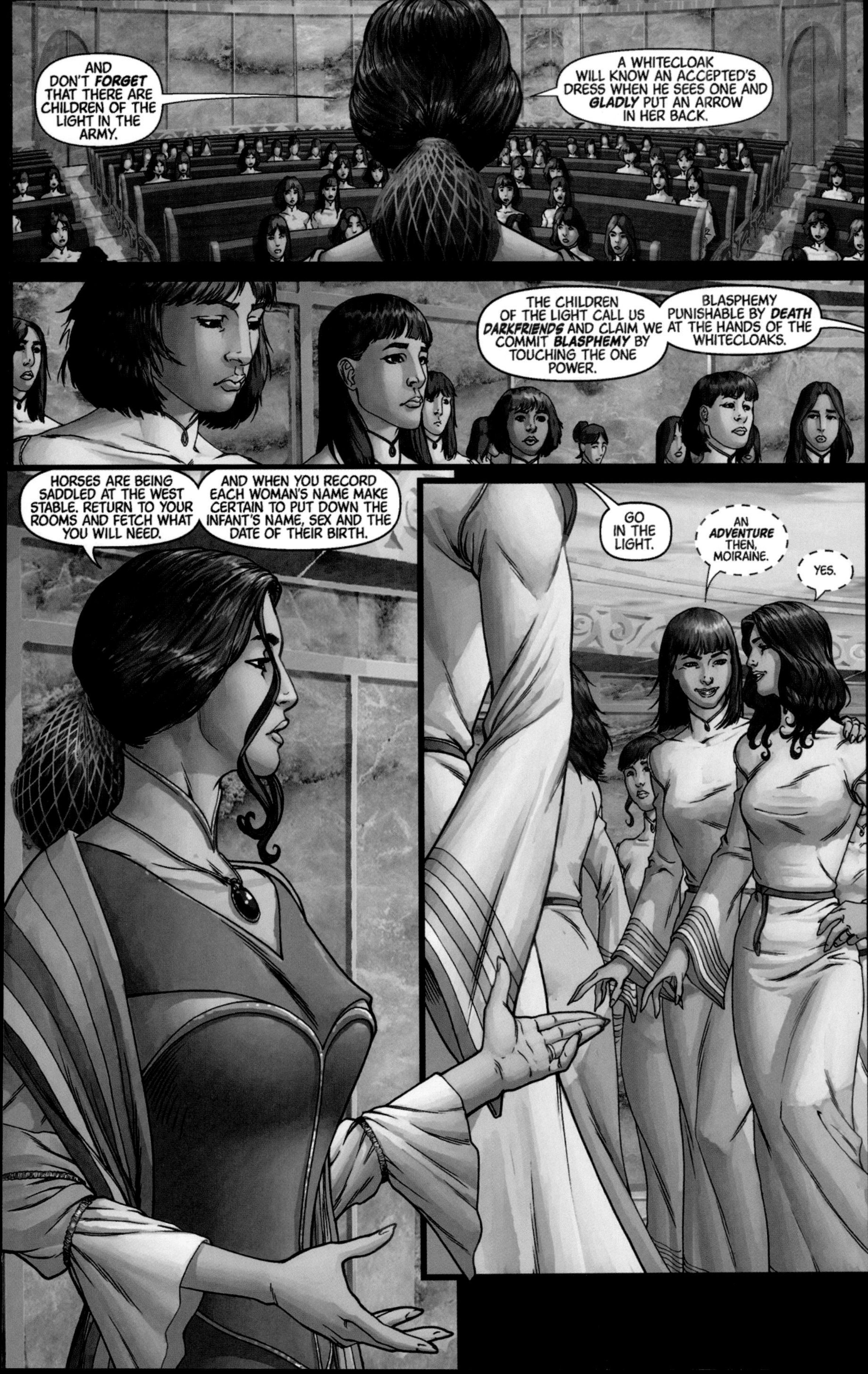
AND DON'T FORGET THAT THERE ARE CHILDREN OF THE LIGHT IN THE ARMY.
A WHITECLOAK WILL KNOW AN ACCEPTED'S DRESS WHEN HE SEES ONE AND GLADLY PUT AN ARROW IN HER BACK.
THE CHILDREN OF THE LIGHT CALL US DARKFRIENDS AND CLAIM WE COMMIT BLASPHEMY BY TOUCHING THE ONE POWER.
BLASPHEMY PUNISHABLE BY DEATH AT THE HANDS OF THE WHITECLOAKS.
HORSES ARE BEING SADDLED AT THE WEST STABLE. RETURN TO YOUR ROOMS AND FETCH WHAT YOU WILL NEED.
AND WHEN YOU RECORD EACH WOMAN'S NAME MAKE CERTAIN TO PUT DOWN THE INFANT'S NAME, SEX AND THE DATE OF THEIR BIRTH.
GO IN THE LIGHT.
AN ADVENTURE THEN, MOIRAINE.
YES.

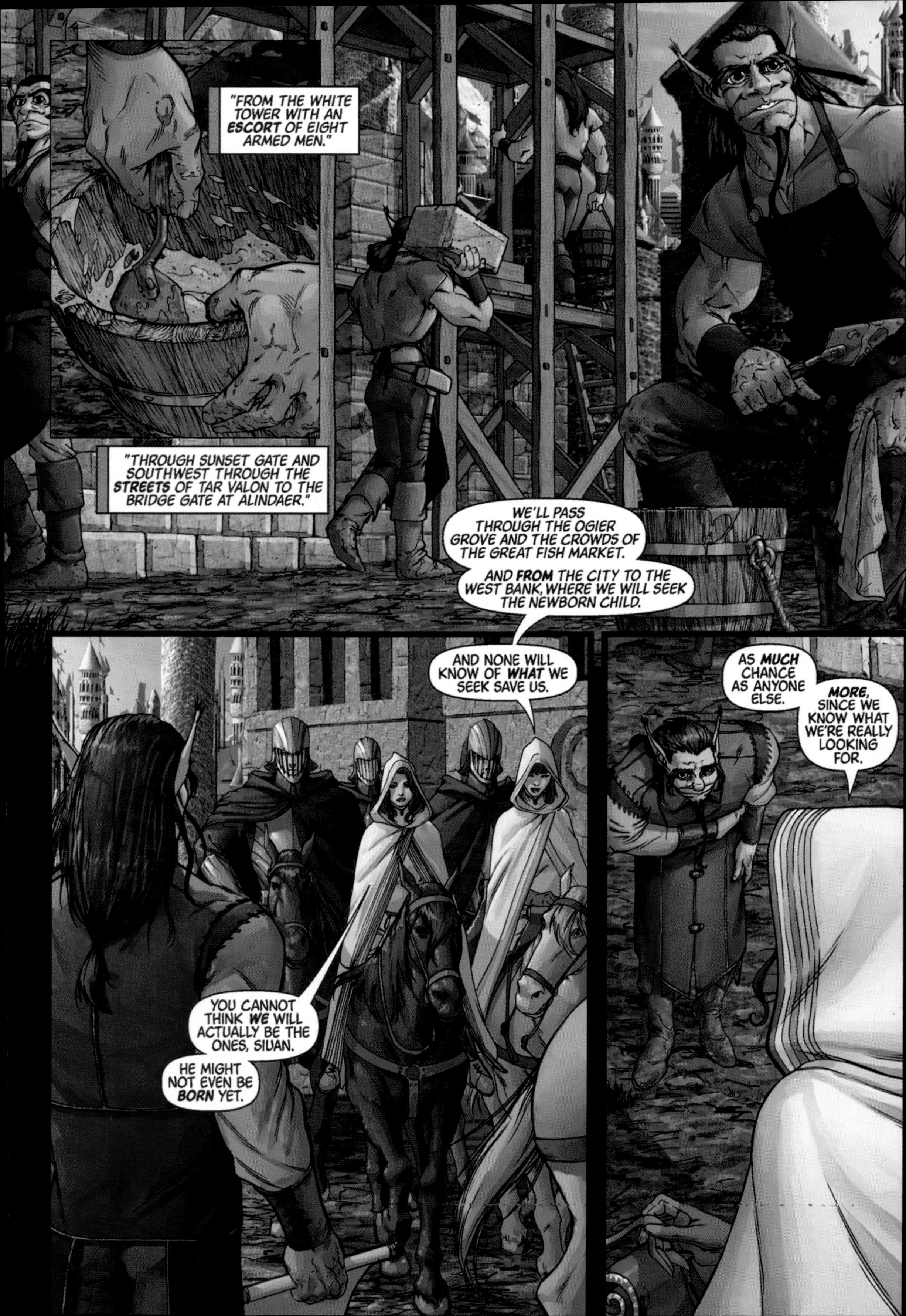
"FROM THE WHITE TOWER WITH AN ESCORT OF EIGHT ARMED MEN."
"THROUGH SUNSET GATE AND SOUTHWEST THROUGH THE STREETS OF TAR VALON TO THE BRIDGE GATE AT ALINDAER."
WE'LL PASS THROUGH THE OGIER GROVE AND THE CROWDS OF THE GREAT FISH MARKET.
AND FROM THE CITY TO THE WEST BANK, WHERE WE WILL SEEK THE NEWBORN CHILD.
AND NONE WILL KNOW OF WHAT WE SEEK SAVE US.
YOU CANNOT THINK WE WILL ACTUALLY BE THE ONES, SIUAN.
HE MIGHT NOT EVEN BE BORN YET.
AS MUCH CHANCE AS ANYONE ELSE.
MORE, SINCE WE KNOW WHAT WE'RE REALLY LOOKING FOR.

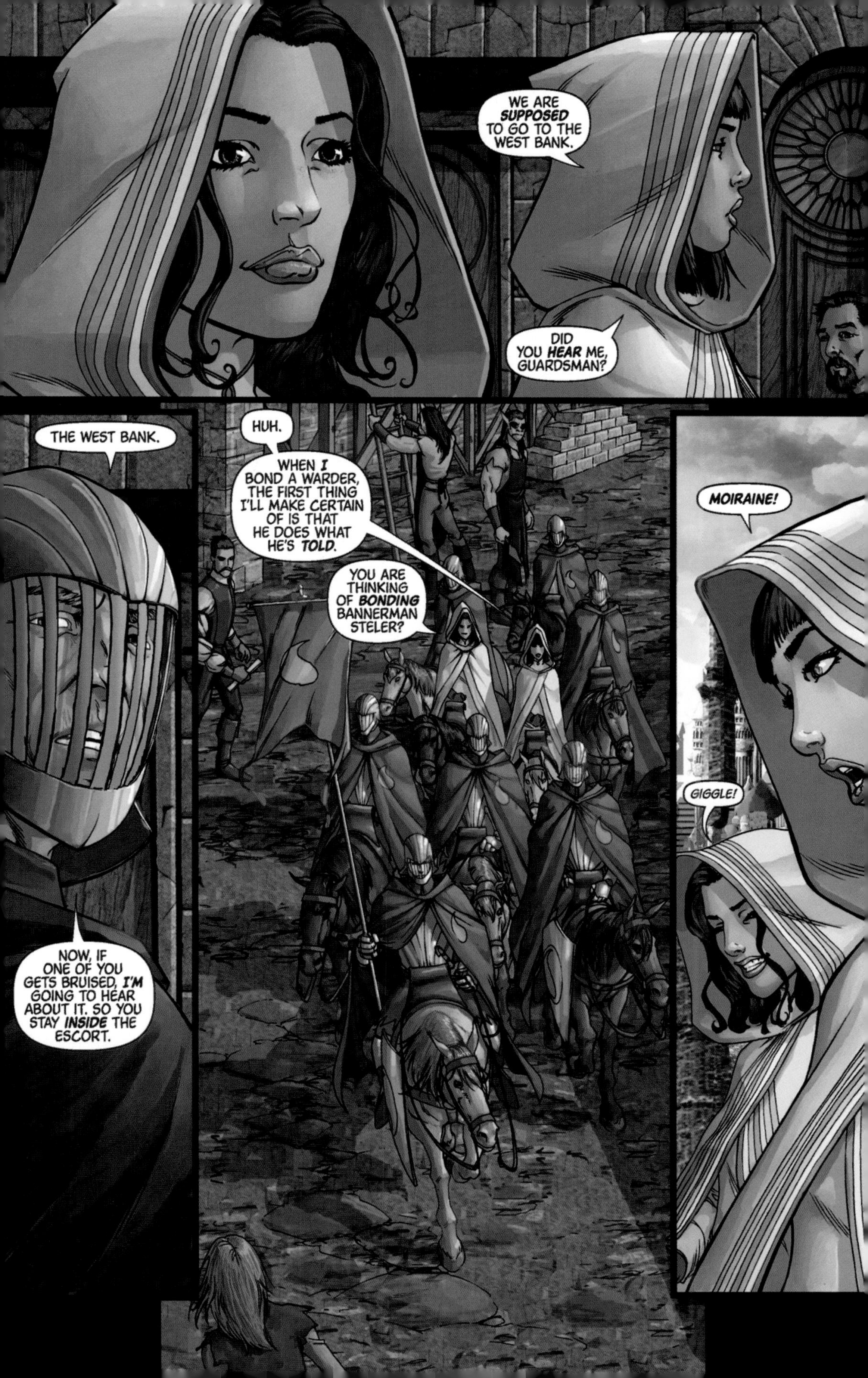
WE ARE SUPPOSED TO GO TO THE WEST BANK.
DID YOU HEAR ME, GUARDSMAN?
THE WEST BANK.
NOW, IF ONE OF YOU GETS BRUISED, I'M GOING TO HEAR ABOUT IT. SO YOU STAY INSIDE THE ESCORT.
HUH.
WHEN I BOND A WARDER, THE FIRST THING I'LL MAKE CERTAIN OF IS THAT HE DOES WHAT HE'S TOLD.
YOU ARE THINKING OF BONDING BANNERMAN STELER?
MOIRAINE!
GIGGLE!

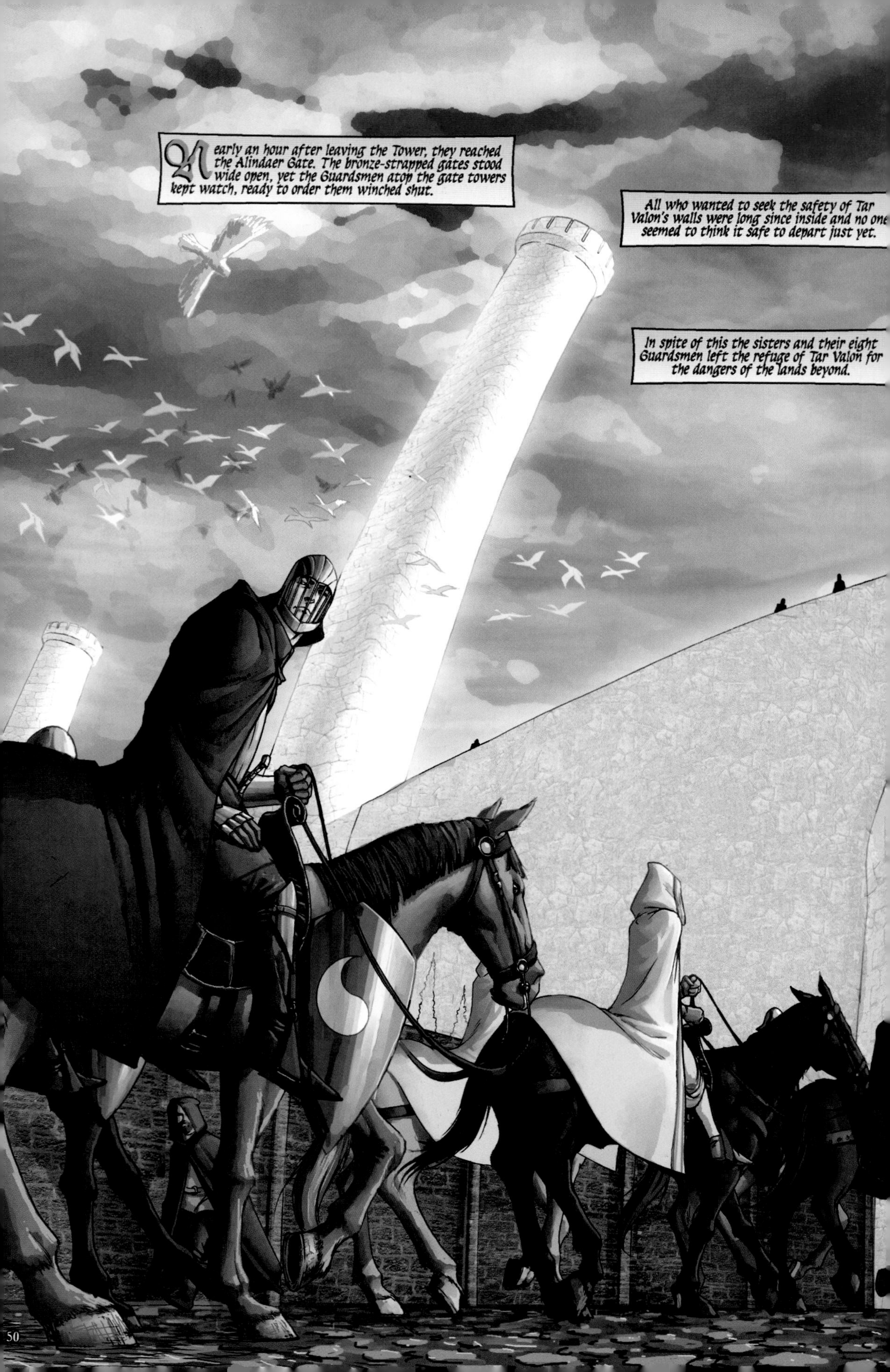

Nearly an hour after leaving the Tower, they reached the Alindaer Gate. The bronze-strapped gates stood wide open, yet the Guardsmen atop the gate towers kept watch, ready to order them winched shut.
All who wanted to seek the safety of Tar Valon's walls were long since inside and no one seemed to think it safe to depart just yet.
In spite of this the sisters and their eight Guardsmen left the refuge of Tar Valon for the dangers of the lands beyond.

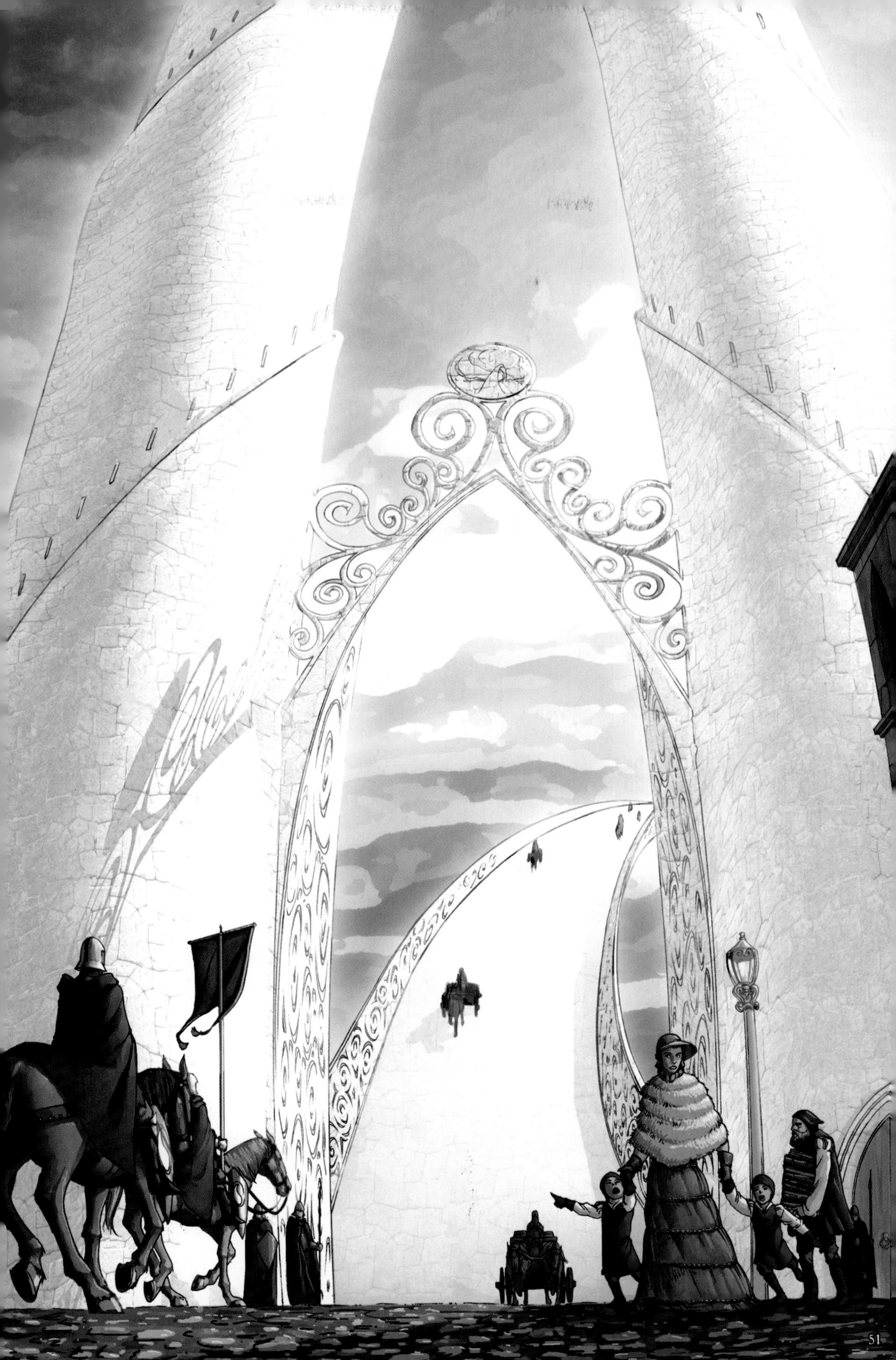

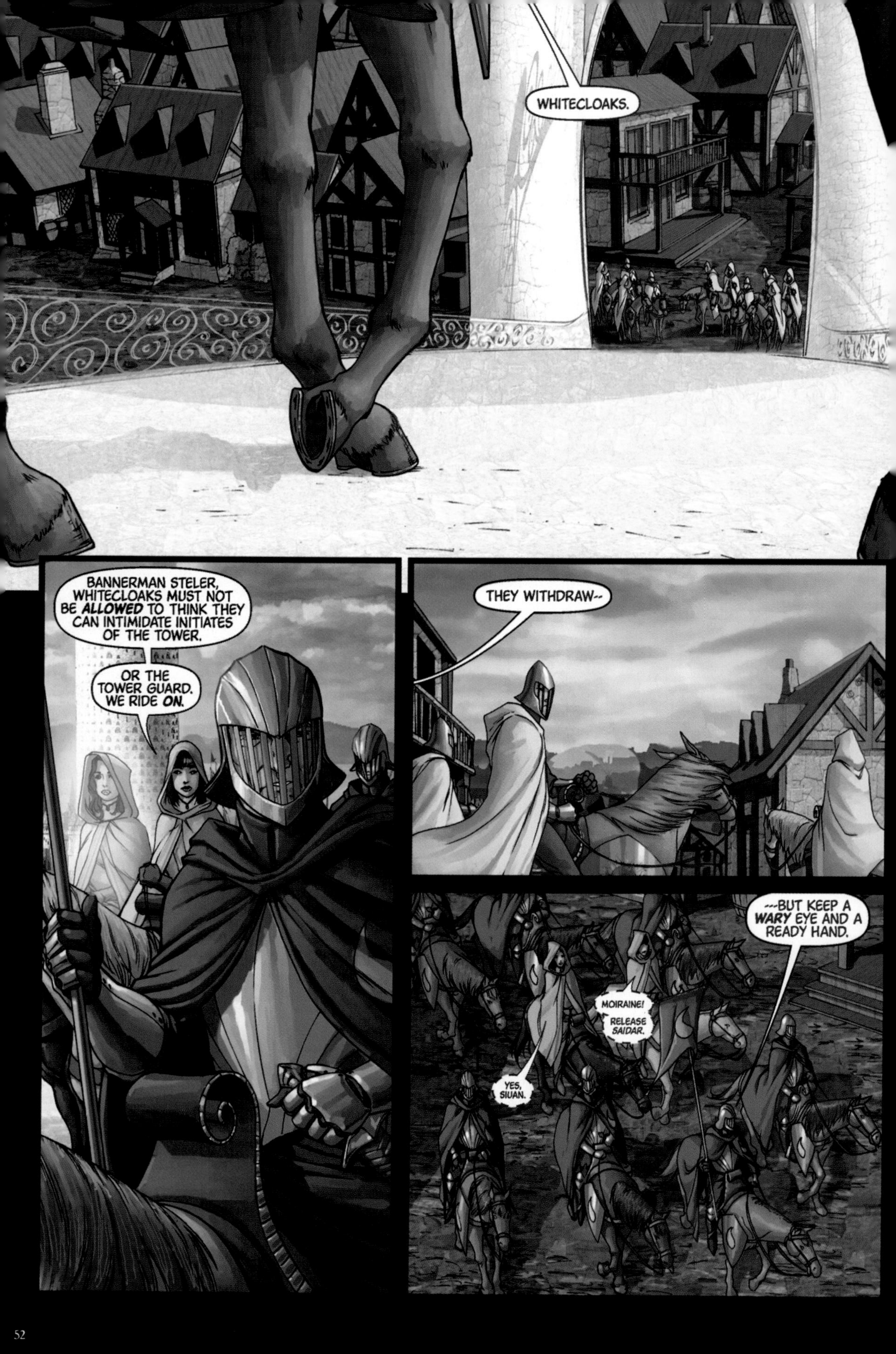
WHITECLOAKS.
BANNERMAN STELER, WHITECLOAKS MUST NOT BE ALLOWED TO THINK THEY CAN INTIMIDATE INITIATES OF THE TOWER.
OR THE TOWER GUARD. WE RIDE ON.
THEY WITHDRAW--
---BUT KEEP A WARY EYE AND A READY HAND.
MOIRAINE! RELEASE SAIDAR.
YES, SIUAN.

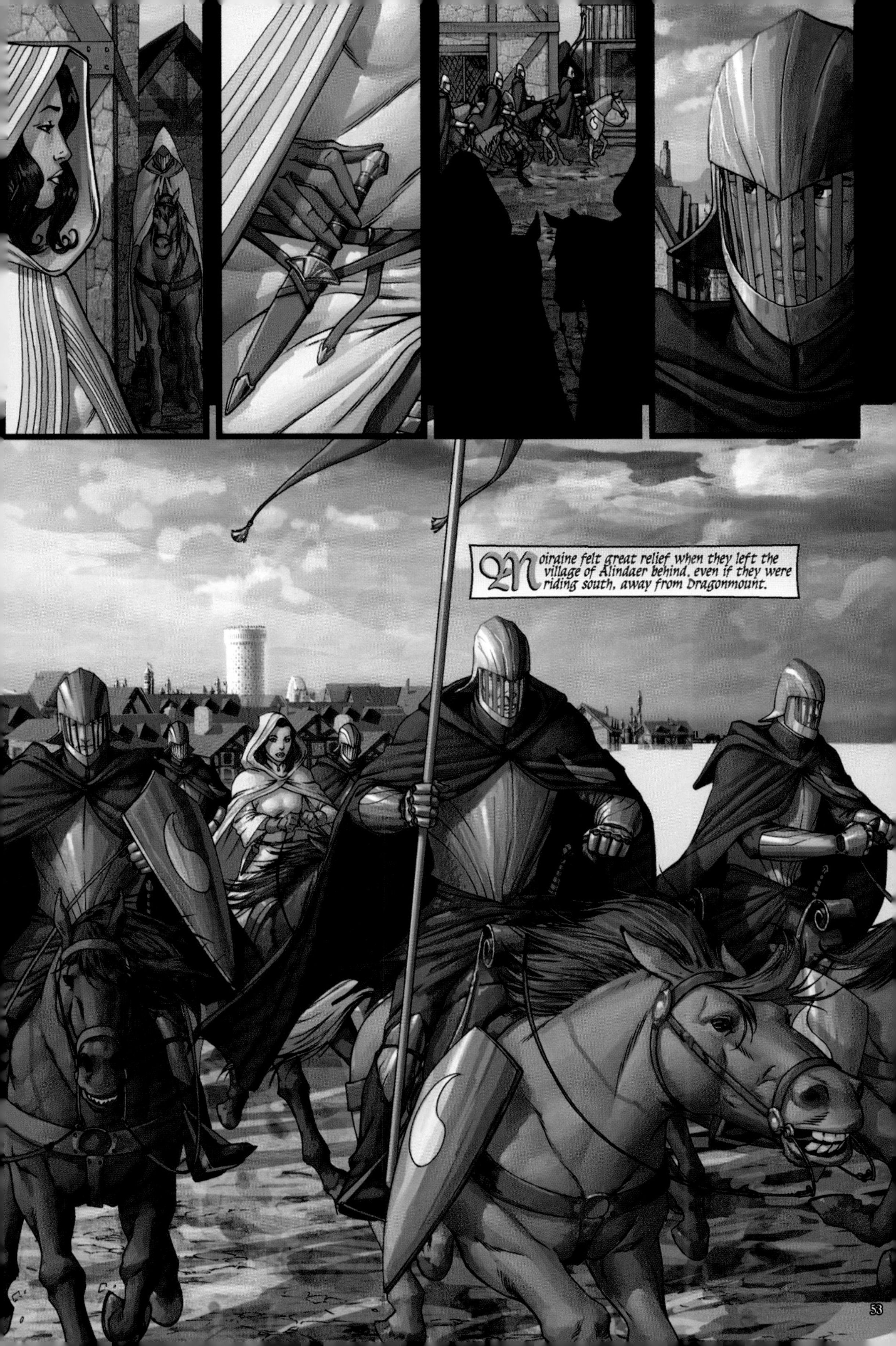
Moiraine felt great relief when they left the village of Alindaer behind, even if they were riding south, away from Dragonmount.

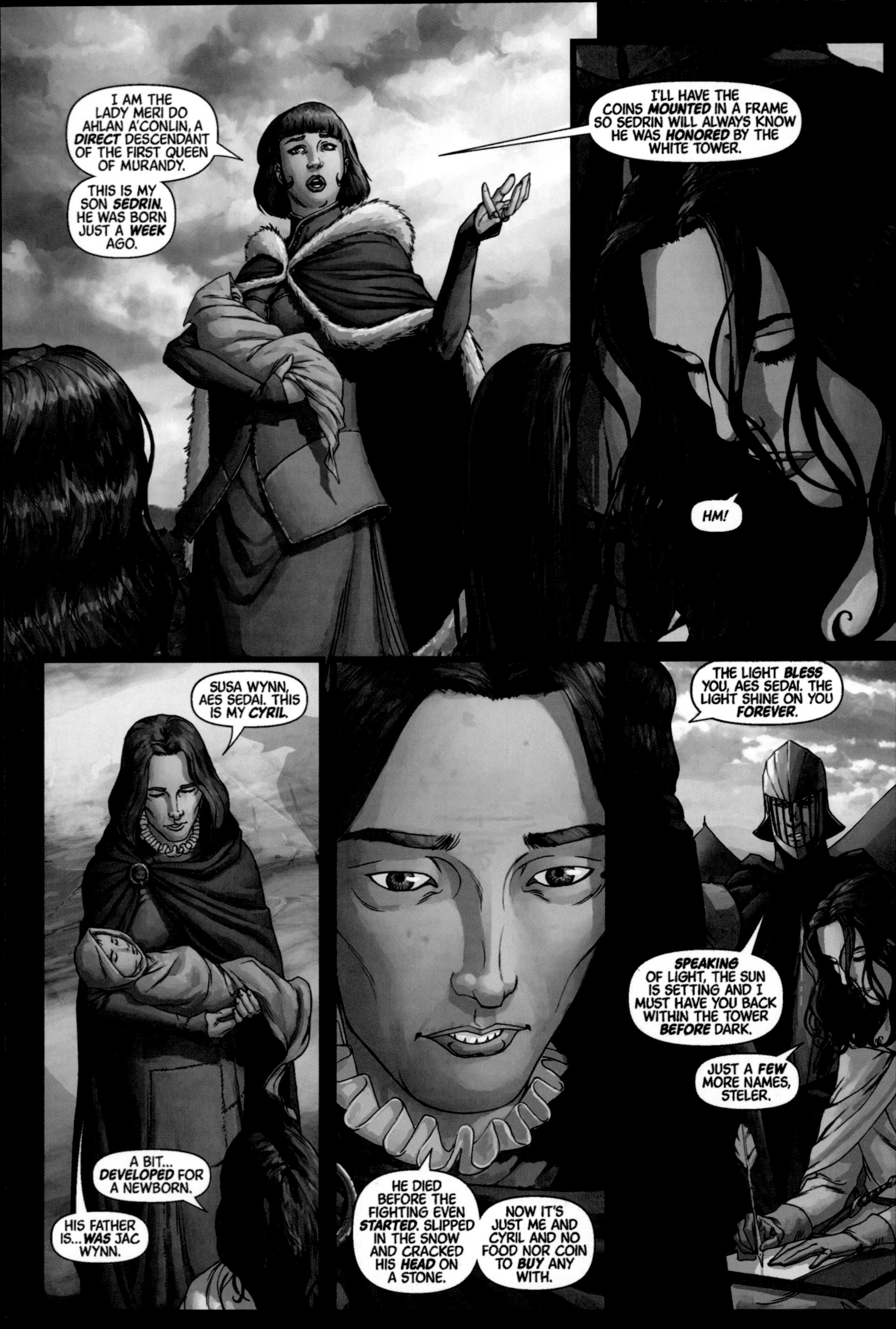
I AM THE LADY MERI DO AHLAN A'CONLIN, A DIRECT DESCENDANT OF THE FIRST QUEEN OF MURANDY.
THIS IS MY SON SEDRIN. HE WAS BORN JUST A WEEK AGO.
I'LL HAVE THE COINS MOUNTED IN A FRAME SO SEDRIN WILL ALWAYS KNOW HE WAS HONORED BY THE WHITE TOWER.
HM!
SUSA WYNN, AES SEDAI. THIS IS MY CYRIL.
A BIT... DEVELOPED FOR A NEWBORN.
HIS FATHER IS...WAS JAC WYNN.
HE DIED BEFORE THE FIGHTING EVEN STARTED. SLIPPED IN THE SNOW AND CRACKED HIS HEAD ON A STONE.
NOW IT'S JUST ME AND CYRIL AND NO FOOD NOR COIN TO BUY ANY WITH.
THE LIGHT BLESS YOU, AES SEDAI. THE LIGHT SHINE ON YOU FOREVER.
SPEAKING OF LIGHT, THE SUN IS SETTING AND I MUST HAVE YOU BACK WITHIN THE TOWER BEFORE DARK.
JUST A FEW MORE NAMES, STELER.

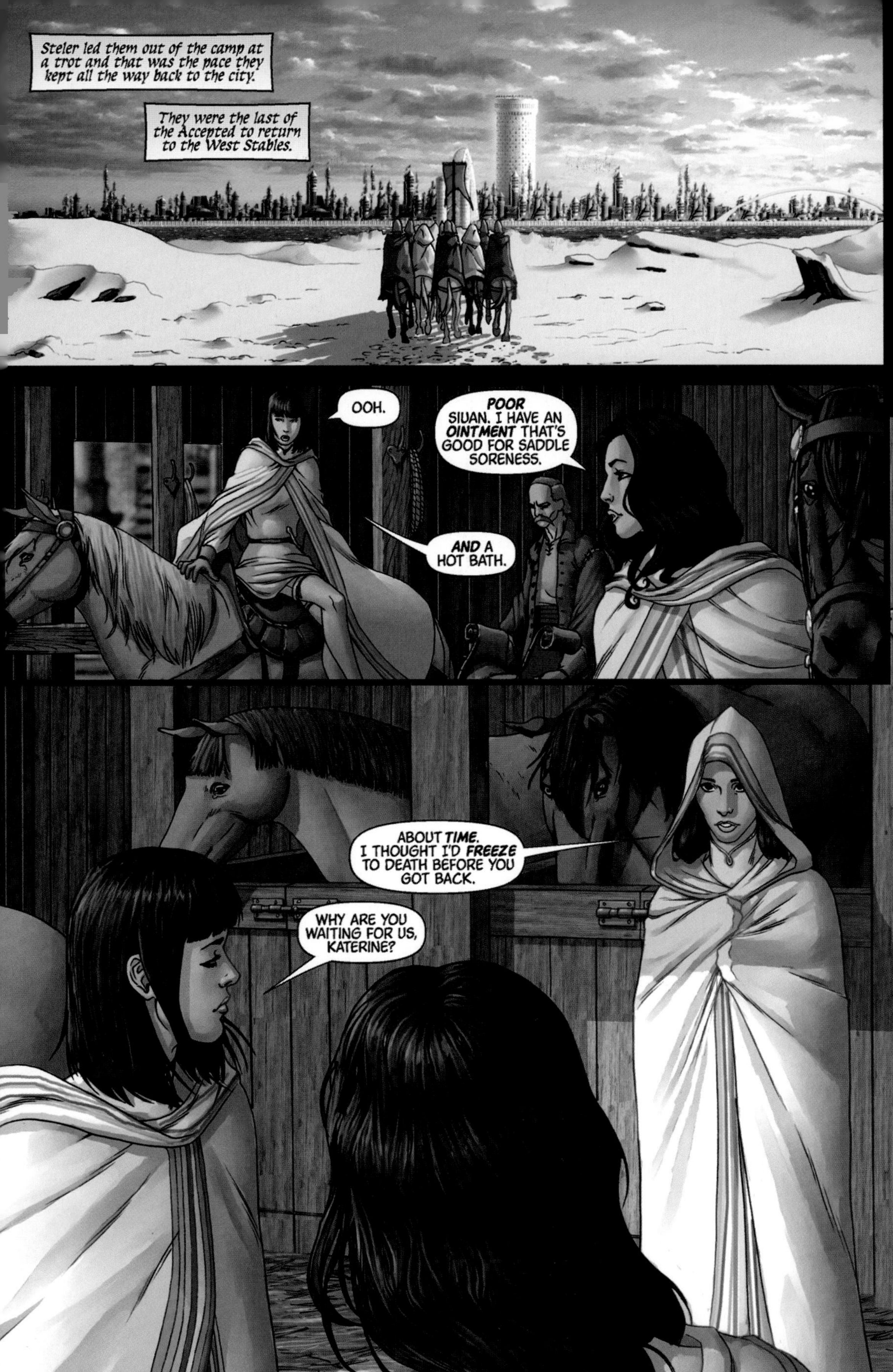

Steler led them out of the camp at a trot and that was the pace they kept all the way back to the city.
They were the last of the Accepted to return to the West Stables.
OOH.
POOR SIUAN. I HAVE AN OINTMENT THAT'S GOOD FOR SADDLE SORENESS.
AND A HOT BATH.
ABOUT TIME. I THOUGHT I'D FREEZE TO DEATH BEFORE YOU GOT BACK.
WHY ARE YOU WAITING FOR US, KATERINE?

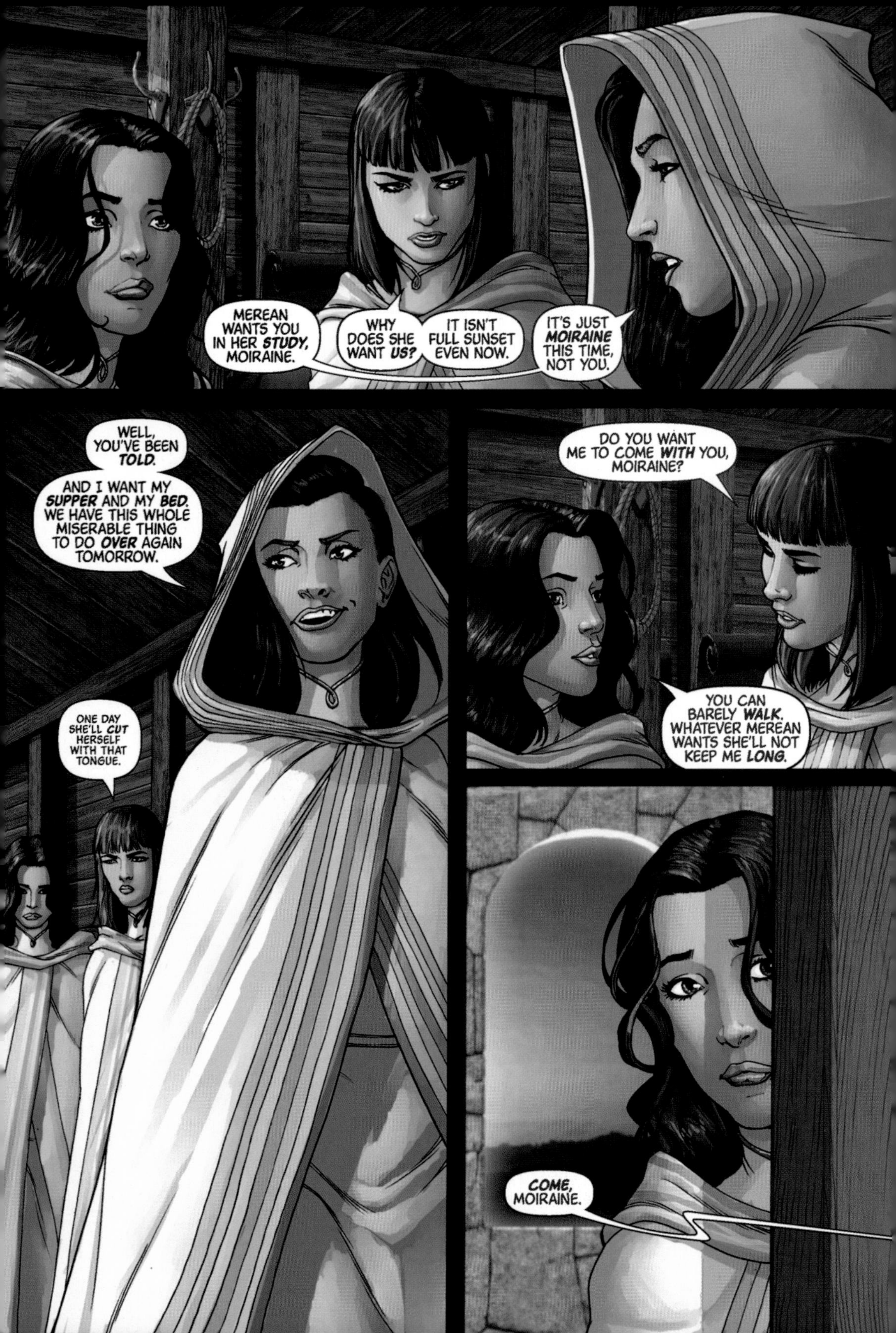
MEREAN WANTS YOU IN HER STUDY, MOIRAINE.
WHY DOES SHE WANT US?
IT ISN'T FULL SUNSET EVEN NOW.
IT'S JUST MOIRAINE THIS TIME, NOT YOU.
WELL, YOU'VE BEEN TOLD.
AND I WANT MY SUPPER AND MY BED. WE HAVE THIS WHOLE MISERABLE THING TO DO OVER AGAIN TOMORROW.
ONE DAY SHE'LL CUT HERSELF WITH THAT TONGUE.
DO YOU WANT ME TO COME WITH YOU, MOIRAINE?
YOU CAN BARELY WALK. WHATEVER MEREAN WANTS SHE'LL NOT KEEP ME LONG.
COME, MOIRAINE.

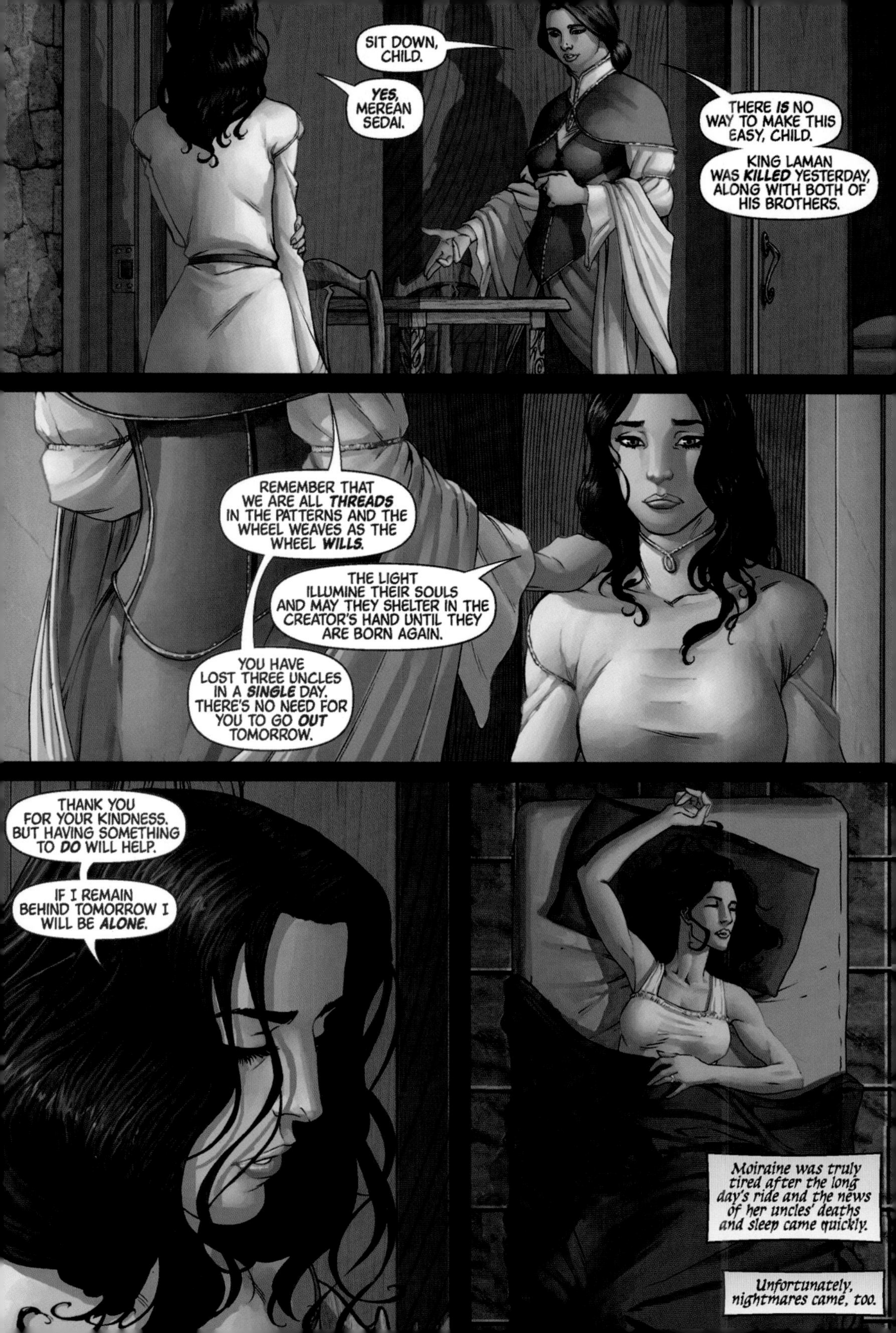
SIT DOWN, CHILD.
YES, MEREAN SEDAI.
THERE IS NO WAY TO MAKE THIS EASY, CHILD.
KING LAMAN WAS KILLED YESTERDAY, ALONG WITH BOTH OF HIS BROTHERS.
REMEMBER THAT WE ARE ALL THREADS IN THE PATTERNS AND THE WHEEL WEAVES AS THE WHEEL WILLS.
THE LIGHT ILLUMINE THEIR SOULS AND MAY THEY SHELTER IN THE CREATOR'S HAND UNTIL THEY ARE BORN AGAIN.
YOU HAVE LOST THREE UNCLES IN A SINGLE DAY. THERE'S NO NEED FOR YOU TO GO OUT TOMORROW.
THANK YOU FOR YOUR KINDNESS. BUT HAVING SOMETHING TO DO WILL HELP.
IF I REMAIN BEHIND TOMORROW I WILL BE ALONE.
Moiraine was truly tired after the long day's ride and the news of her uncles' deaths and sleep came quickly.
Unfortunately, nightmares came, too.

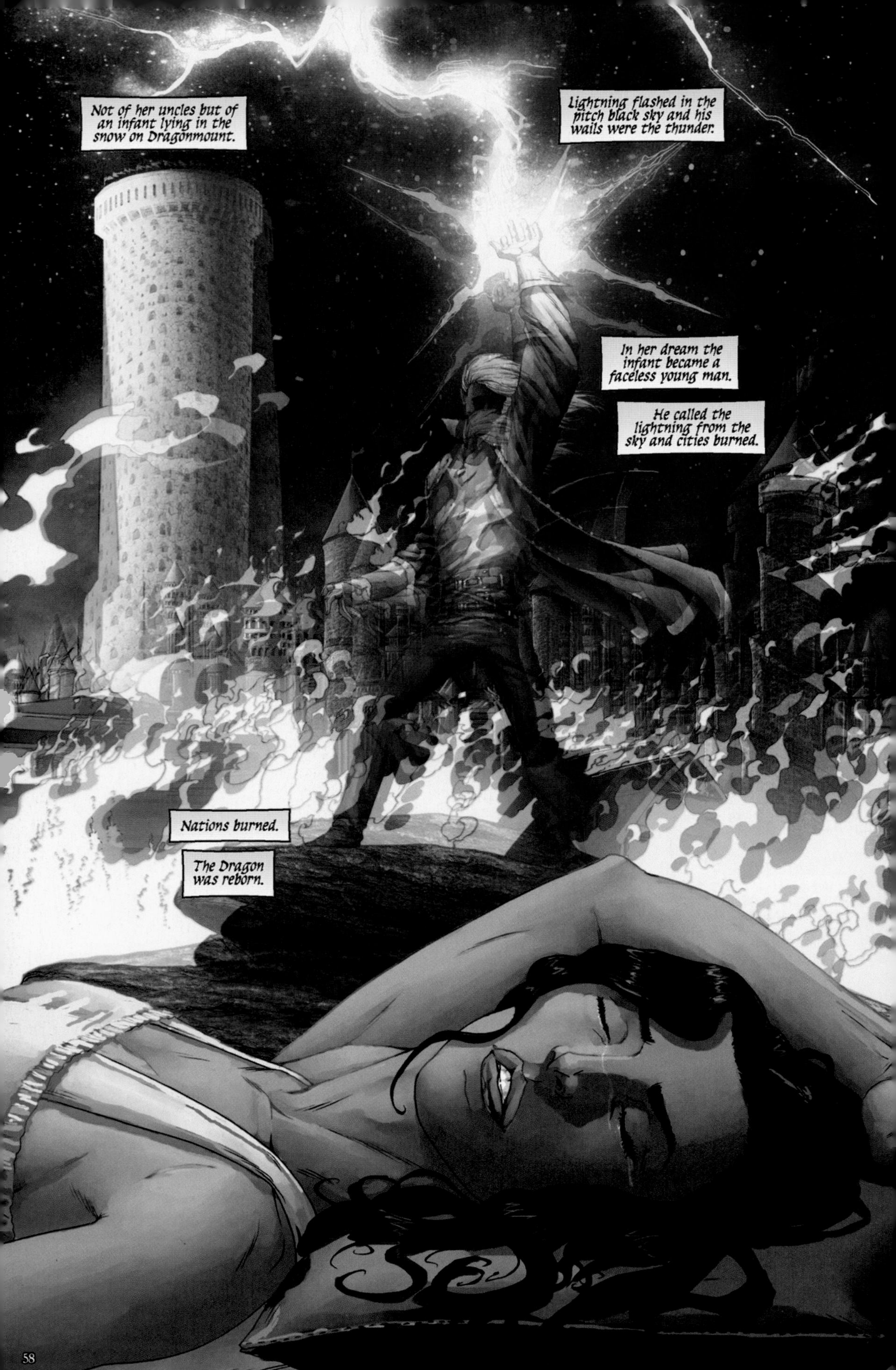
Not of her uncles but of an infant lying in the snow on Dragonmount.
Lightning flashed in the pitch black sky and his wails were the thunder.
In her dream the infant became a faceless young man.
He called the lightning from the sky and cities burned.
Nations burned.
The Dragon was reborn.

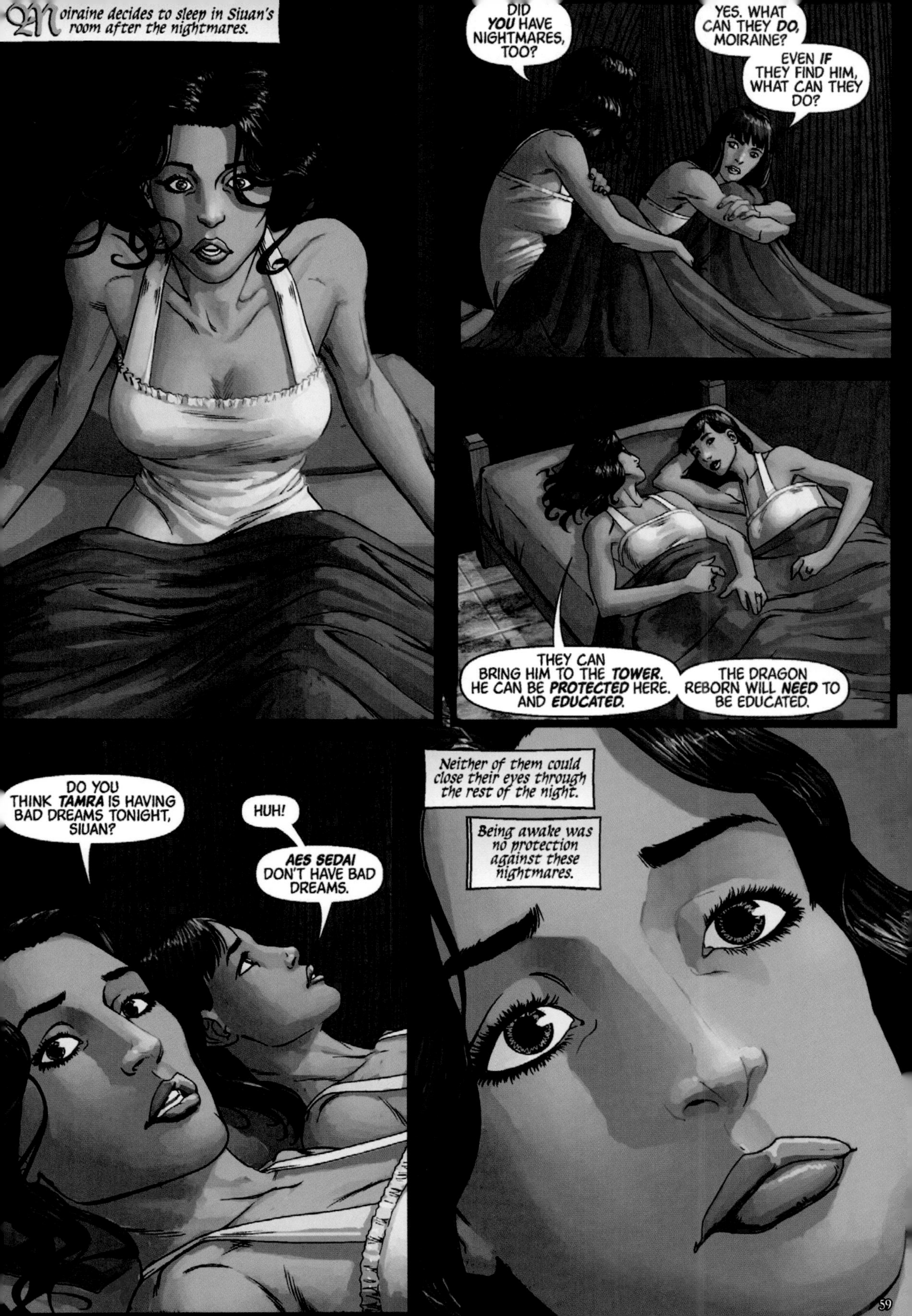
Moiraine decides to sleep in Siuan's room after the nightmares.
DID YOU HAVE NIGHTMARES, TOO?
YES. WHAT CAN THEY DO, MOIRAINE?
EVEN IF THEY FIND HIM, WHAT CAN THEY DO?
THEY CAN BRING HIM TO THE TOWER. HE CAN BE PROTECTED HERE. AND EDUCATED.
THE DRAGON REBORN WILL NEED TO BE EDUCATED.
DO YOU THINK TAMRA IS HAVING BAD DREAMS TONIGHT, SIUAN?
HUH!
AES SEDAI DON'T HAVE BAD DREAMS.
Neither of them could close their eyes through the rest of the night.
Being awake was no protection against these nightmares.

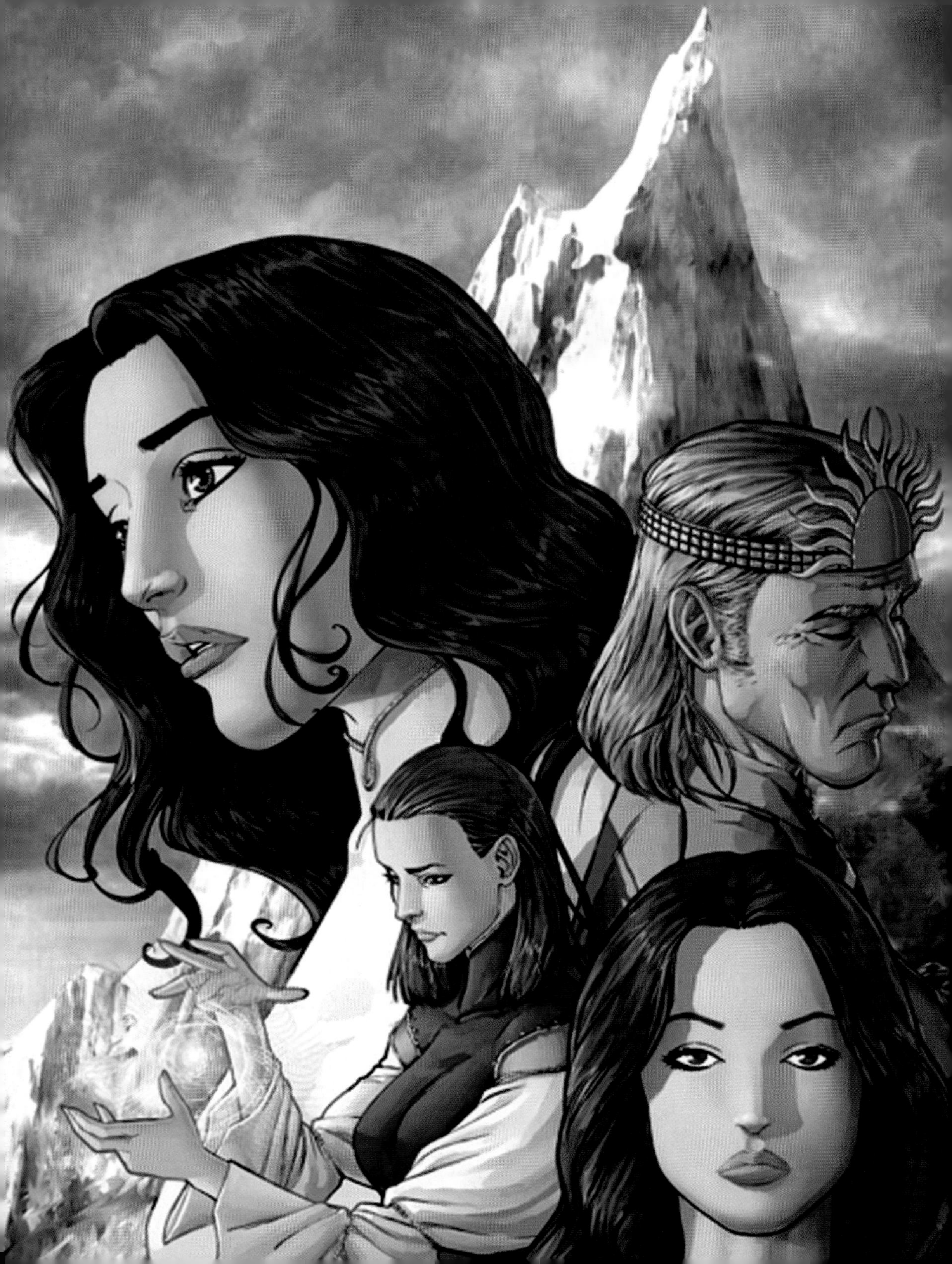

chapter three

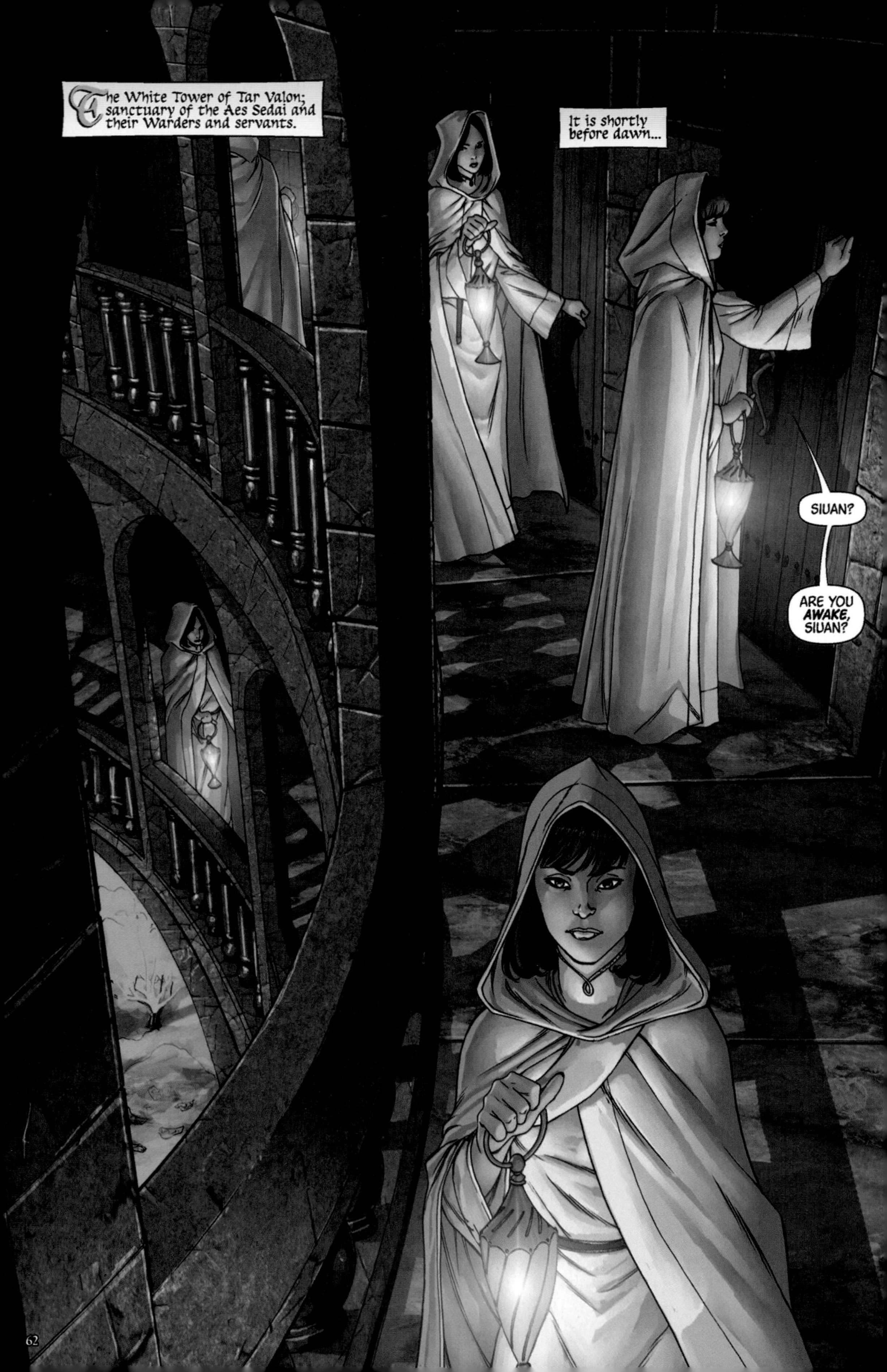
The White Tower of Tar Valon; sanctuary of the Aes Sedai and their Warders and servants.
It is shortly before dawn...
SIUAN?
ARE YOU AWAKE, SIUAN?

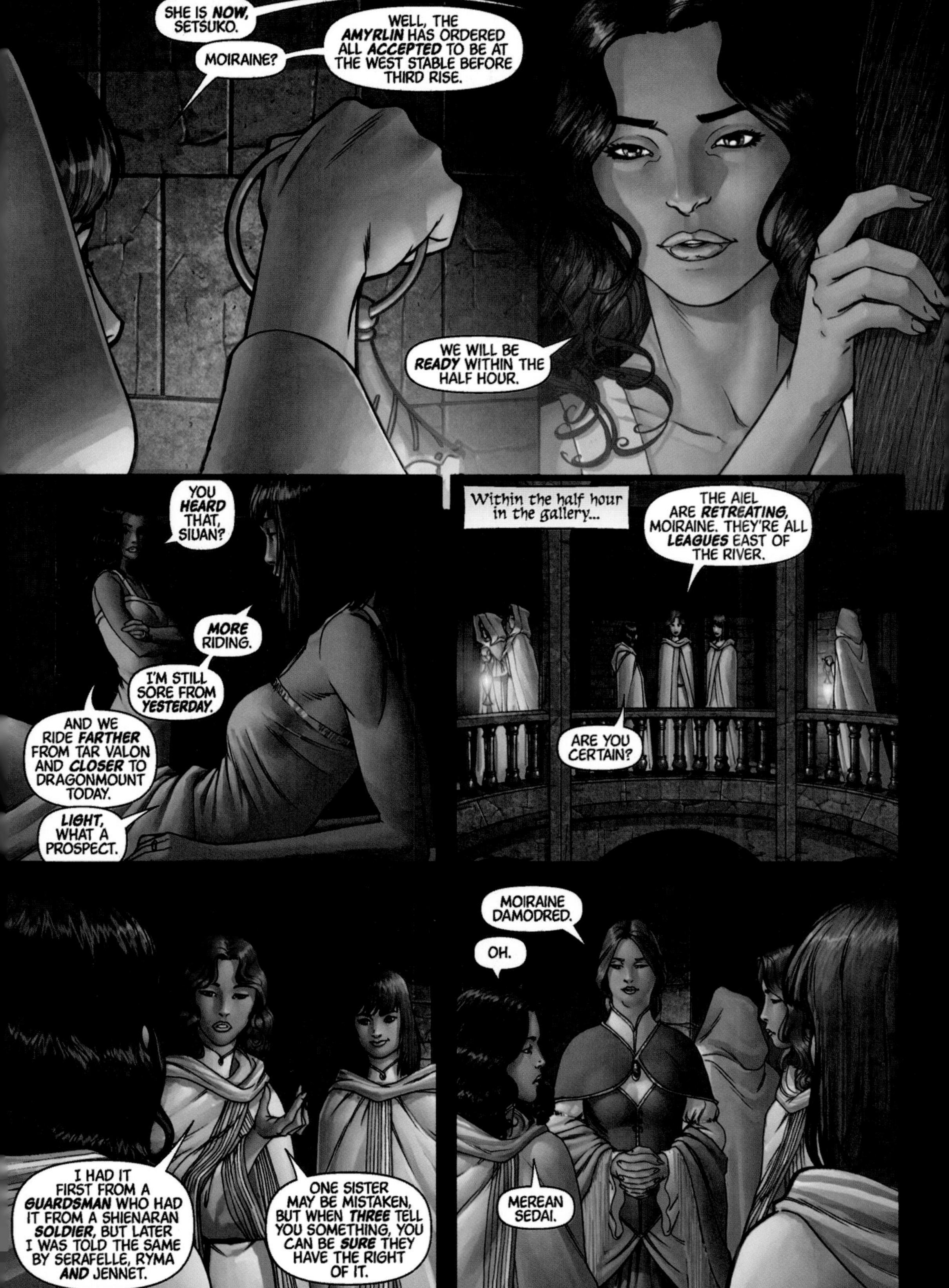

SHE IS NOW, SETSUKO.
MOIRAINE?
WELL, THE AMYRLIN HAS ORDERED ALL ACCEPTED TO BE AT THE WEST STABLE BEFORE THIRD RISE.
WE WILL BE READY WITHIN THE HALF HOUR.
YOU HEARD THAT, SIUAN?
MORE RIDING.
I'M STILL SORE FROM YESTERDAY.
AND WE RIDE FARTHER FROM TAR VALON AND CLOSER TO DRAGONMOUNT TODAY.
LIGHT, WHAT A PROSPECT.
Within the half hour in the gallery...
THE AIEL ARE RETREATING, MOIRAINE. THEY'RE ALL LEAGUES EAST OF THE RIVER.
ARE YOU CERTAIN?
I HAD IT FIRST FROM A GUARDSMAN WHO HAD IT FROM A SHIENARAN SOLDIER, BUT LATER I WAS TOLD THE SAME BY SERAFELLE, RYMA AND JENNET.
ONE SISTER MAY BE MISTAKEN, BUT WHEN THREE TELL YOU SOMETHING, YOU CAN BE SURE THEY HAVE THE RIGHT OF IT.
MOIRAINE DAMODRED.
OH.
MEREAN SEDAI.

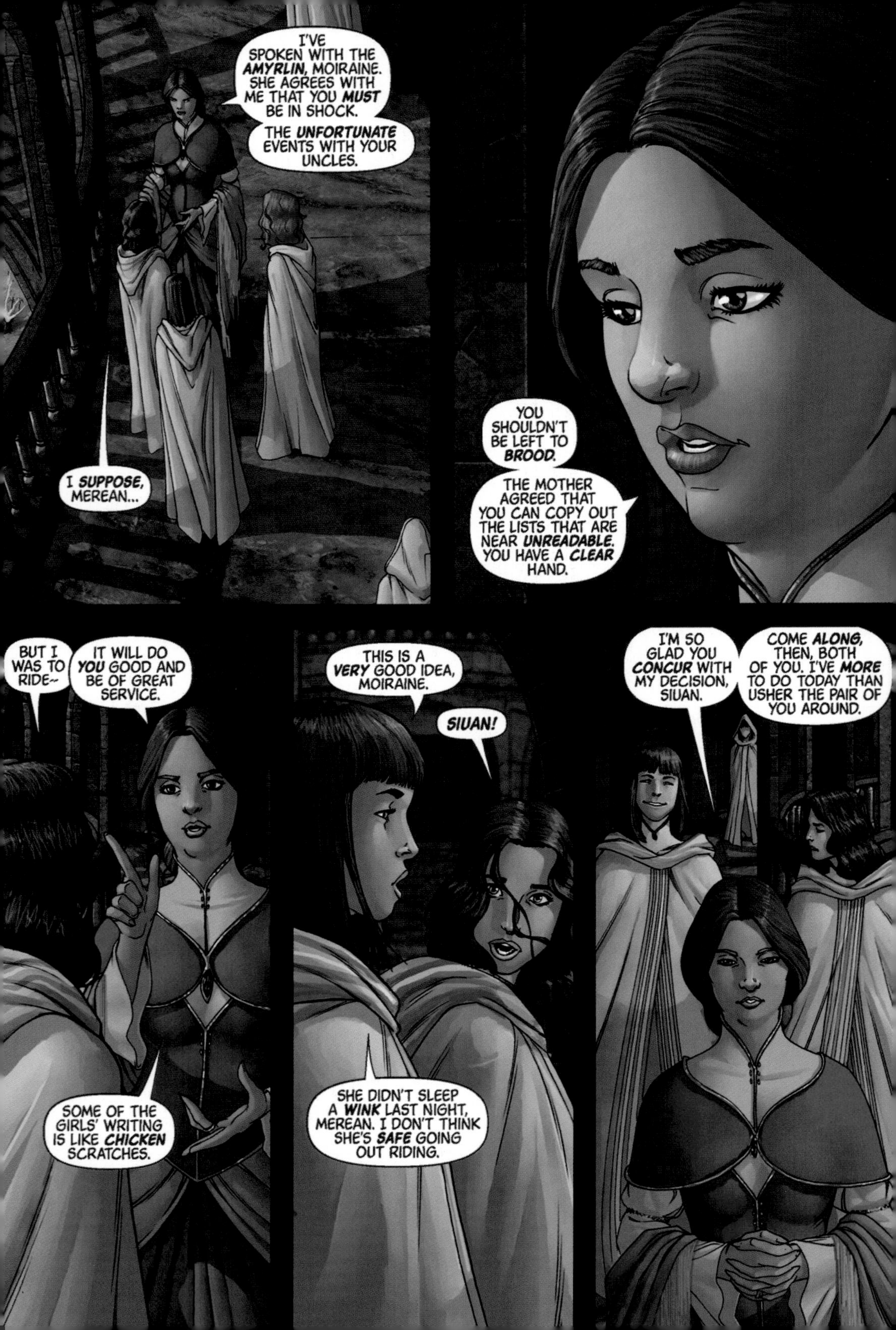
I'VE SPOKEN WITH THE AMYRLIN, MOIRAINE. SHE AGREES WITH ME THAT YOU MUST BE IN SHOCK.
THE UNFORTUNATE EVENTS WITH YOUR UNCLES.
I SUPPOSE, MEREAN...
YOU SHOULDN'T BE LEFT TO BROOD.
THE MOTHER AGREED THAT YOU CAN COPY OUT THE LISTS THAT ARE NEAR UNREADABLE. YOU HAVE A CLEAR HAND.
BUT I WAS TO RIDE--
IT WILL DO YOU GOOD AND BE OF GREAT SERVICE.
SOME OF THE GIRLS' WRITING IS LIKE CHICKEN SCRATCHES.
THIS IS A VERY GOOD IDEA, MOIRAINE.
SIUAN!
SHE DIDN'T SLEEP A WINK LAST NIGHT, MEREAN. I DON'T THINK SHE'S SAFE GOING OUT RIDING.
I'M SO GLAD YOU CONCUR WITH MY DECISION, SIUAN.
COME ALONG, THEN, BOTH OF YOU. I'VE MORE TO DO TODAY THAN USHER THE PAIR OF YOU AROUND.

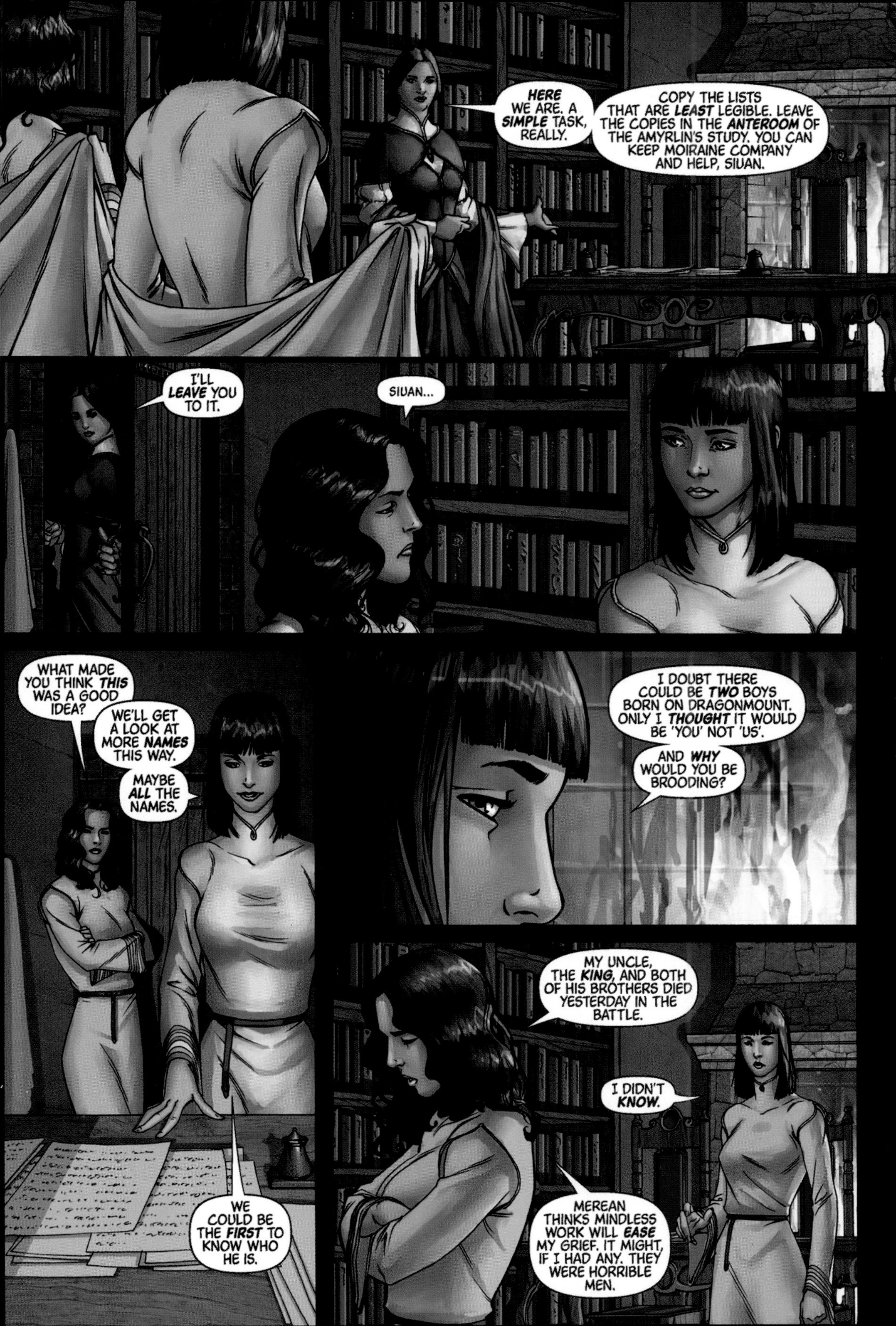
HERE WE ARE. A SIMPLE TASK, REALLY.
COPY THE LISTS THAT ARE LEAST LEGIBLE. LEAVE THE COPIES IN THE ANTEROOM OF THE AMYRLIN'S STUDY. YOU CAN KEEP MOIRAINE COMPANY AND HELP, SIUAN.
I'LL LEAVE YOU TO IT.
SIUAN...
WHAT MADE YOU THINK THIS WAS A GOOD IDEA?
WE'LL GET A LOOK AT MORE NAMES THIS WAY.
MAYBE ALL THE NAMES.
WE COULD BE THE FIRST TO KNOW WHO HE IS.
I DOUBT THERE COULD BE TWO BOYS BORN ON DRAGONMOUNT. ONLY I THOUGHT IT WOULD BE 'YOU' NOT 'US'.
AND WHY WOULD YOU BE BROODING?
MY UNCLE, THE KING, AND BOTH OF HIS BROTHERS DIED YESTERDAY IN THE BATTLE.
I DIDN'T KNOW.
MEREAN THINKS MINDLESS WORK WILL EASE MY GRIEF. IT MIGHT, IF I HAD ANY. THEY WERE HORRIBLE MEN.

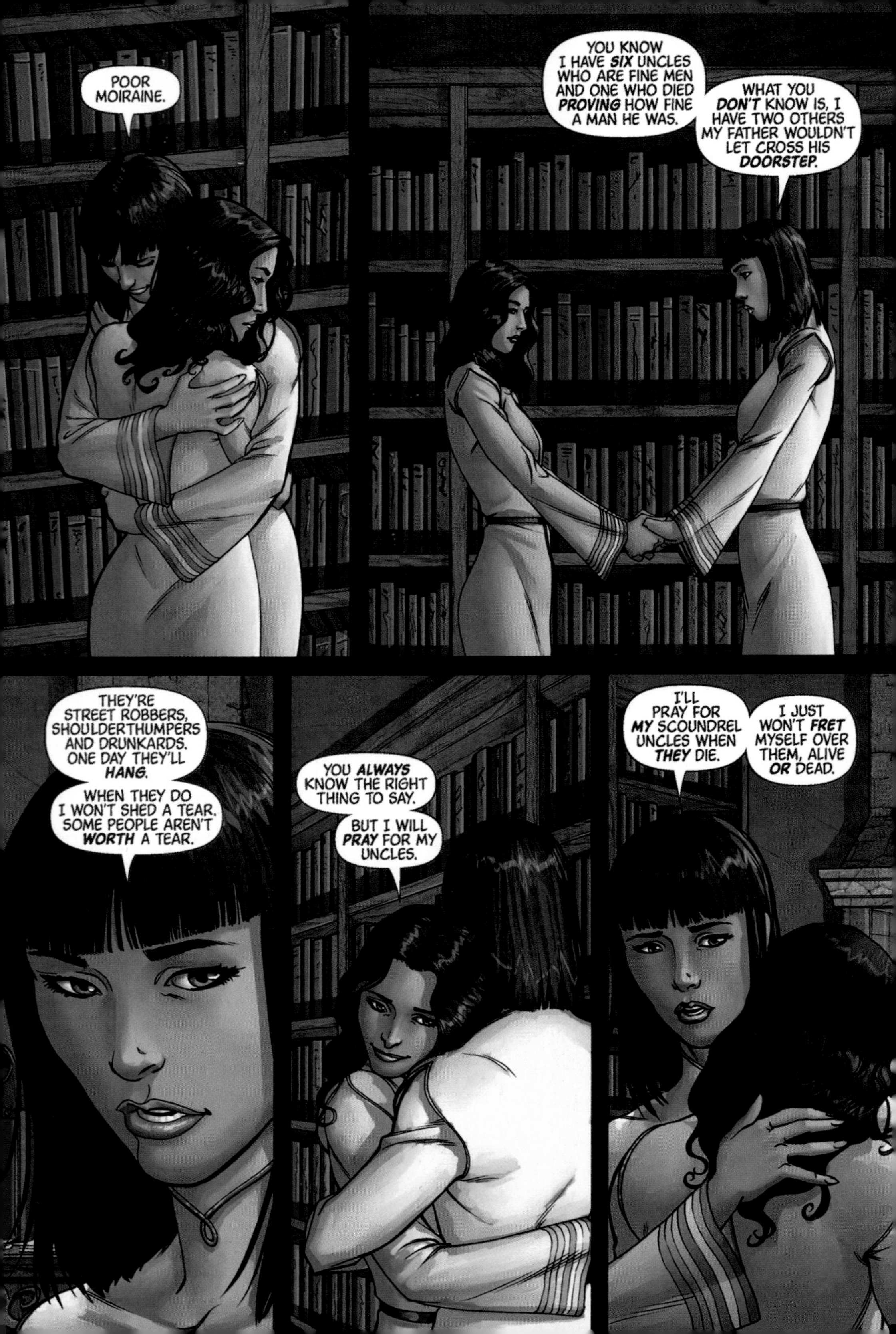
POOR MOIRAINE.
YOU KNOW I HAVE SIX UNCLES WHO ARE FINE MEN AND ONE WHO DIED PROVING HOW FINE A MAN HE WAS.
WHAT YOU DON'T KNOW IS, I HAVE TWO OTHERS MY FATHER WOULDN'T LET CROSS HIS DOORSTEP.
THEY'RE STREET ROBBERS, SHOULDERTHUMPERS AND DRUNKARDS. ONE DAY THEY'LL HANG.
WHEN THEY DO I WON'T SHED A TEAR. SOME PEOPLE AREN'T WORTH A TEAR.
YOU ALWAYS KNOW THE RIGHT THING TO SAY.
BUT I WILL PRAY FOR MY UNCLES.
I'LL PRAY FOR MY SCOUNDREL UNCLES WHEN THEY DIE.
I JUST WON'T FRET MYSELF OVER THEM, ALIVE OR DEAD.

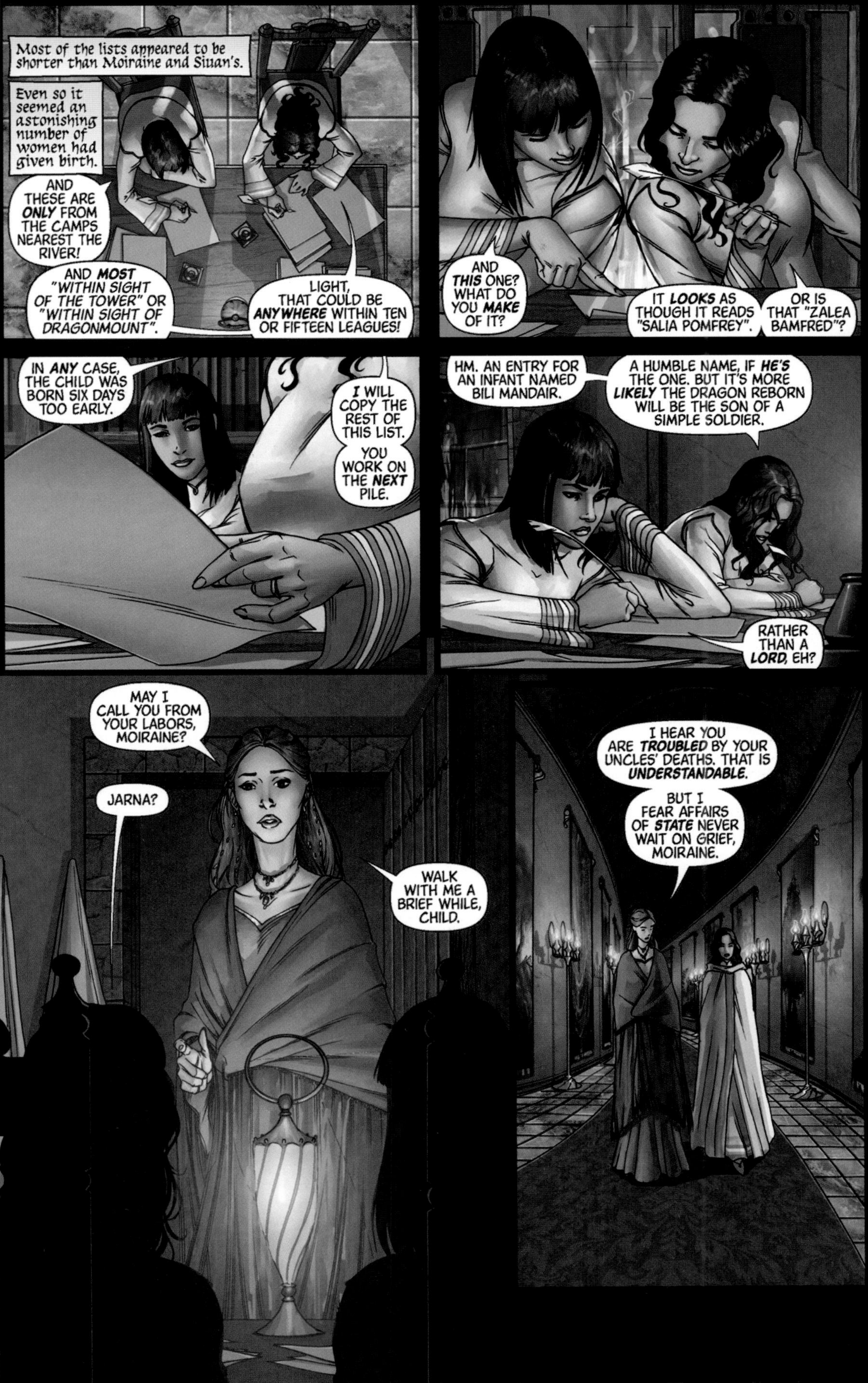

Most of the lists appeared to be shorter than Moiraine and Siuan's.
Even so it seemed an astonishing number of women had given birth.
AND THESE ARE ONLY FROM THE CAMPS NEAREST THE RIVER!
AND MOST "WITHIN SIGHT OF THE TOWER" OR "WITHIN SIGHT OF DRAGONMOUNT".
LIGHT, THAT COULD BE ANYWHERE WITHIN TEN OR FIFTEEN LEAGUES!
AND THIS ONE? WHAT DO YOU MAKE OF IT?
IT LOOKS AS THOUGH IT READS "SALIA POMFREY".
OR IS THAT "ZALEA BAMFRED"?
IN ANY CASE, THE CHILD WAS BORN SIX DAYS TOO EARLY.
I WILL COPY THE REST OF THIS LIST.
YOU WORK ON THE NEXT PILE.
HM. AN ENTRY FOR AN INFANT NAMED BILI MANDAIR.
A HUMBLE NAME, IF HE'S THE ONE. BUT IT'S MORE LIKELY THE DRAGON REBORN WILL BE THE SON OF A SIMPLE SOLDIER.
RATHER THAN A LORD, EH?
MAY I CALL YOU FROM YOUR LABORS, MOIRAINE?
JARNA?
WALK WITH ME A BRIEF WHILE, CHILD.
I HEAR YOU ARE TROUBLED BY YOUR UNCLES' DEATHS. THAT IS UNDERSTANDABLE.
BUT I FEAR AFFAIRS OF STATE NEVER WAIT ON GRIEF, MOIRAINE.

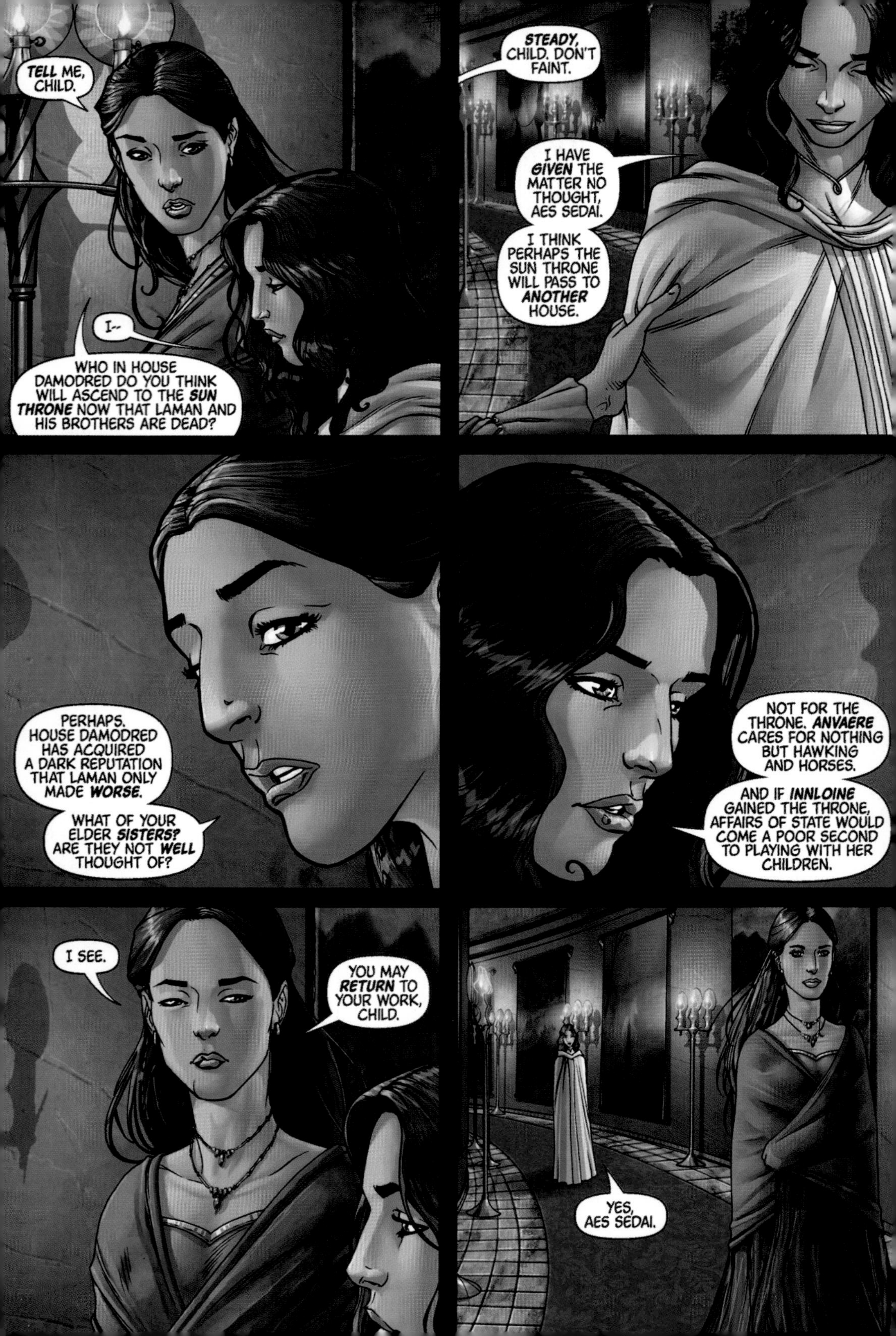
TELL ME, CHILD.
I--
WHO IN HOUSE DAMODRED DO YOU THINK WILL ASCEND TO THE SUN THRONE NOW THAT LAMAN AND HIS BROTHERS ARE DEAD?
STEADY, CHILD. DON'T FAINT.
I HAVE GIVEN THE MATTER NO THOUGHT, AES SEDAI.
I THINK PERHAPS THE SUN THRONE WILL PASS TO ANOTHER HOUSE.
PERHAPS. HOUSE DAMODRED HAS ACQUIRED A DARK REPUTATION THAT LAMAN ONLY MADE WORSE.
WHAT OF YOUR ELDER SISTERS? ARE THEY NOT WELL THOUGHT OF?
NOT FOR THE THRONE. ANVAERE CARES FOR NOTHING BUT HAWKING AND HORSES.
AND IF INNLOINE GAINED THE THRONE, AFFAIRS OF STATE WOULD COME A POOR SECOND TO PLAYING WITH HER CHILDREN.
I SEE.
YOU MAY RETURN TO YOUR WORK, CHILD.
YES, AES SEDAI.

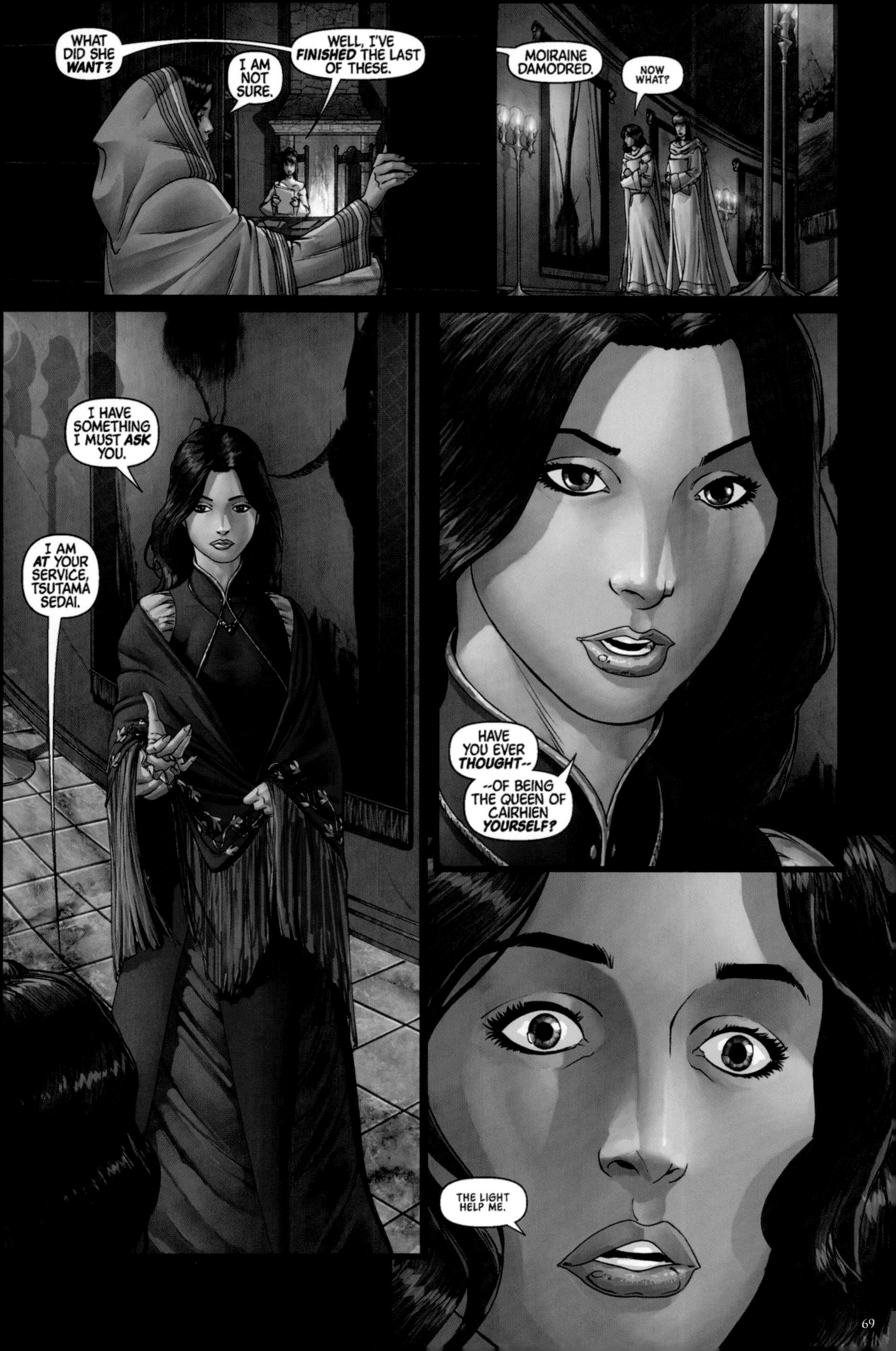
WHAT DID SHE WANT?
I AM NOT SURE.
WELL, I'VE FINISHED THE LAST OF THESE.
MOIRAINE DAMODRED.
NOW WHAT?
I HAVE SOMETHING I MUST ASK YOU.
I AM AT YOUR SERVICE, TSUTAMA SEDAI.
HAVE YOU EVER THOUGHT--
--OF BEING THE QUEEN OF CAIRHIEN YOURSELF?
THE LIGHT HELP ME.

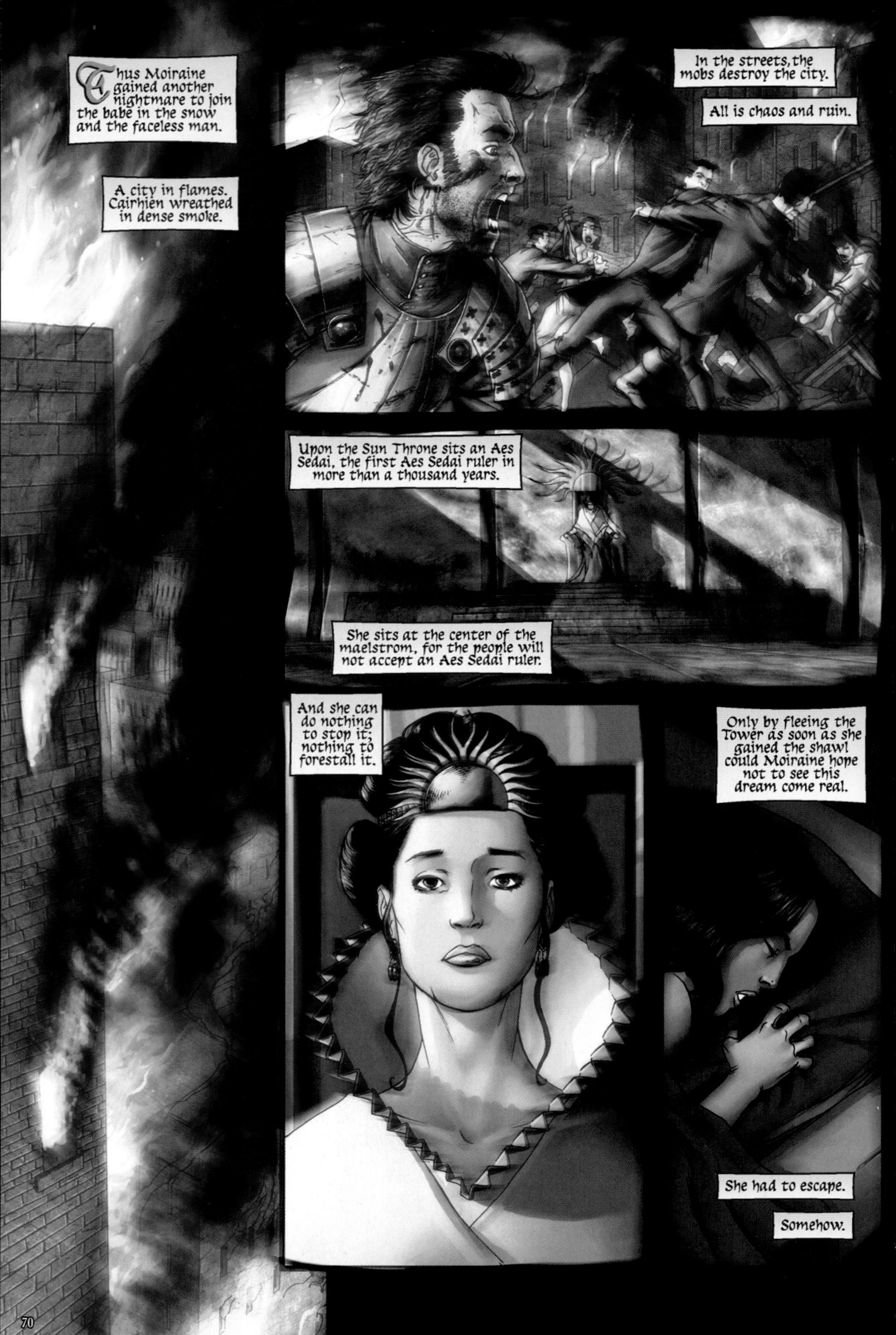
Thus Moiraine gained another nightmare to join the babe in the snow and the faceless man.
A city in flames. Cairhien wreathed in dense smoke.
In the streets, the mobs destroy the city.
All is chaos and ruin.
Upon the Sun Throne sits an Aes Sedai, the first Aes Sedai ruler in more than a thousand years.
She sits at the center of the maelstrom, for the people will not accept an Aes Sedai ruler.
And she can do nothing to stop it; nothing to forestall it.
Only by fleeing the Tower as soon as she gained the shawl could Moiraine hope not to see this dream come real.
She had to escape.
Somehow.

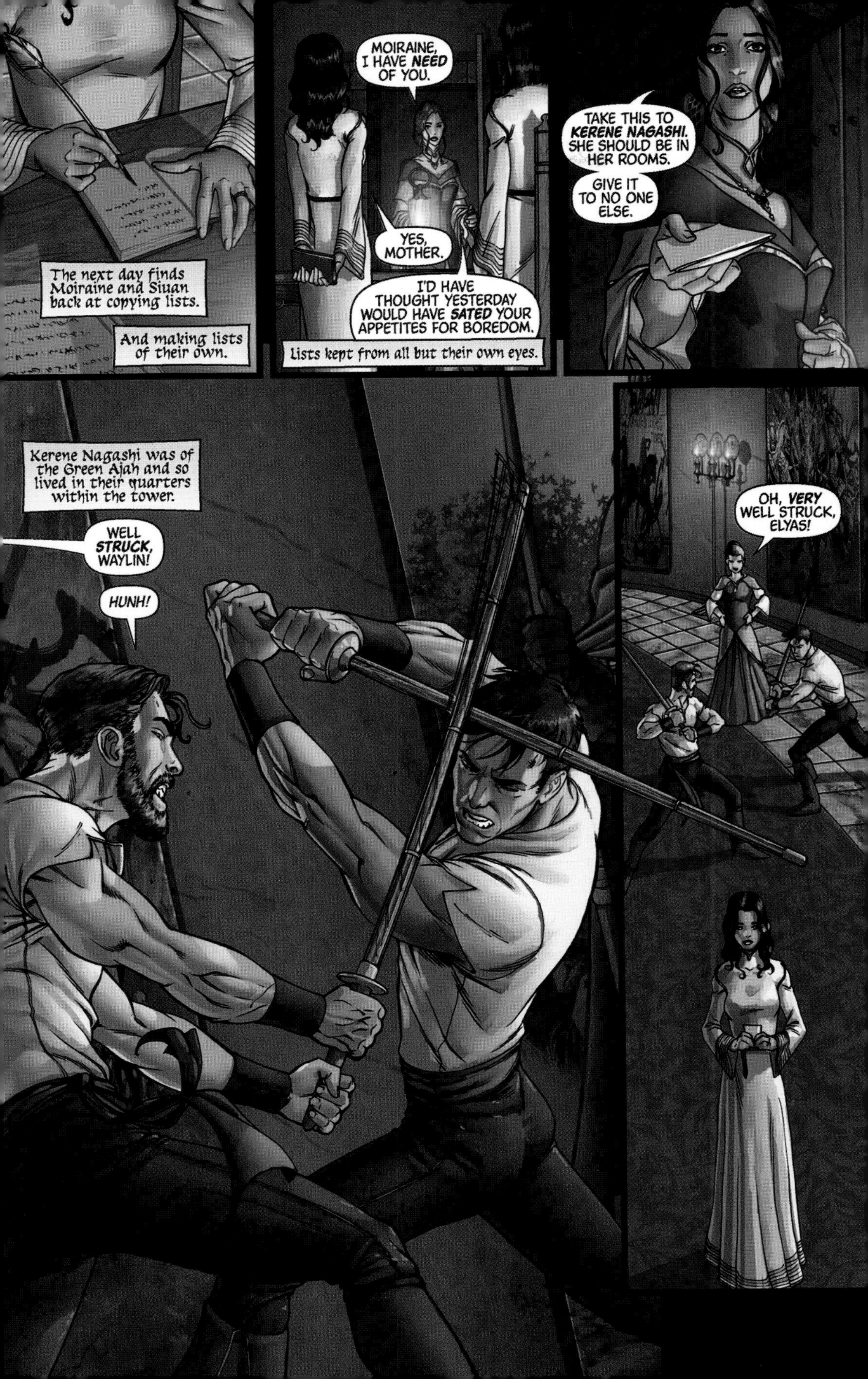

The next day finds Moiraine and Siuan back at copying lists.
And making lists of their own.
MOIRAINE, I HAVE NEED OF YOU.
YES, MOTHER.
I'D HAVE THOUGHT YESTERDAY WOULD HAVE SATED YOUR APPETITES FOR BOREDOM.
Lists kept from all but their own eyes.
TAKE THIS TO KERENE NAGASHI. SHE SHOULD BE IN HER ROOMS.
GIVE IT TO NO ONE ELSE.
Kerene Nagashi was of the Green Ajah and so lived in their quarters within the tower.
WELL STRUCK, WAYLIN!
HUNH!
OH, VERY WELL STRUCK, ELYAS!

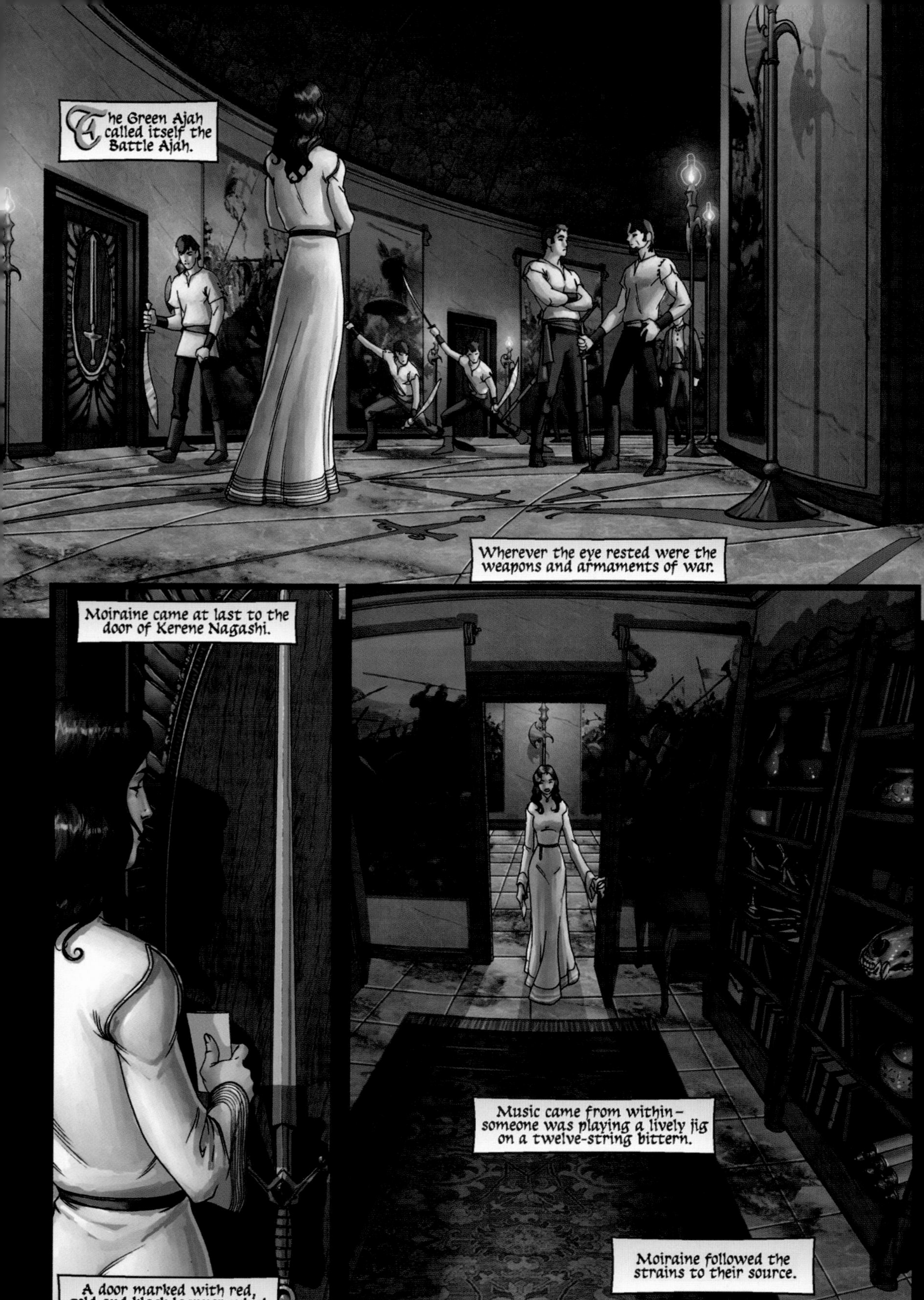
The Green Ajah called itself the Battle Ajah.
Wherever the eye rested were the weapons and armaments of war.
Moiraine came at last to the door of Kerene Nagashi.
A door marked with red, gold, and black lacquer, which Moiraine found curious.
Music came from within–someone was playing a lively jig on a twelve-string bittern.
Moiraine followed the strains to their source.

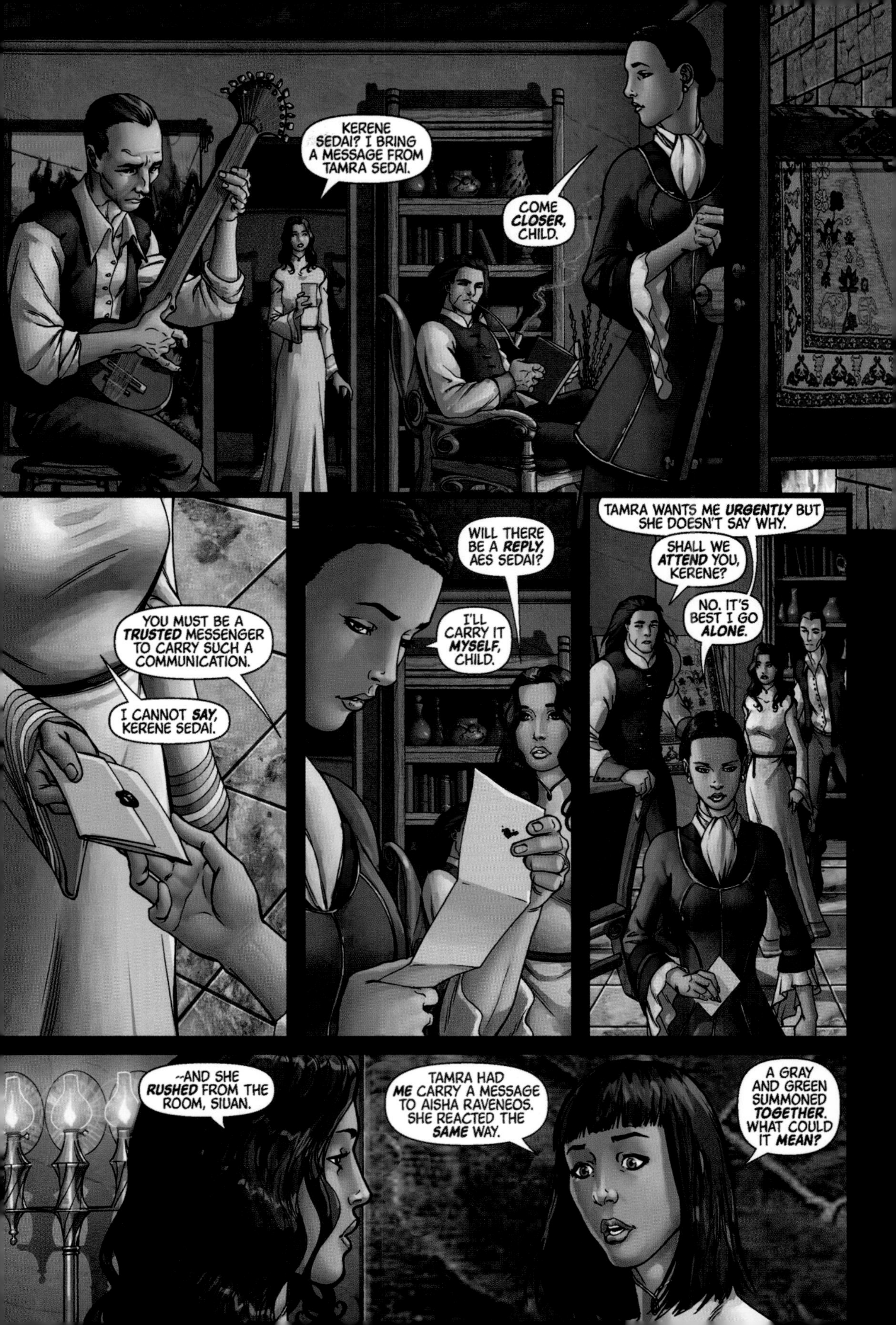
KERENE SEDAI? I BRING A MESSAGE FROM TAMRA SEDAI.
COME CLOSER, CHILD.
YOU MUST BE A TRUSTED MESSENGER TO CARRY SUCH A COMMUNICATION.
I CANNOT SAY, KERENE SEDAI.
WILL THERE BE A REPLY, AES SEDAI?
I'LL CARRY IT MYSELF, CHILD.
TAMRA WANTS ME URGENTLY BUT SHE DOESN'T SAY WHY.
SHALL WE ATTEND YOU, KERENE?
NO. IT'S BEST I GO ALONE.
--AND SHE RUSHED FROM THE ROOM, SIUAN.
TAMRA HAD ME CARRY A MESSAGE TO AISHA RAVENEOS. SHE REACTED THE SAME WAY.
A GRAY AND GREEN SUMMONED TOGETHER. WHAT COULD IT MEAN?

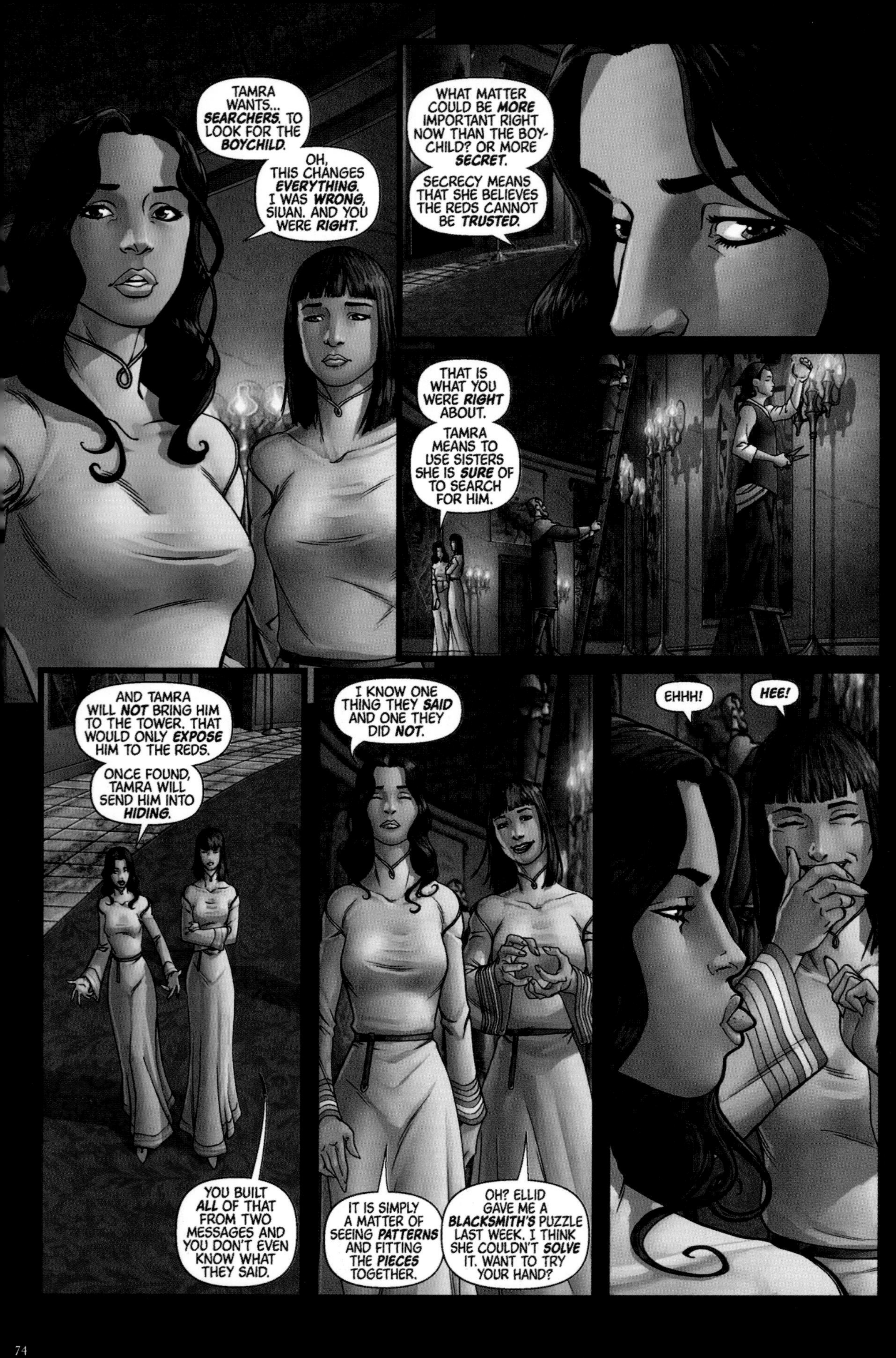
TAMRA WANTS... SEARCHERS, TO LOOK FOR THE BOYCHILD.
OH, THIS CHANGES EVERYTHING. I WAS WRONG, SIUAN. AND YOU WERE RIGHT.
WHAT MATTER COULD BE MORE IMPORTANT RIGHT NOW THAN THE BOY-CHILD? OR MORE SECRET.
SECRECY MEANS THAT SHE BELIEVES THE REDS CANNOT BE TRUSTED.
THAT IS WHAT YOU WERE RIGHT ABOUT.
TAMRA MEANS TO USE SISTERS SHE IS SURE OF TO SEARCH FOR HIM.
AND TAMRA WILL NOT BRING HIM TO THE TOWER. THAT WOULD ONLY EXPOSE HIM TO THE REDS.
ONCE FOUND, TAMRA WILL SEND HIM INTO HIDING.
YOU BUILT ALL OF THAT FROM TWO MESSAGES AND YOU DON'T EVEN KNOW WHAT THEY SAID.
I KNOW ONE THING THEY SAID AND ONE THEY DID NOT.
IT IS SIMPLY A MATTER OF SEEING PATTERNS AND FITTING THE PIECES TOGETHER.
OH? ELLID GAVE ME A BLACKSMITH'S PUZZLE LAST WEEK. I THINK SHE COULDN'T SOLVE IT. WANT TO TRY YOUR HAND?
EHHH!
HEE!

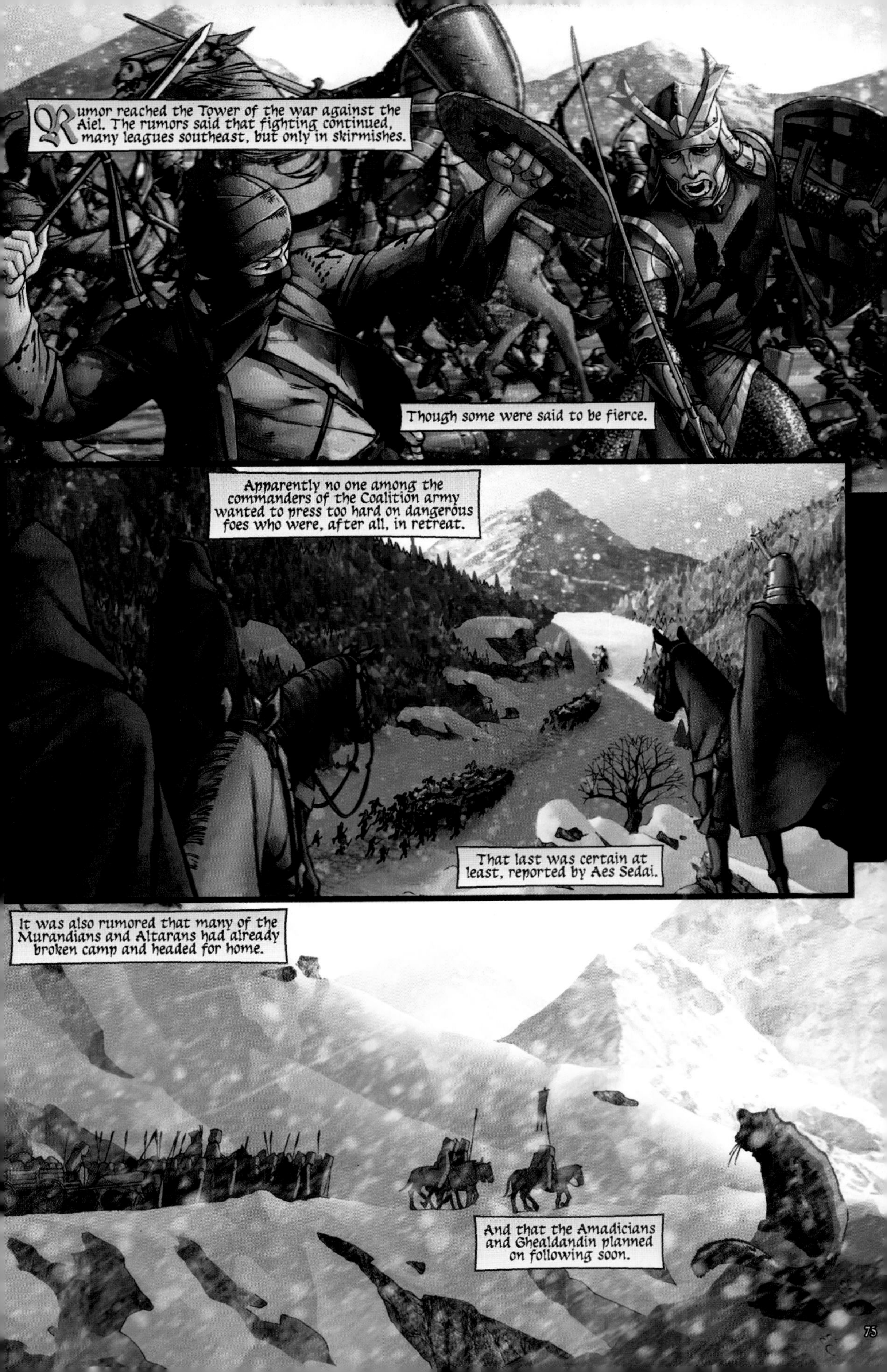
Rumor reached the Tower of the war against the Aiel. The rumors said that fighting continued, many leagues southeast, but only in skirmishes.
Though some were said to be fierce.
Apparently no one among the commanders of the Coalition army wanted to press too hard on dangerous foes who were, after all, in retreat.
That last was certain at least, reported by Aes Sedai.
It was also rumored that many of the Murandians and Altarans had already broken camp and headed for home.
And that the Amadicians and Ghealdandin planned on following soon.

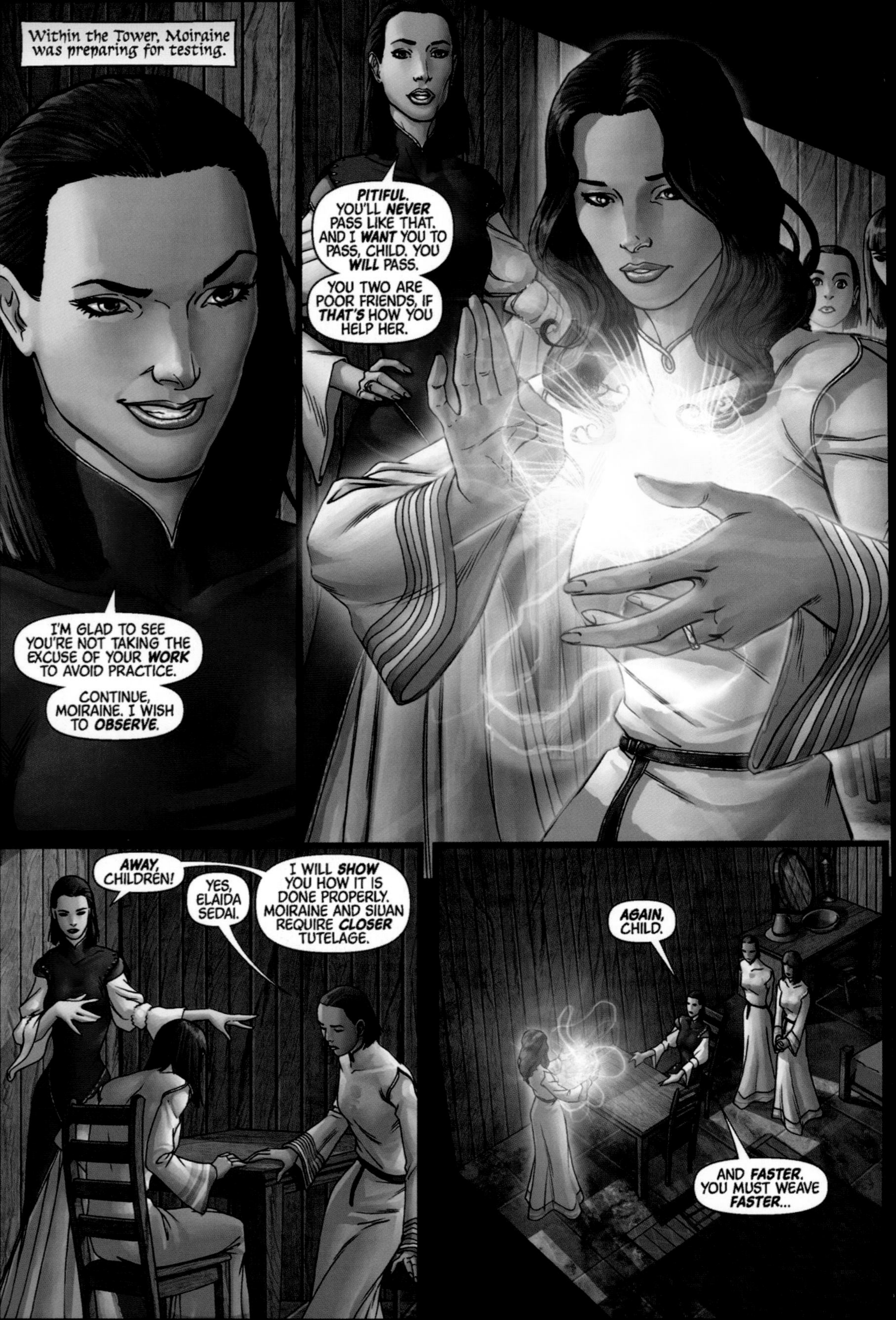
Within the Tower, Moiraine was preparing for testing.
PITIFUL. YOU'LL NEVER PASS LIKE THAT. AND I WANT YOU TO PASS, CHILD. YOU WILL PASS.
YOU TWO ARE POOR FRIENDS, IF THAT'S HOW YOU HELP HER.
I'M GLAD TO SEE YOU'RE NOT TAKING THE EXCUSE OF YOUR WORK TO AVOID PRACTICE.
CONTINUE, MOIRAINE. I WISH TO OBSERVE.
AWAY, CHILDREN!
YES, ELAIDA SEDAI.
I WILL SHOW YOU HOW IT IS DONE PROPERLY. MOIRAINE AND SIUAN REQUIRE CLOSER TUTELAGE.
AGAIN, CHILD.
AND FASTER. YOU MUST WEAVE FASTER...

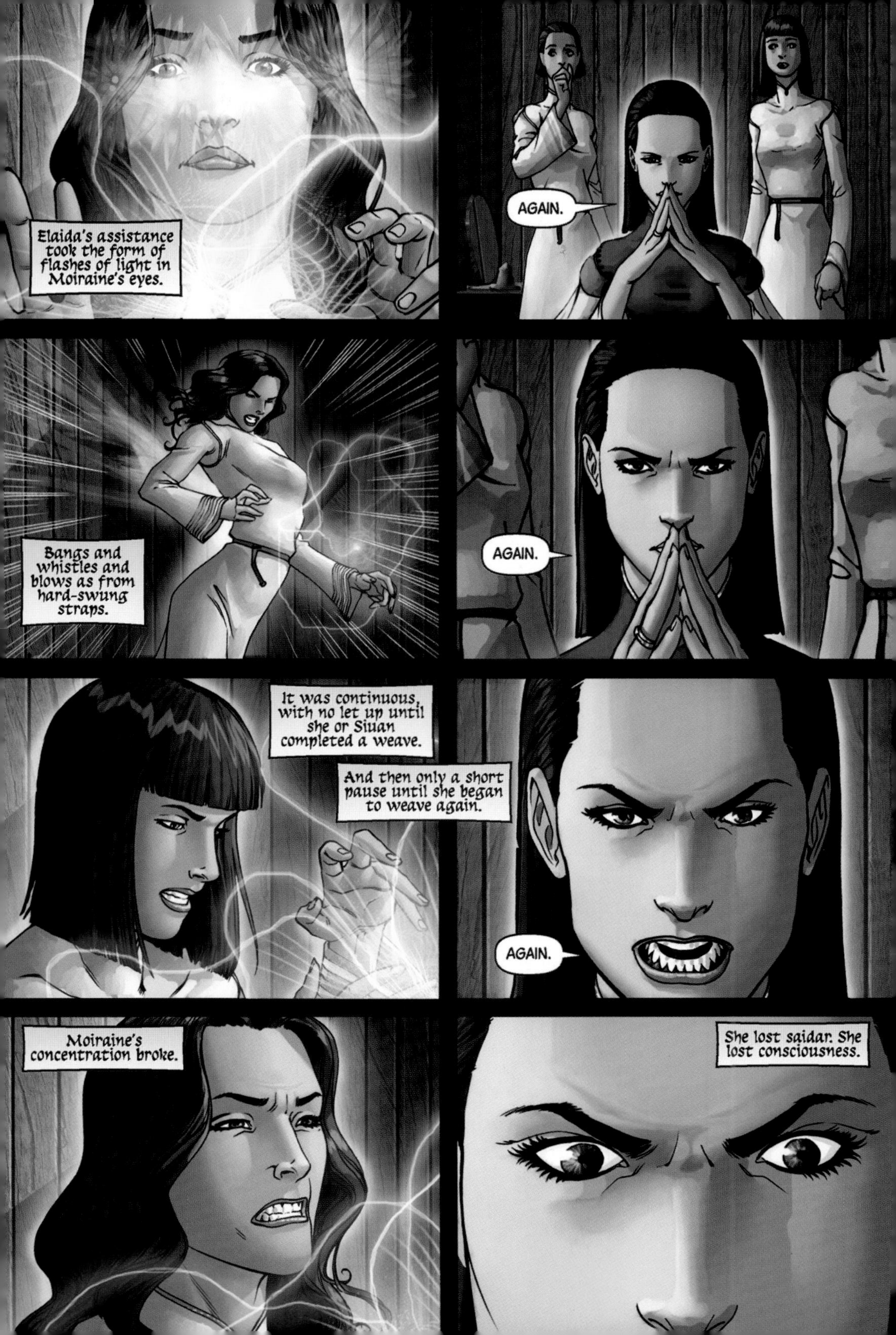

Elaida's assistance took the form of flashes of light in Moiraine's eyes.
AGAIN.
Bangs and whistles and blows as from hard-swung straps.
AGAIN.
It was continuous, with no let up until she or Siuan completed a weave.
And then only a short pause until she began to weave again.
AGAIN.
Moiraine's concentration broke.
She lost saidar. She lost consciousness.

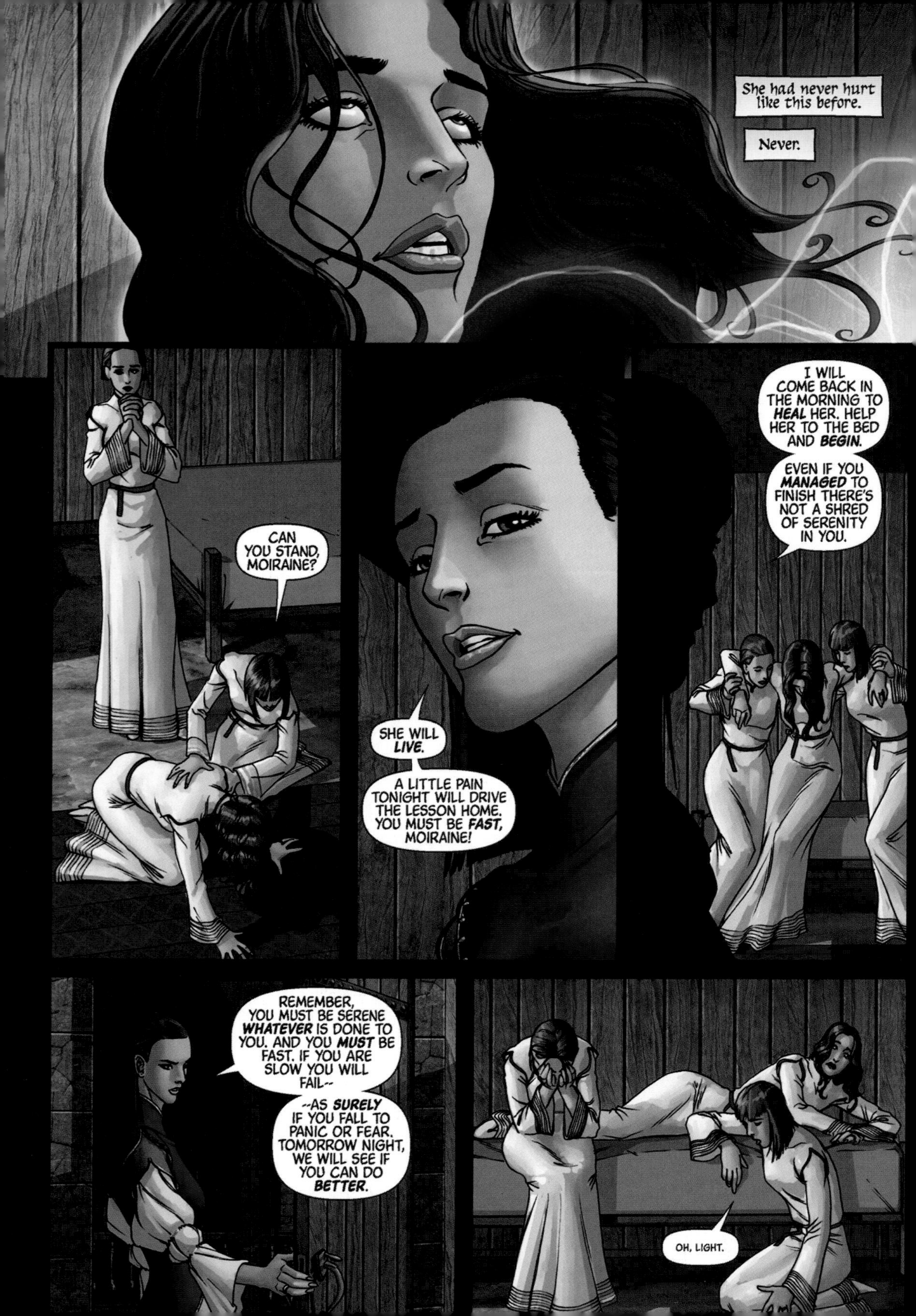
She had never hurt like this before.
Never.
CAN YOU STAND, MOIRAINE?
SHE WILL LIVE.
A LITTLE PAIN TONIGHT WILL DRIVE THE LESSON HOME. YOU MUST BE FAST, MOIRAINE!
I WILL COME BACK IN THE MORNING TO HEAL HER. HELP HER TO THE BED AND BEGIN.
EVEN IF YOU MANAGED TO FINISH THERE'S NOT A SHRED OF SERENITY IN YOU.
REMEMBER, YOU MUST BE SERENE WHATEVER IS DONE TO YOU. AND YOU MUST BE FAST. IF YOU ARE SLOW YOU WILL FAIL--
--AS SURELY IF YOU FALL TO PANIC OR FEAR. TOMORROW NIGHT, WE WILL SEE IF YOU CAN DO BETTER.
OH, LIGHT.

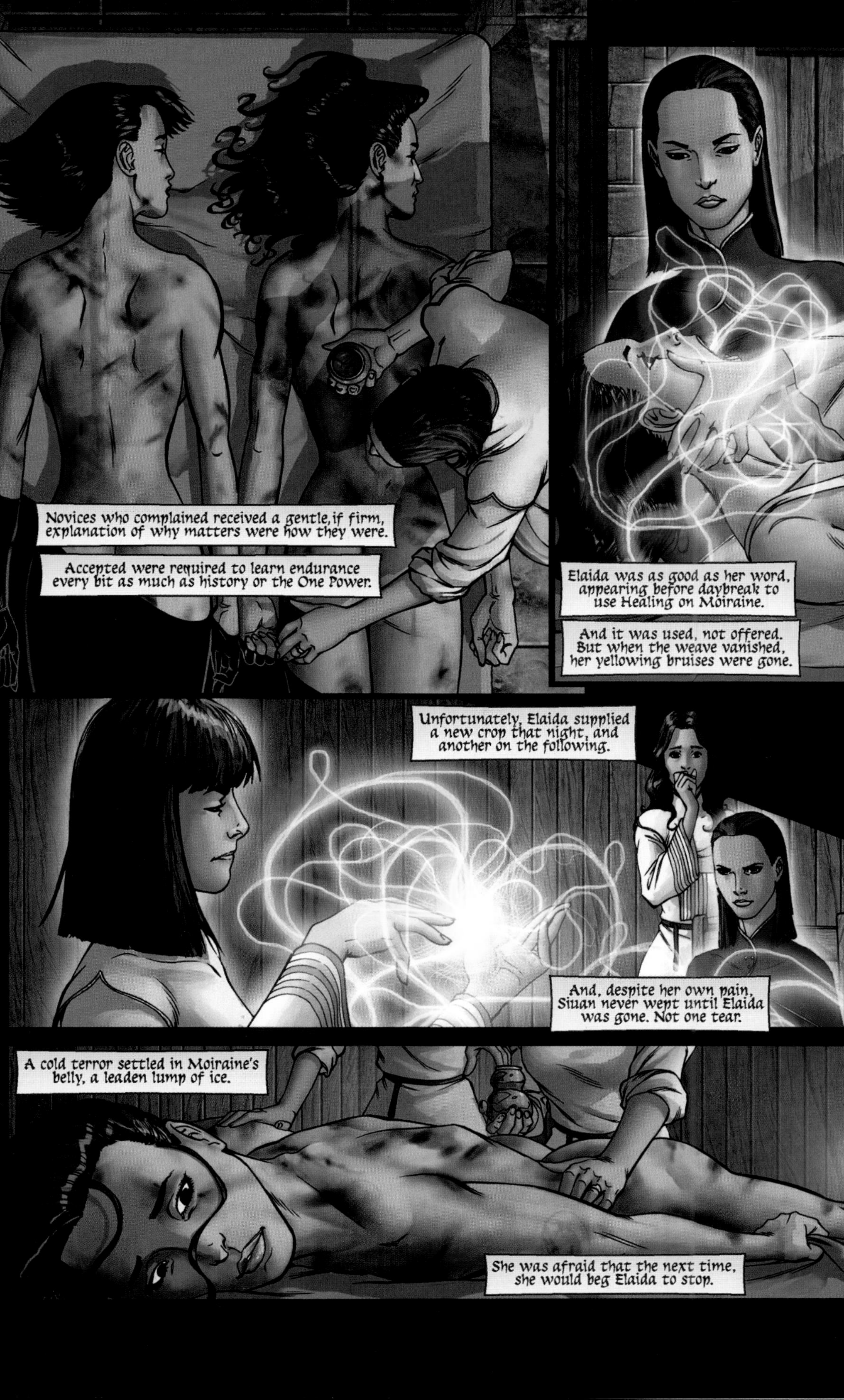
Novices who complained received a gentle, if firm, explanation of why matters were how they were.
Accepted were required to learn endurance every bit as much as history or the One Power.
Elaida was as good as her word, appearing before daybreak to use Healing on Moiraine.
And it was used, not offered. But when the weave vanished, her yellowing bruises were gone.
Unfortunately, Elaida supplied a new crop that night, and another on the following.
And, despite her own pain, Siuan never wept until Elaida was gone. Not one tear.
A cold terror settled in Moiraine's belly, a leaden lump of ice.
She was afraid that the next time, she would beg Elaida to stop.

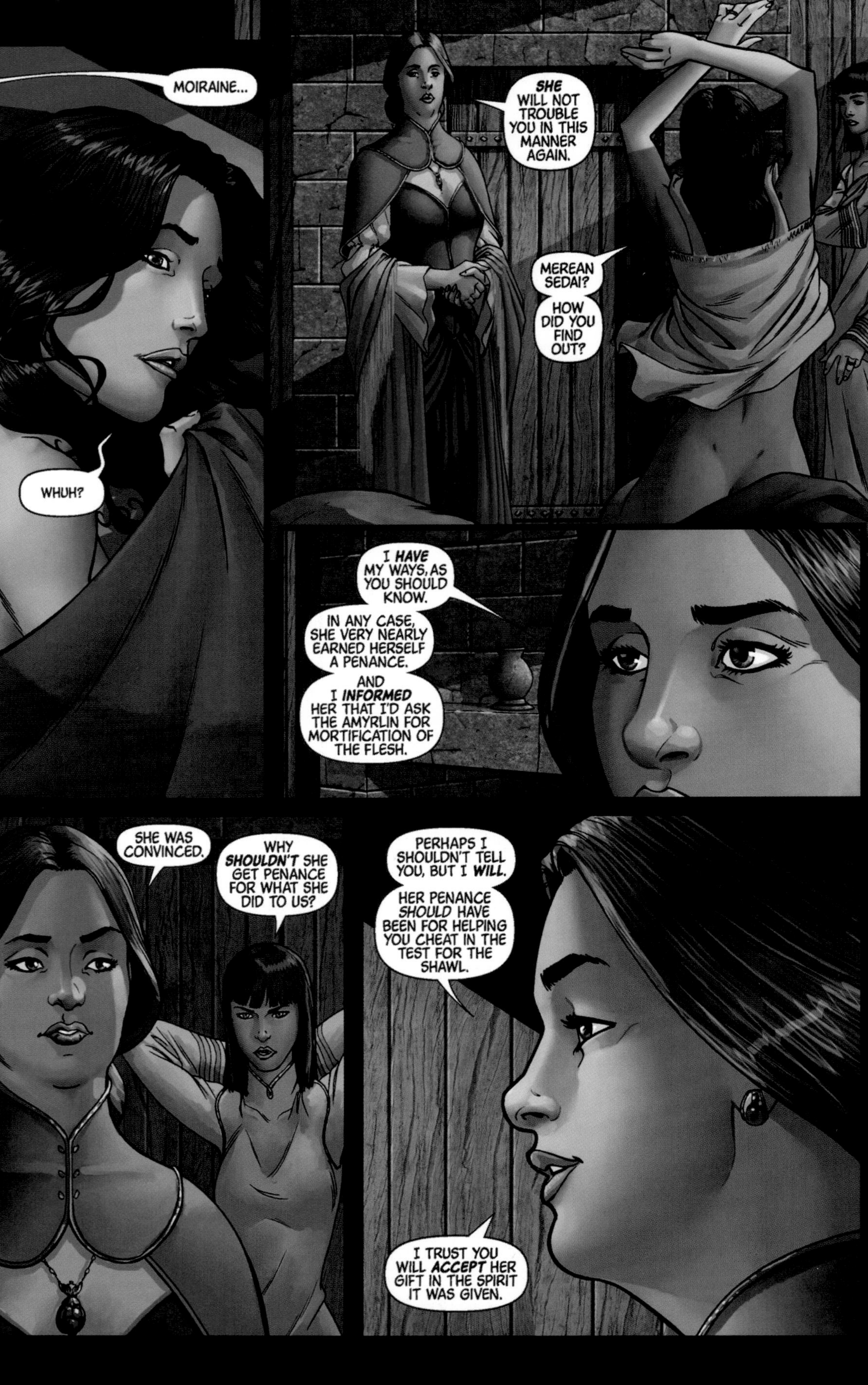

MOIRAINE...
WHUH?
SHE WILL NOT TROUBLE YOU IN THIS MANNER AGAIN.
MEREAN SEDAI?
HOW DID YOU FIND OUT?
I HAVE MY WAYS, AS YOU SHOULD KNOW.
IN ANY CASE, SHE VERY NEARLY EARNED HERSELF A PENANCE.
AND I INFORMED HER THAT I'D ASK THE AMYRLIN FOR MORTIFICATION OF THE FLESH.
SHE WAS CONVINCED.
WHY SHOULDN'T SHE GET PENANCE FOR WHAT SHE DID TO US?
PERHAPS I SHOULDN'T TELL YOU, BUT I WILL.
HER PENANCE SHOULD HAVE BEEN FOR HELPING YOU CHEAT IN THE TEST FOR THE SHAWL.
I TRUST YOU WILL ACCEPT HER GIFT IN THE SPIRIT IT WAS GIVEN.

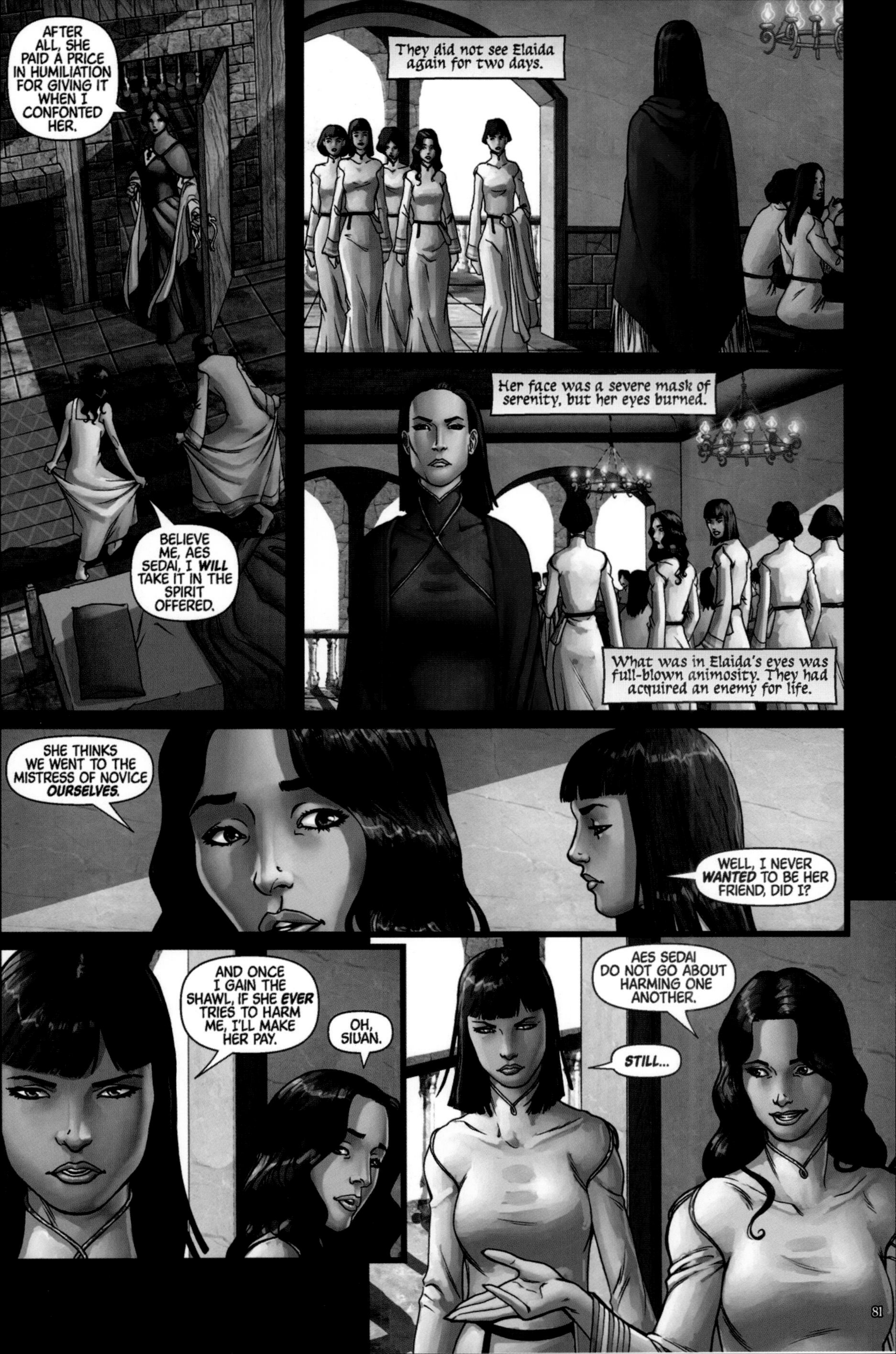
AFTER ALL, SHE PAID A PRICE IN HUMILIATION FOR GIVING IT WHEN I CONFONTED HER.
BELIEVE ME, AES SEDAI, I WILL TAKE IT IN THE SPIRIT OFFERED.
They did not see Elaida again for two days.
Her face was a severe mask of serenity, but her eyes burned.
What was in Elaida's eyes was full-blown animosity. They had acquired an enemy for life.
SHE THINKS WE WENT TO THE MISTRESS OF NOVICE OURSELVES.
WELL, I NEVER WANTED TO BE HER FRIEND, DID I?
AND ONCE I GAIN THE SHAWL, IF SHE EVER TRIES TO HARM ME, I'LL MAKE HER PAY.
OH, SIUAN.
AES SEDAI DO NOT GO ABOUT HARMING ONE ANOTHER.
STILL...

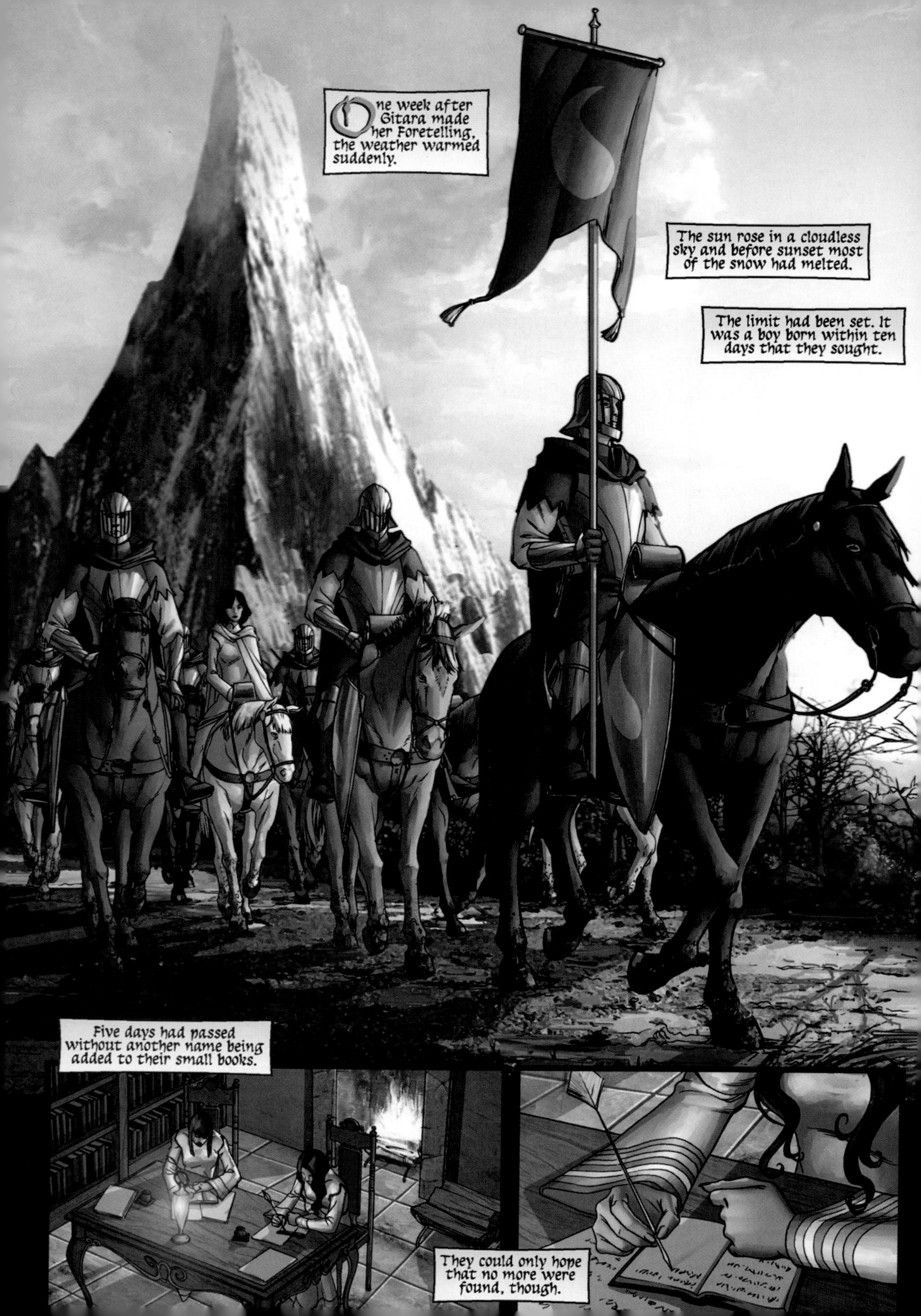
One week after Gitara made her Foretelling, the weather warmed suddenly.
The sun rose in a cloudless sky and before sunset most of the snow had melted.
The limit had been set. It was a boy born within ten days that they sought.
Five days had passed without another name being added to their small books.
They could only hope that no more were found, though.

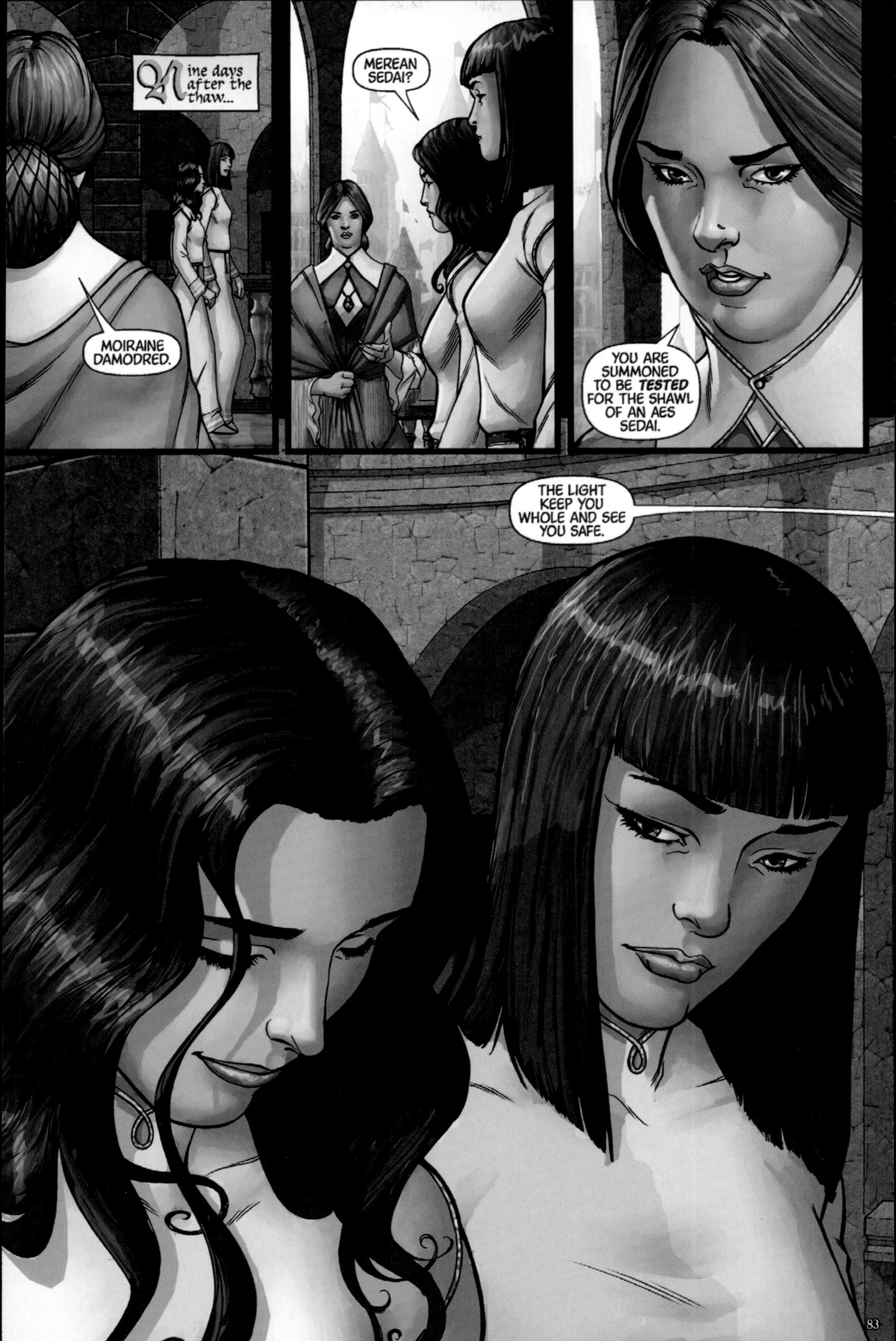
Nine days after the thaw...
MOIRAINE DAMODRED.
MEREAN SEDAI?
YOU ARE SUMMONED TO BE TESTED FOR THE SHAWL OF AN AES SEDAI.
THE LIGHT KEEP YOU WHOLE AND SEE YOU SAFE.

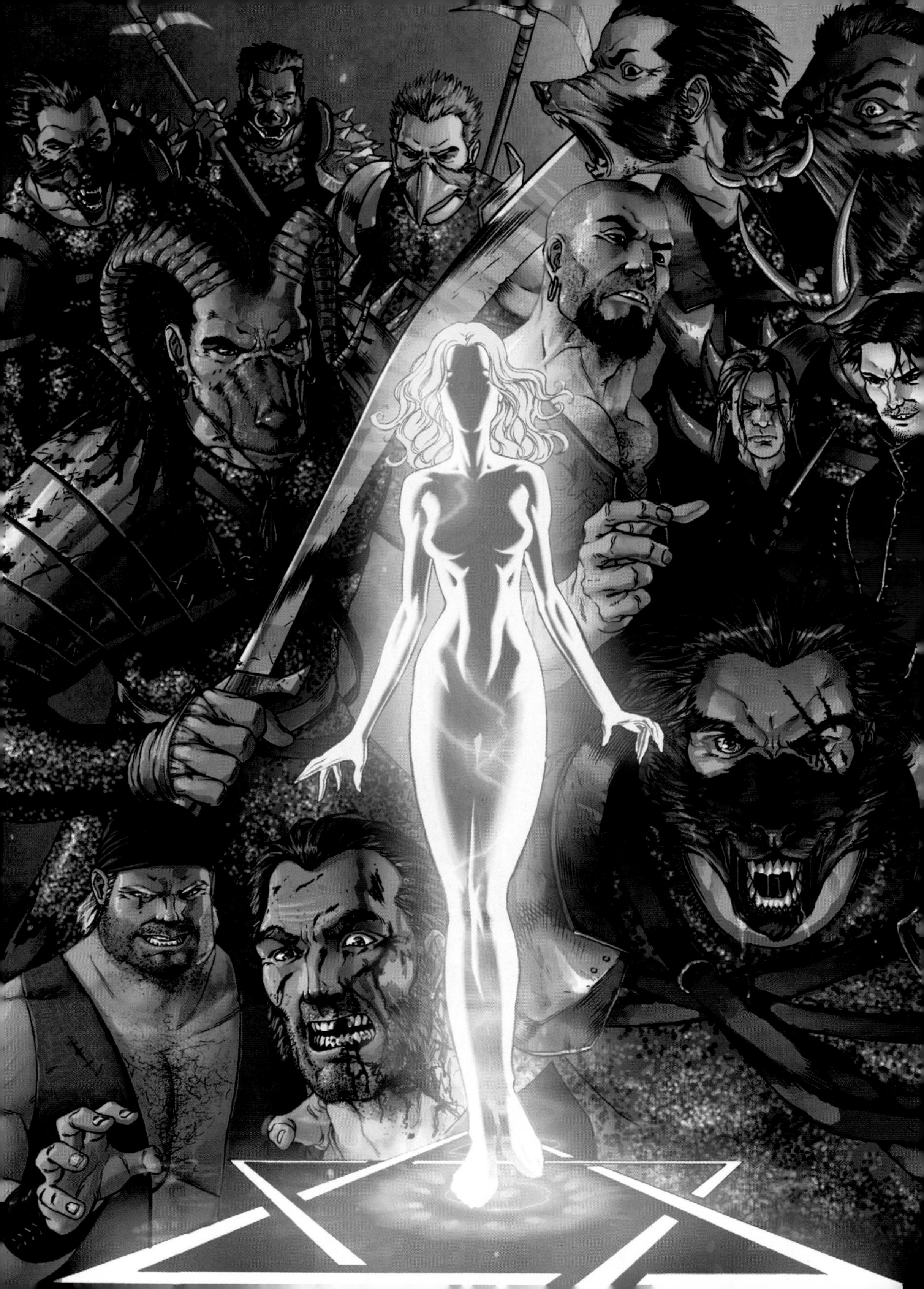

chapter four

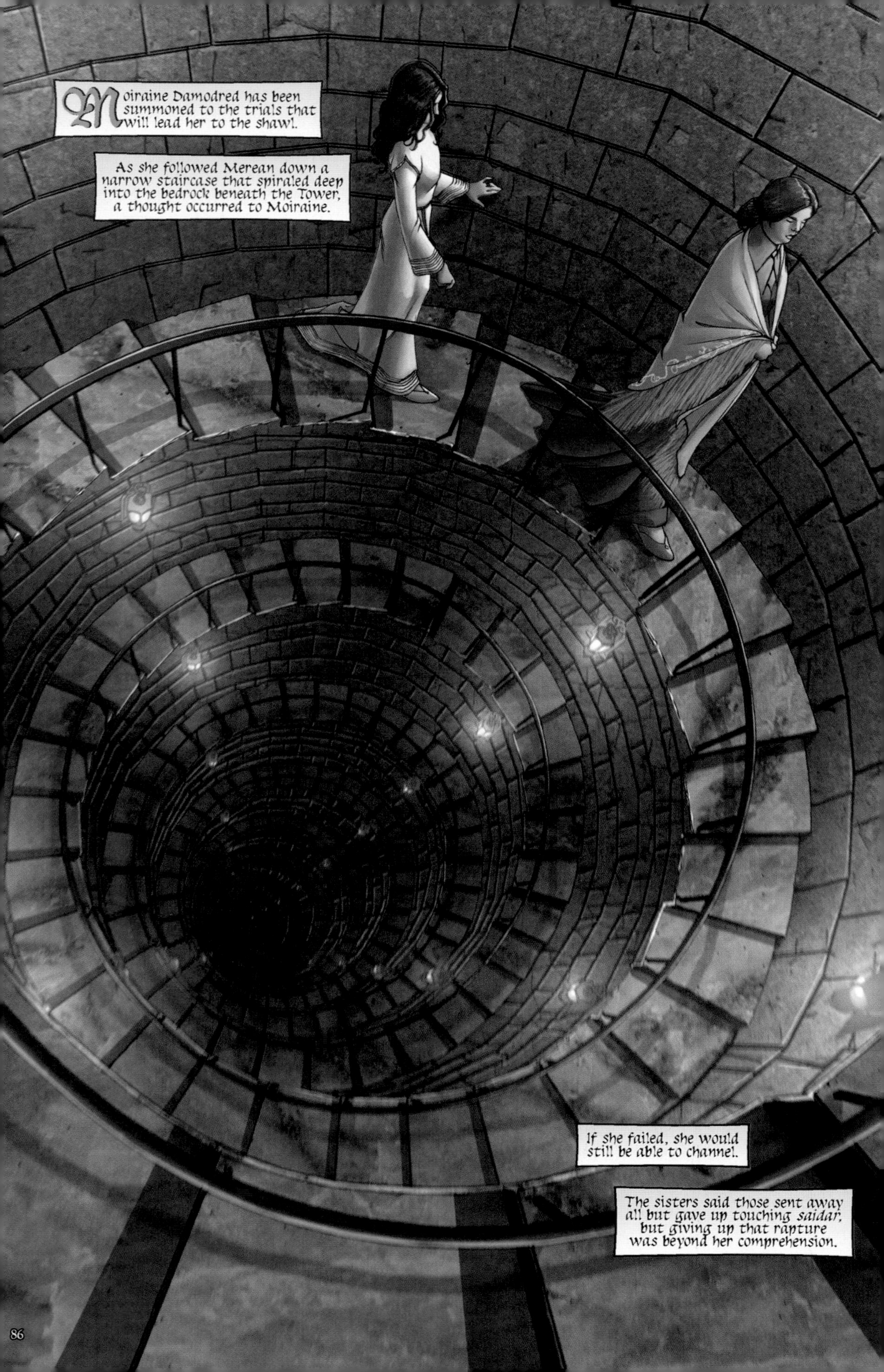
Moiraine Damodred has been summoned to the trials that will lead her to the shawl.
As she followed Merean down a narrow staircase that spiraled deep into the bedrock beneath the Tower, a thought occurred to Moiraine.
If she failed, she would still be able to channel.
The sisters said those sent away all but gave up touching *saidar*, but giving up that rapture was beyond her comprehension.

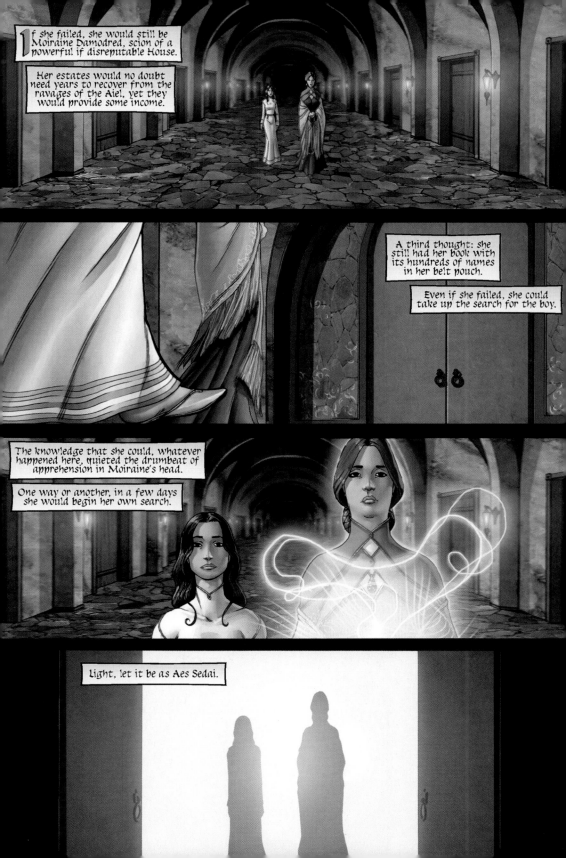

If she failed, she would still be Moiraine Damodred, scion of a powerful if disreputable House.

Her estates would no doubt need years to recover from the ravages of the Aiel, yet they would provide some income.

A third thought: she still had her book with its hundreds of names in her belt pouch.

Even if she failed, she could take up the search for the boy.

The knowledge that she could, whatever happened here, quieted the drumbeat of apprehension in Moiraine's head.

One way or another, in a few days she would begin her own search.

Light, let it be as Aes Sedai.

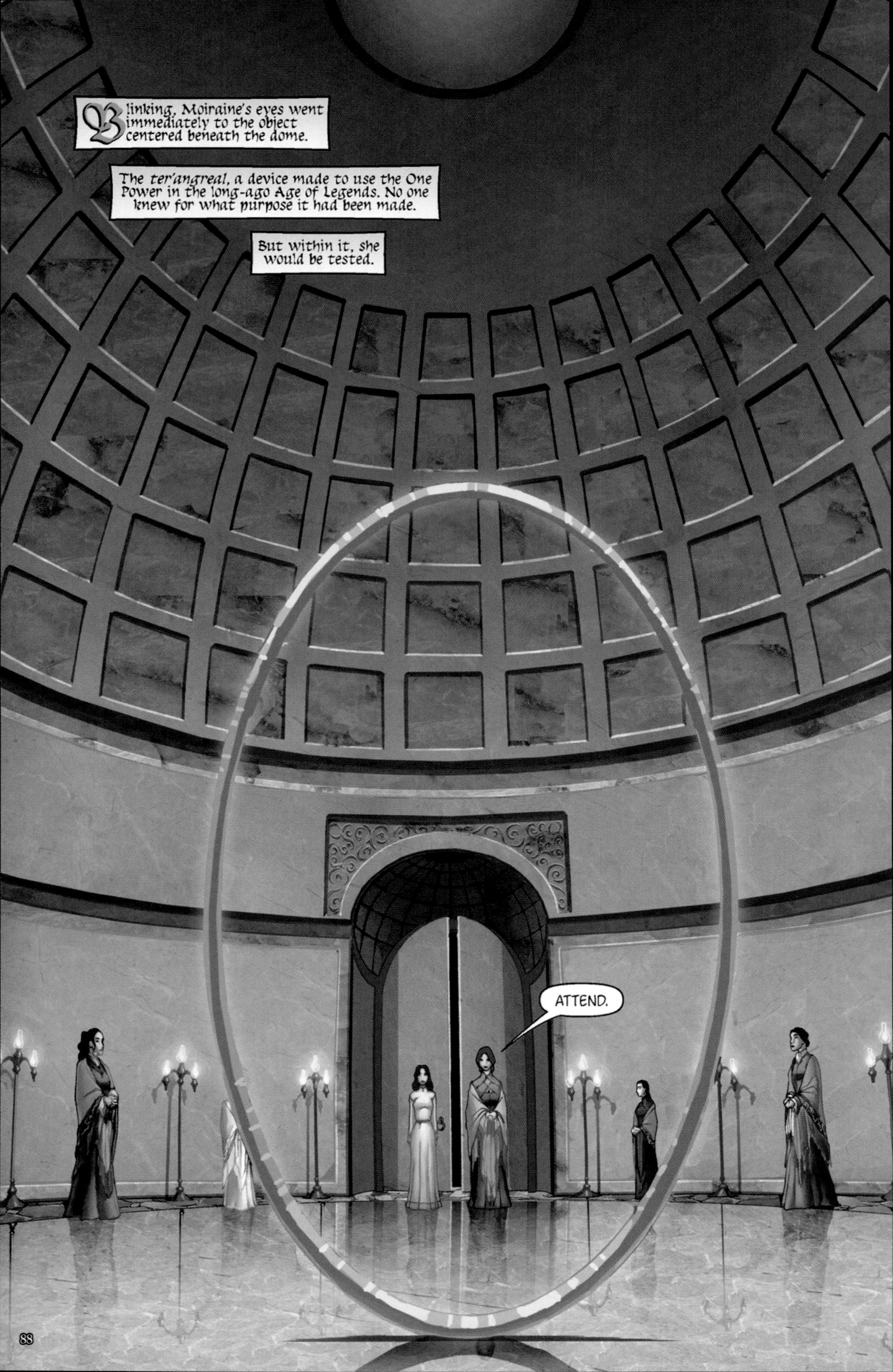
Blinking, Moiraine's eyes went immediately to the object centered beneath the dome.
The *ter'angreal*, a device made to use the One Power in the long-ago Age of Legends. No one knew for what purpose it had been made.
But within it, she would be tested.
ATTEND.

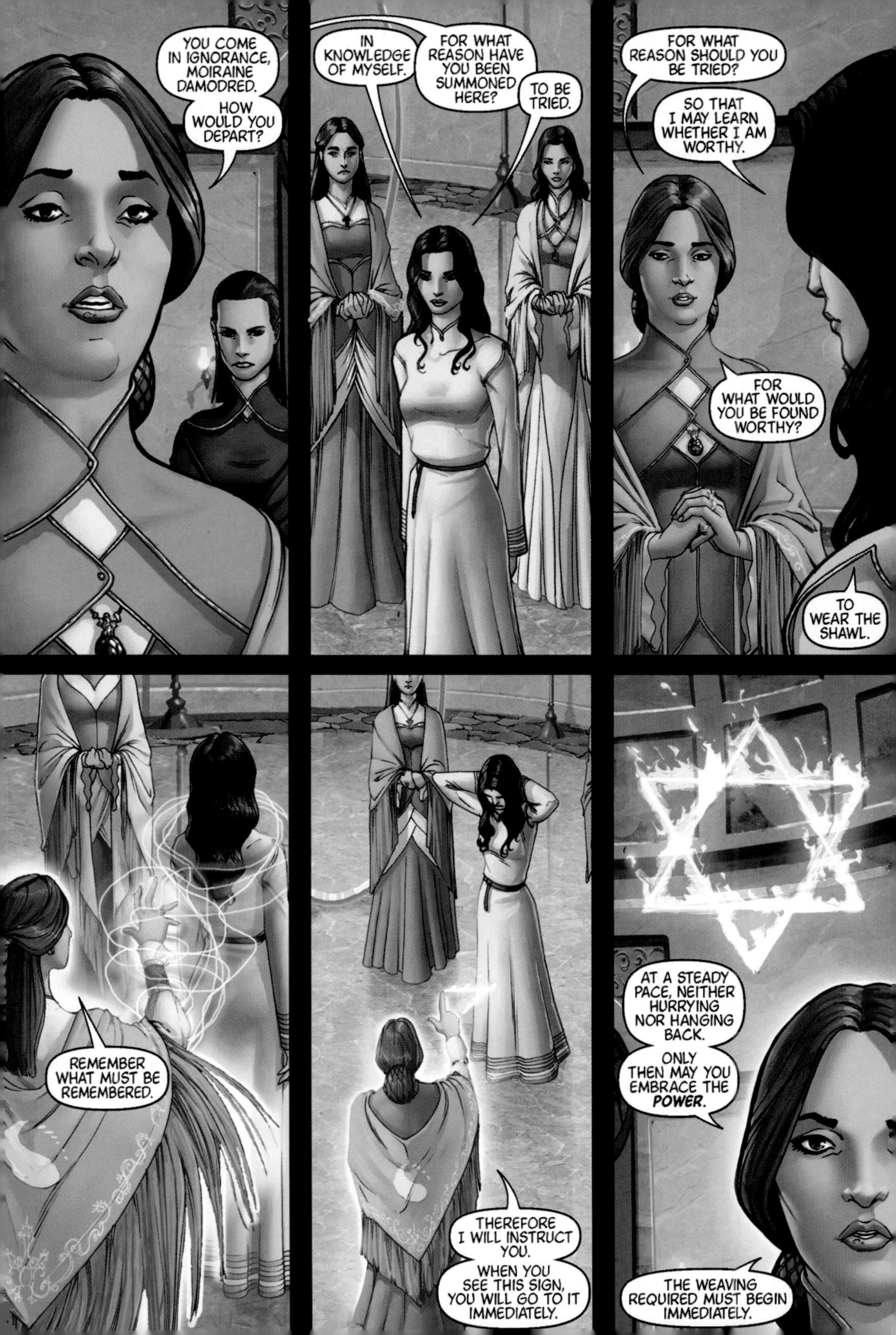
YOU COME IN IGNORANCE, MOIRAINE DAMODRED.
HOW WOULD YOU DEPART?
IN KNOWLEDGE OF MYSELF.
FOR WHAT REASON HAVE YOU BEEN SUMMONED HERE?
TO BE TRIED.
FOR WHAT REASON SHOULD YOU BE TRIED?
SO THAT I MAY LEARN WHETHER I AM WORTHY.
FOR WHAT WOULD YOU BE FOUND WORTHY?
TO WEAR THE SHAWL.
REMEMBER WHAT MUST BE REMEMBERED.
THEREFORE I WILL INSTRUCT YOU.
WHEN YOU SEE THIS SIGN, YOU WILL GO TO IT IMMEDIATELY.
AT A STEADY PACE, NEITHER HURRYING NOR HANGING BACK.
ONLY THEN MAY YOU EMBRACE THE POWER.
THE WEAVING REQUIRED MUST BEGIN IMMEDIATELY.

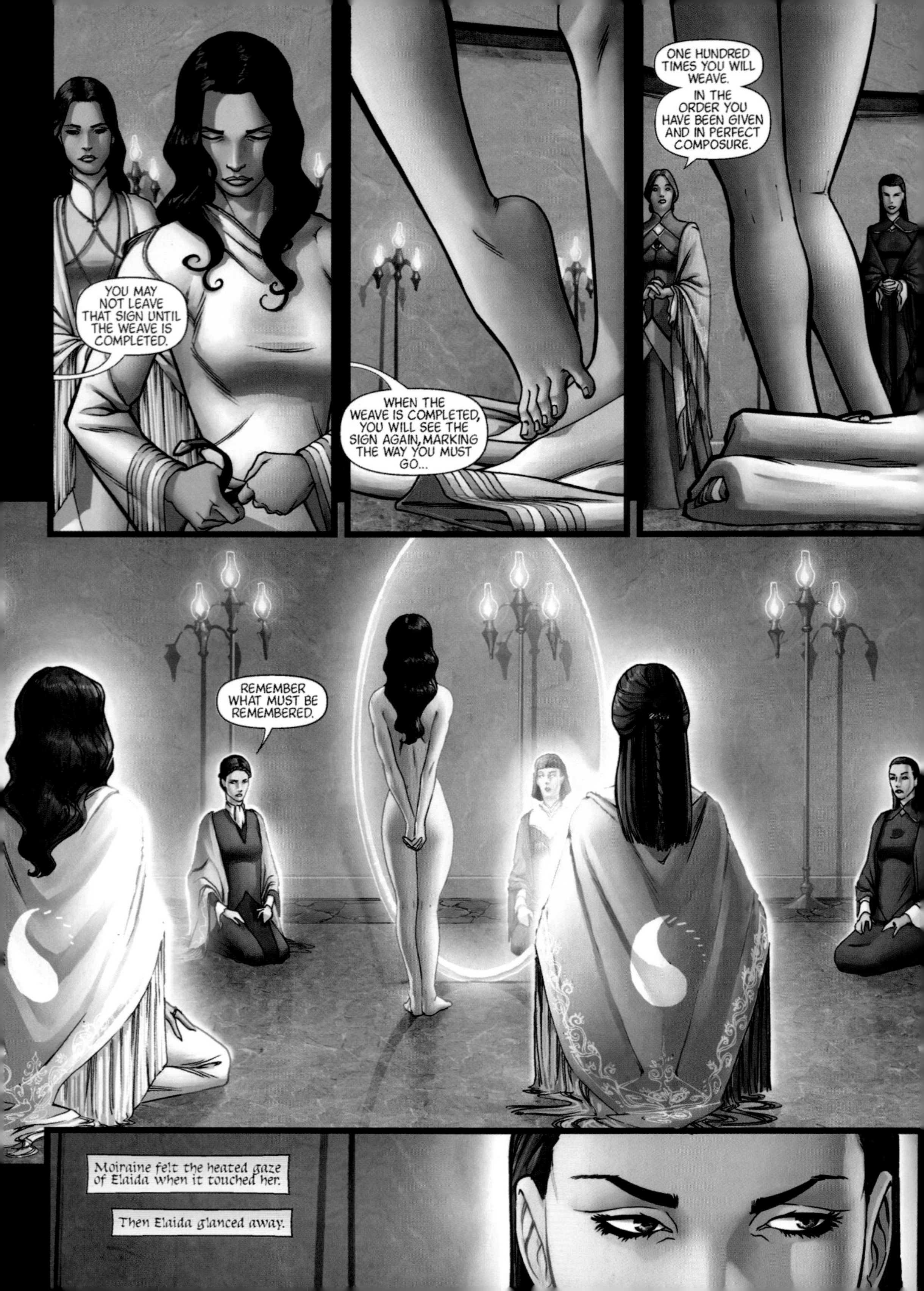
YOU MAY NOT LEAVE THAT SIGN UNTIL THE WEAVE IS COMPLETED.
WHEN THE WEAVE IS COMPLETED, YOU WILL SEE THE SIGN AGAIN, MARKING THE WAY YOU MUST GO...
ONE HUNDRED TIMES YOU WILL WEAVE.
IN THE ORDER YOU HAVE BEEN GIVEN AND IN PERFECT COMPOSURE.
REMEMBER WHAT MUST BE REMEMBERED.
Moiraine felt the heated gaze of Elaida when it touched her.
Then Elaida glanced away.

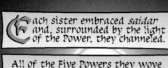
Each sister embraced *saidar* and, surrounded by the light of the Power, they channeled.

All of the Five Powers they wove and the *ter'angreal* glowed white.

She would pass, whatever Elaida did.

She would!

VERY STRANGE. WHERE AM I?

AND WHY AM I-- UNCLOTHED?

A *DRESS* IN *MY* HOUSE COLORS.

HOW HAS *THIS* COME TO BE HERE?

I WISH I KNEW WHAT WAS HAPPENING HERE.

THESE GARMENTS FIT AS THOUGH MY OWN SEAMSTRESS HAD MADE THEM.

WHAT *IS* THIS PLACE?

A *PALACE?*

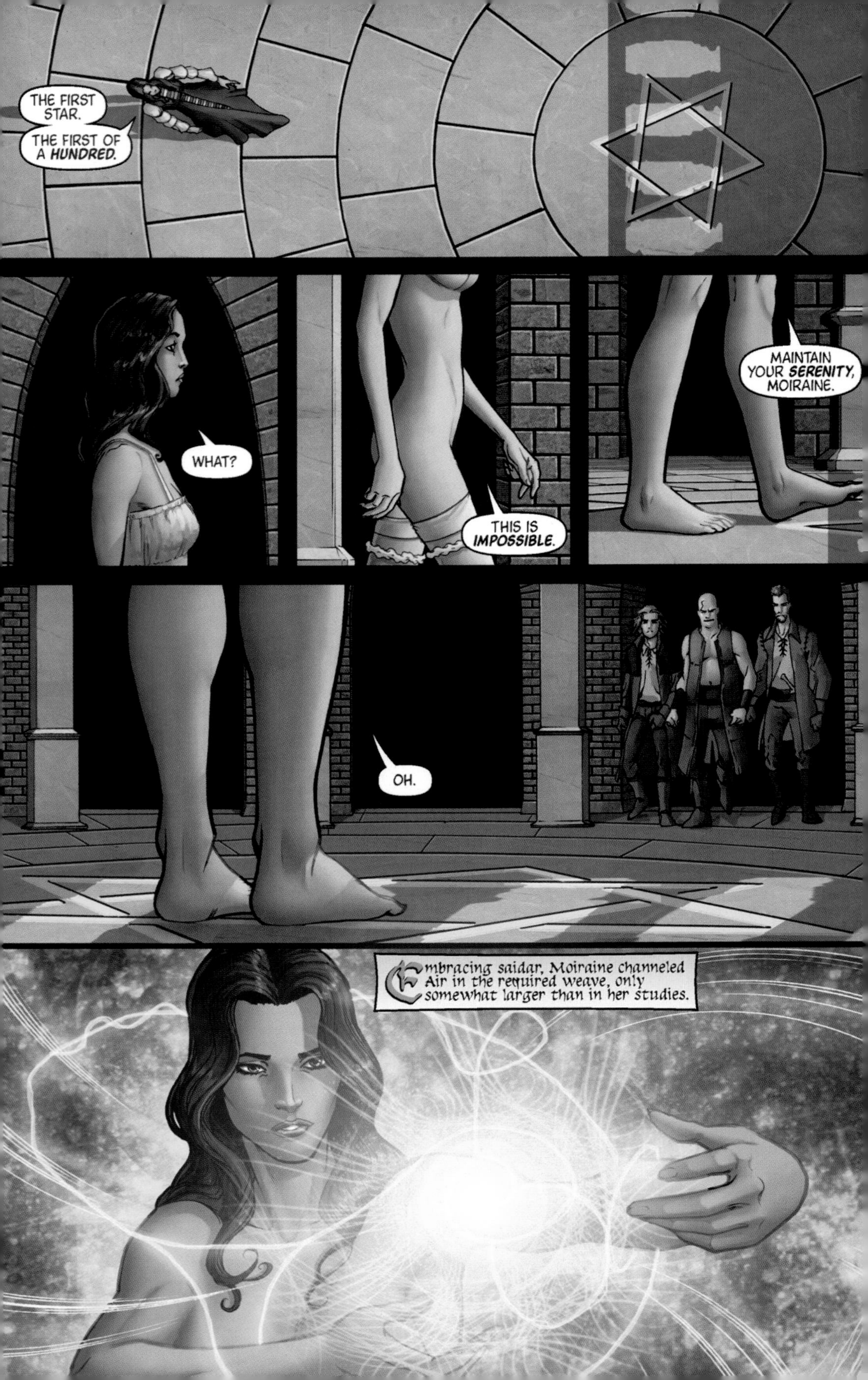
THE FIRST STAR.
THE FIRST OF A HUNDRED.
WHAT?
THIS IS IMPOSSIBLE.
MAINTAIN YOUR SERENITY, MOIRAINE.
OH.
Embracing saidar, Moiraine channeled Air in the required weave, only somewhat larger than in her studies.

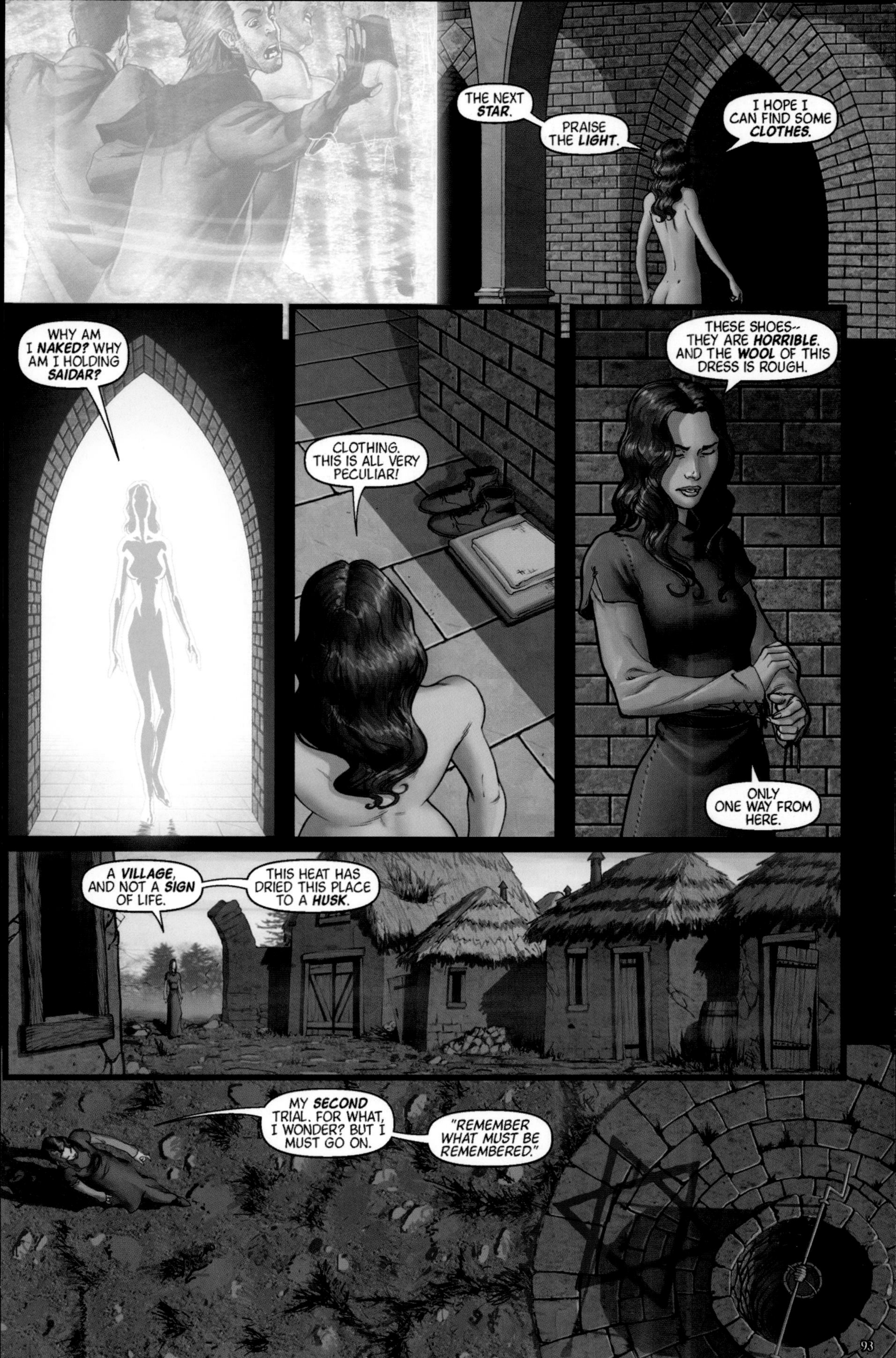
THE NEXT STAR.
PRAISE THE LIGHT.
I HOPE I CAN FIND SOME CLOTHES.
WHY AM I NAKED? WHY AM I HOLDING SAIDAR?
CLOTHING. THIS IS ALL VERY PECULIAR!
THESE SHOES-- THEY ARE HORRIBLE. AND THE WOOL OF THIS DRESS IS ROUGH.
ONLY ONE WAY FROM HERE.
A VILLAGE, AND NOT A SIGN OF LIFE.
THIS HEAT HAS DRIED THIS PLACE TO A HUSK.
MY SECOND TRIAL. FOR WHAT, I WONDER? BUT I MUST GO ON.
"REMEMBER WHAT MUST BE REMEMBERED."

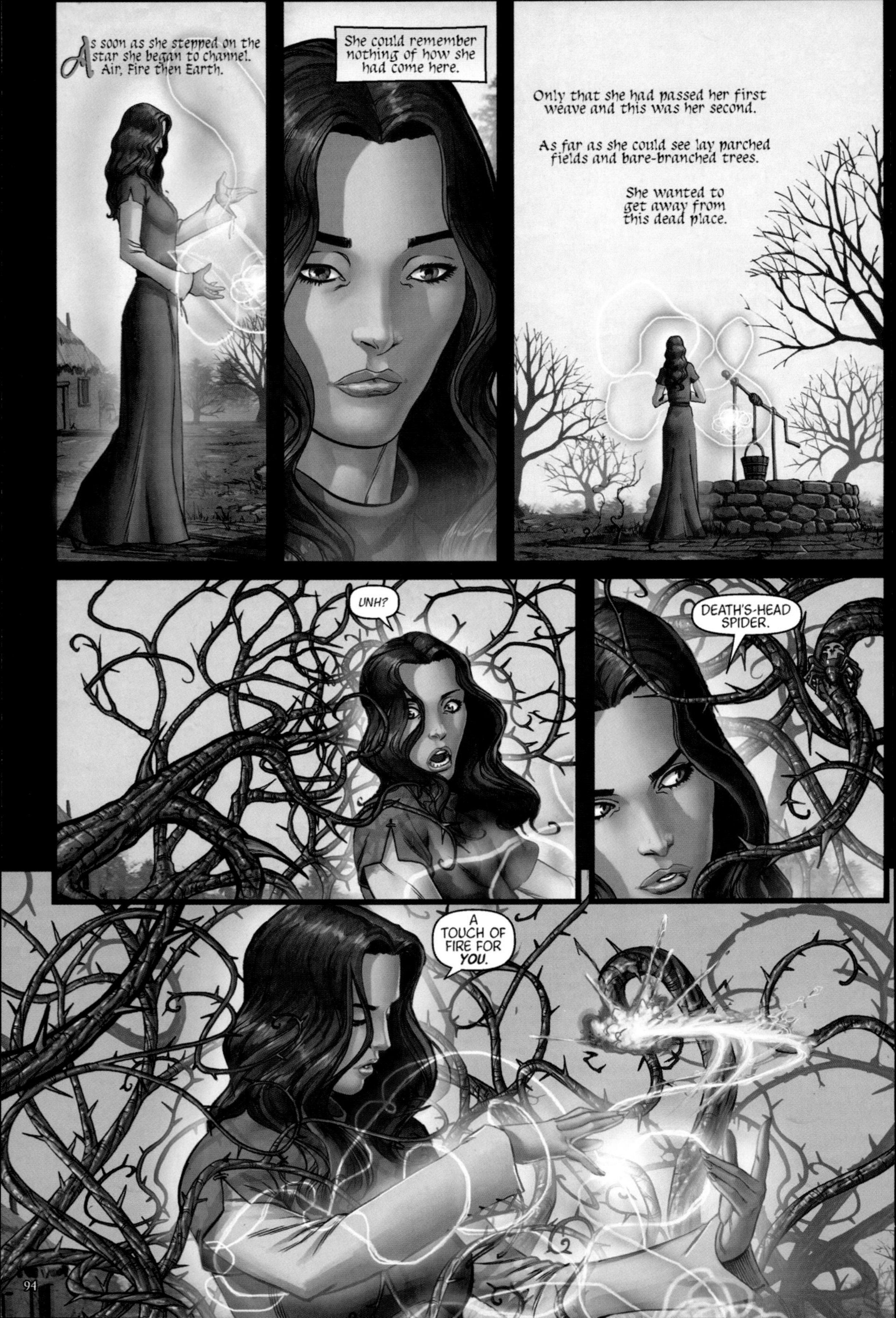

As soon as she stepped on the star she began to channel. Air, Fire then Earth.
She could remember nothing of how she had come here.
Only that she had passed her first weave and this was her second.
As far as she could see lay parched fields and bare-branched trees.
She wanted to get away from this dead place.
UNH?
DEATH'S-HEAD SPIDER.
A TOUCH OF FIRE FOR *YOU*.

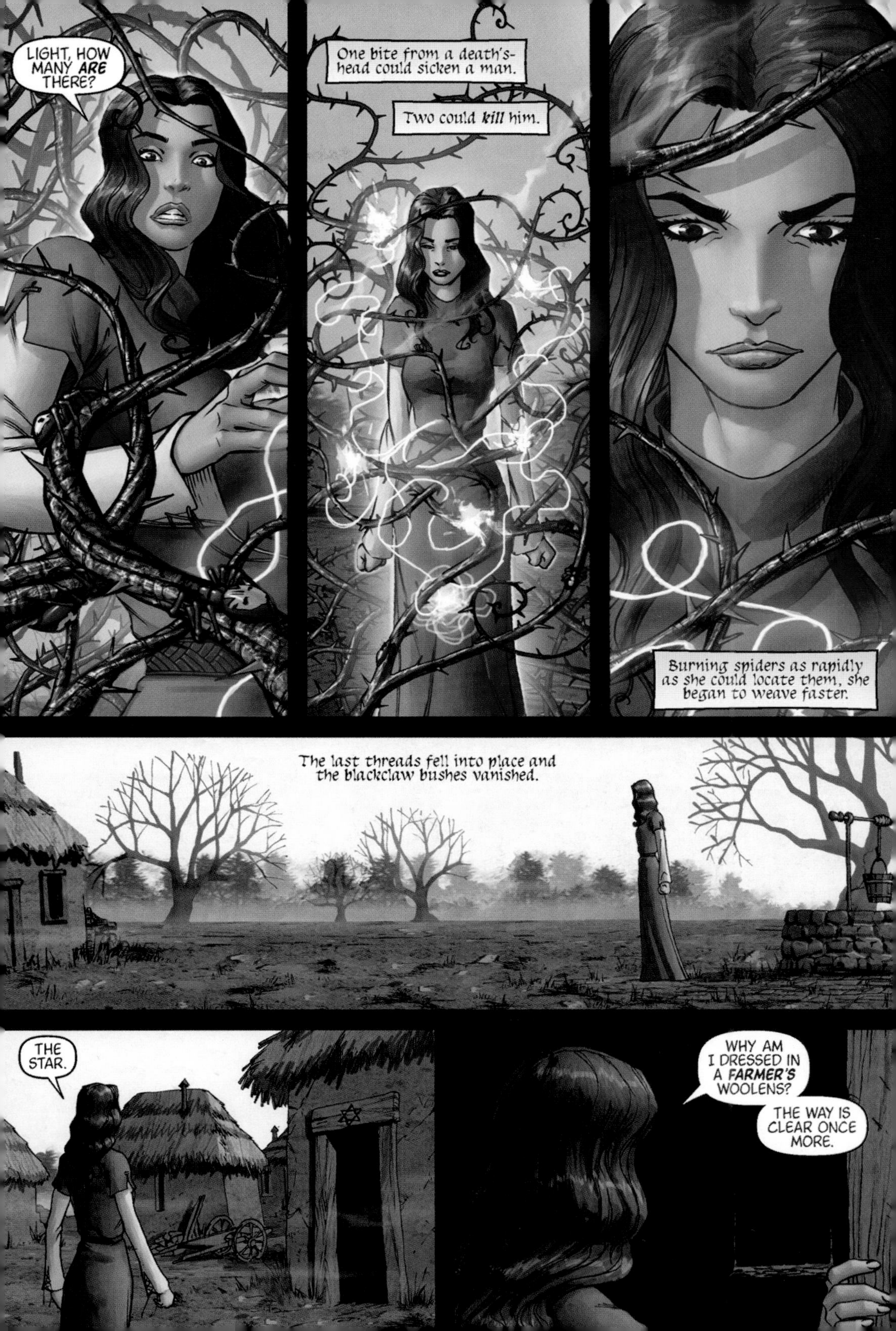
LIGHT, HOW MANY ARE THERE?
One bite from a death's-head could sicken a man.
Two could kill him.
Burning spiders as rapidly as she could locate them, she began to weave faster.
The last threads fell into place and the blackclaw bushes vanished.
THE STAR.
WHY AM I DRESSED IN A FARMER'S WOOLENS?
THE WAY IS CLEAR ONCE MORE.

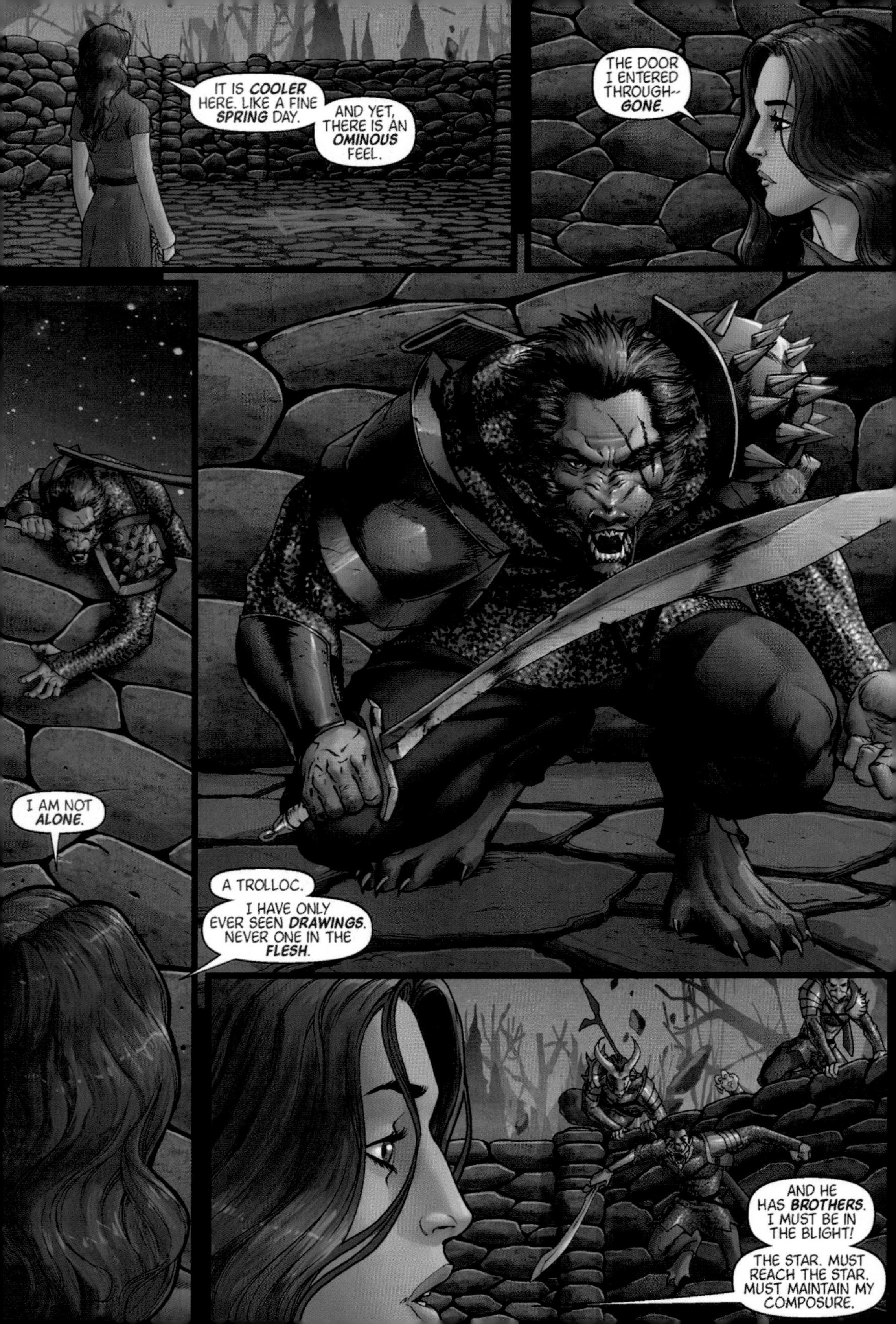
IT IS **COOLER** HERE. LIKE A FINE **SPRING** DAY.
AND YET, THERE IS AN **OMINOUS** FEEL.
THE DOOR I ENTERED THROUGH-- **GONE**.
I AM NOT **ALONE**.
A TROLLOC.
I HAVE ONLY EVER SEEN **DRAWINGS**. NEVER ONE IN THE **FLESH**.
AND HE HAS **BROTHERS**. I MUST BE IN THE BLIGHT!
THE STAR. MUST REACH THE STAR. MUST MAINTAIN MY COMPOSURE.

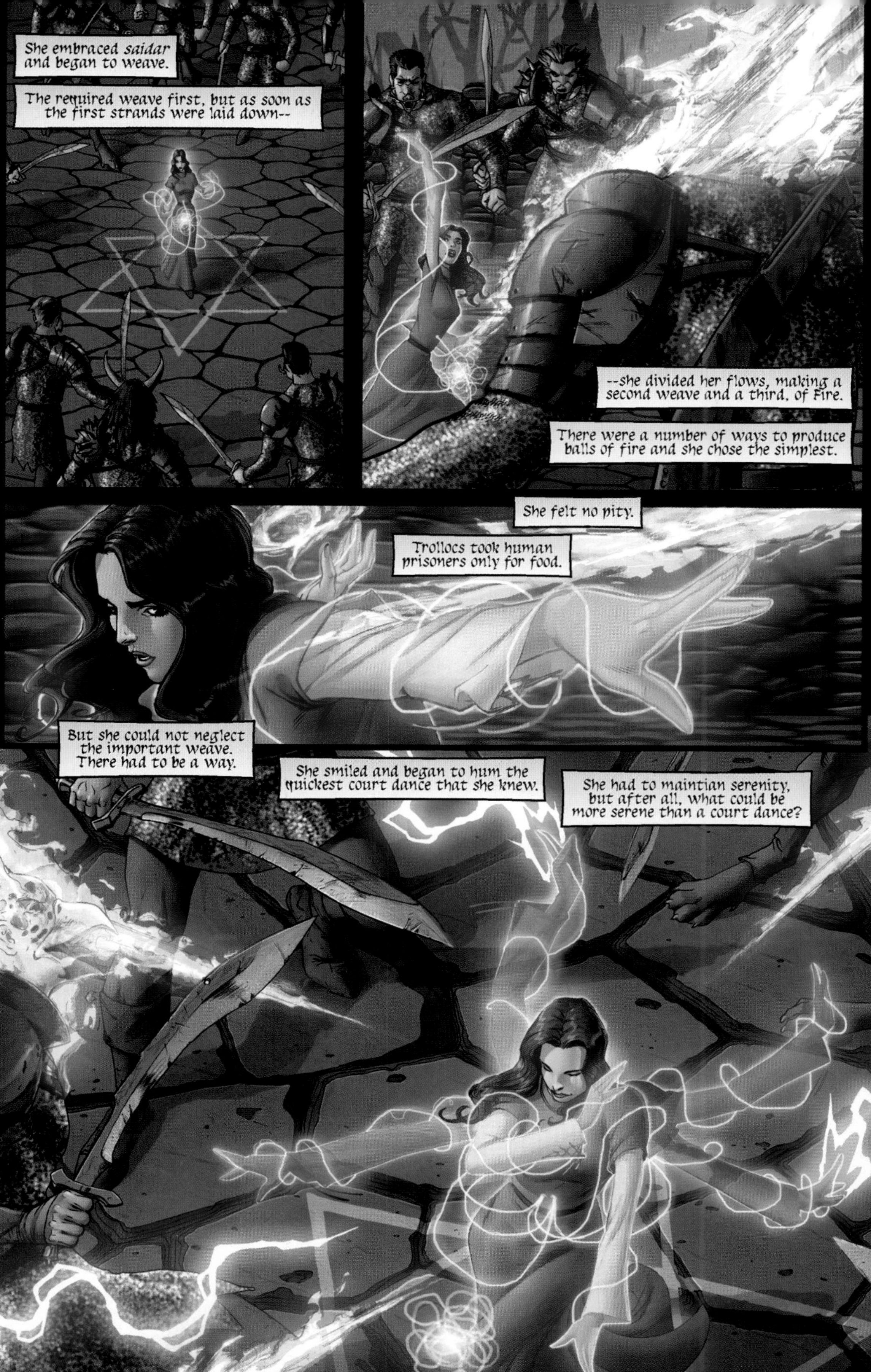

She embraced *saidar* and began to weave.
The required weave first, but as soon as the first strands were laid down--
--she divided her flows, making a second weave and a third, of Fire.
There were a number of ways to produce balls of fire and she chose the simplest.
She felt no pity.
Trollocs took human prisoners only for food.
But she could not neglect the important weave. There had to be a way.
She smiled and began to hum the quickest court dance that she knew.
She had to maintian serenity, but after all, what could be more serene than a court dance?

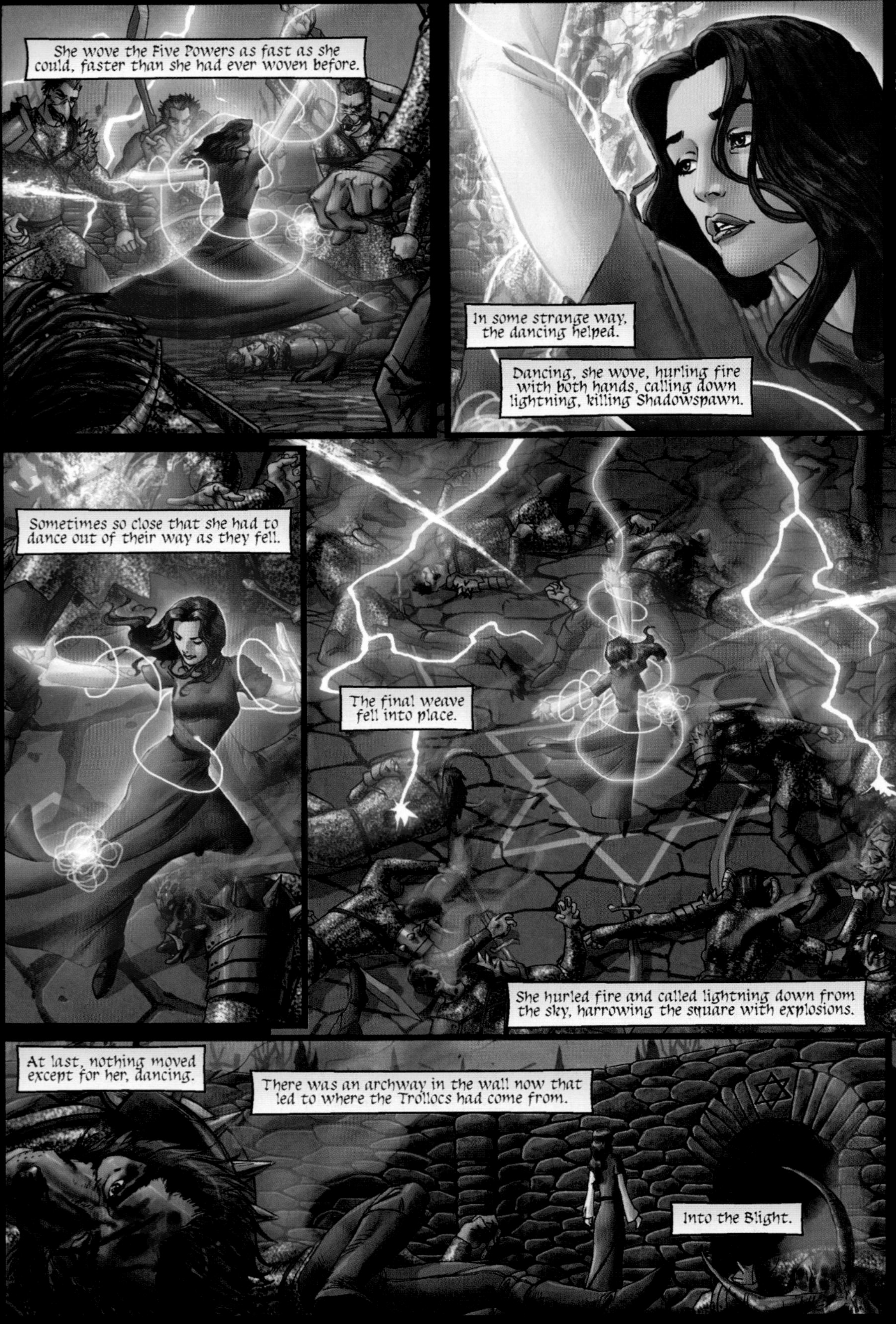

She wove the Five Powers as fast as she could, faster than she had ever woven before.
In some strange way, the dancing helped.
Dancing, she wove, hurling fire with both hands, calling down lightning, killing Shadowspawn.
Sometimes so close that she had to dance out of their way as they fell.
The final weave fell into place.
She hurled fire and called lightning down from the sky, harrowing the square with explosions.
At last, nothing moved except for her, dancing.
There was an archway in the wall now that led to where the Trollocs had come from.
Into the Blight.

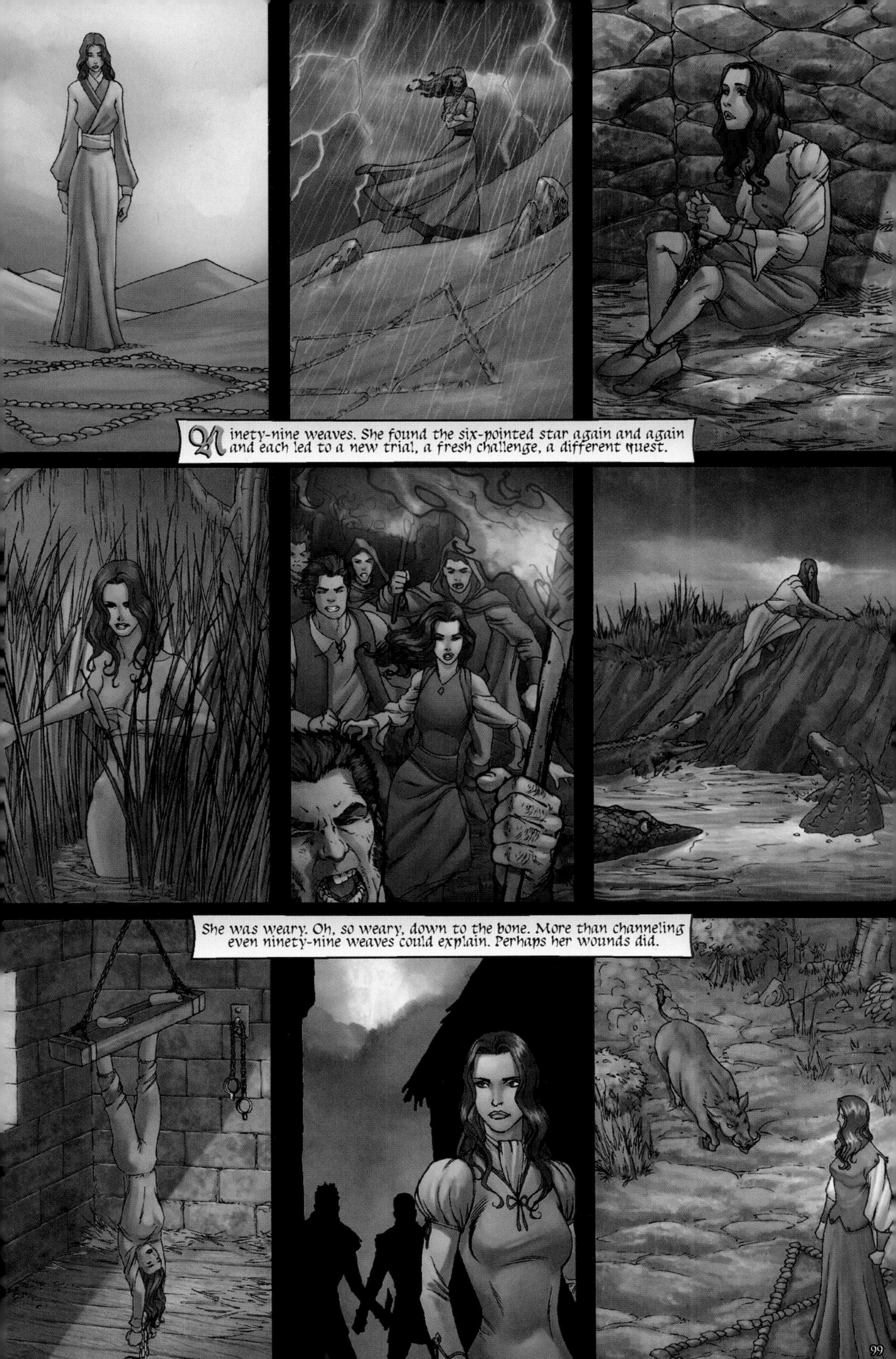
Ninety-nine weaves. She found the six-pointed star again and again and each led to a new trial, a fresh challenge, a different quest.
She was weary. Oh, so weary, down to the bone. More than channeling even ninety-nine weaves could explain. Perhaps her wounds did.

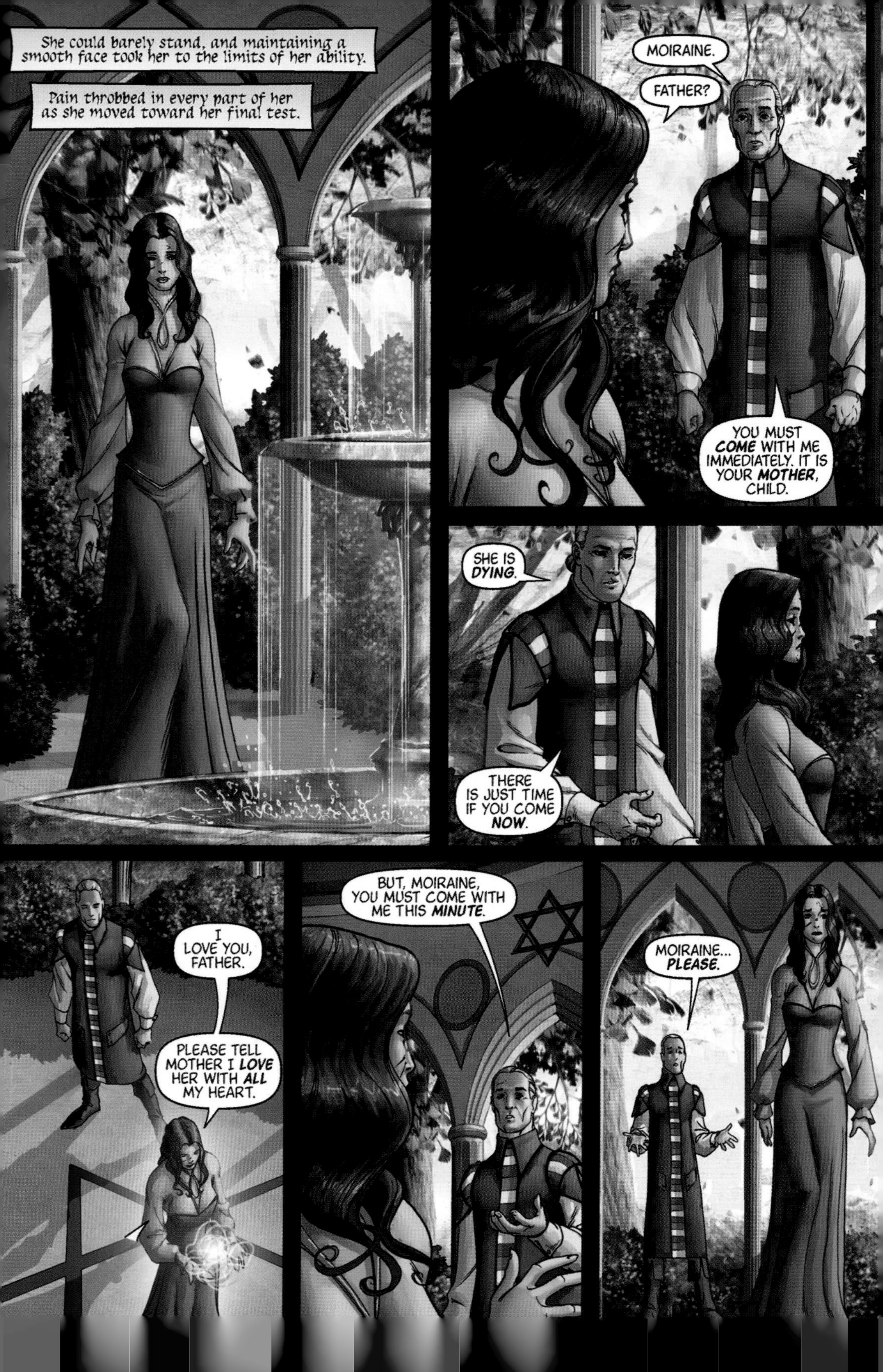
She could barely stand, and maintaining a smooth face took her to the limits of her ability.
Pain throbbed in every part of her as she moved toward her final test.
MOIRAINE.
FATHER?
YOU MUST COME WITH ME IMMEDIATELY. IT IS YOUR MOTHER, CHILD.
SHE IS DYING.
THERE IS JUST TIME IF YOU COME NOW.
I LOVE YOU, FATHER.
PLEASE TELL MOTHER I LOVE HER WITH ALL MY HEART.
BUT, MOIRAINE, YOU MUST COME WITH ME THIS MINUTE.
MOIRAINE... PLEASE.

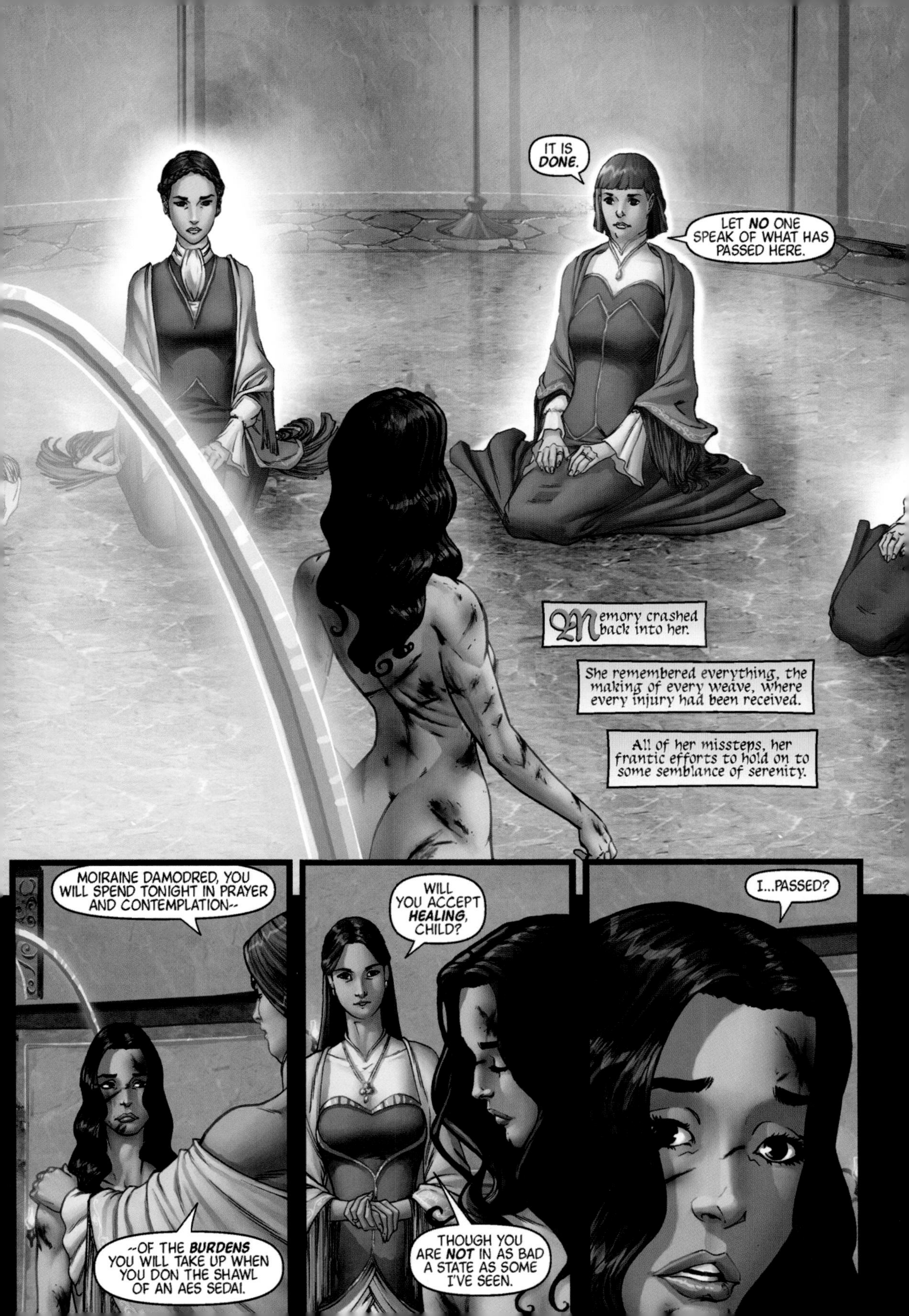

IT IS DONE.
LET NO ONE SPEAK OF WHAT HAS PASSED HERE.
Memory crashed back into her.
She remembered everything, the making of every weave, where every injury had been received.
All of her missteps, her frantic efforts to hold on to some semblance of serenity.
MOIRAINE DAMODRED, YOU WILL SPEND TONIGHT IN PRAYER AND CONTEMPLATION--
--OF THE BURDENS YOU WILL TAKE UP WHEN YOU DON THE SHAWL OF AN AES SEDAI.
WILL YOU ACCEPT HEALING, CHILD?
THOUGH YOU ARE NOT IN AS BAD A STATE AS SOME I'VE SEEN.
I...PASSED?

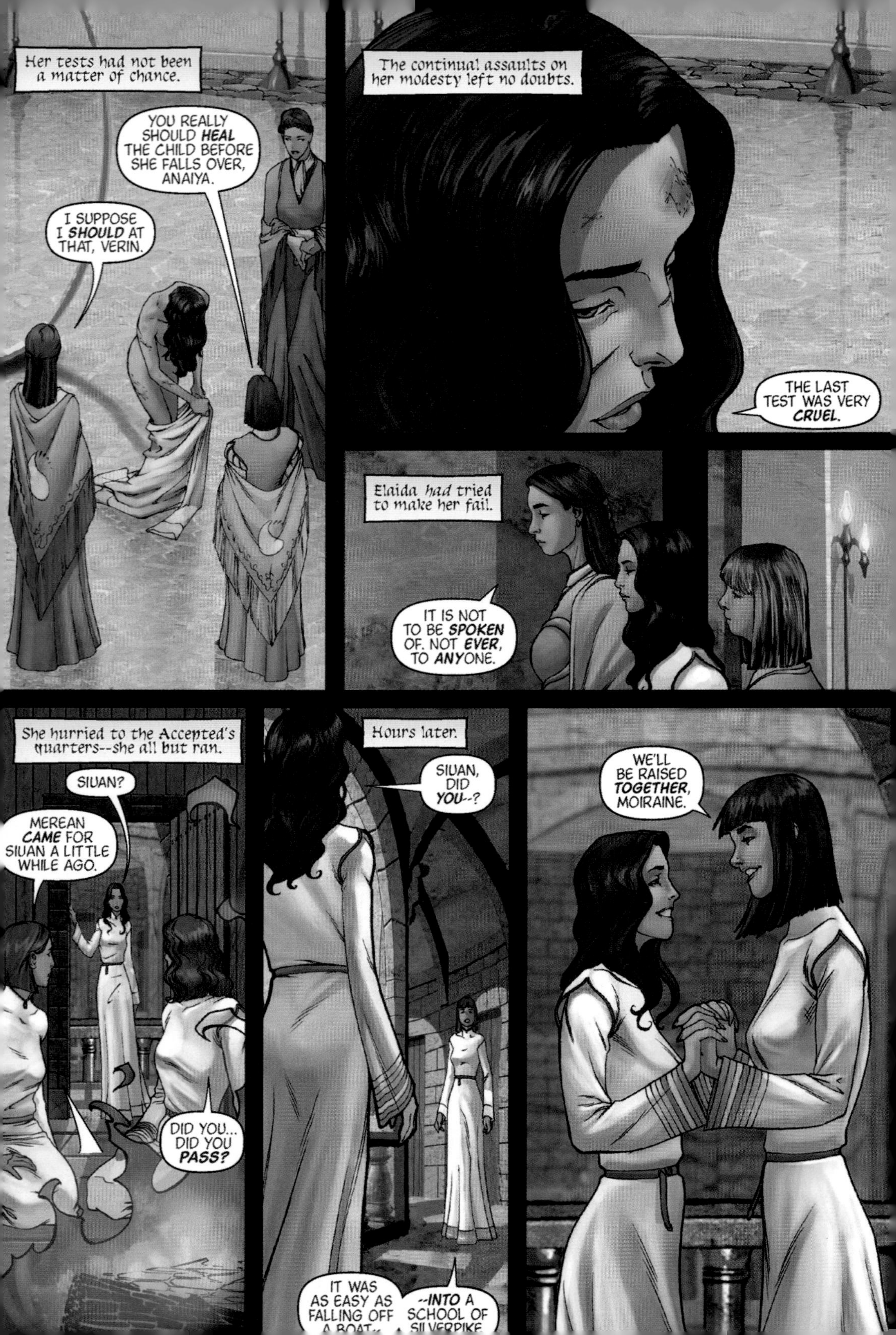
Her tests had not been a matter of chance.
YOU REALLY SHOULD HEAL THE CHILD BEFORE SHE FALLS OVER, ANAIYA.
I SUPPOSE I SHOULD AT THAT, VERIN.
The continual assaults on her modesty left no doubts.
THE LAST TEST WAS VERY CRUEL.
Elaida had tried to make her fail.
IT IS NOT TO BE SPOKEN OF. NOT EVER, TO ANYONE.
She hurried to the Accepted's quarters--she all but ran.
SIUAN?
MEREAN CAME FOR SIUAN A LITTLE WHILE AGO.
DID YOU... DID YOU PASS?
Hours later.
SIUAN, DID YOU--?
IT WAS AS EASY AS FALLING OFF A BOAT--
--INTO A SCHOOL OF SILVERPIKE
WE'LL BE RAISED TOGETHER, MOIRAINE.

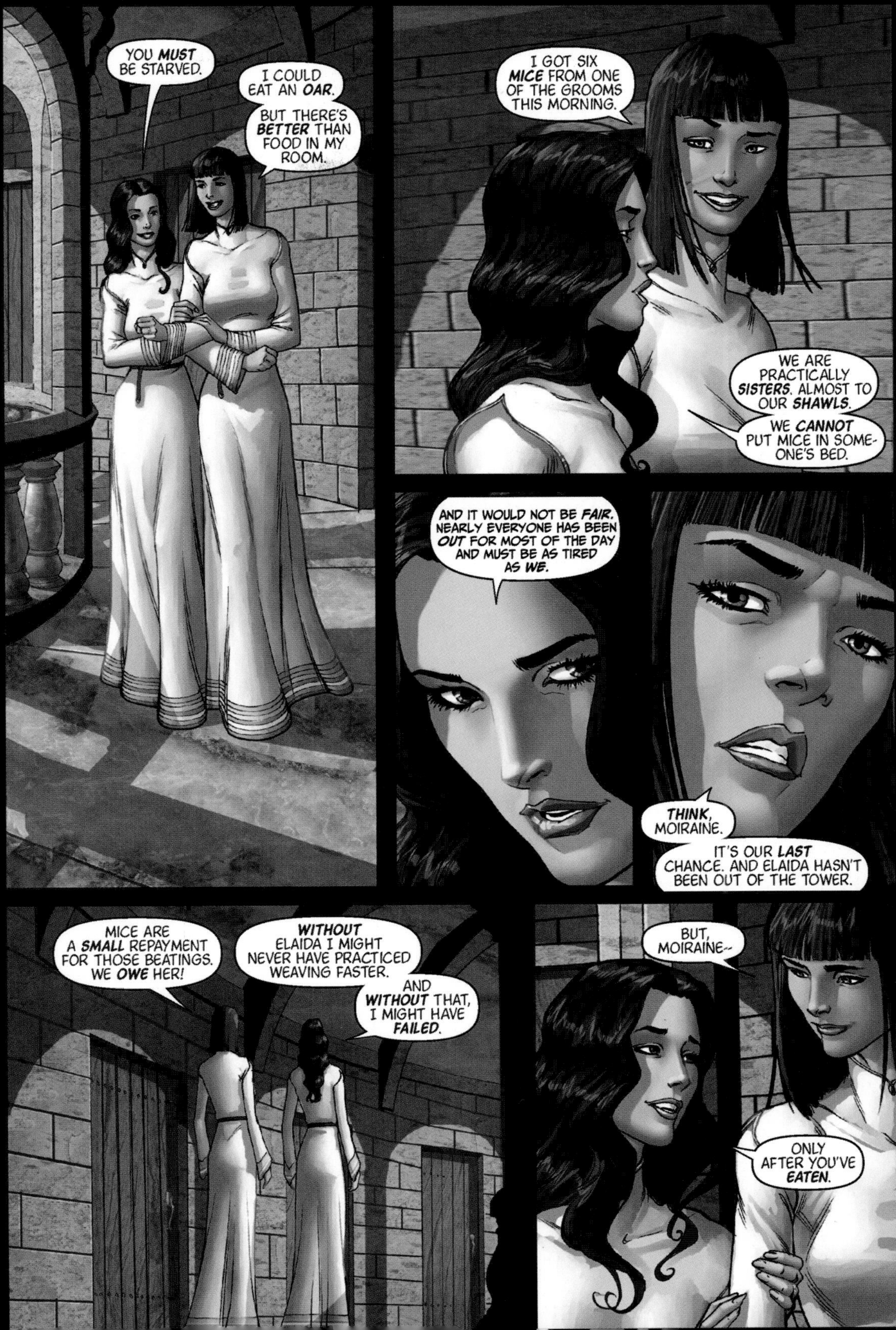
YOU MUST BE STARVED.
I COULD EAT AN OAR.
BUT THERE'S BETTER THAN FOOD IN MY ROOM.
I GOT SIX MICE FROM ONE OF THE GROOMS THIS MORNING.
WE ARE PRACTICALLY SISTERS. ALMOST TO OUR SHAWLS.
WE CANNOT PUT MICE IN SOME-ONE'S BED.
AND IT WOULD NOT BE FAIR. NEARLY EVERYONE HAS BEEN OUT FOR MOST OF THE DAY AND MUST BE AS TIRED AS WE.
THINK, MOIRAINE.
IT'S OUR LAST CHANCE. AND ELAIDA HASN'T BEEN OUT OF THE TOWER.
MICE ARE A SMALL REPAYMENT FOR THOSE BEATINGS. WE OWE HER!
WITHOUT ELAIDA I MIGHT NEVER HAVE PRACTICED WEAVING FASTER.
AND WITHOUT THAT, I MIGHT HAVE FAILED.
BUT, MOIRAINE--
ONLY AFTER YOU'VE EATEN.

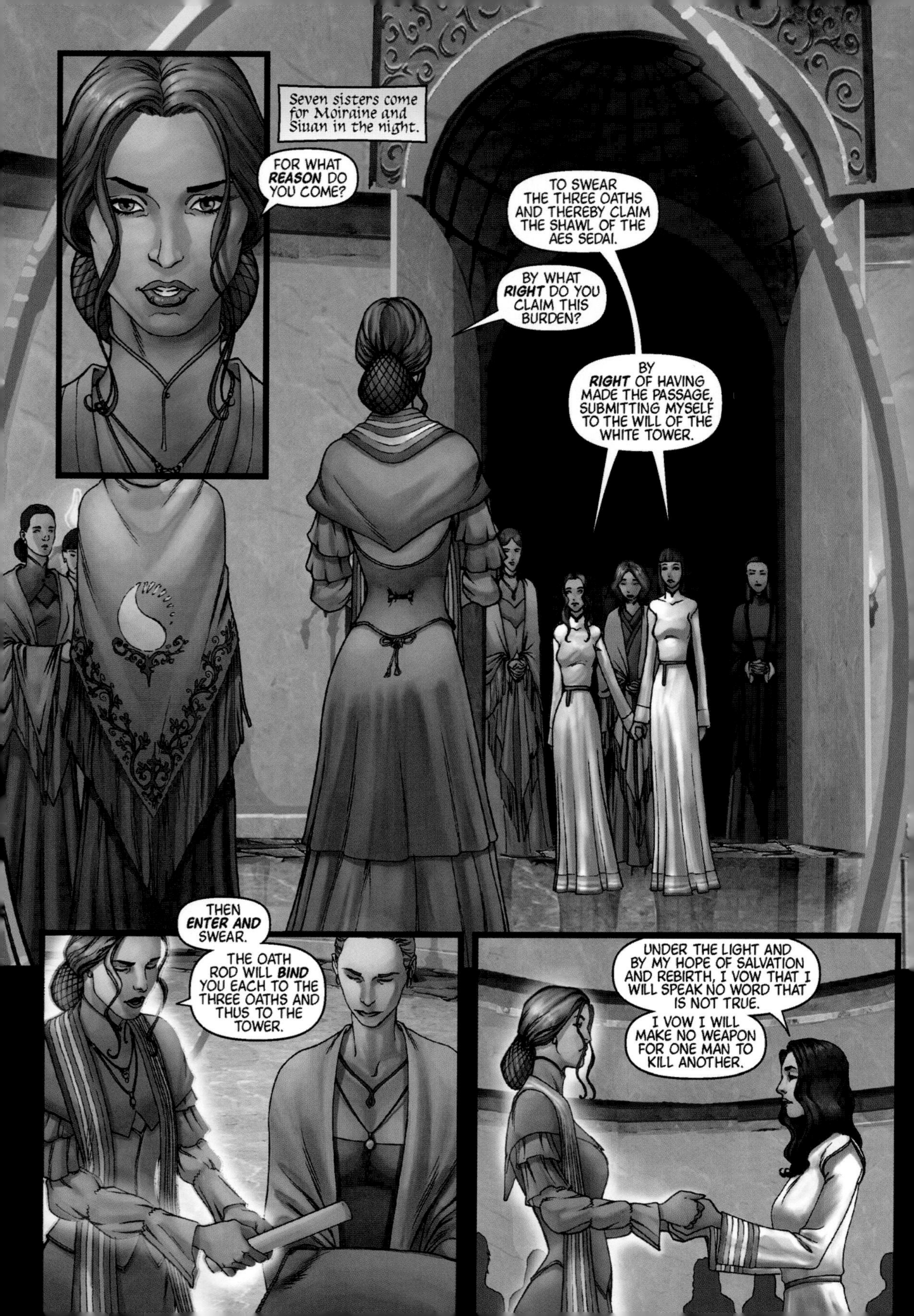
Seven sisters come for Moiraine and Siuan in the night.
FOR WHAT REASON DO YOU COME?
TO SWEAR THE THREE OATHS AND THEREBY CLAIM THE SHAWL OF THE AES SEDAI.
BY WHAT RIGHT DO YOU CLAIM THIS BURDEN?
BY RIGHT OF HAVING MADE THE PASSAGE, SUBMITTING MYSELF TO THE WILL OF THE WHITE TOWER.
THEN ENTER AND SWEAR.
THE OATH ROD WILL BIND YOU EACH TO THE THREE OATHS AND THUS TO THE TOWER.
UNDER THE LIGHT AND BY MY HOPE OF SALVATION AND REBIRTH, I VOW THAT I WILL SPEAK NO WORD THAT IS NOT TRUE.
I VOW I WILL MAKE NO WEAPON FOR ONE MAN TO KILL ANOTHER.

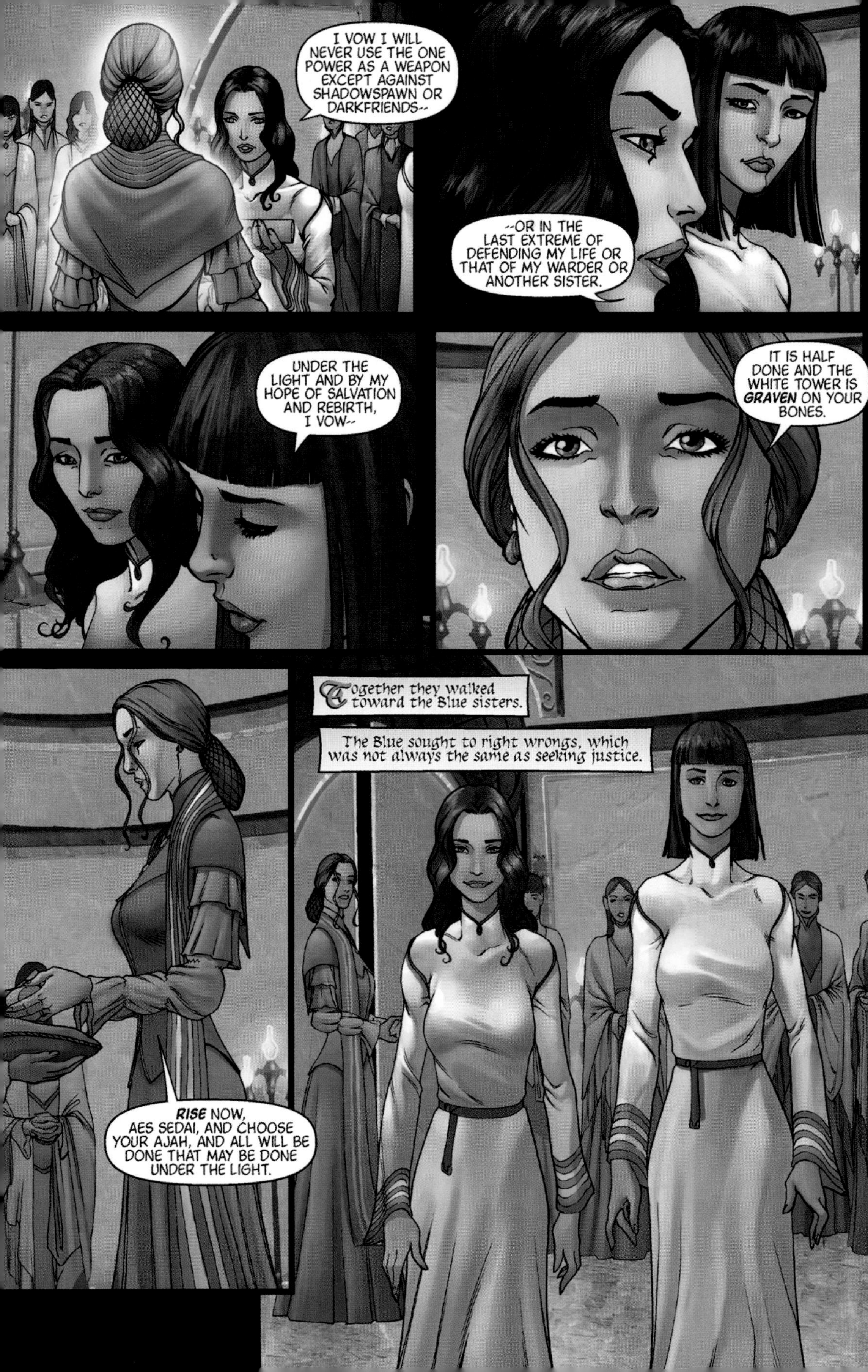
I VOW I WILL NEVER USE THE ONE POWER AS A WEAPON EXCEPT AGAINST SHADOWSPAWN OR DARKFRIENDS--
--OR IN THE LAST EXTREME OF DEFENDING MY LIFE OR THAT OF MY WARDER OR ANOTHER SISTER.
UNDER THE LIGHT AND BY MY HOPE OF SALVATION AND REBIRTH, I VOW--
IT IS HALF DONE AND THE WHITE TOWER IS **GRAVEN** ON YOUR BONES.
RISE NOW, AES SEDAI, AND CHOOSE YOUR AJAH, AND ALL WILL BE DONE THAT MAY BE DONE UNDER THE LIGHT.
Together they walked toward the Blue sisters.
The Blue sought to right wrongs, which was not always the same as seeking justice.

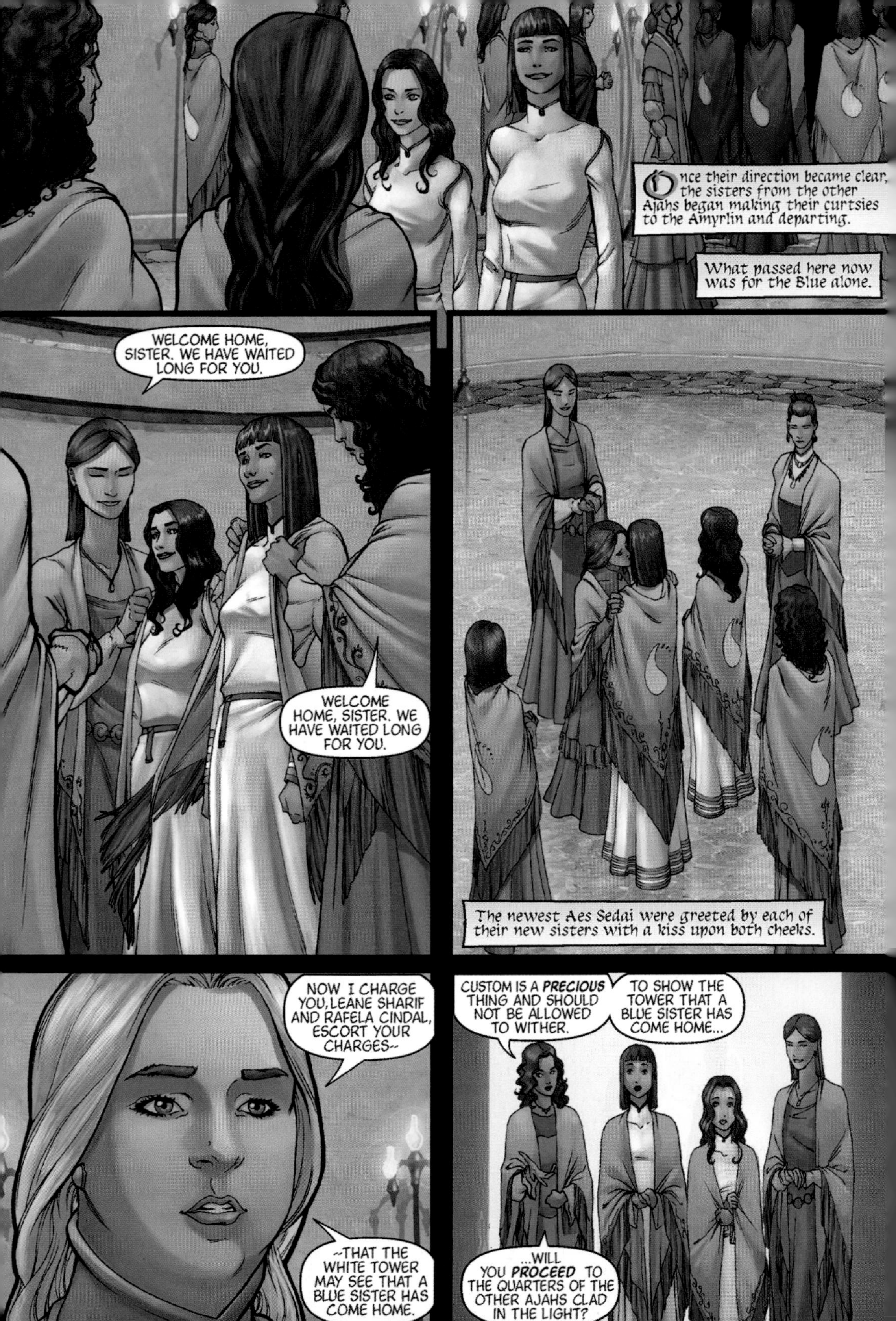
Once their direction became clear, the sisters from the other Ajahs began making their curtsies to the Amyrlin and departing.
What passed here now was for the Blue alone.
WELCOME HOME, SISTER. WE HAVE WAITED LONG FOR YOU.
WELCOME HOME, SISTER. WE HAVE WAITED LONG FOR YOU.
The newest Aes Sedai were greeted by each of their new sisters with a kiss upon both cheeks.
NOW I CHARGE YOU, LEANE SHARIF AND RAFELA CINDAL, ESCORT YOUR CHARGES--
--THAT THE WHITE TOWER MAY SEE THAT A BLUE SISTER HAS COME HOME.
CUSTOM IS A PRECIOUS THING AND SHOULD NOT BE ALLOWED TO WITHER.
TO SHOW THE TOWER THAT A BLUE SISTER HAS COME HOME...
...WILL YOU PROCEED TO THE QUARTERS OF THE OTHER AJAHS CLAD IN THE LIGHT?

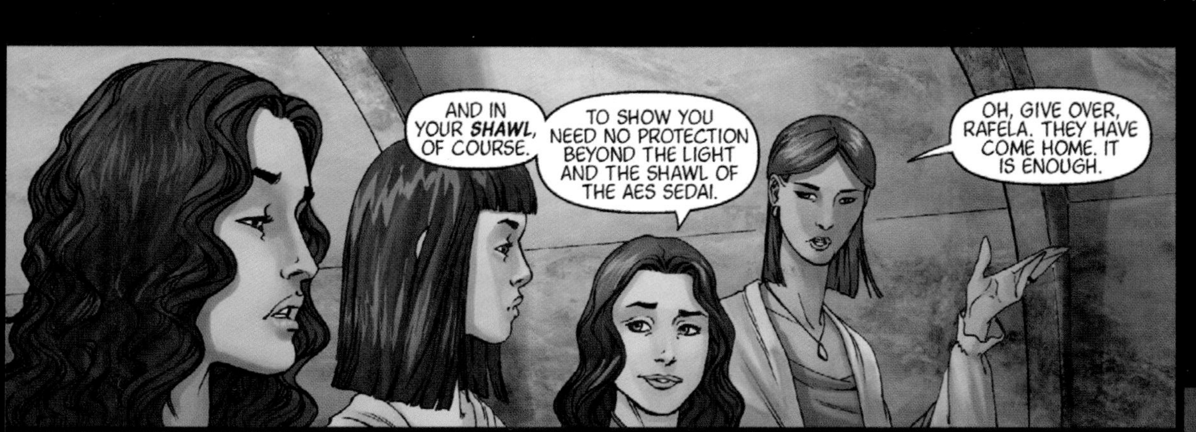
AND IN YOUR SHAWL, OF COURSE.
TO SHOW YOU NEED NO PROTECTION BEYOND THE LIGHT AND THE SHAWL OF THE AES SEDAI.
OH, GIVE OVER, RAFELA. THEY HAVE COME HOME. IT IS ENOUGH.

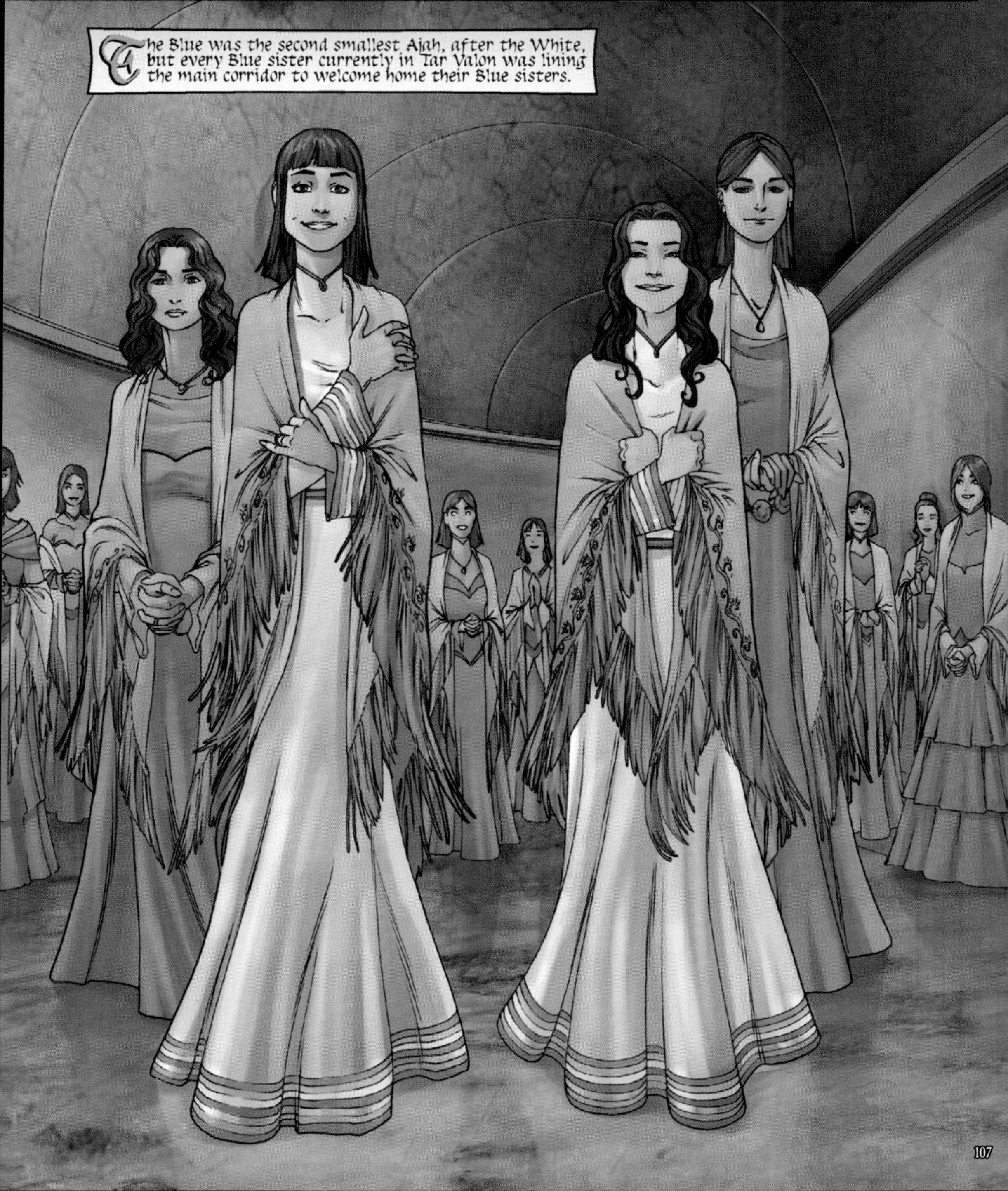
The Blue was the second smallest Ajah, after the White, but every Blue sister currently in Tar Valon was lining the main corridor to welcome home their Blue sisters.

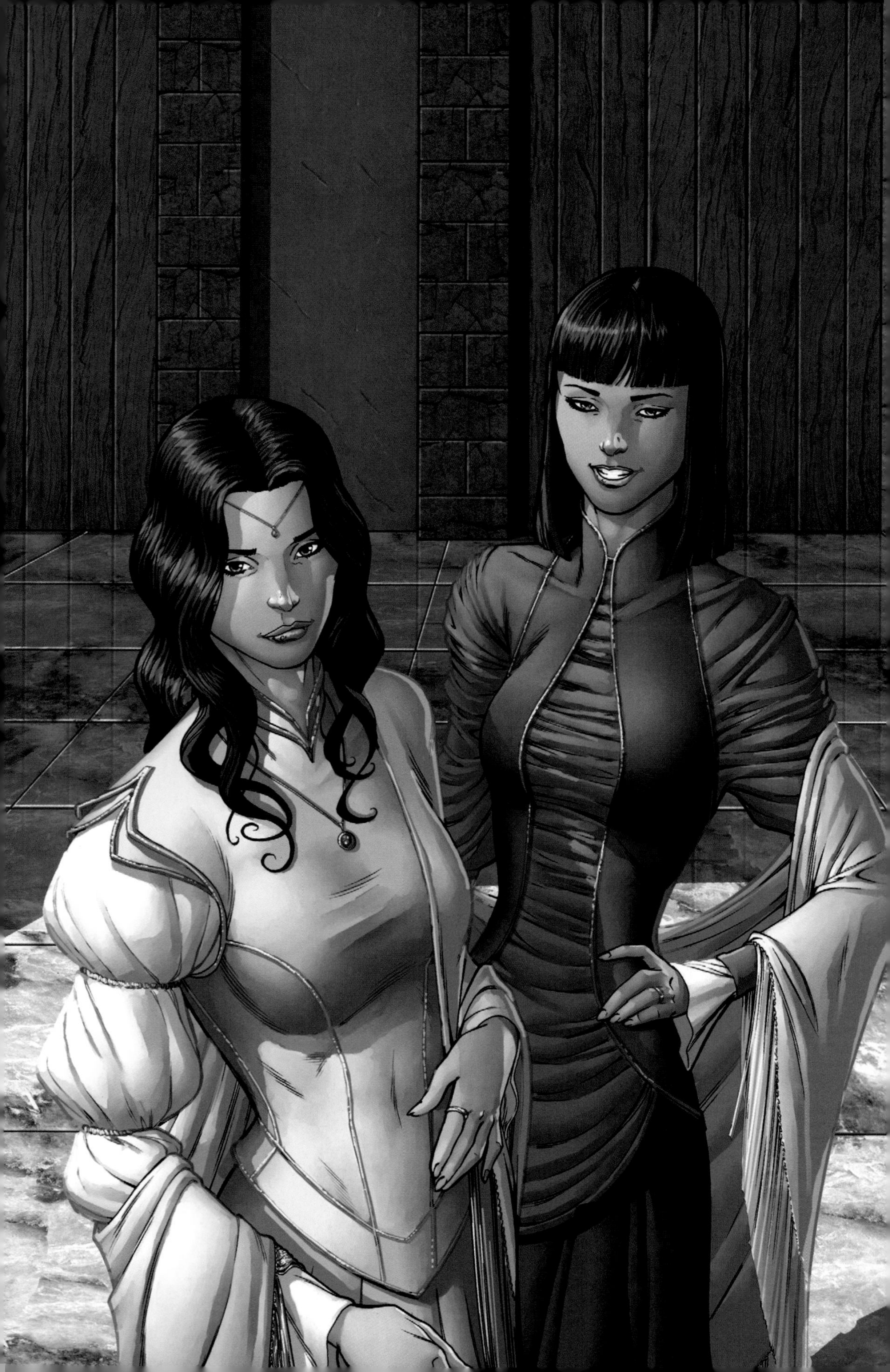

chapter five

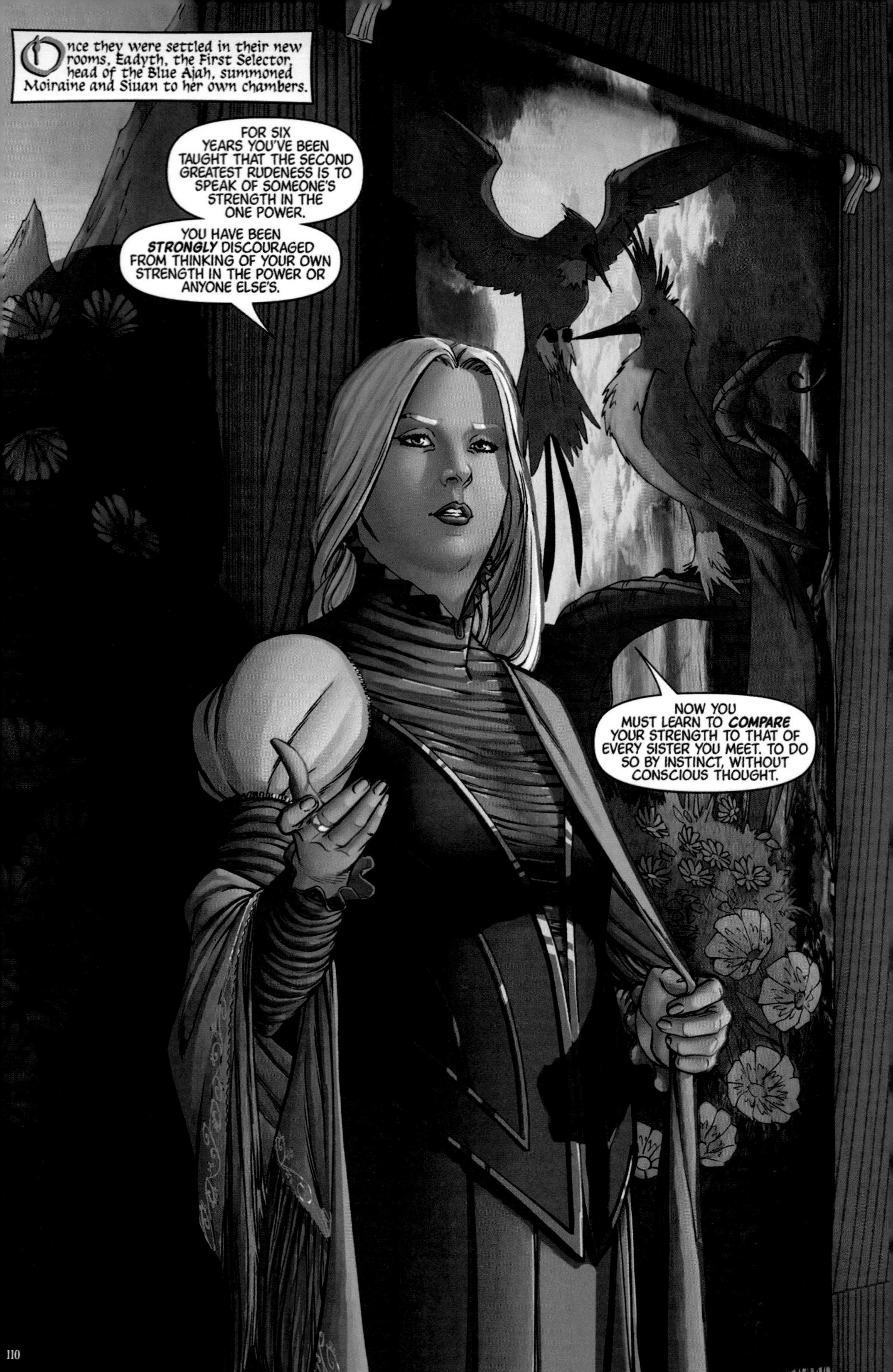
Once they were settled in their new rooms, Eadyth, the First Selector, head of the Blue Ajah, summoned Moiraine and Siuan to her own chambers.
FOR SIX YEARS YOU'VE BEEN TAUGHT THAT THE SECOND GREATEST RUDENESS IS TO SPEAK OF SOMEONE'S STRENGTH IN THE ONE POWER.
YOU HAVE BEEN ***STRONGLY*** DISCOURAGED FROM THINKING OF YOUR OWN STRENGTH IN THE POWER OR ANYONE ELSE'S.
NOW YOU MUST LEARN TO ***COMPARE*** YOUR STRENGTH TO THAT OF EVERY SISTER YOU MEET. TO DO SO BY INSTINCT, WITHOUT CONSCIOUS THOUGHT.

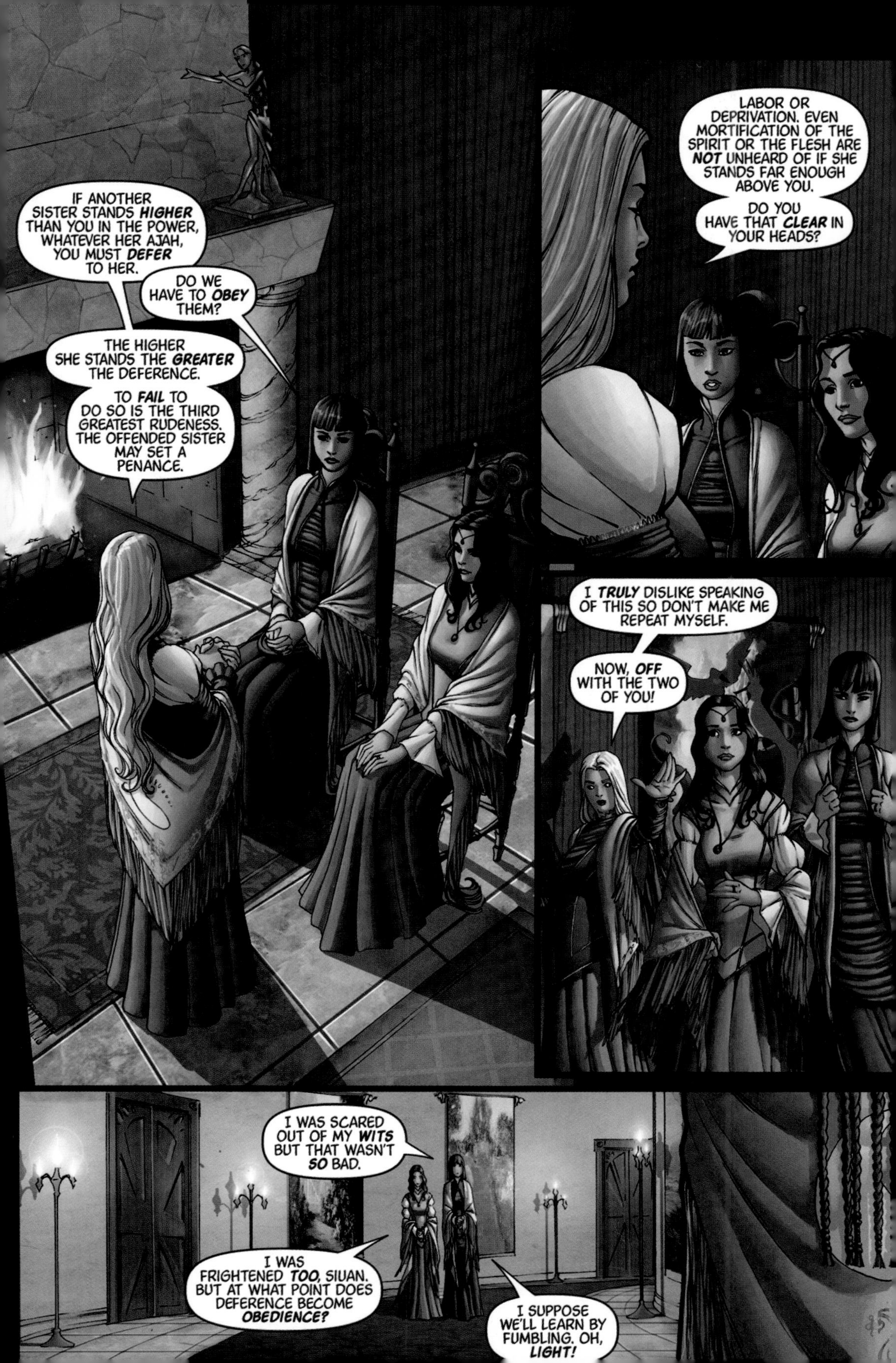
IF ANOTHER SISTER STANDS ***HIGHER*** THAN YOU IN THE POWER, WHATEVER HER AJAH, YOU MUST ***DEFER*** TO HER.
DO WE HAVE TO ***OBEY*** THEM?
THE HIGHER SHE STANDS THE ***GREATER*** THE DEFERENCE.
TO ***FAIL*** TO DO SO IS THE THIRD GREATEST RUDENESS. THE OFFENDED SISTER MAY SET A PENANCE.
LABOR OR DEPRIVATION. EVEN MORTIFICATION OF THE SPIRIT OR THE FLESH ARE ***NOT*** UNHEARD OF IF SHE STANDS FAR ENOUGH ABOVE YOU.
DO YOU HAVE THAT ***CLEAR*** IN YOUR HEADS?
I ***TRULY*** DISLIKE SPEAKING OF THIS SO DON'T MAKE ME REPEAT MYSELF.
NOW, ***OFF*** WITH THE TWO OF YOU!
I WAS SCARED OUT OF MY ***WITS*** BUT THAT WASN'T ***SO*** BAD.
I WAS FRIGHTENED ***TOO***, SIUAN. BUT AT WHAT POINT DOES DEFERENCE BECOME ***OBEDIENCE?***
I SUPPOSE WE'LL LEARN BY FUMBLING. OH, ***LIGHT!***

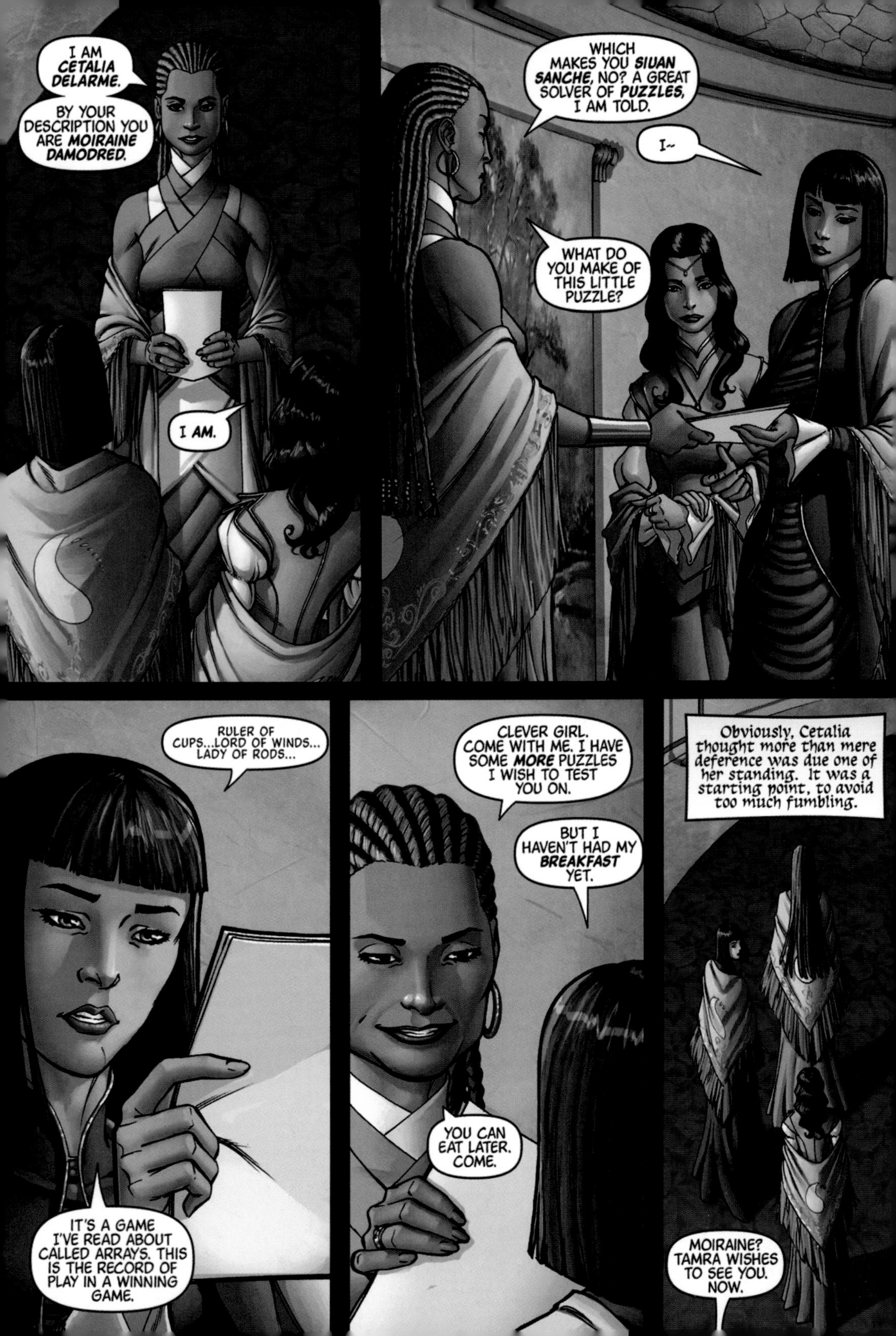
I AM CETALIA DELARME.
BY YOUR DESCRIPTION YOU ARE MOIRAINE DAMODRED.
I AM.
WHICH MAKES YOU SIUAN SANCHE, NO? A GREAT SOLVER OF PUZZLES, I AM TOLD.
I--
WHAT DO YOU MAKE OF THIS LITTLE PUZZLE?
RULER OF CUPS...LORD OF WINDS... LADY OF RODS...
IT'S A GAME I'VE READ ABOUT CALLED ARRAYS. THIS IS THE RECORD OF PLAY IN A WINNING GAME.
CLEVER GIRL. COME WITH ME. I HAVE SOME MORE PUZZLES I WISH TO TEST YOU ON.
BUT I HAVEN'T HAD MY BREAKFAST YET.
YOU CAN EAT LATER. COME.
Obviously, Cetalia thought more than mere deference was due one of her standing. It was a starting point, to avoid too much fumbling.
MOIRAINE? TAMRA WISHES TO SEE YOU. NOW.

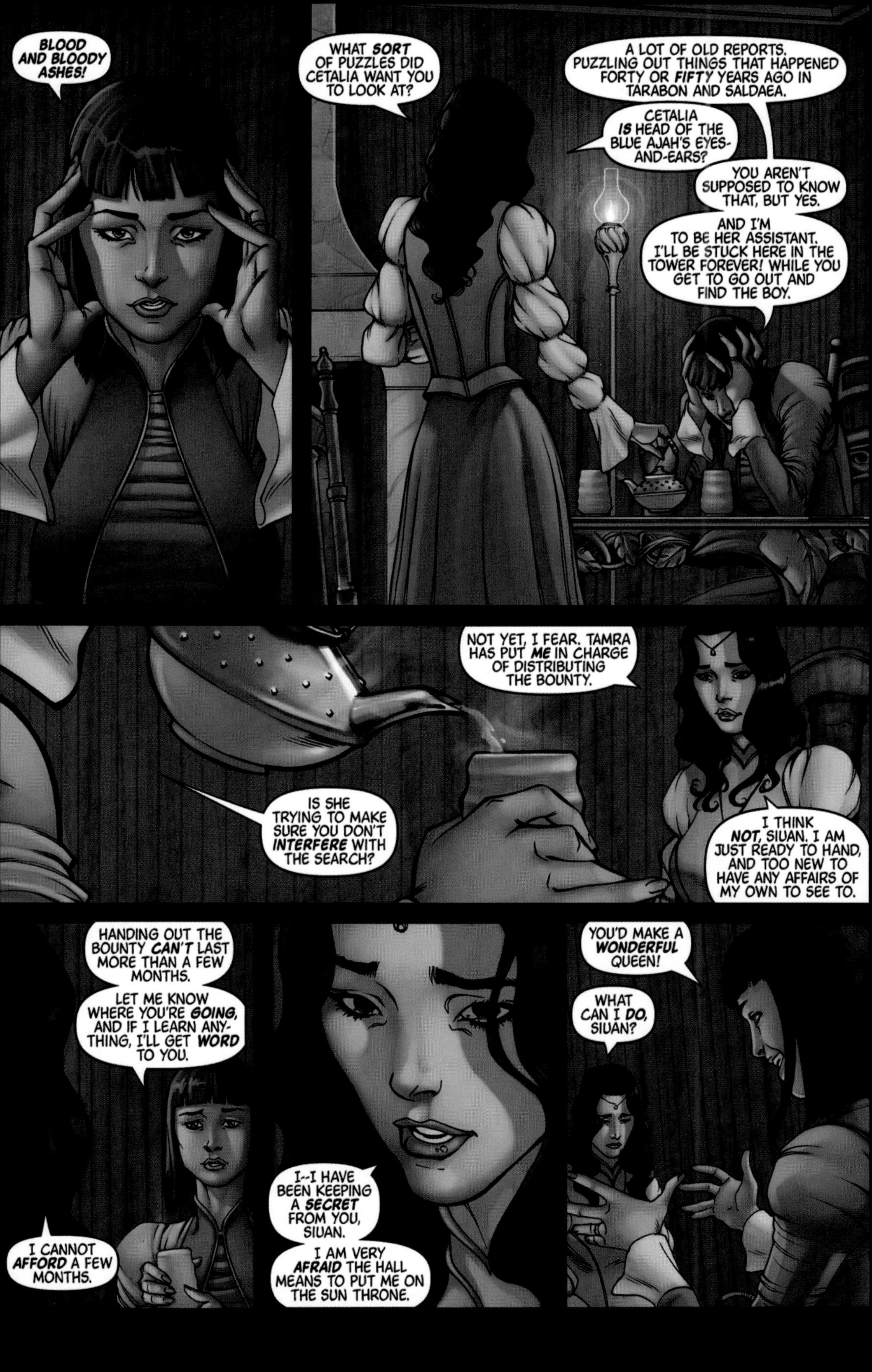
BLOOD AND BLOODY ASHES!
WHAT SORT OF PUZZLES DID CETALIA WANT YOU TO LOOK AT?
A LOT OF OLD REPORTS. PUZZLING OUT THINGS THAT HAPPENED FORTY OR FIFTY YEARS AGO IN TARABON AND SALDAEA.
CETALIA IS HEAD OF THE BLUE AJAH'S EYES-AND-EARS?
YOU AREN'T SUPPOSED TO KNOW THAT, BUT YES.
AND I'M TO BE HER ASSISTANT. I'LL BE STUCK HERE IN THE TOWER FOREVER! WHILE YOU GET TO GO OUT AND FIND THE BOY.
NOT YET, I FEAR. TAMRA HAS PUT ME IN CHARGE OF DISTRIBUTING THE BOUNTY.
IS SHE TRYING TO MAKE SURE YOU DON'T INTERFERE WITH THE SEARCH?
I THINK NOT, SIUAN. I AM JUST READY TO HAND, AND TOO NEW TO HAVE ANY AFFAIRS OF MY OWN TO SEE TO.
HANDING OUT THE BOUNTY CAN'T LAST MORE THAN A FEW MONTHS.
LET ME KNOW WHERE YOU'RE GOING, AND IF I LEARN ANYTHING, I'LL GET WORD TO YOU.
I CANNOT AFFORD A FEW MONTHS.
I--I HAVE BEEN KEEPING A SECRET FROM YOU, SIUAN.
I AM VERY AFRAID THE HALL MEANS TO PUT ME ON THE SUN THRONE.
YOU'D MAKE A WONDERFUL QUEEN!
WHAT CAN I DO, SIUAN?

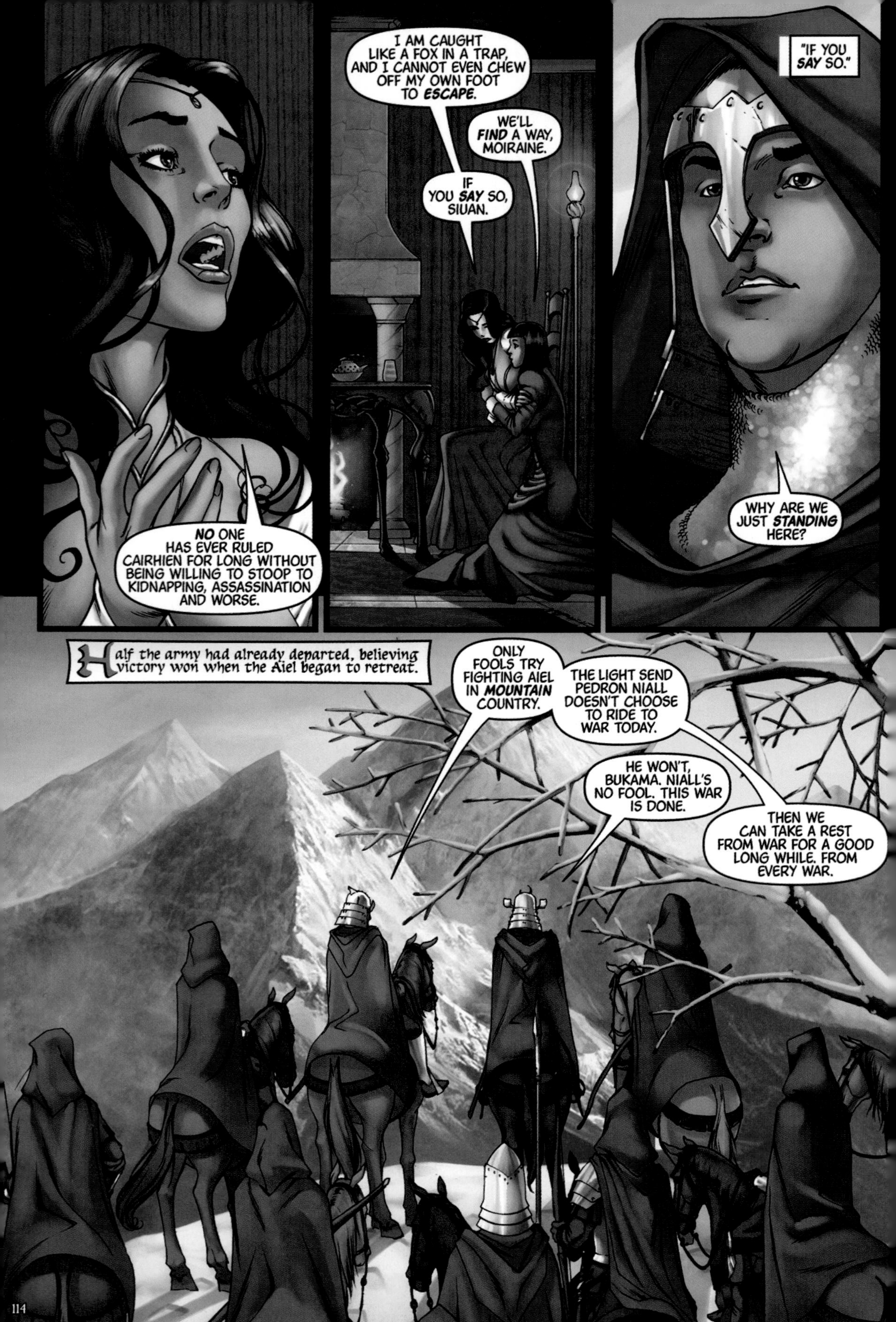
NO ONE HAS EVER RULED CAIRHIEN FOR LONG WITHOUT BEING WILLING TO STOOP TO KIDNAPPING, ASSASSINATION AND WORSE.
I AM CAUGHT LIKE A FOX IN A TRAP, AND I CANNOT EVEN CHEW OFF MY OWN FOOT TO ESCAPE.
WE'LL FIND A WAY, MOIRAINE.
IF YOU SAY SO, SIUAN.
"IF YOU SAY SO."
WHY ARE WE JUST STANDING HERE?
Half the army had already departed, believing victory won when the Aiel began to retreat.
ONLY FOOLS TRY FIGHTING AIEL IN MOUNTAIN COUNTRY.
THE LIGHT SEND PEDRON NIALL DOESN'T CHOOSE TO RIDE TO WAR TODAY.
HE WON'T, BUKAMA. NIALL'S NO FOOL. THIS WAR IS DONE.
THEN WE CAN TAKE A REST FROM WAR FOR A GOOD LONG WHILE. FROM EVERY WAR.

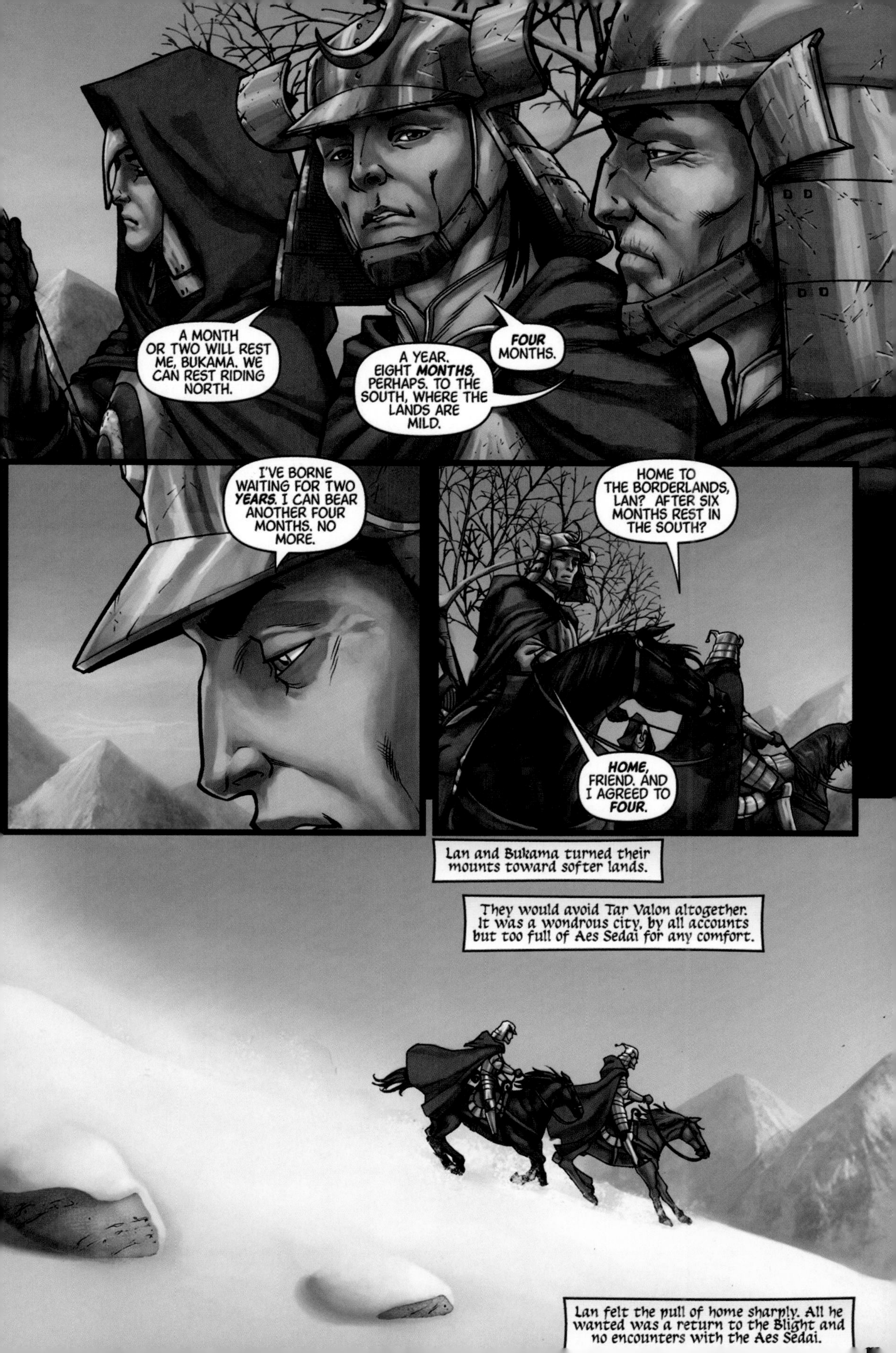
A MONTH OR TWO WILL REST ME, BUKAMA. WE CAN REST RIDING NORTH.
A YEAR. EIGHT MONTHS, PERHAPS. TO THE SOUTH, WHERE THE LANDS ARE MILD.
FOUR MONTHS.
I'VE BORNE WAITING FOR TWO YEARS. I CAN BEAR ANOTHER FOUR MONTHS. NO MORE.
HOME TO THE BORDERLANDS, LAN? AFTER SIX MONTHS REST IN THE SOUTH?
HOME, FRIEND. AND I AGREED TO FOUR.
Lan and Bukama turned their mounts toward softer lands.
They would avoid Tar Valon altogether. It was a wondrous city, by all accounts but too full of Aes Sedai for any comfort.
Lan felt the pull of home sharply. All he wanted was a return to the Blight and no encounters with the Aes Sedai.

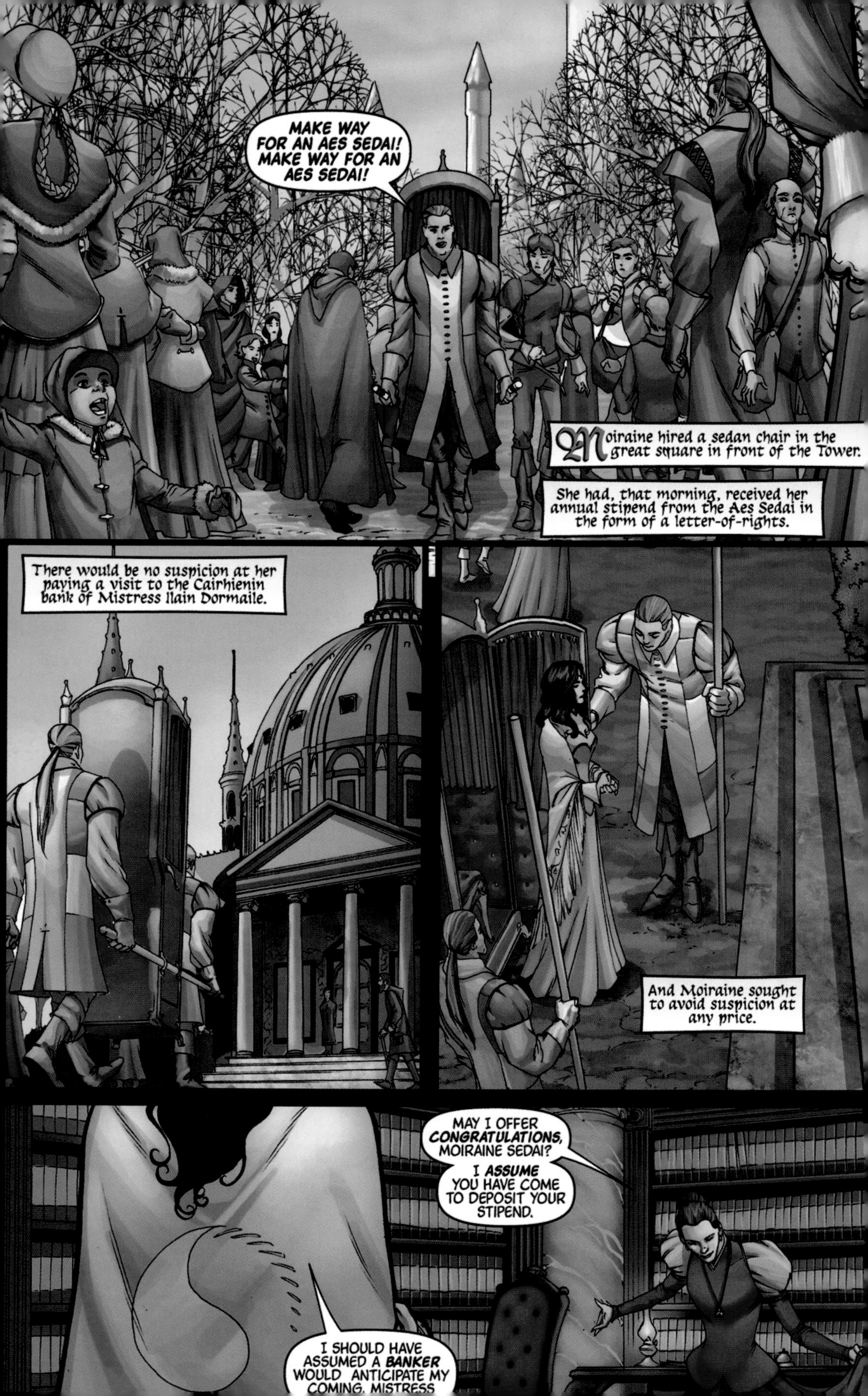
MAKE WAY FOR AN AES SEDAI! MAKE WAY FOR AN AES SEDAI!
Moiraine hired a sedan chair in the great square in front of the Tower.
She had, that morning, received her annual stipend from the Aes Sedai in the form of a letter-of-rights.
There would be no suspicion at her paying a visit to the Cairhienin bank of Mistress Ilain Dormaile.
And Moiraine sought to avoid suspicion at any price.
MAY I OFFER CONGRATULATIONS, MOIRAINE SEDAI?
I ASSUME YOU HAVE COME TO DEPOSIT YOUR STIPEND.
I SHOULD HAVE ASSUMED A BANKER WOULD ANTICIPATE MY COMING, MISTRESS

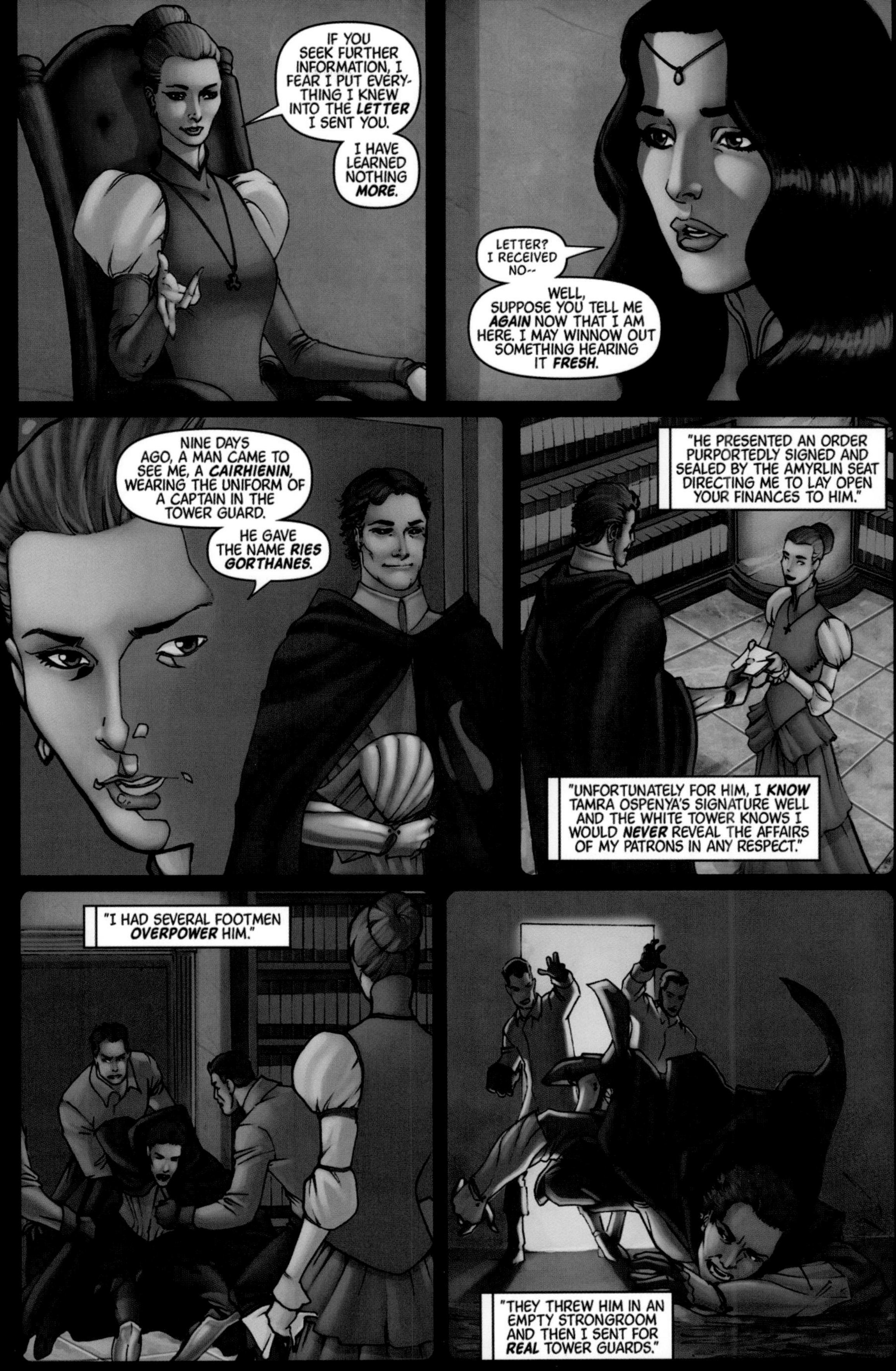
IF YOU SEEK FURTHER INFORMATION, I FEAR I PUT EVERY-THING I KNEW INTO THE LETTER I SENT YOU.
I HAVE LEARNED NOTHING MORE.
LETTER? I RECEIVED NO--
WELL, SUPPOSE YOU TELL ME AGAIN NOW THAT I AM HERE. I MAY WINNOW OUT SOMETHING HEARING IT FRESH.
NINE DAYS AGO, A MAN CAME TO SEE ME, A CAIRHIENIN, WEARING THE UNIFORM OF A CAPTAIN IN THE TOWER GUARD.
HE GAVE THE NAME RIES GORTHANES.
"HE PRESENTED AN ORDER PURPORTEDLY SIGNED AND SEALED BY THE AMYRLIN SEAT DIRECTING ME TO LAY OPEN YOUR FINANCES TO HIM."
"UNFORTUNATELY FOR HIM, I KNOW TAMRA OSPENYA'S SIGNATURE WELL AND THE WHITE TOWER KNOWS I WOULD NEVER REVEAL THE AFFAIRS OF MY PATRONS IN ANY RESPECT."
"I HAD SEVERAL FOOTMEN OVERPOWER HIM."
"THEY THREW HIM IN AN EMPTY STRONGROOM AND THEN I SENT FOR REAL TOWER GUARDS."

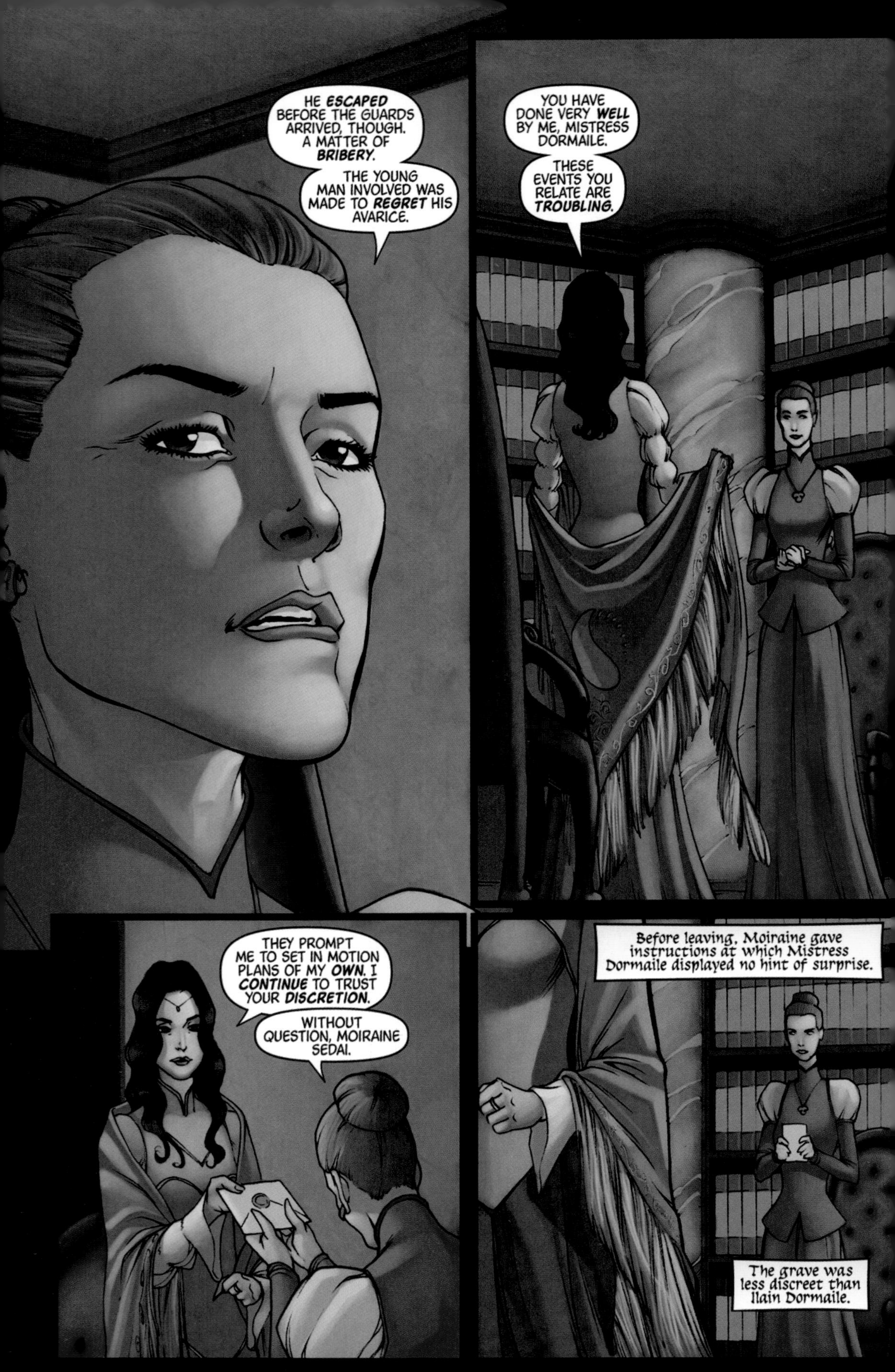
HE ESCAPED BEFORE THE GUARDS ARRIVED, THOUGH. A MATTER OF BRIBERY.
THE YOUNG MAN INVOLVED WAS MADE TO REGRET HIS AVARICE.
YOU HAVE DONE VERY WELL BY ME, MISTRESS DORMAILE.
THESE EVENTS YOU RELATE ARE TROUBLING.
THEY PROMPT ME TO SET IN MOTION PLANS OF MY OWN. I CONTINUE TO TRUST YOUR DISCRETION.
WITHOUT QUESTION, MOIRAINE SEDAI.
Before leaving, Moiraine gave instructions at which Mistress Dormaile displayed no hint of surprise.
The grave was less discreet than Ilain Dormaile.

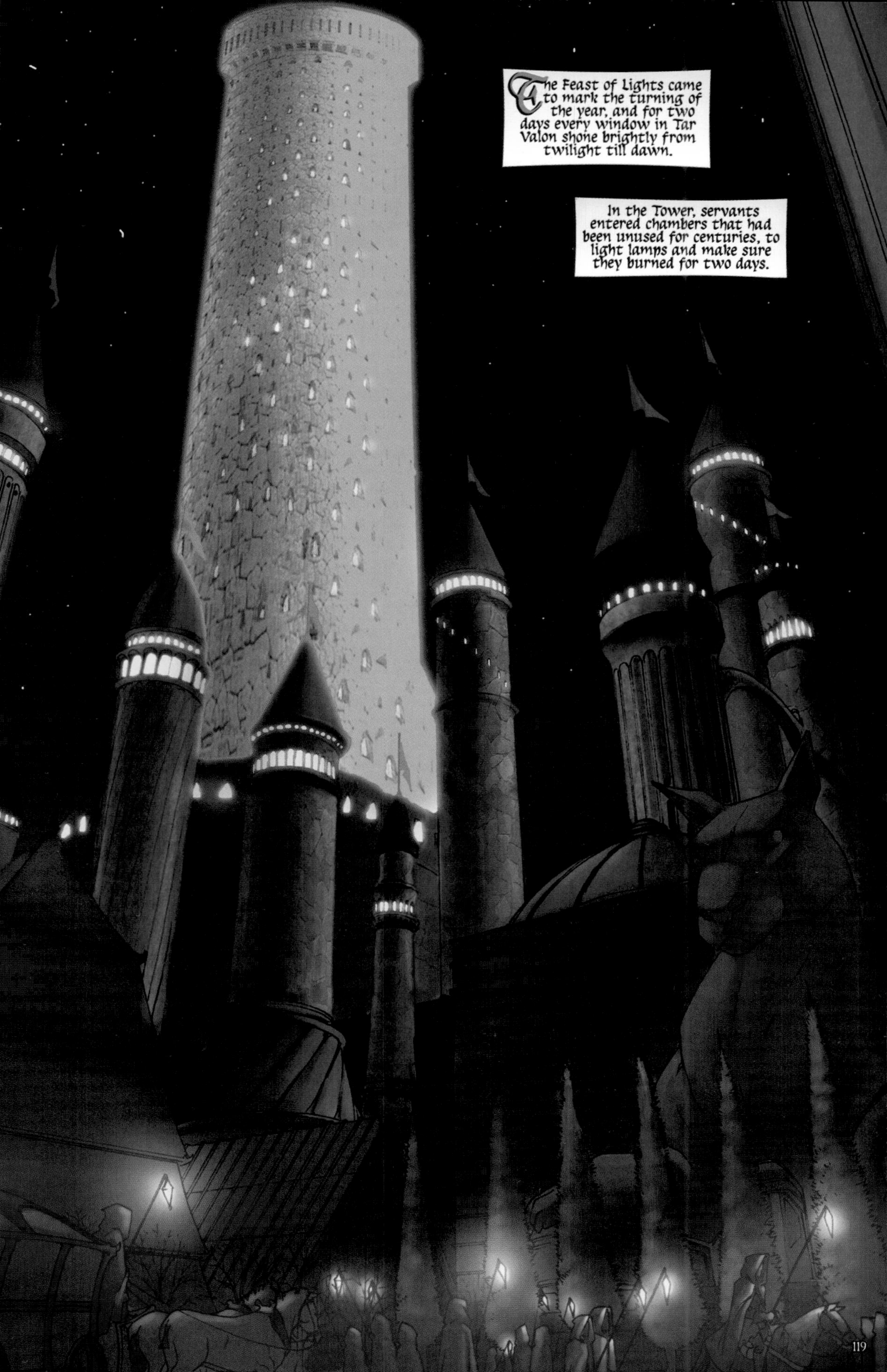
The Feast of Lights came to mark the turning of the year, and for two days every window in Tar Valon shone brightly from twilight till dawn.
In the Tower, servants entered chambers that had been unused for centuries, to light lamps and make sure they burned for two days.

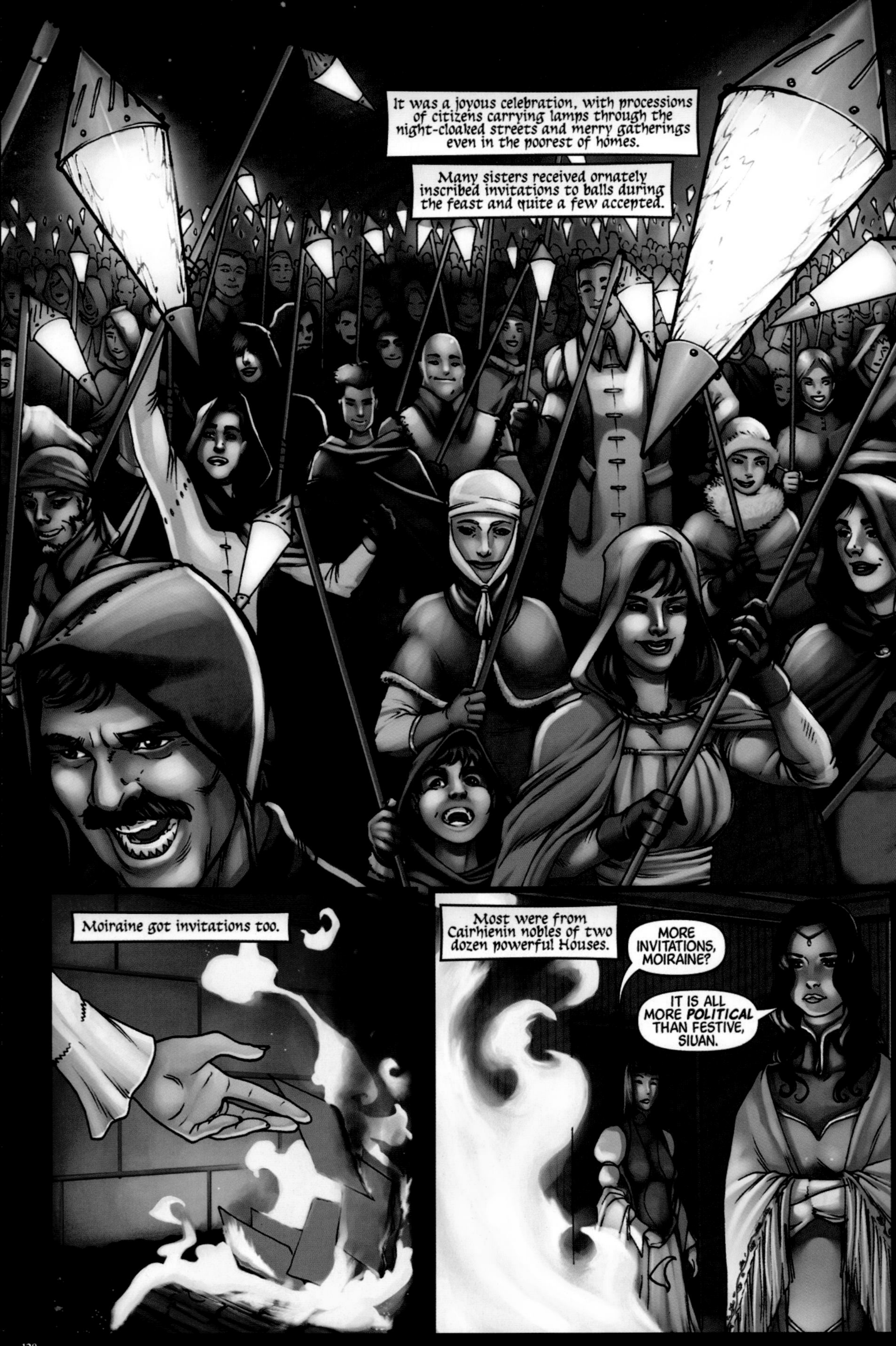
It was a joyous celebration, with processions of citizens carrying lamps through the night-cloaked streets and merry gatherings even in the poorest of homes.
Many sisters received ornately inscribed invitations to balls during the feast and quite a few accepted.
Moiraine got invitations too.
Most were from Cairhienin nobles of two dozen powerful Houses.
MORE INVITATIONS, MOIRAINE?
IT IS ALL MORE *POLITICAL* THAN FESTIVE, SIUAN.

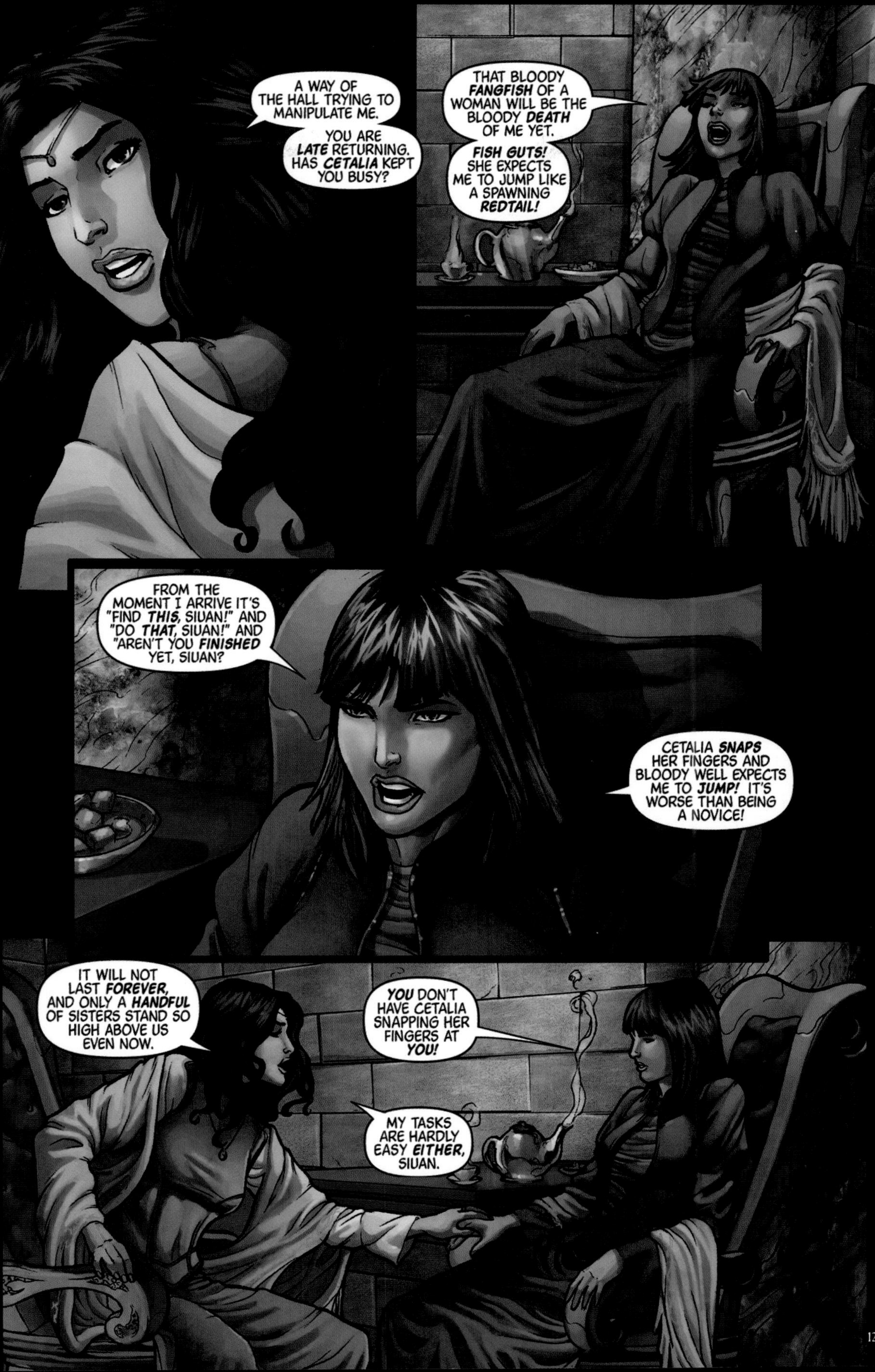
A WAY OF THE HALL TRYING TO MANIPULATE ME.
YOU ARE LATE RETURNING. HAS CETALIA KEPT YOU BUSY?
THAT BLOODY FANGFISH OF A WOMAN WILL BE THE BLOODY DEATH OF ME YET.
FISH GUTS! SHE EXPECTS ME TO JUMP LIKE A SPAWNING REDTAIL!
FROM THE MOMENT I ARRIVE IT'S "FIND THIS, SIUAN!" AND "DO THAT, SIUAN!" AND "AREN'T YOU FINISHED YET, SIUAN?
CETALIA SNAPS HER FINGERS AND BLOODY WELL EXPECTS ME TO JUMP! IT'S WORSE THAN BEING A NOVICE!
IT WILL NOT LAST FOREVER, AND ONLY A HANDFUL OF SISTERS STAND SO HIGH ABOVE US EVEN NOW.
YOU DON'T HAVE CETALIA SNAPPING HER FINGERS AT YOU!
MY TASKS ARE HARDLY EASY EITHER, SIUAN.

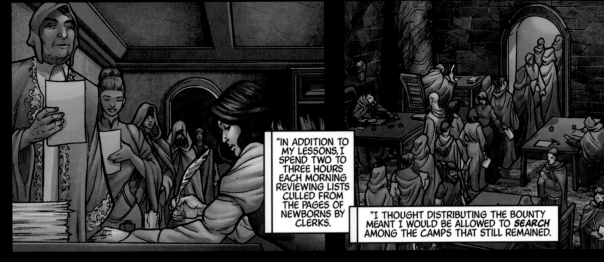

"IN ADDITION TO MY LESSONS, I SPEND TWO TO THREE HOURS EACH MORNING REVIEWING LISTS CULLED FROM THE PAGES OF NEWBORNS BY CLERKS."

"I THOUGHT DISTRIBUTING THE BOUNTY MEANT I WOULD BE ALLOWED TO *SEARCH* AMONG THE CAMPS THAT STILL REMAINED.

"INSTEAD I MUST READ EACH PAGE AND SIGN MY NAME TO IT IN APPROVAL."

"BOREDOM *AND* FRUSTRATION IN ONE TASK.

"EVEN *SLEEP* IS NO RESPITE. MY DREAMS ARE PLAGUED WITH THE FACELESS MAN, THE BABE IN THE SNOW AND THE SUN THRONE."

The day following the Feast of Lights, Ellid was summoned to her testing.

The beautiful Accepted who wanted to become a Green failed to come out of the *ter'angreal*.

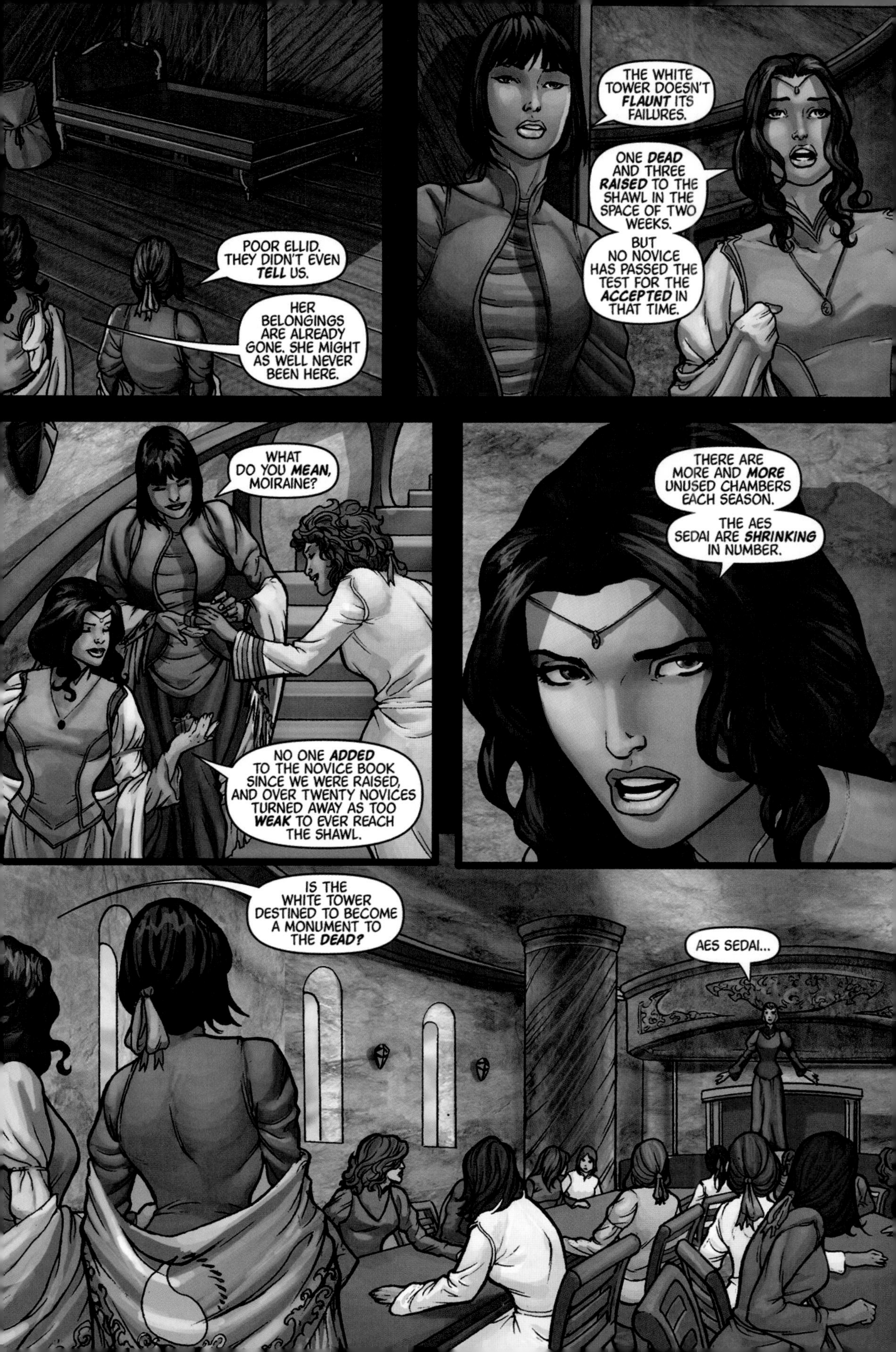

POOR ELLID. THEY DIDN'T EVEN TELL US.
HER BELONGINGS ARE ALREADY GONE. SHE MIGHT AS WELL NEVER BEEN HERE.
THE WHITE TOWER DOESN'T FLAUNT ITS FAILURES.
ONE DEAD AND THREE RAISED TO THE SHAWL IN THE SPACE OF TWO WEEKS.
BUT NO NOVICE HAS PASSED THE TEST FOR THE ACCEPTED IN THAT TIME.
WHAT DO YOU MEAN, MOIRAINE?
NO ONE ADDED TO THE NOVICE BOOK SINCE WE WERE RAISED, AND OVER TWENTY NOVICES TURNED AWAY AS TOO WEAK TO EVER REACH THE SHAWL.
THERE ARE MORE AND MORE UNUSED CHAMBERS EACH SEASON.
THE AES SEDAI ARE SHRINKING IN NUMBER.
IS THE WHITE TOWER DESTINED TO BECOME A MONUMENT TO THE DEAD?
AES SEDAI...

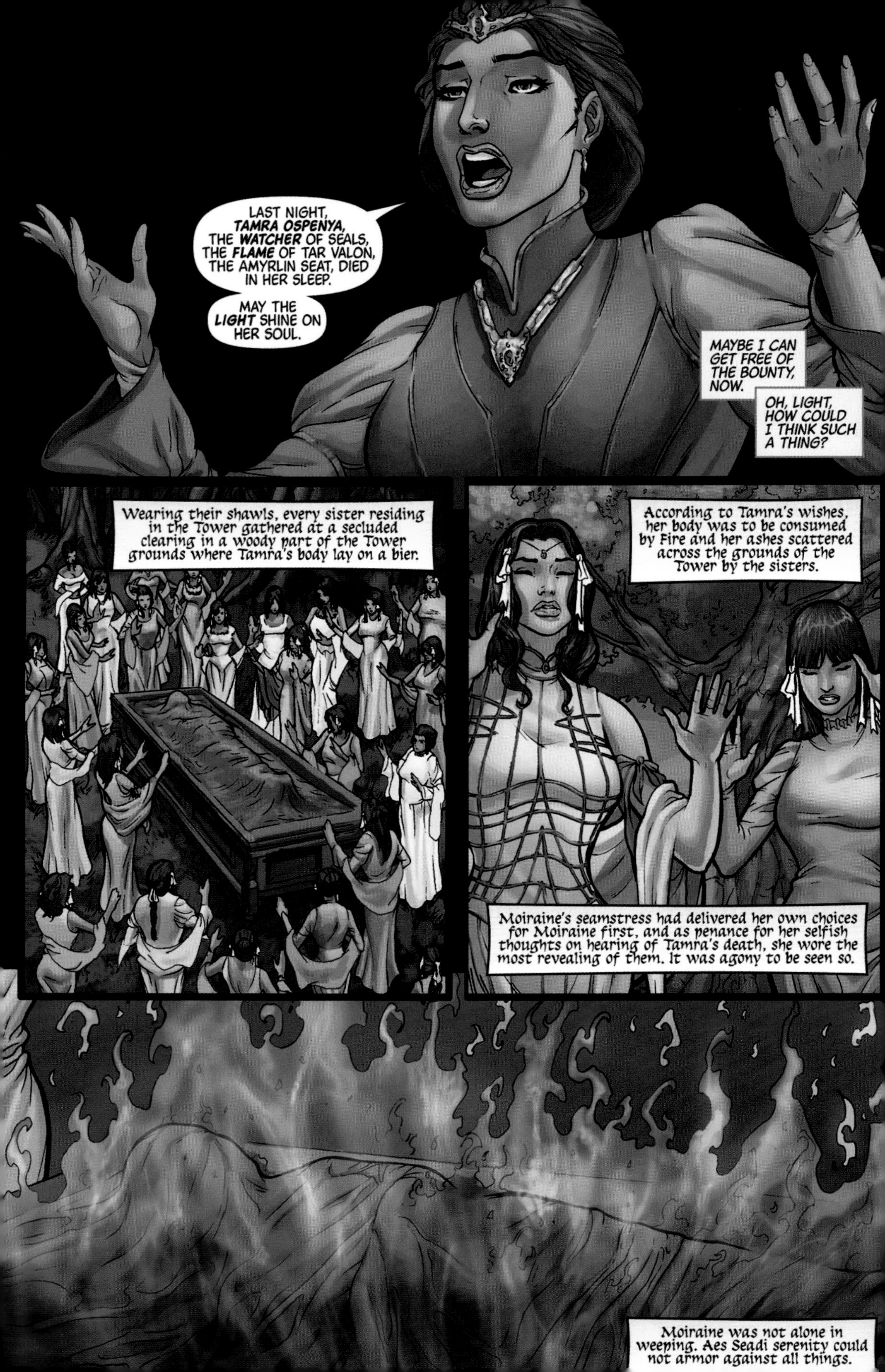
LAST NIGHT, TAMRA OSPENYA, THE WATCHER OF SEALS, THE FLAME OF TAR VALON, THE AMYRLIN SEAT, DIED IN HER SLEEP.
MAY THE LIGHT SHINE ON HER SOUL.
MAYBE I CAN GET FREE OF THE BOUNTY, NOW.
OH, LIGHT, HOW COULD I THINK SUCH A THING?
Wearing their shawls, every sister residing in the Tower gathered at a secluded clearing in a woody part of the Tower grounds where Tamra's body lay on a bier.
According to Tamra's wishes, her body was to be consumed by Fire and her ashes scattered across the grounds of the Tower by the sisters.
Moiraine's seamstress had delivered her own choices for Moiraine first, and as penance for her selfish thoughts on hearing of Tamra's death, she wore the most revealing of them. It was agony to be seen so.
Moiraine was not alone in weeping. Aes Seadi serenity could not armor against all things.

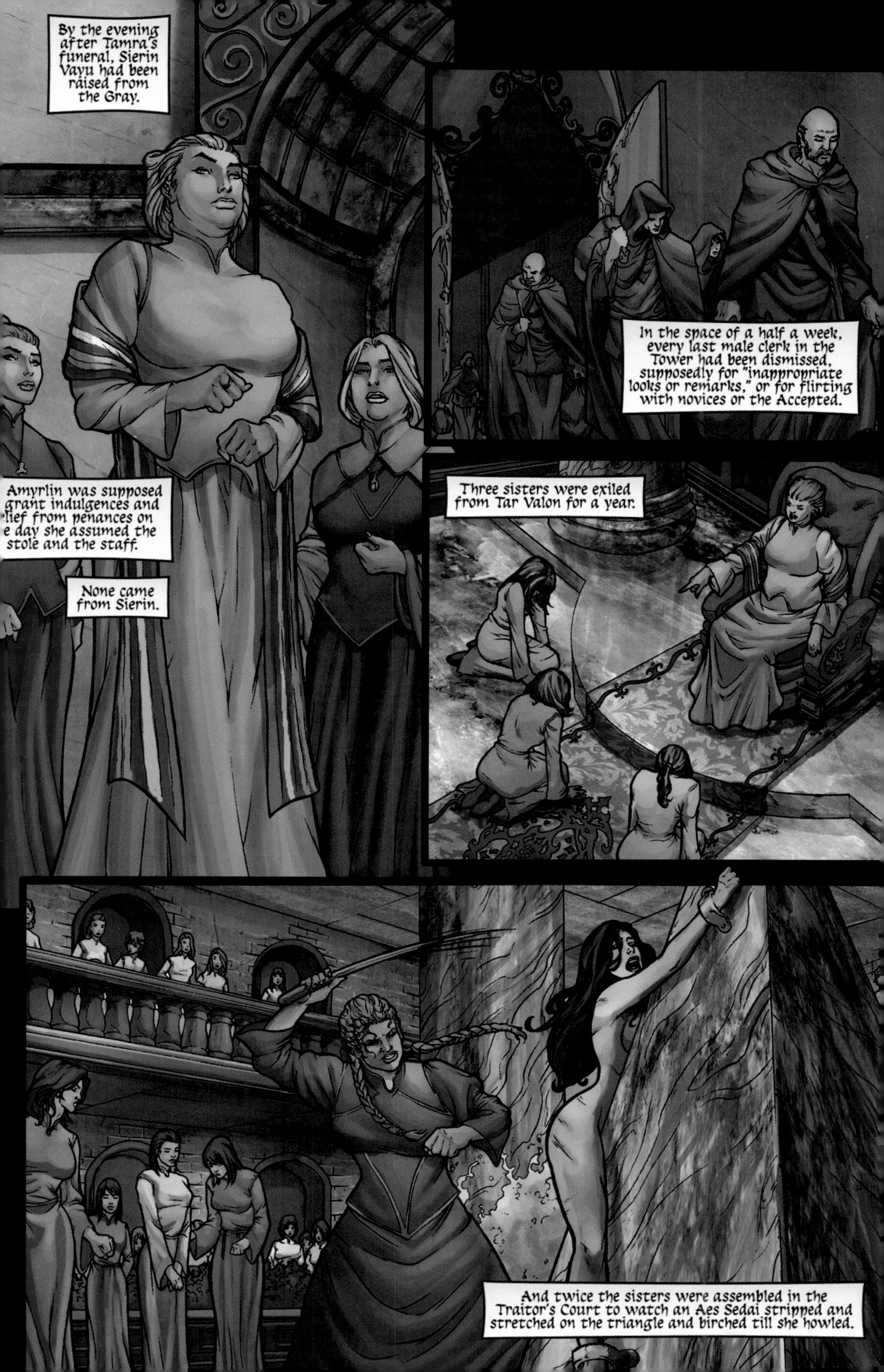
By the evening after Tamra's funeral, Sierin Vayu had been raised from the Gray.
In the space of a half a week, every last male clerk in the Tower had been dismissed, supposedly for "inappropriate looks or remarks," or for flirting with novices or the Accepted.
Amyrlin was supposed grant indulgences and lief from penances on e day she assumed the stole and the staff.
None came from Sierin.
Three sisters were exiled from Tar Valon for a year.
And twice the sisters were assembled in the Traitor's Court to watch an Aes Sedai stripped and stretched on the triangle and birched till she howled.

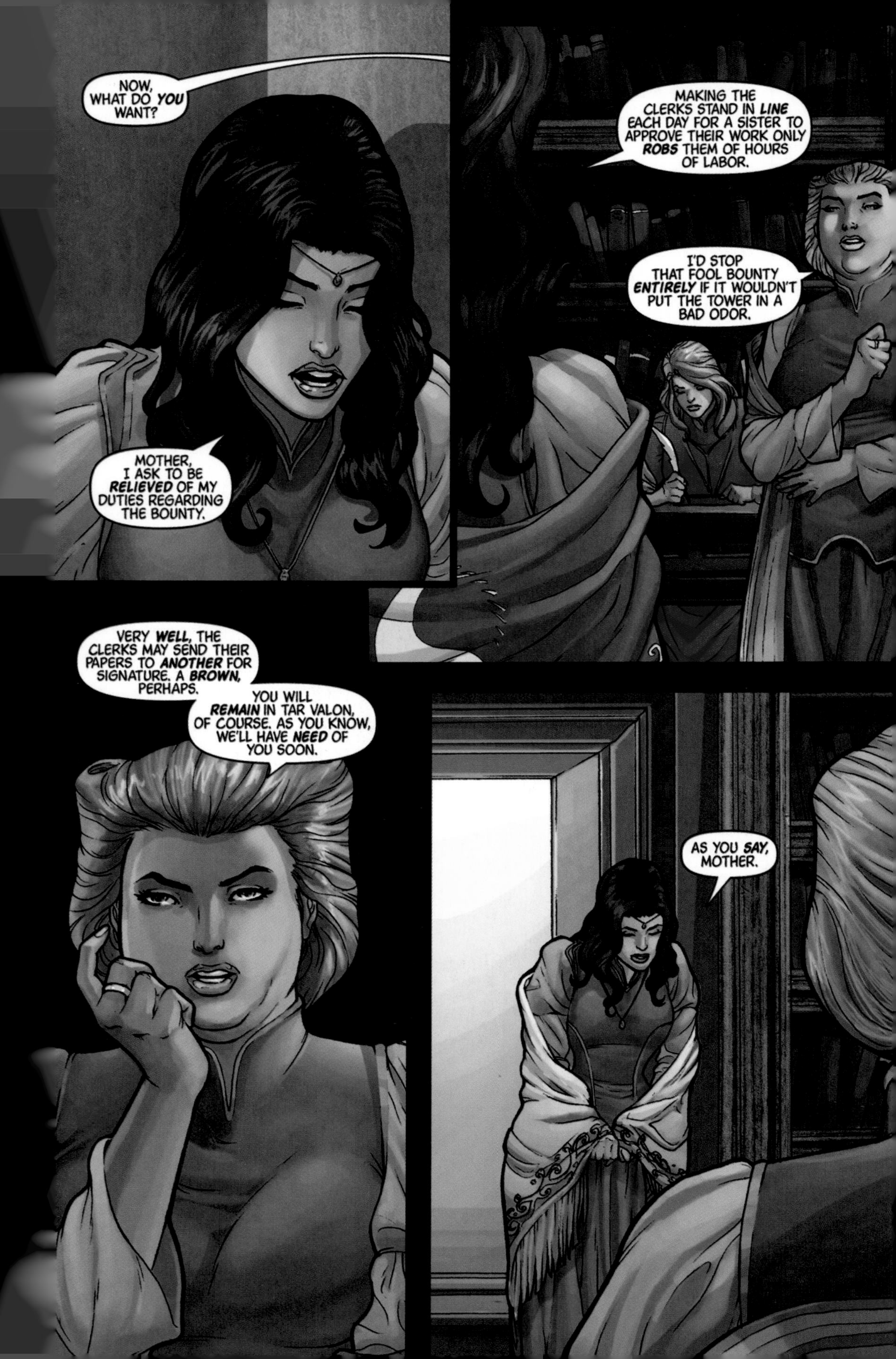
NOW, WHAT DO YOU WANT?
MOTHER, I ASK TO BE RELIEVED OF MY DUTIES REGARDING THE BOUNTY.
MAKING THE CLERKS STAND IN LINE EACH DAY FOR A SISTER TO APPROVE THEIR WORK ONLY ROBS THEM OF HOURS OF LABOR.
I'D STOP THAT FOOL BOUNTY ENTIRELY IF IT WOULDN'T PUT THE TOWER IN A BAD ODOR.
VERY WELL, THE CLERKS MAY SEND THEIR PAPERS TO ANOTHER FOR SIGNATURE. A BROWN, PERHAPS.
YOU WILL REMAIN IN TAR VALON, OF COURSE. AS YOU KNOW, WE'LL HAVE NEED OF YOU SOON.
AS YOU SAY, MOTHER.

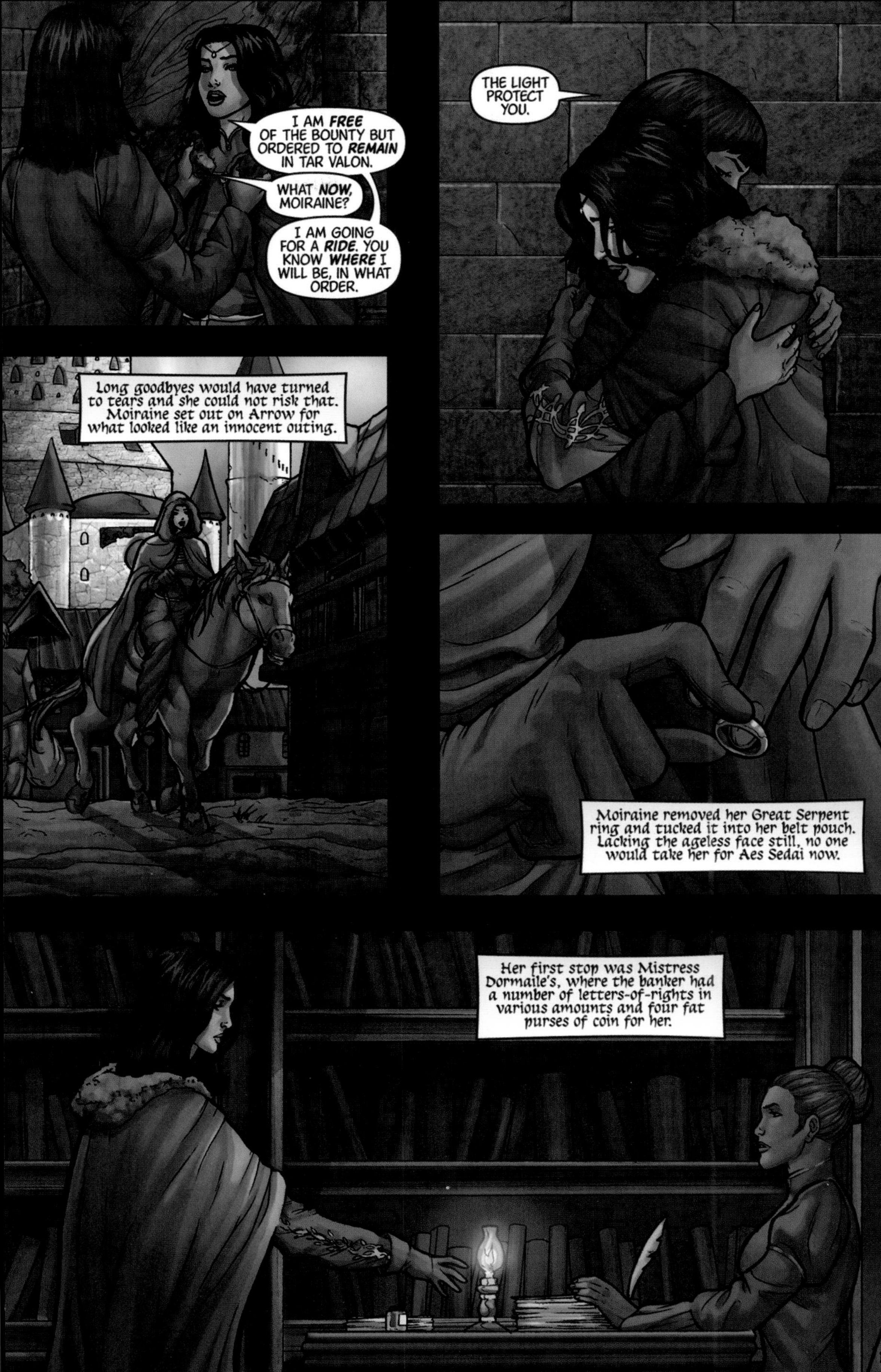
I AM FREE OF THE BOUNTY BUT ORDERED TO REMAIN IN TAR VALON.
WHAT NOW, MOIRAINE?
I AM GOING FOR A RIDE. YOU KNOW WHERE I WILL BE, IN WHAT ORDER.
THE LIGHT PROTECT YOU.
Long goodbyes would have turned to tears and she could not risk that. Moiraine set out on Arrow for what looked like an innocent outing.
Moiraine removed her Great Serpent ring and tucked it into her belt pouch. Lacking the ageless face still, no one would take her for Aes Sedai now.
Her first stop was Mistress Dormaile's, where the banker had a number of letters-of-rights in various amounts and four fat purses of coin for her.

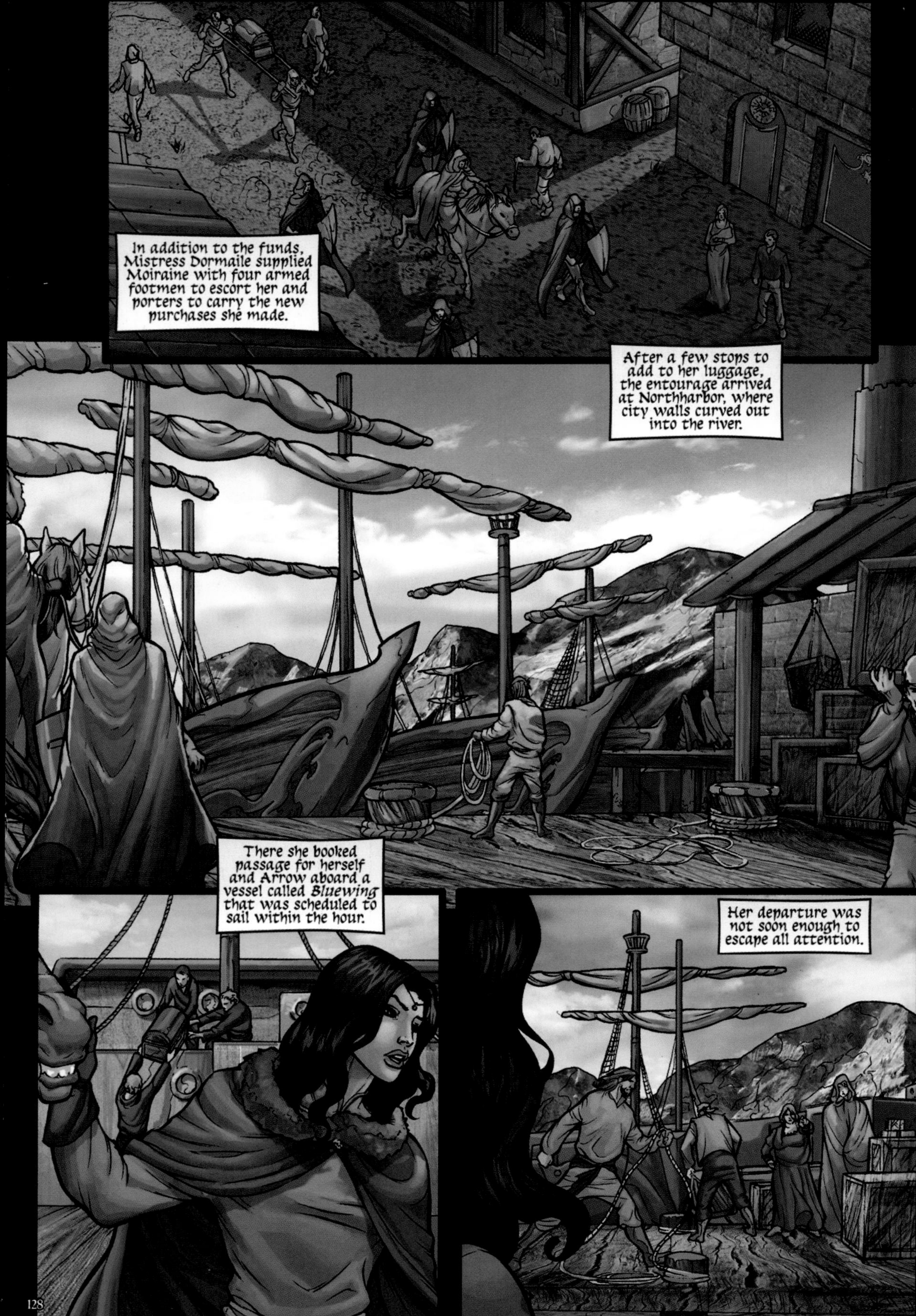
In addition to the funds, Mistress Dormaile supplied Moiraine with four armed footmen to escort her and porters to carry the new purchases she made.
After a few stops to add to her luggage, the entourage arrived at Northharbor, where city walls curved out into the river.
There she booked passage for herself and Arrow aboard a vessel called *Bluewing* that was scheduled to sail within the hour.
Her departure was not soon enough to escape all attention.

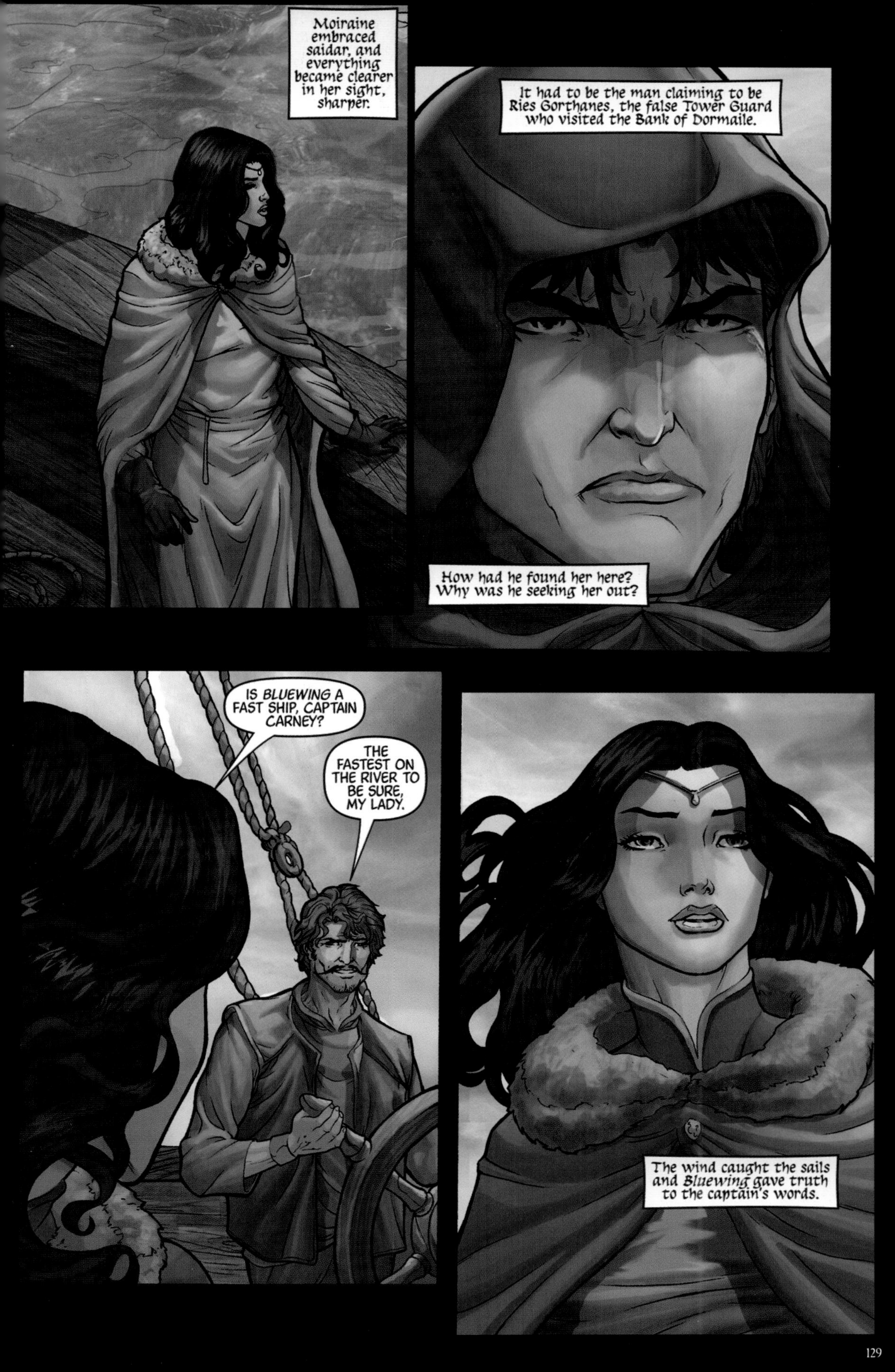

Moiraine embraced *saidar*, and everything became clearer in her sight, sharper.
It had to be the man claiming to be Ries Gorthanes, the false Tower Guard who visited the Bank of Dormaile.
How had he found her here? Why was he seeking her out?
IS *BLUEWING* A FAST SHIP, CAPTAIN CARNEY?
THE FASTEST ON THE RIVER TO BE SURE, MY LADY.
The wind caught the sails and *Bluewing* gave truth to the captain's words.

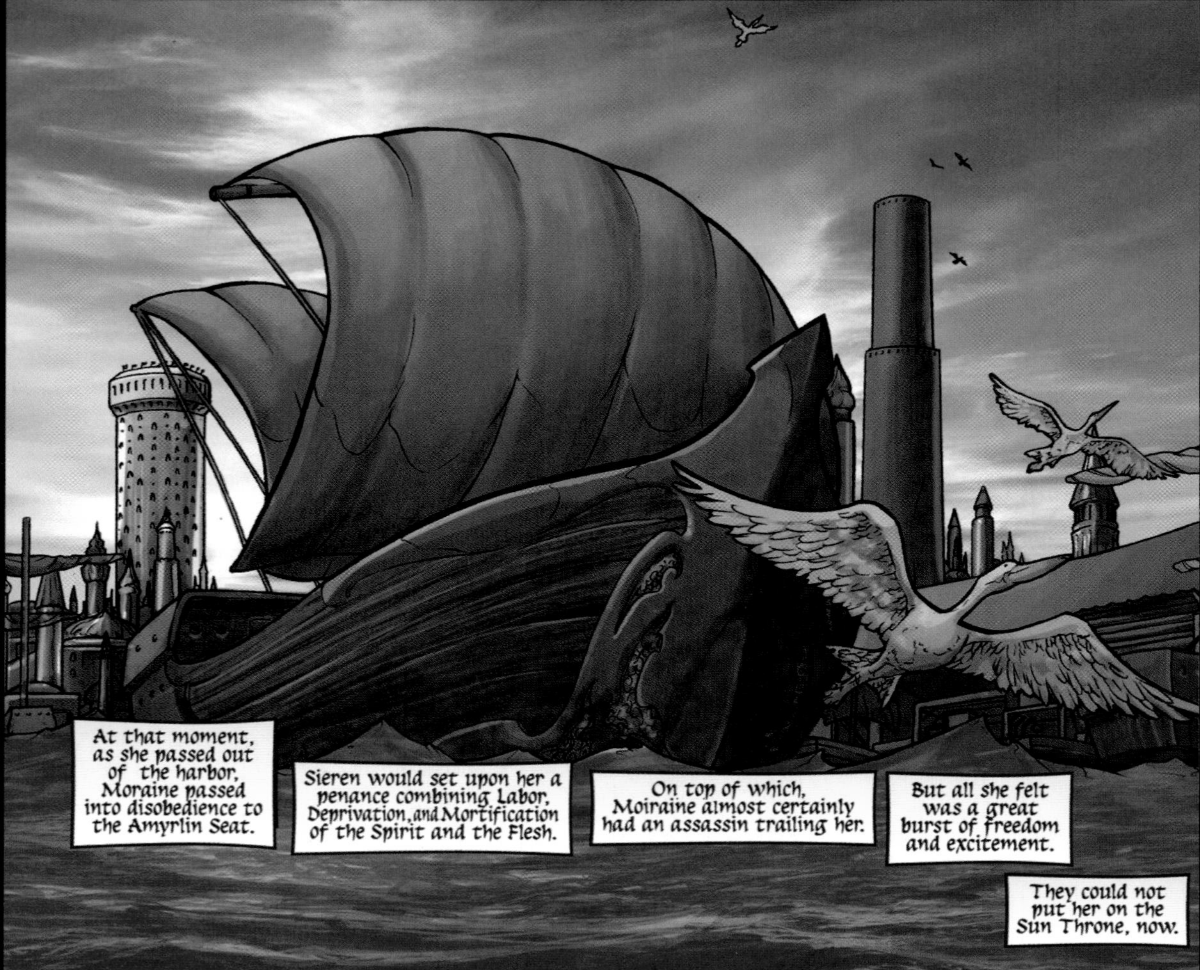
At that moment, as she passed out of the harbor, Moraine passed into disobedience to the Amyrlin Seat.
Sieren would set upon her a penance combining Labor, Deprivation, and Mortification of the Spirit and the Flesh.
On top of which, Moiraine almost certainly had an assassin trailing her.
But all she felt was a great burst of freedom and excitement.
They could not put her on the Sun Throne, now.

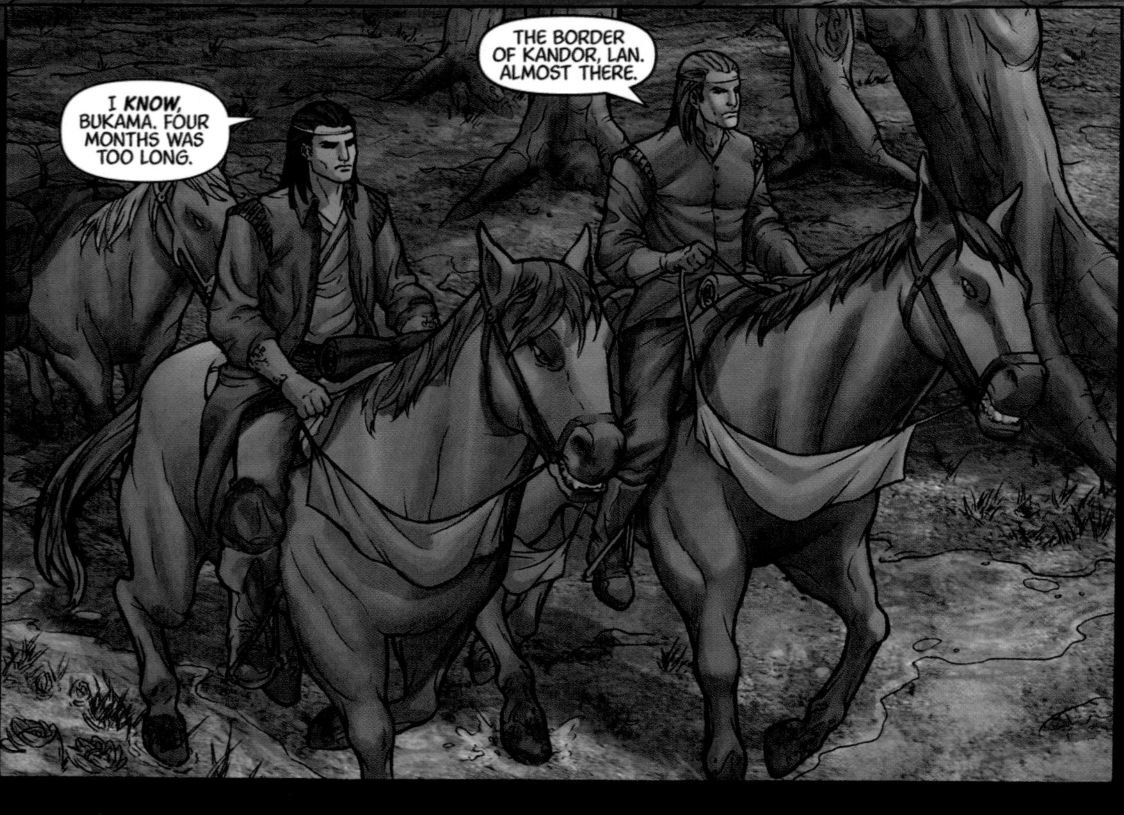
THE BORDER OF KANDOR, LAN. ALMOST THERE.
I *KNOW*, BUKAMA. FOUR MONTHS WAS TOO LONG.

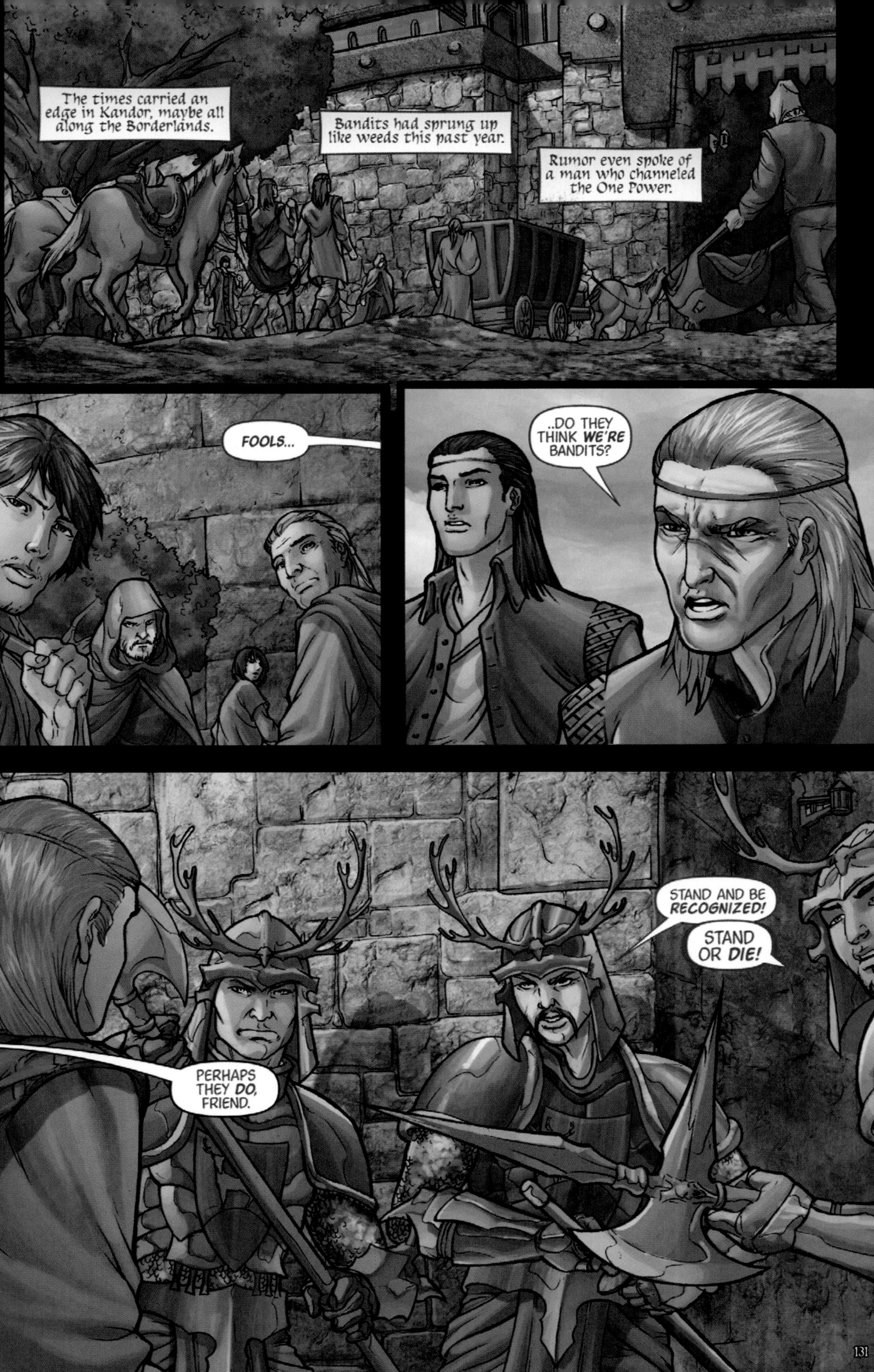
The times carried an edge in Kandor, maybe all along the Borderlands.
Bandits had sprung up like weeds this past year.
Rumor even spoke of a man who channeled the One Power.
FOOLS...
..DO THEY THINK WE'RE BANDITS?
PERHAPS THEY DO, FRIEND.
STAND AND BE RECOGNIZED!
STAND OR DIE!

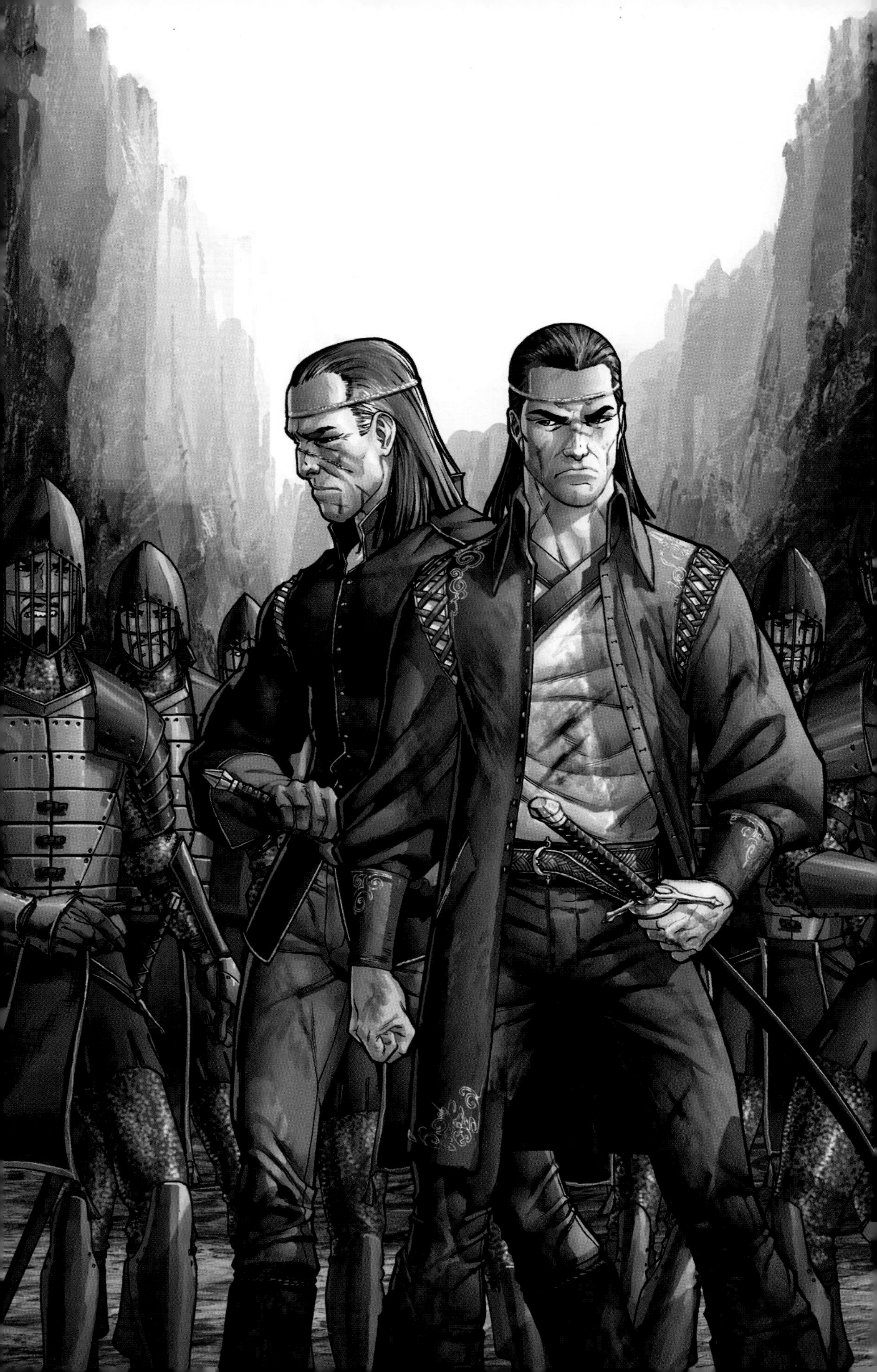

chapter six

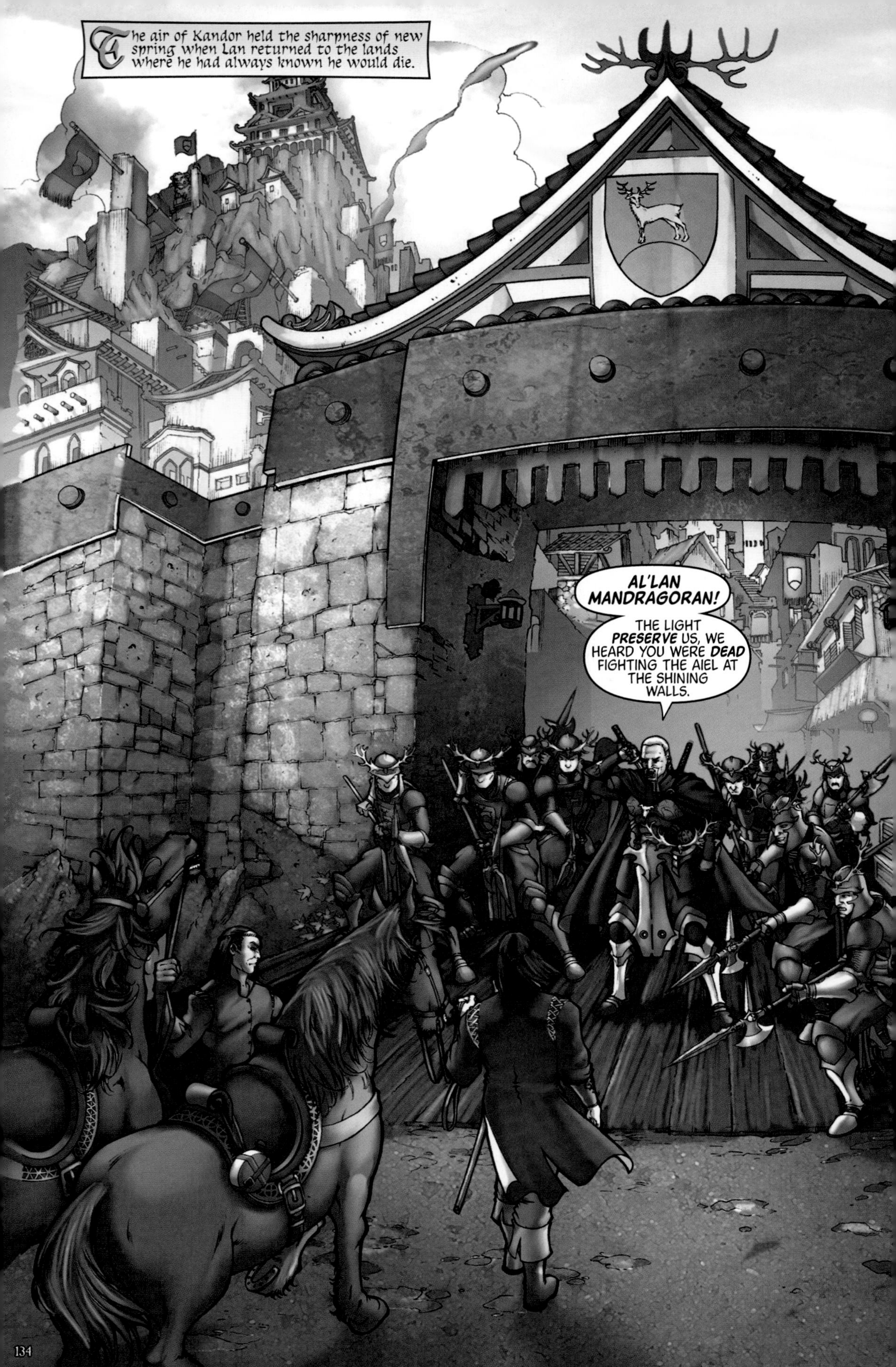
The air of Kandor held the sharpness of new spring when Lan returned to the lands where he had always known he would die.
AL'LAN MANDRAGORAN!
THE LIGHT PRESERVE US, WE HEARD YOU WERE DEAD FIGHTING THE AIEL AT THE SHINING WALLS.

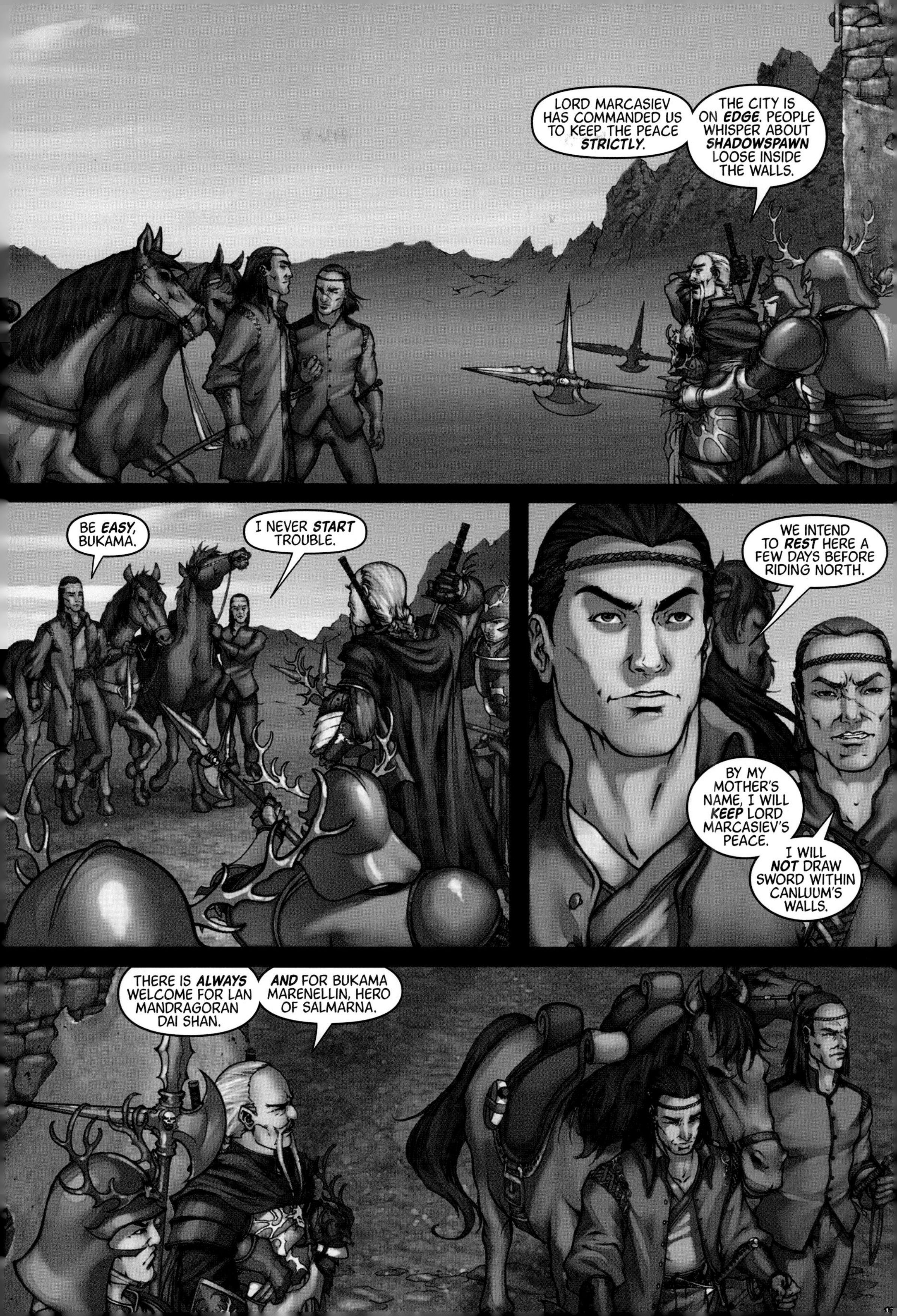
LORD MARCASIEV HAS COMMANDED US TO KEEP THE PEACE STRICTLY.
THE CITY IS ON EDGE. PEOPLE WHISPER ABOUT SHADOWSPAWN LOOSE INSIDE THE WALLS.
BE EASY, BUKAMA.
I NEVER START TROUBLE.
WE INTEND TO REST HERE A FEW DAYS BEFORE RIDING NORTH.
BY MY MOTHER'S NAME, I WILL KEEP LORD MARCASIEV'S PEACE.
I WILL NOT DRAW SWORD WITHIN CANLUUM'S WALLS.
THERE IS ALWAYS WELCOME FOR LAN MANDRAGORAN DAI SHAN.
AND FOR BUKAMA MARENELLIN, HERO OF SALMARNA.

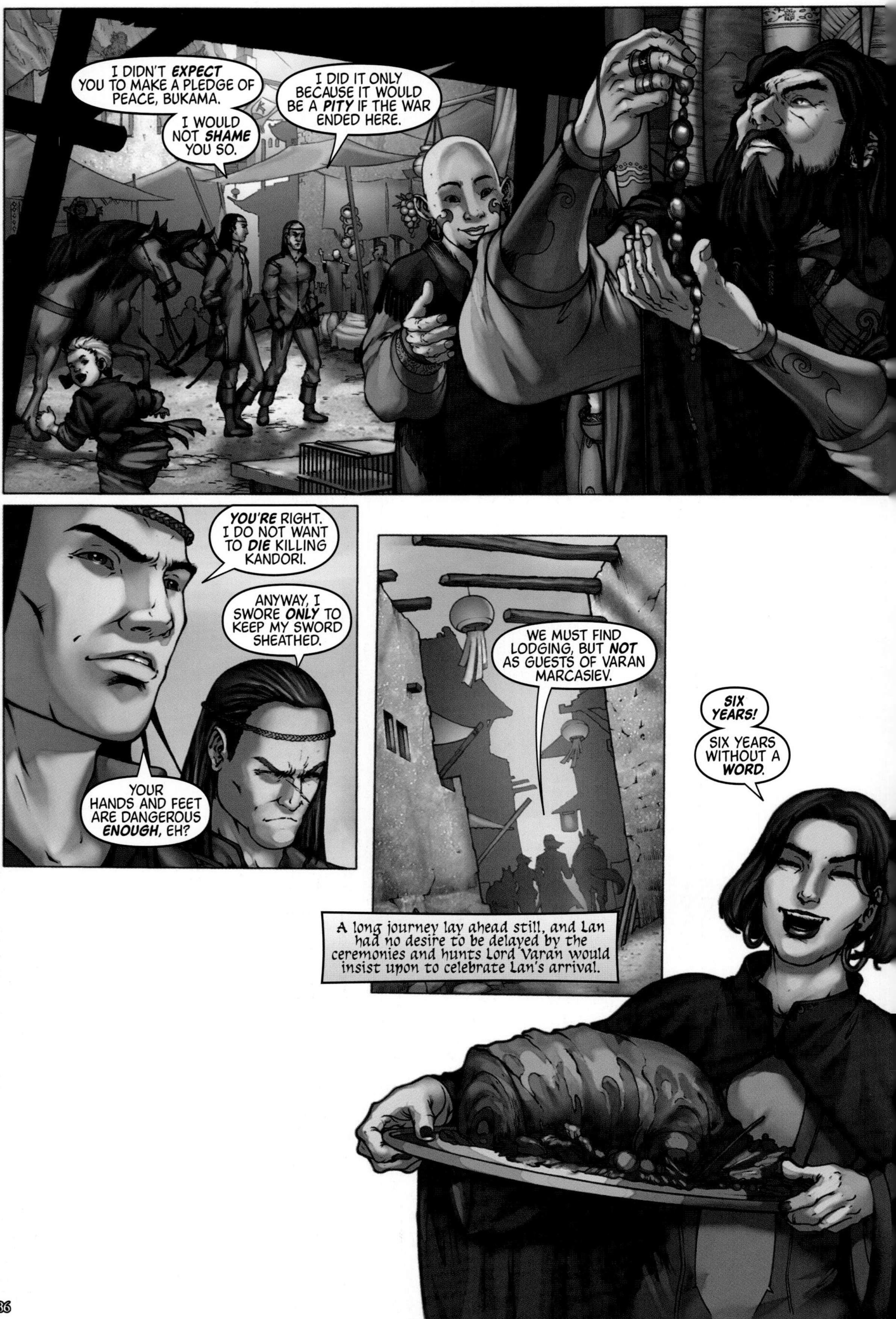
I DIDN'T EXPECT YOU TO MAKE A PLEDGE OF PEACE, BUKAMA.
I WOULD NOT SHAME YOU SO.
I DID IT ONLY BECAUSE IT WOULD BE A PITY IF THE WAR ENDED HERE.
YOU'RE RIGHT. I DO NOT WANT TO DIE KILLING KANDORI.
ANYWAY, I SWORE ONLY TO KEEP MY SWORD SHEATHED.
YOUR HANDS AND FEET ARE DANGEROUS ENOUGH, EH?
WE MUST FIND LODGING, BUT NOT AS GUESTS OF VARAN MARCASIEV.
A long journey lay ahead still, and Lan had no desire to be delayed by the ceremonies and hunts Lord Varan would insist upon to celebrate Lan's arrival.
SIX YEARS!
SIX YEARS WITHOUT A WORD.

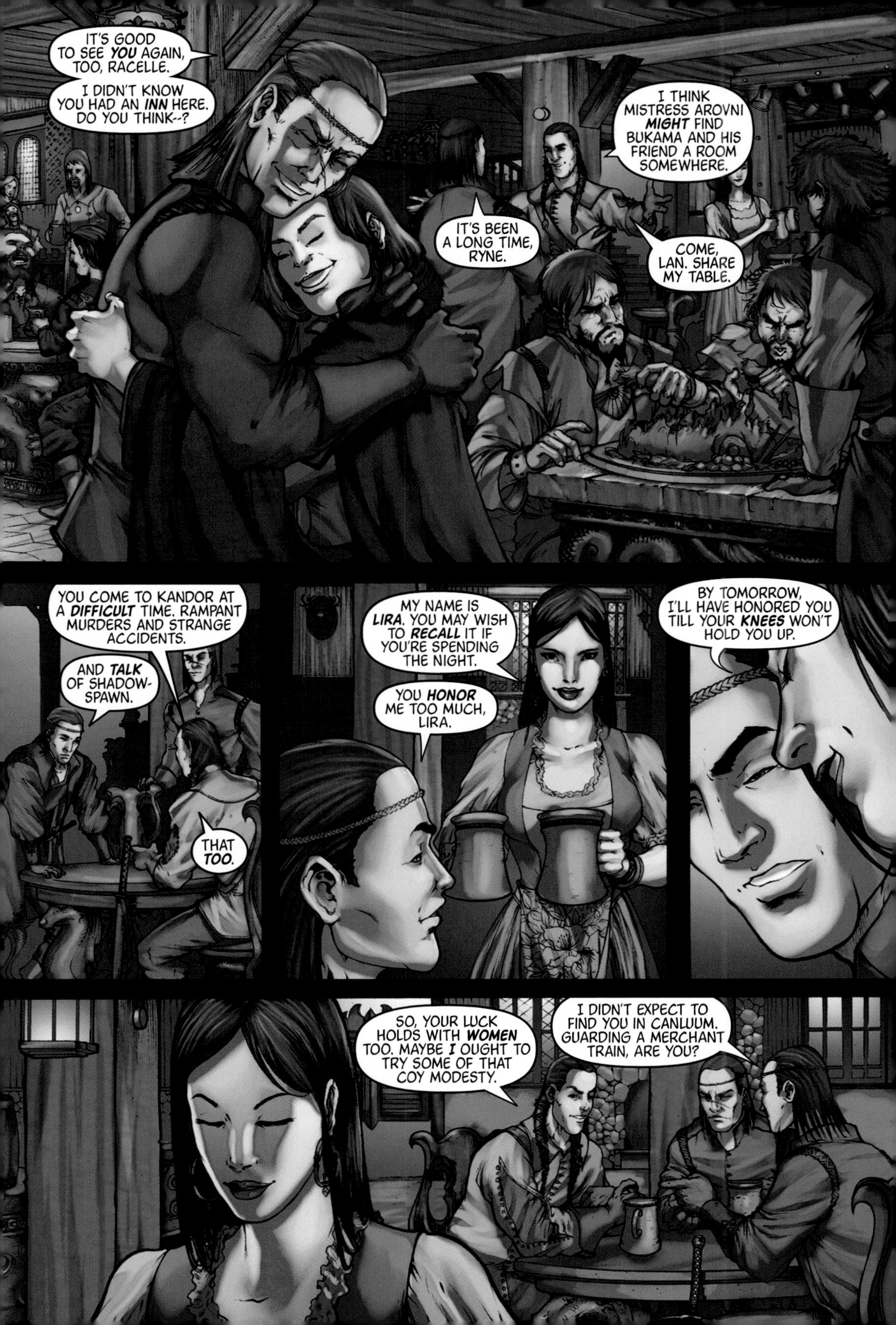
IT'S GOOD TO SEE YOU AGAIN, TOO, RACELLE.
I DIDN'T KNOW YOU HAD AN INN HERE. DO YOU THINK--?
IT'S BEEN A LONG TIME, RYNE.
I THINK MISTRESS AROVNI MIGHT FIND BUKAMA AND HIS FRIEND A ROOM SOMEWHERE.
COME, LAN. SHARE MY TABLE.
YOU COME TO KANDOR AT A DIFFICULT TIME. RAMPANT MURDERS AND STRANGE ACCIDENTS.
AND TALK OF SHADOW-SPAWN.
THAT TOO.
MY NAME IS LIRA. YOU MAY WISH TO RECALL IT IF YOU'RE SPENDING THE NIGHT.
YOU HONOR ME TOO MUCH, LIRA.
BY TOMORROW, I'LL HAVE HONORED YOU TILL YOUR KNEES WON'T HOLD YOU UP.
SO, YOUR LUCK HOLDS WITH WOMEN TOO. MAYBE I OUGHT TO TRY SOME OF THAT COY MODESTY.
I DIDN'T EXPECT TO FIND YOU IN CANLUUM. GUARDING A MERCHANT TRAIN, ARE YOU?

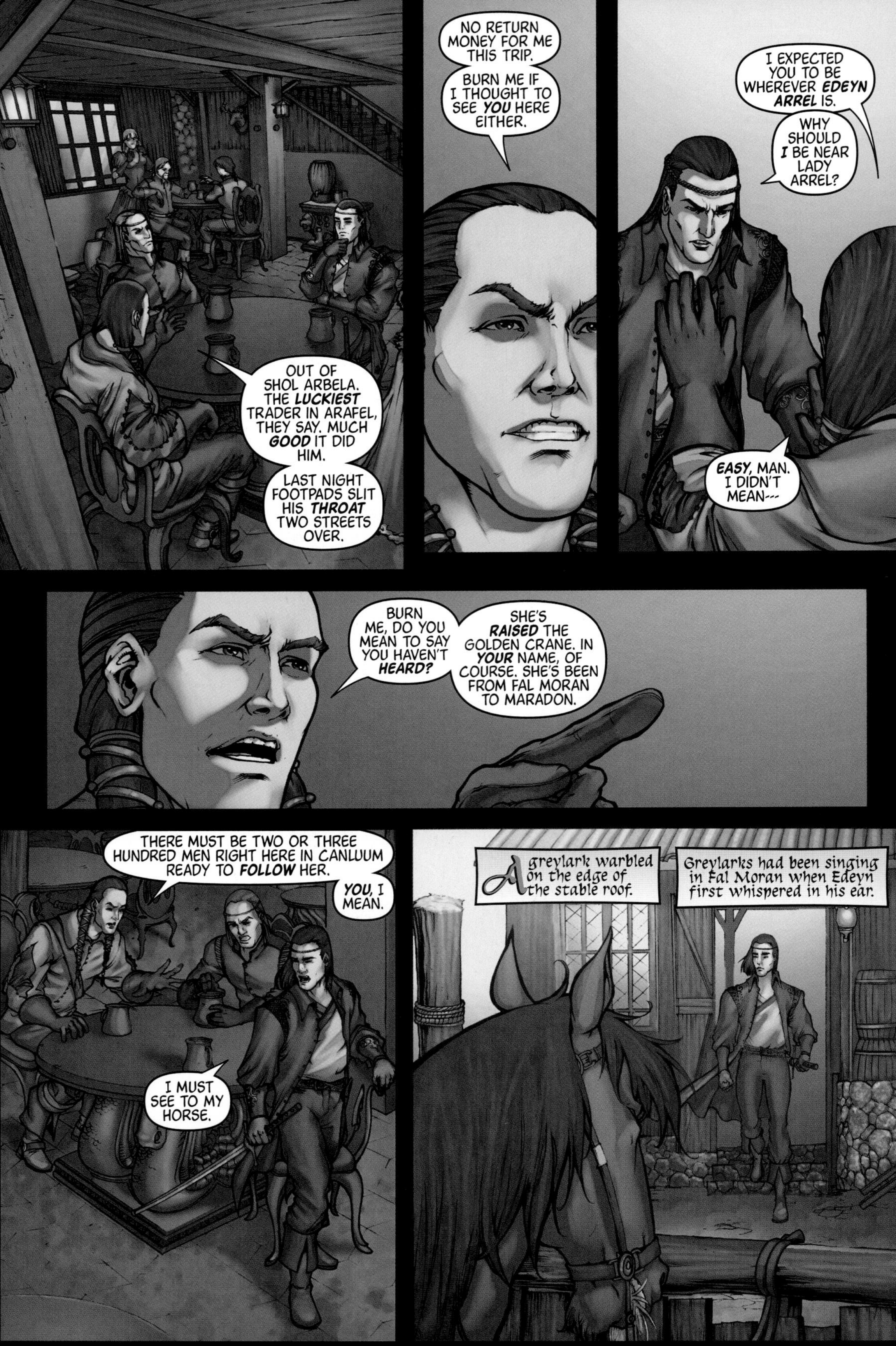
OUT OF SHOL ARBELA. THE LUCKIEST TRADER IN ARAFEL, THEY SAY. MUCH GOOD IT DID HIM.
LAST NIGHT FOOTPADS SLIT HIS THROAT TWO STREETS OVER.
NO RETURN MONEY FOR ME THIS TRIP.
BURN ME IF I THOUGHT TO SEE YOU HERE EITHER.
I EXPECTED YOU TO BE WHEREVER EDEYN ARREL IS.
WHY SHOULD I BE NEAR LADY ARREL?
EASY, MAN. I DIDN'T MEAN---
BURN ME, DO YOU MEAN TO SAY YOU HAVEN'T HEARD?
SHE'S RAISED THE GOLDEN CRANE. IN YOUR NAME, OF COURSE. SHE'S BEEN FROM FAL MORAN TO MARADON.
THERE MUST BE TWO OR THREE HUNDRED MEN RIGHT HERE IN CANLUUM READY TO FOLLOW HER.
YOU, I MEAN.
I MUST SEE TO MY HORSE.
A greylark warbled on the edge of the stable roof.
Greylarks had been singing in Fal Moran when Edeyn first whispered in his ear.

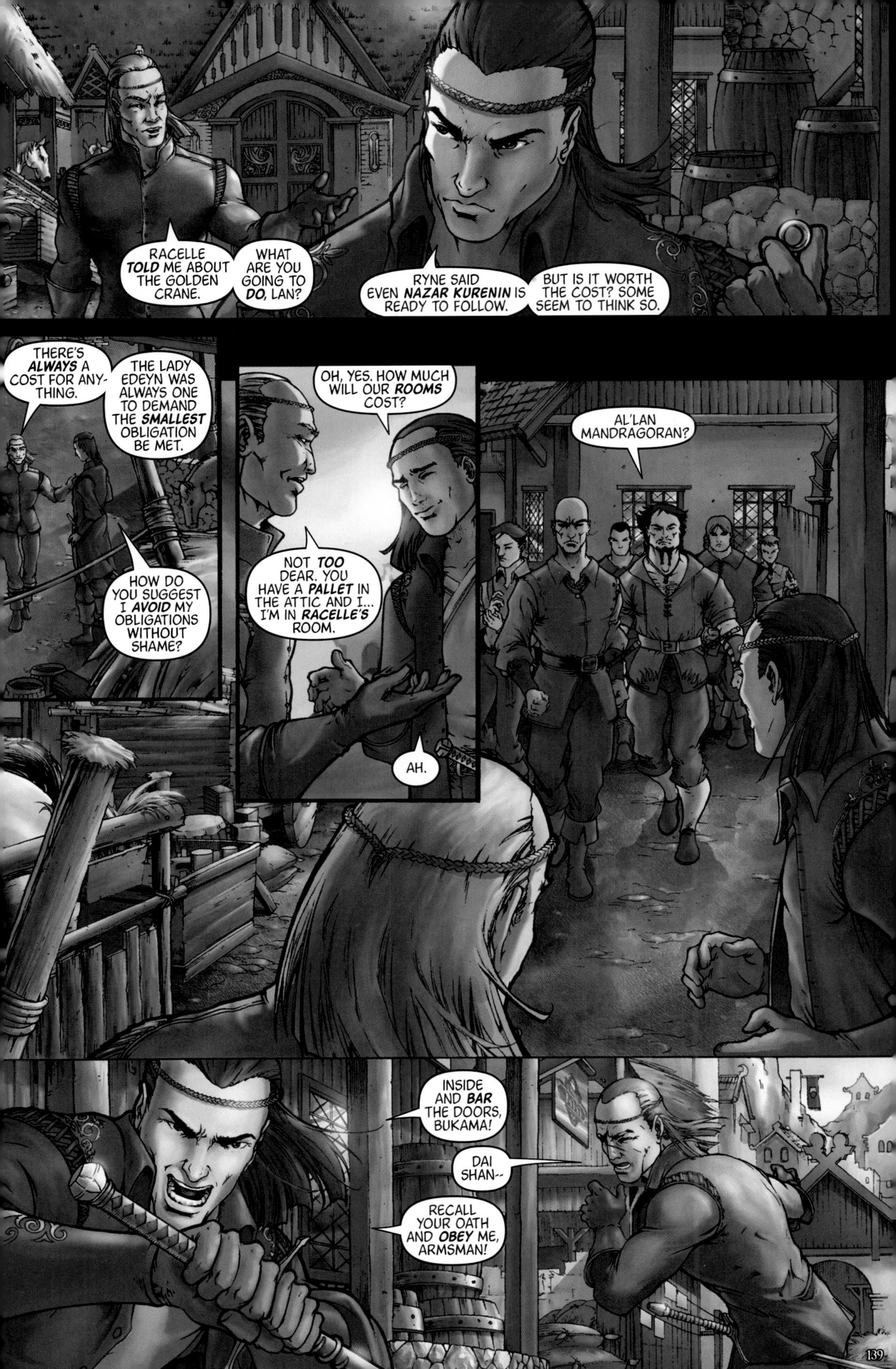
RACELLE TOLD ME ABOUT THE GOLDEN CRANE.
WHAT ARE YOU GOING TO DO, LAN?
RYNE SAID EVEN NAZAR KURENIN IS READY TO FOLLOW.
BUT IS IT WORTH THE COST? SOME SEEM TO THINK SO.
THERE'S ALWAYS A COST FOR ANY-THING.
THE LADY EDEYN WAS ALWAYS ONE TO DEMAND THE SMALLEST OBLIGATION BE MET.
HOW DO YOU SUGGEST I AVOID MY OBLIGATIONS WITHOUT SHAME?
OH, YES. HOW MUCH WILL OUR ROOMS COST?
NOT TOO DEAR. YOU HAVE A PALLET IN THE ATTIC AND I... I'M IN RACELLE'S ROOM.
AH.
AL'LAN MANDRAGORAN?
INSIDE AND BAR THE DOORS, BUKAMA!
DAI SHAN--
RECALL YOUR OATH AND OBEY ME, ARMSMAN!

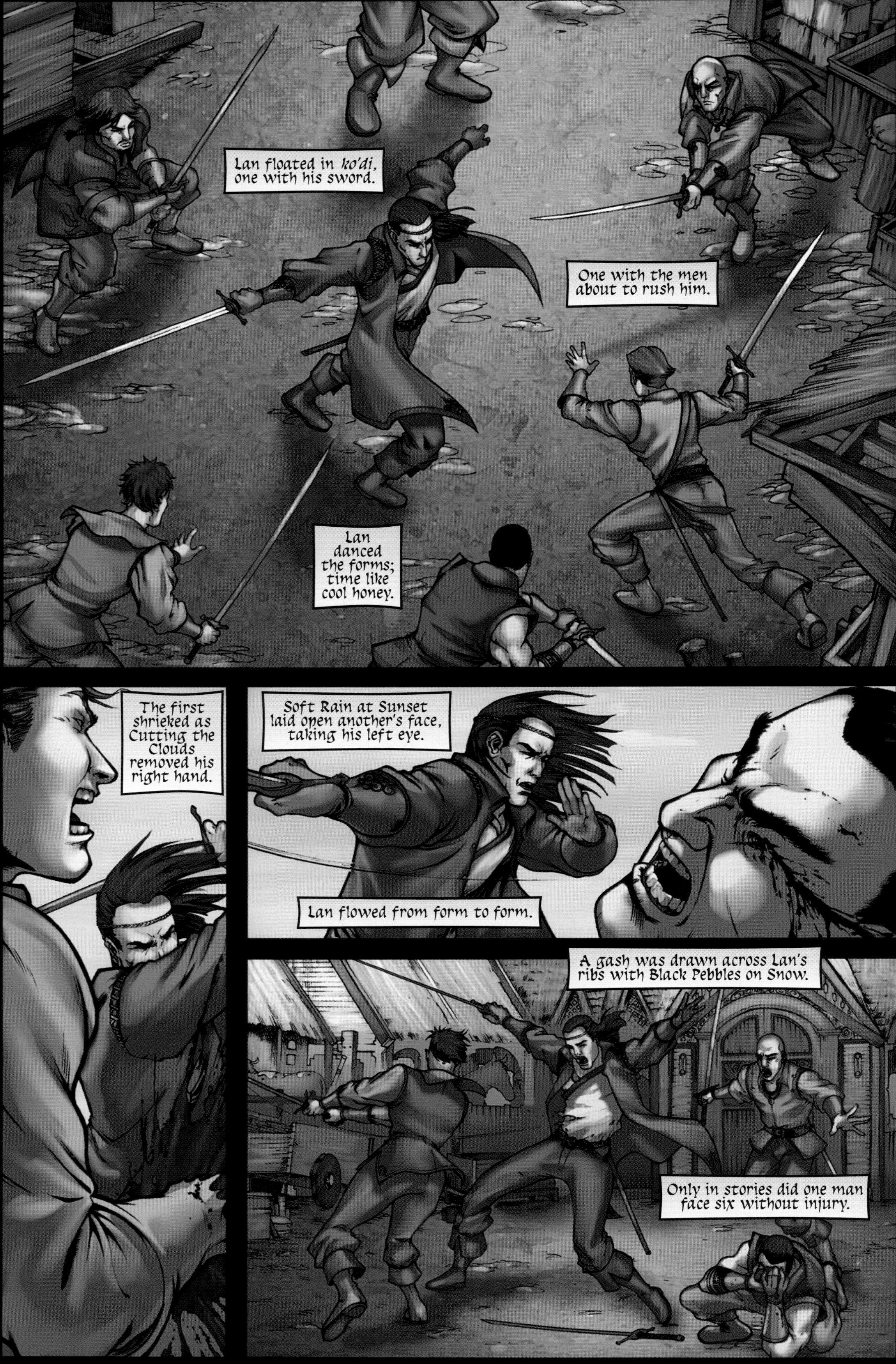
Lan floated in *ko'di*, one with his sword.
One with the men about to rush him.
Lan danced the forms; time like cool honey.
The first shrieked as Cutting the Clouds removed his right hand.
Soft Rain at Sunset laid open another's face, taking his left eye.
Lan flowed from form to form.
A gash was drawn across Lan's ribs with Black Pebbles on Snow.
Only in stories did one man face six without injury.

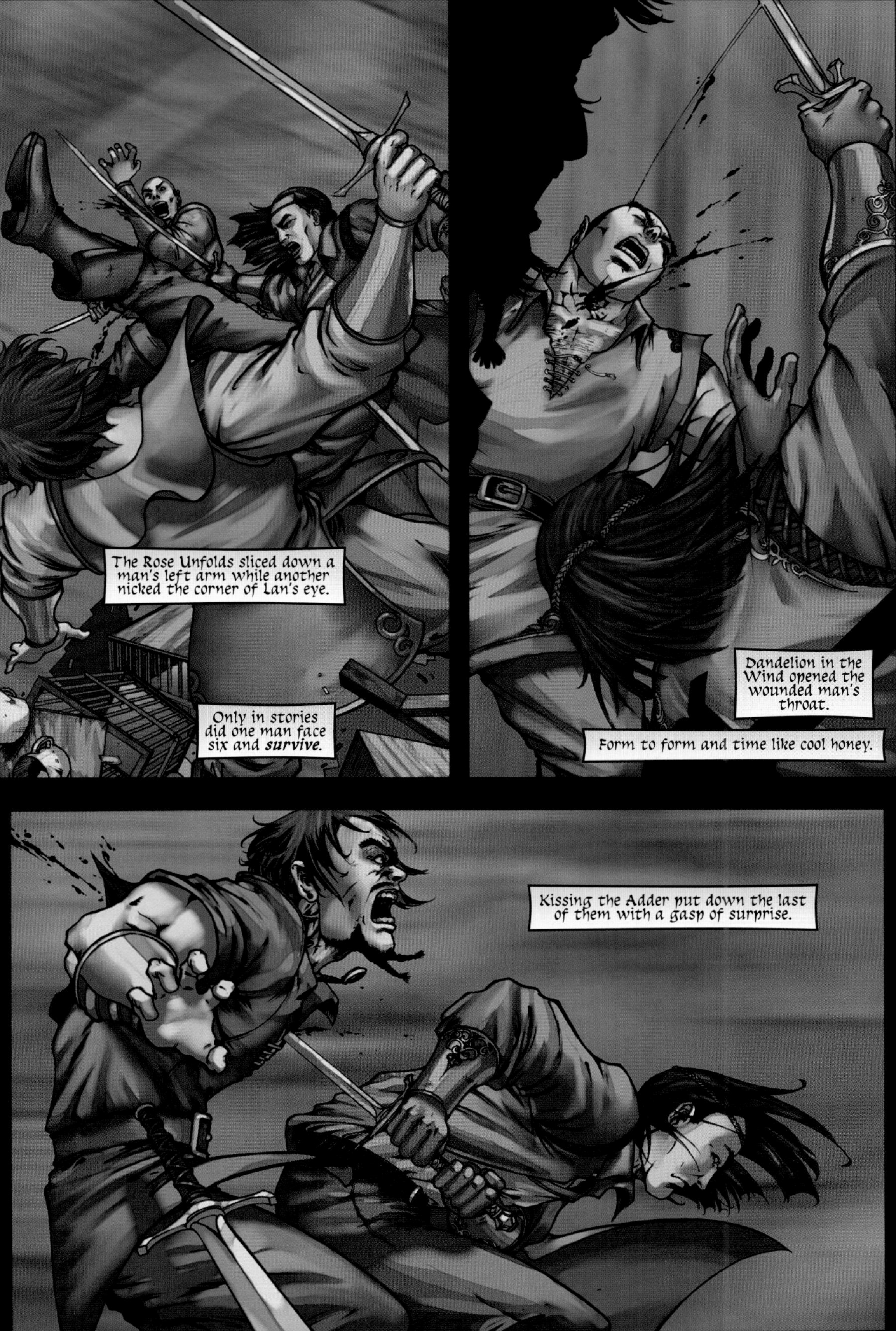
The Rose Unfolds sliced down a man's left arm while another nicked the corner of Lan's eye.
Only in stories did one man face six and *survive*.
Dandelion in the Wind opened the wounded man's throat.
Form to form and time like cool honey.
Kissing the Adder put down the last of them with a gasp of surprise.

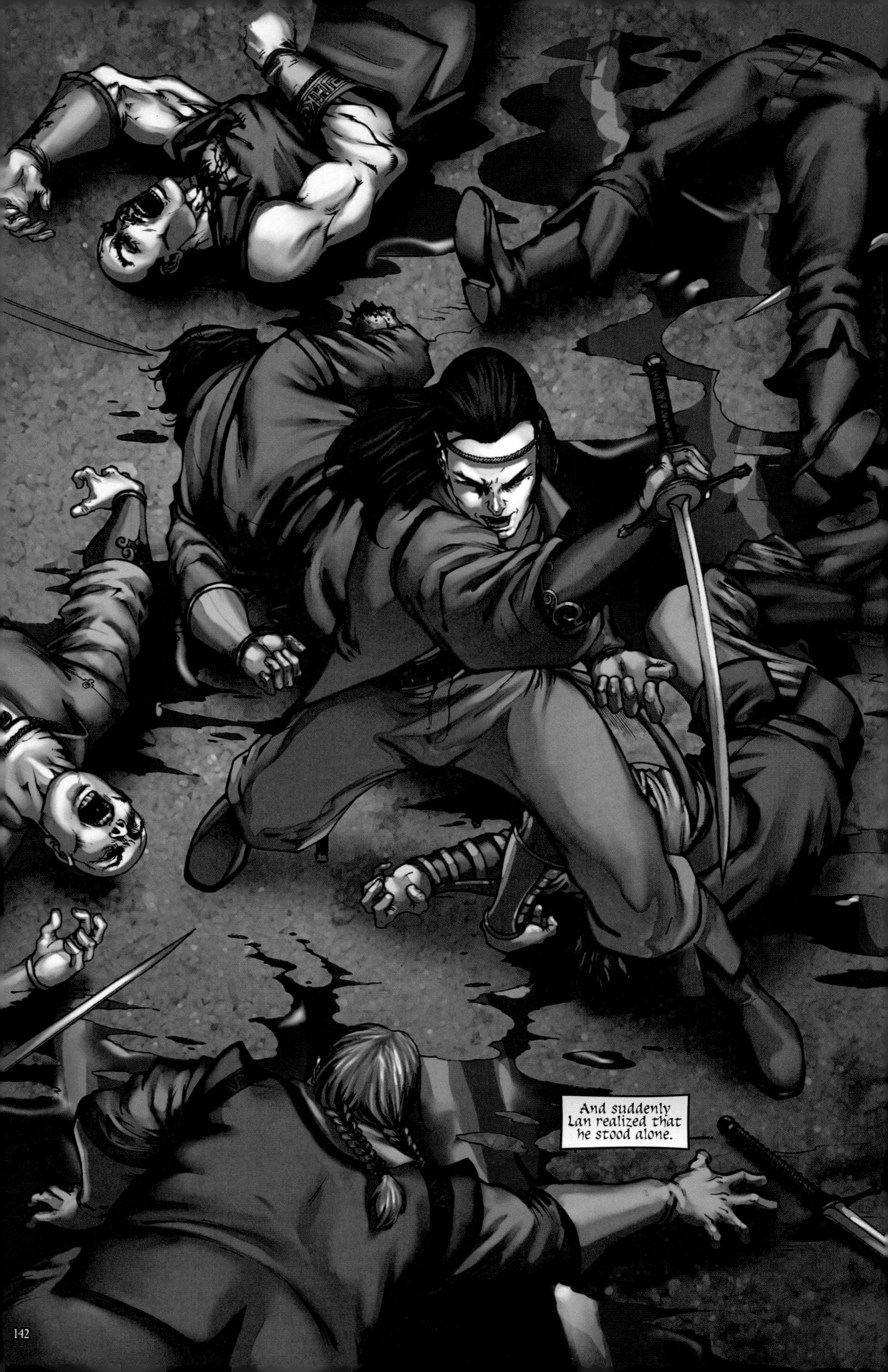
And suddenly Lan realized that he stood alone.

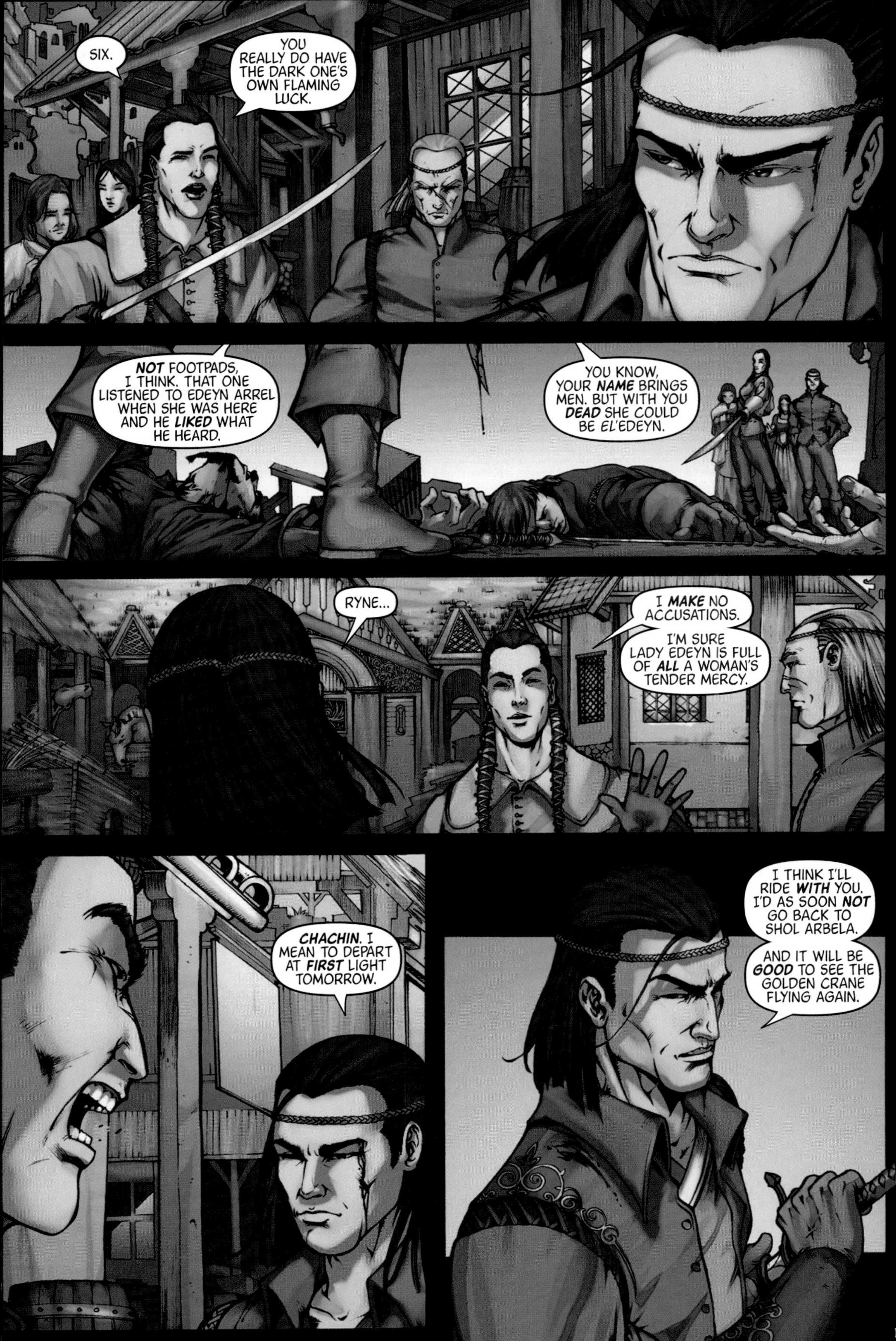
SIX.
YOU REALLY DO HAVE THE DARK ONE'S OWN FLAMING LUCK.
NOT FOOTPADS, I THINK. THAT ONE LISTENED TO EDEYN ARREL WHEN SHE WAS HERE AND HE **LIKED** WHAT HE HEARD.
YOU KNOW, YOUR **NAME** BRINGS MEN. BUT WITH YOU **DEAD** SHE COULD BE EL'EDEYN.
RYNE...
I **MAKE** NO ACCUSATIONS.
I'M SURE LADY EDEYN IS FULL OF **ALL** A WOMAN'S TENDER MERCY.
CHACHIN. I MEAN TO DEPART AT **FIRST** LIGHT TOMORROW.
I THINK I'LL RIDE **WITH** YOU. I'D AS SOON **NOT** GO BACK TO SHOL ARBELA.
AND IT WILL BE **GOOD** TO SEE THE GOLDEN CRANE FLYING AGAIN.

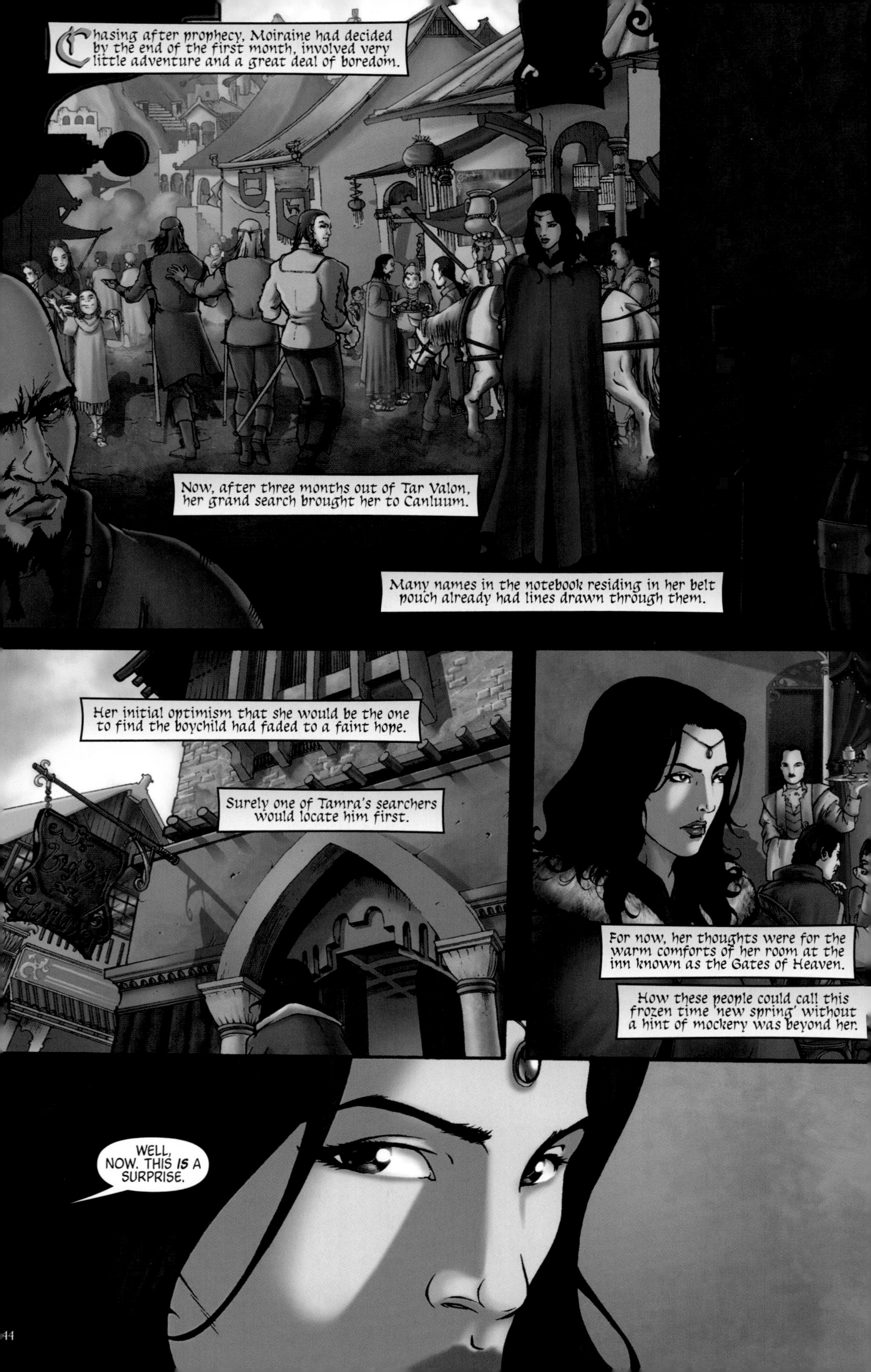
Chasing after prophecy, Moiraine had decided by the end of the first month, involved very little adventure and a great deal of boredom.
Now, after three months out of Tar Valon, her grand search brought her to Canluum.
Many names in the notebook residing in her belt pouch already had lines drawn through them.
Her initial optimism that she would be the one to find the boychild had faded to a faint hope.
Surely one of Tamra's searchers would locate him first.
For now, her thoughts were for the warm comforts of her room at the inn known as the Gates of Heaven.
How these people could call this frozen time 'new spring' without a hint of mockery was beyond her.
WELL, NOW. THIS *IS* A SURPRISE.

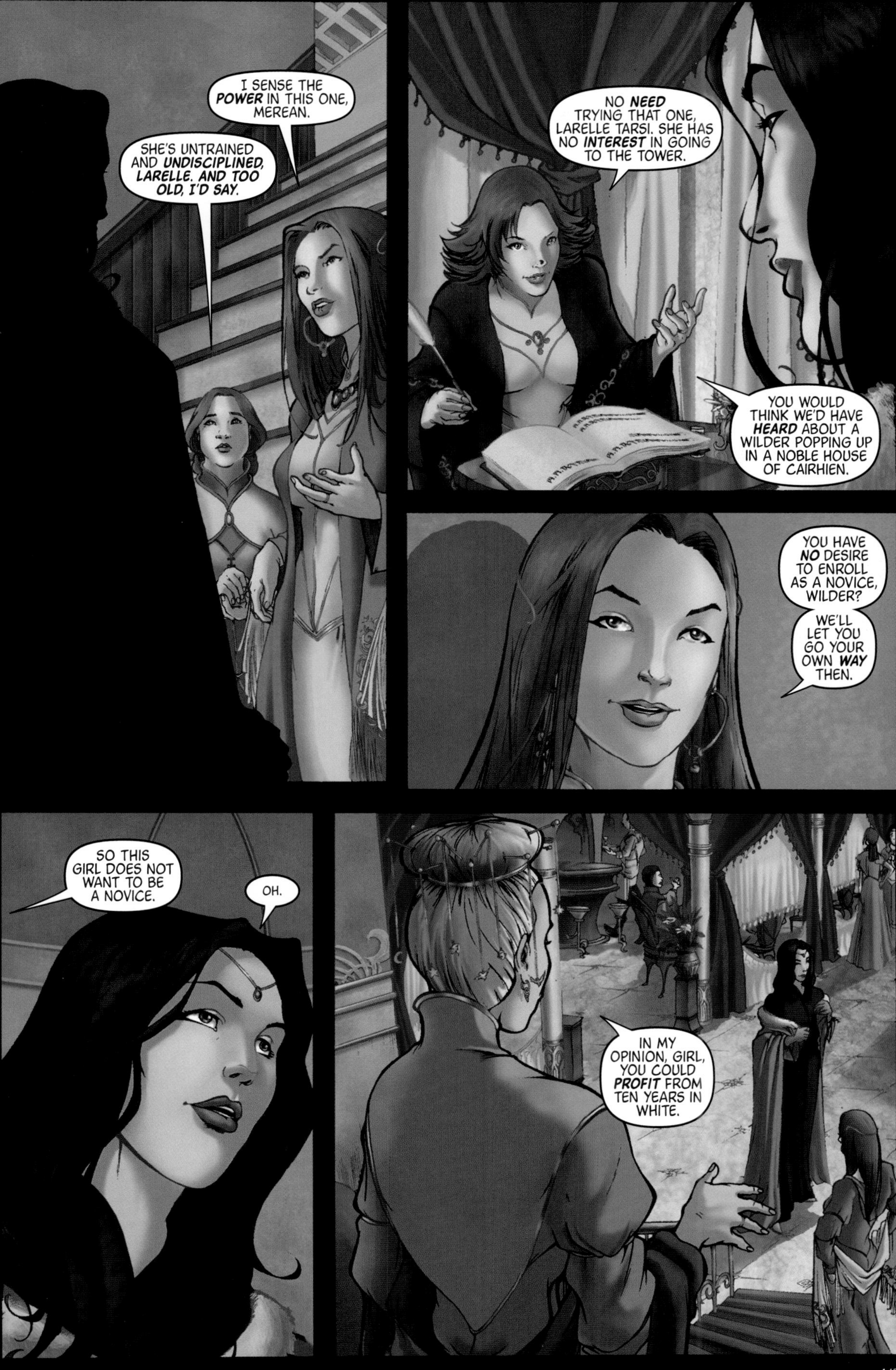
I SENSE THE POWER IN THIS ONE, MEREAN.
SHE'S UNTRAINED AND UNDISCIPLINED, LARELLE. AND TOO OLD, I'D SAY.
NO NEED TRYING THAT ONE, LARELLE TARSI. SHE HAS NO INTEREST IN GOING TO THE TOWER.
YOU WOULD THINK WE'D HAVE HEARD ABOUT A WILDER POPPING UP IN A NOBLE HOUSE OF CAIRHIEN.
YOU HAVE NO DESIRE TO ENROLL AS A NOVICE, WILDER?
WE'LL LET YOU GO YOUR OWN WAY THEN.
SO THIS GIRL DOES NOT WANT TO BE A NOVICE.
OH.
IN MY OPINION, GIRL, YOU COULD PROFIT FROM TEN YEARS IN WHITE.

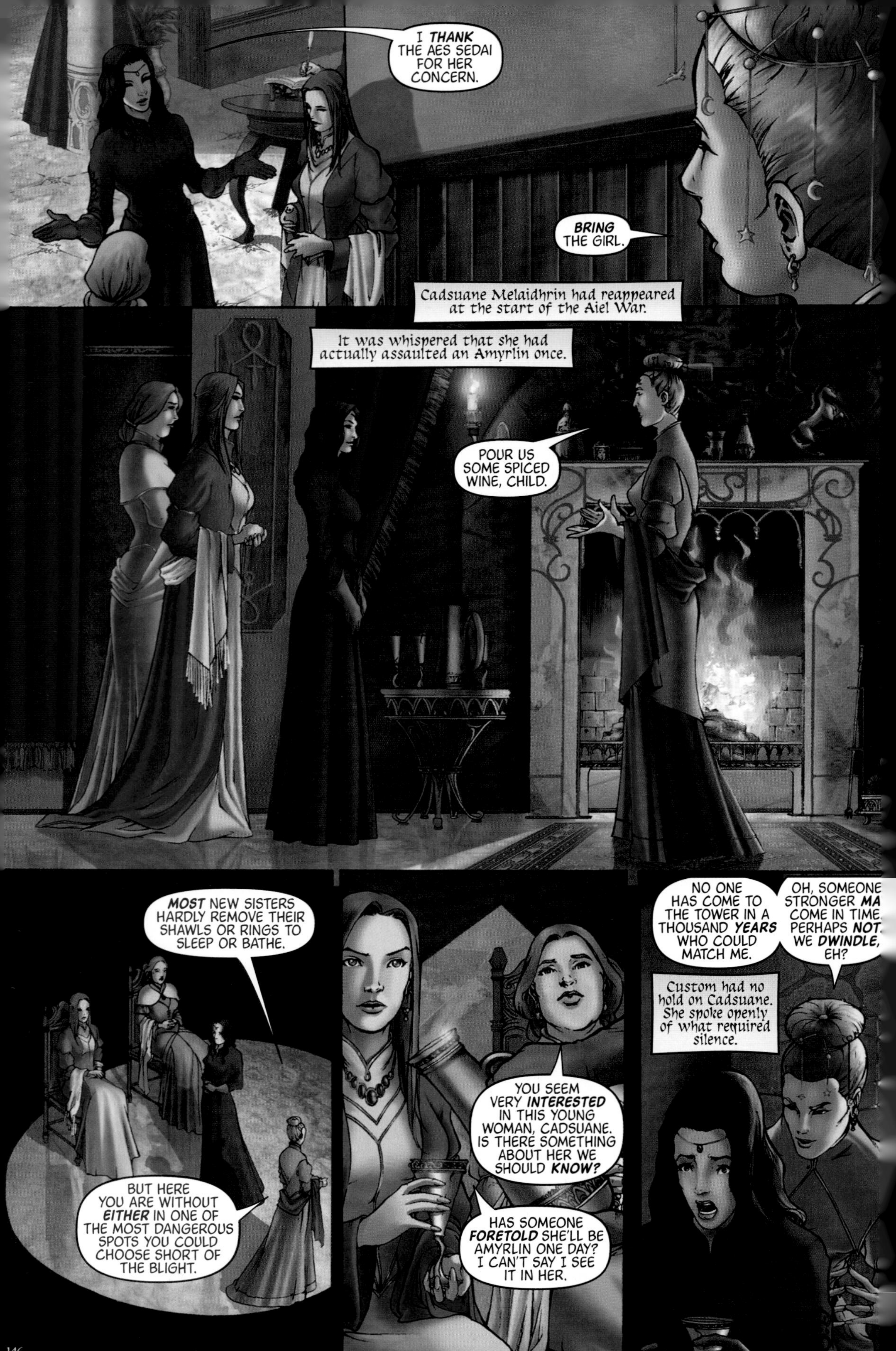
I THANK THE AES SEDAI FOR HER CONCERN.
BRING THE GIRL.
Cadsuane Melaidhrin had reappeared at the start of the Aiel War.
It was whispered that she had actually assaulted an Amyrlin once.
POUR US SOME SPICED WINE, CHILD.
MOST NEW SISTERS HARDLY REMOVE THEIR SHAWLS OR RINGS TO SLEEP OR BATHE.
BUT HERE YOU ARE WITHOUT EITHER IN ONE OF THE MOST DANGEROUS SPOTS YOU COULD CHOOSE SHORT OF THE BLIGHT.
YOU SEEM VERY INTERESTED IN THIS YOUNG WOMAN, CADSUANE. IS THERE SOMETHING ABOUT HER WE SHOULD KNOW?
HAS SOMEONE FORETOLD SHE'LL BE AMYRLIN ONE DAY? I CAN'T SAY I SEE IT IN HER.
NO ONE HAS COME TO THE TOWER IN A THOUSAND YEARS WHO COULD MATCH ME.
OH, SOMEONE STRONGER MA COME IN TIME. PERHAPS NOT. WE DWINDLE, EH?
Custom had no hold on Cadsuane. She spoke openly of what required silence.

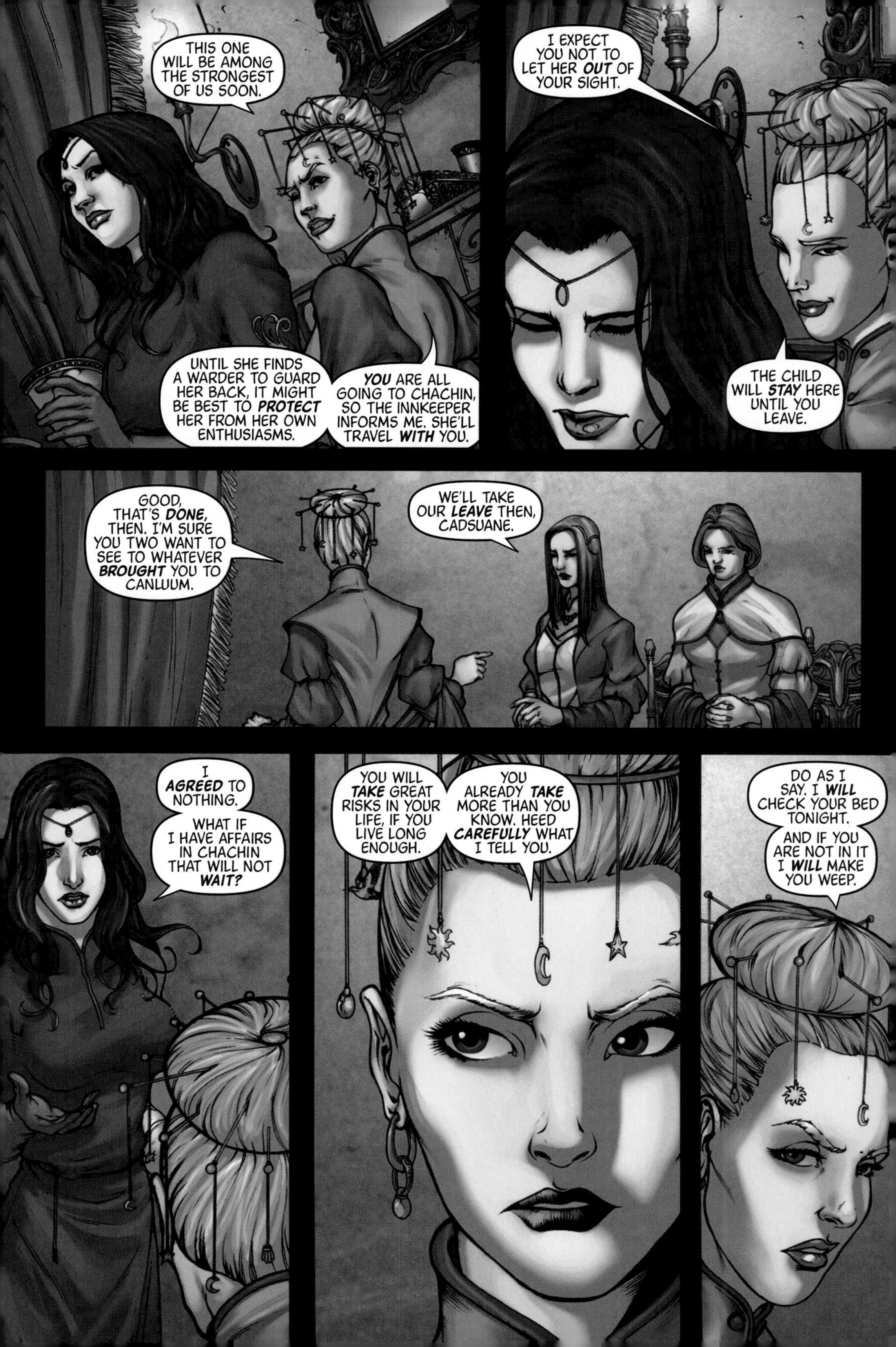

THIS ONE WILL BE AMONG THE STRONGEST OF US SOON.
UNTIL SHE FINDS A WARDER TO GUARD HER BACK, IT MIGHT BE BEST TO PROTECT HER FROM HER OWN ENTHUSIASMS.
YOU ARE ALL GOING TO CHACHIN, SO THE INNKEEPER INFORMS ME. SHE'LL TRAVEL WITH YOU.
I EXPECT YOU NOT TO LET HER OUT OF YOUR SIGHT.
THE CHILD WILL STAY HERE UNTIL YOU LEAVE.
GOOD, THAT'S DONE, THEN. I'M SURE YOU TWO WANT TO SEE TO WHATEVER BROUGHT YOU TO CANLUUM.
WE'LL TAKE OUR LEAVE THEN, CADSUANE.
I AGREED TO NOTHING.
WHAT IF I HAVE AFFAIRS IN CHACHIN THAT WILL NOT WAIT?
YOU WILL TAKE GREAT RISKS IN YOUR LIFE, IF YOU LIVE LONG ENOUGH.
YOU ALREADY TAKE MORE THAN YOU KNOW. HEED CAREFULLY WHAT I TELL YOU.
DO AS I SAY. I WILL CHECK YOUR BED TONIGHT.
AND IF YOU ARE NOT IN IT I WILL MAKE YOU WEEP.

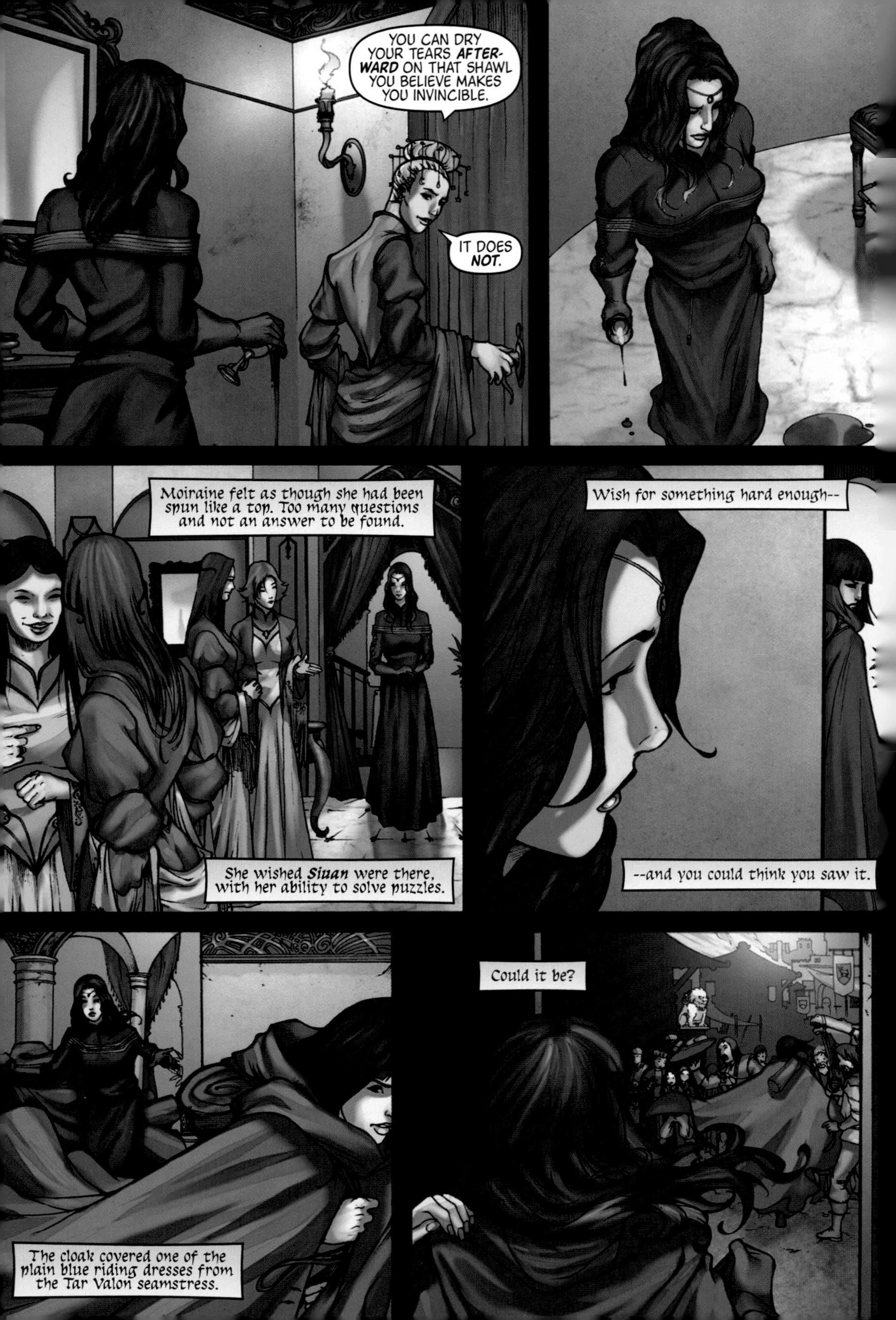
YOU CAN DRY YOUR TEARS AFTERWARD ON THAT SHAWL YOU BELIEVE MAKES YOU INVINCIBLE.
IT DOES NOT.
Moiraine felt as though she had been spun like a top. Too many questions and not an answer to be found.
She wished Siuan were there, with her ability to solve puzzles.
Wish for something hard enough--
--and you could think you saw it.
The cloak covered one of the plain blue riding dresses from the Tar Valon seamstress.
Could it be?

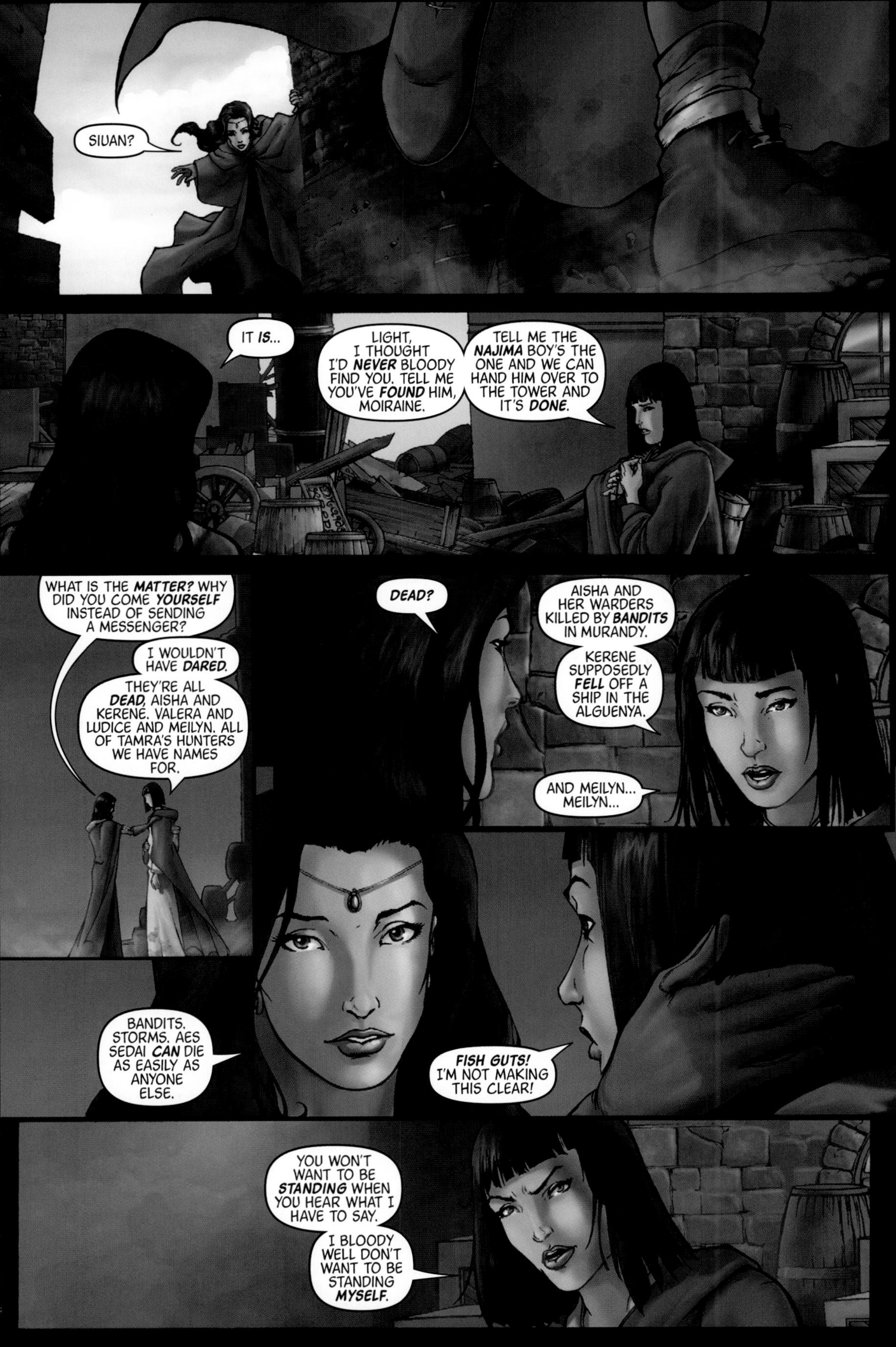
SIUAN?
IT IS...
LIGHT, I THOUGHT I'D NEVER BLOODY FIND YOU. TELL ME YOU'VE FOUND HIM, MOIRAINE.
TELL ME THE NAJIMA BOY'S THE ONE AND WE CAN HAND HIM OVER TO THE TOWER AND IT'S DONE.
WHAT IS THE MATTER? WHY DID YOU COME YOURSELF INSTEAD OF SENDING A MESSENGER?
I WOULDN'T HAVE DARED.
THEY'RE ALL DEAD, AISHA AND KERENE. VALERA AND LUDICE AND MEILYN. ALL OF TAMRA'S HUNTERS WE HAVE NAMES FOR.
DEAD?
AISHA AND HER WARDERS KILLED BY BANDITS IN MURANDY.
KERENE SUPPOSEDLY FELL OFF A SHIP IN THE ALGUENYA.
AND MEILYN... MEILYN...
BANDITS. STORMS. AES SEDAI CAN DIE AS EASILY AS ANYONE ELSE.
FISH GUTS! I'M NOT MAKING THIS CLEAR!
YOU WON'T WANT TO BE STANDING WHEN YOU HEAR WHAT I HAVE TO SAY.
I BLOODY WELL DON'T WANT TO BE STANDING MYSELF.

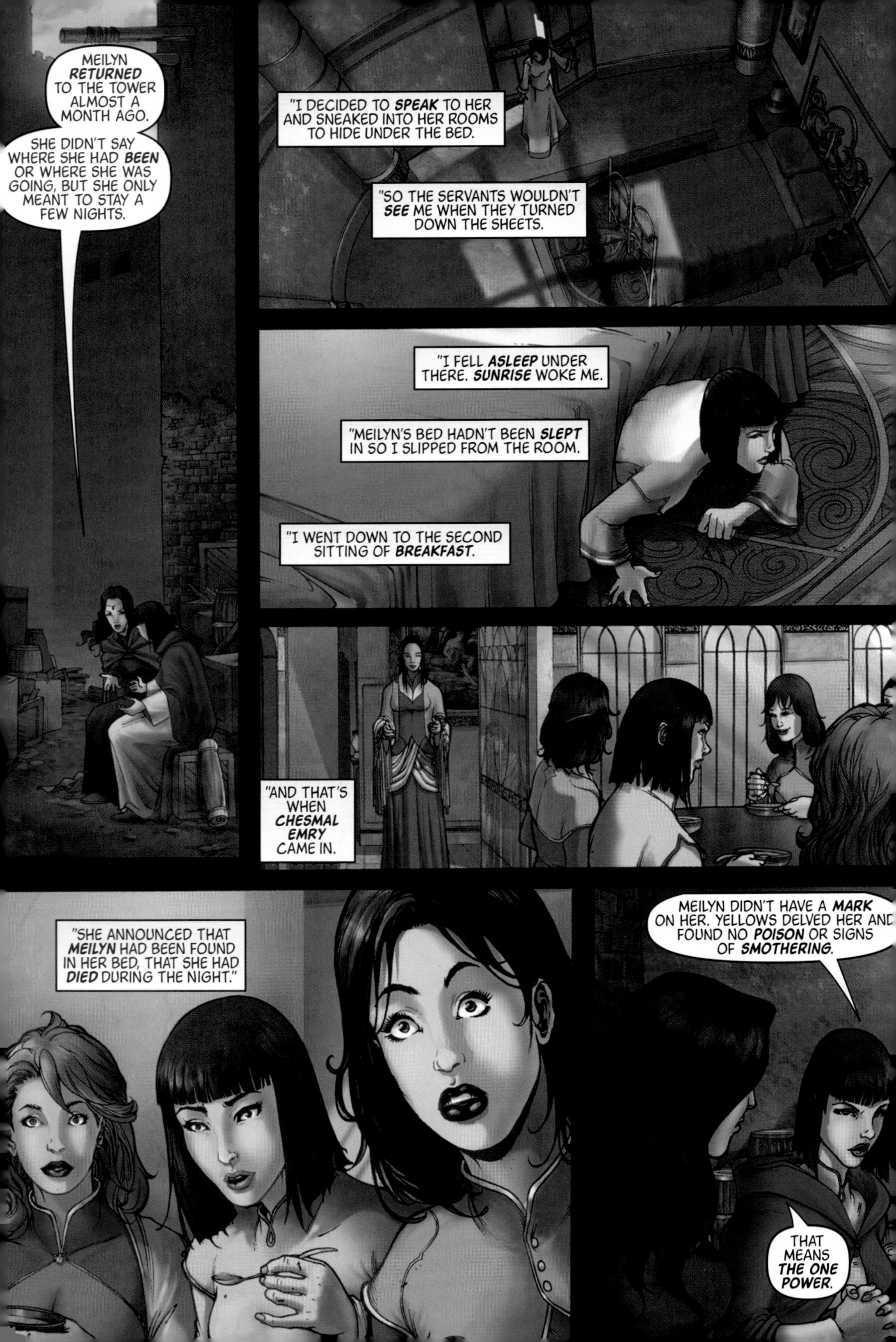
MEILYN RETURNED TO THE TOWER ALMOST A MONTH AGO.
SHE DIDN'T SAY WHERE SHE HAD BEEN OR WHERE SHE WAS GOING, BUT SHE ONLY MEANT TO STAY A FEW NIGHTS.
"I DECIDED TO SPEAK TO HER AND SNEAKED INTO HER ROOMS TO HIDE UNDER THE BED.
"SO THE SERVANTS WOULDN'T SEE ME WHEN THEY TURNED DOWN THE SHEETS.
"I FELL ASLEEP UNDER THERE. SUNRISE WOKE ME.
"MEILYN'S BED HADN'T BEEN SLEPT IN SO I SLIPPED FROM THE ROOM.
"I WENT DOWN TO THE SECOND SITTING OF BREAKFAST.
"AND THAT'S WHEN CHESMAL EMRY CAME IN.
"SHE ANNOUNCED THAT MEILYN HAD BEEN FOUND IN HER BED, THAT SHE HAD DIED DURING THE NIGHT."
MEILYN DIDN'T HAVE A MARK ON HER. YELLOWS DELVED HER AND FOUND NO POISON OR SIGNS OF SMOTHERING.
THAT MEANS THE ONE POWER.

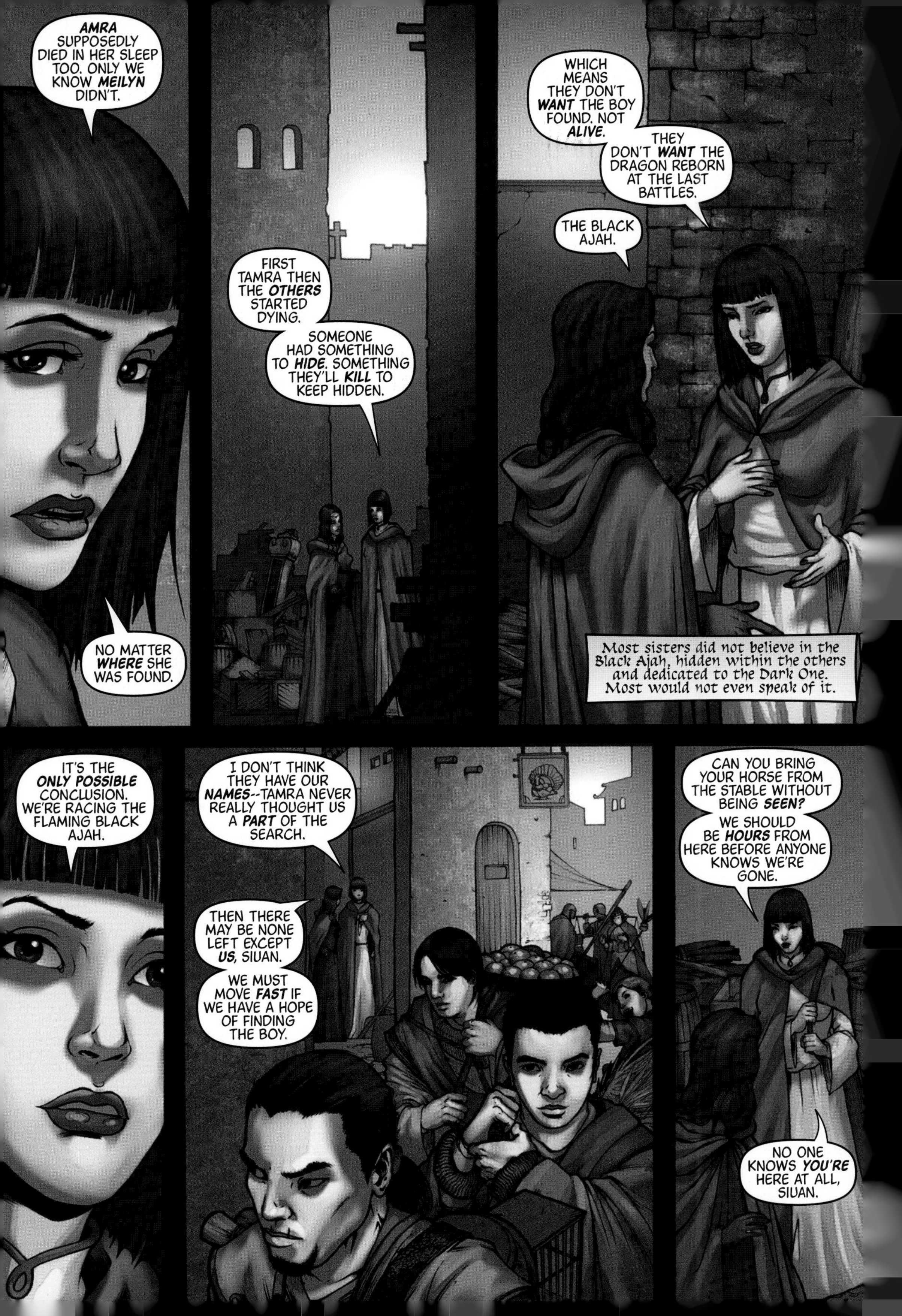
AMRA SUPPOSEDLY DIED IN HER SLEEP TOO. ONLY WE KNOW MEILYN DIDN'T.
NO MATTER WHERE SHE WAS FOUND.
FIRST TAMRA THEN THE OTHERS STARTED DYING.
SOMEONE HAD SOMETHING TO HIDE. SOMETHING THEY'LL KILL TO KEEP HIDDEN.
WHICH MEANS THEY DON'T WANT THE BOY FOUND. NOT ALIVE.
THEY DON'T WANT THE DRAGON REBORN AT THE LAST BATTLES.
THE BLACK AJAH.
Most sisters did not believe in the Black Ajah, hidden within the others and dedicated to the Dark One. Most would not even speak of it.
IT'S THE ONLY POSSIBLE CONCLUSION. WE'RE RACING THE FLAMING BLACK AJAH.
I DON'T THINK THEY HAVE OUR NAMES--TAMRA NEVER REALLY THOUGHT US A PART OF THE SEARCH.
THEN THERE MAY BE NONE LEFT EXCEPT US, SIUAN.
WE MUST MOVE FAST IF WE HAVE A HOPE OF FINDING THE BOY.
CAN YOU BRING YOUR HORSE FROM THE STABLE WITHOUT BEING SEEN?
WE SHOULD BE HOURS FROM HERE BEFORE ANYONE KNOWS WE'RE GONE.
NO ONE KNOWS YOU'RE HERE AT ALL, SIUAN.

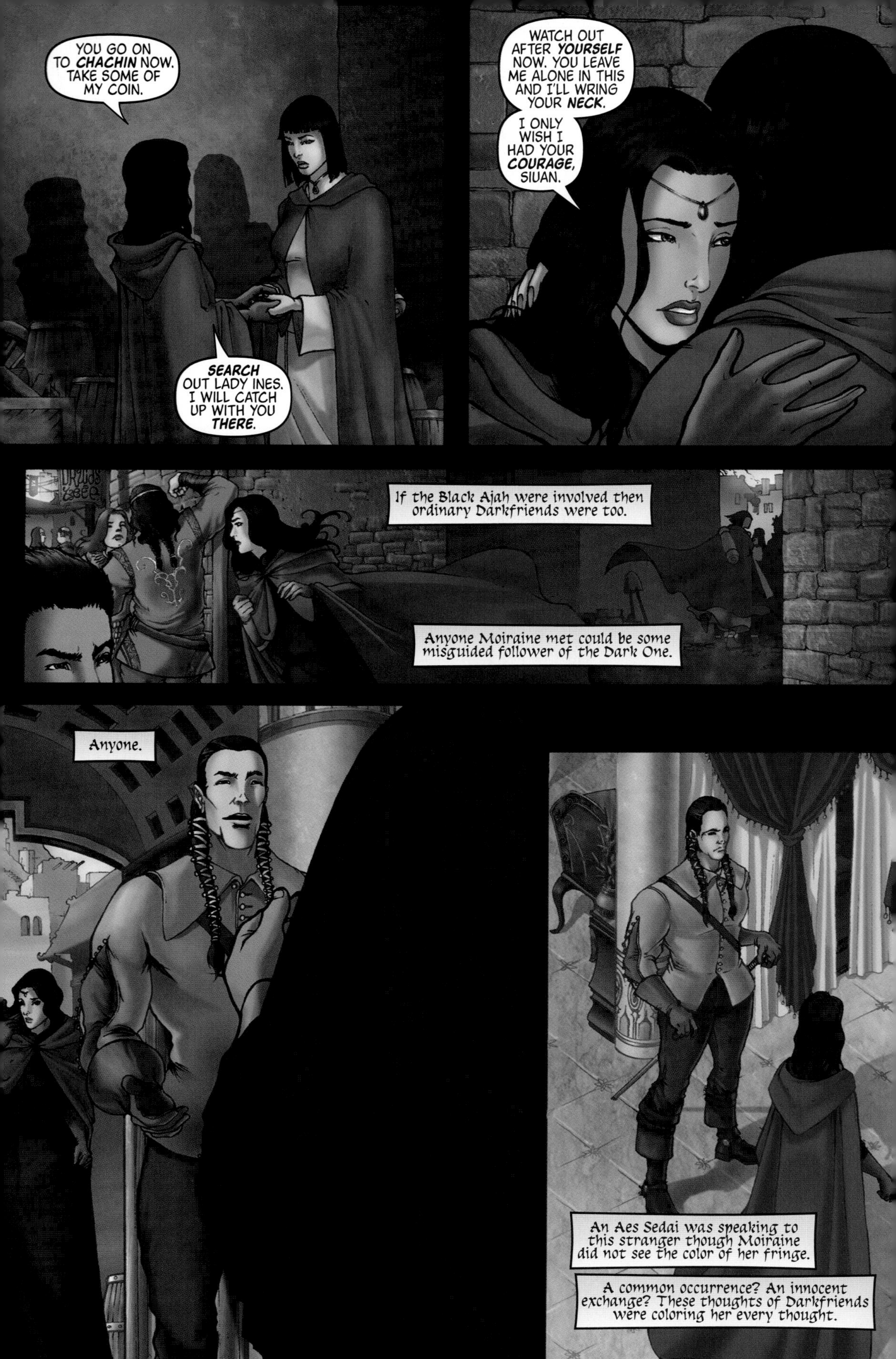
YOU GO ON TO CHACHIN NOW. TAKE SOME OF MY COIN.
SEARCH OUT LADY INES. I WILL CATCH UP WITH YOU THERE.
WATCH OUT AFTER YOURSELF NOW. YOU LEAVE ME ALONE IN THIS AND I'LL WRING YOUR NECK.
I ONLY WISH I HAD YOUR COURAGE, SIUAN.
If the Black Ajah were involved then ordinary Darkfriends were too.
Anyone Moiraine met could be some misguided follower of the Dark One.
Anyone.
An Aes Sedai was speaking to this stranger though Moiraine did not see the color of her fringe.
A common occurrence? An innocent exchange? These thoughts of Darkfriends were coloring her every thought.

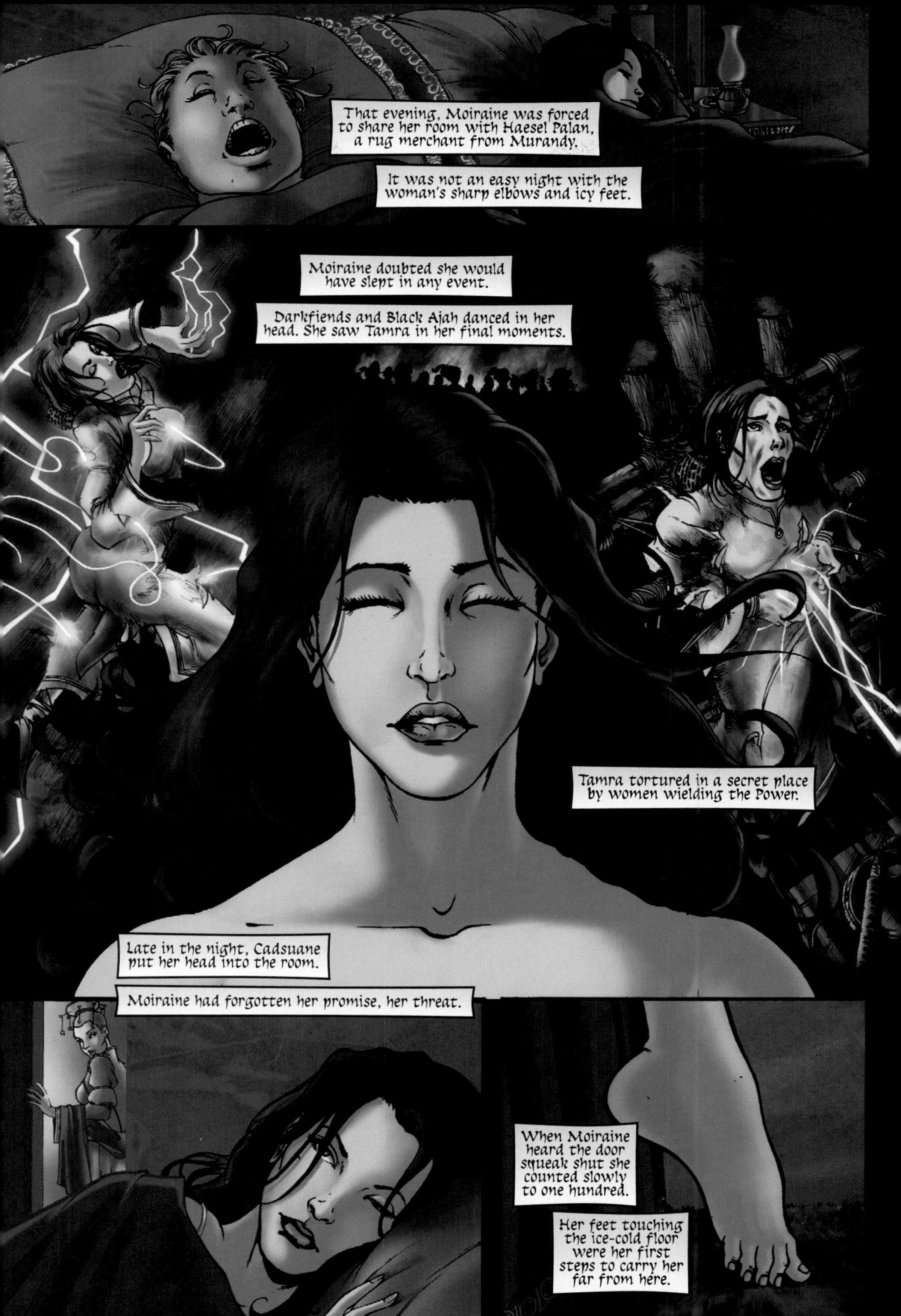
That evening, Moiraine was forced to share her room with Haesel Palan, a rug merchant from Murandy.
It was not an easy night with the woman's sharp elbows and icy feet.
Moiraine doubted she would have slept in any event.
Darkfiends and Black Ajah danced in her head. She saw Tamra in her final moments.
Tamra tortured in a secret place by women wielding the Power.
Late in the night, Cadsuane put her head into the room.
Moiraine had forgotten her promise, her threat.
When Moiraine heard the door squeak shut she counted slowly to one hundred.
Her feet touching the ice-cold floor were her first steps to carry her far from here.

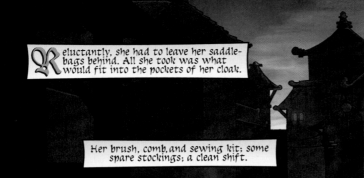

Reluctantly, she had to leave her saddle-bags behind. All she took was what would fit into the pockets of her cloak.

Her brush, comb, and sewing kit; some spare stockings; a clean shift.

It was enough, with the letters-of-rights and the remaining gold in her belt pouch.

She regretted leaving her packhorse behind.

But this way, no one would suspect anything until she failed to return that night.

Night Watchmen eyed her with surprise as she rode by. No one went out at night.

Which is why she was surprised to see she was not the first to reach the western gates.

Several merchant trains with their armored outriders.

And three riders, not armored, wearing swords on their hips and carrying heavy horsebows.

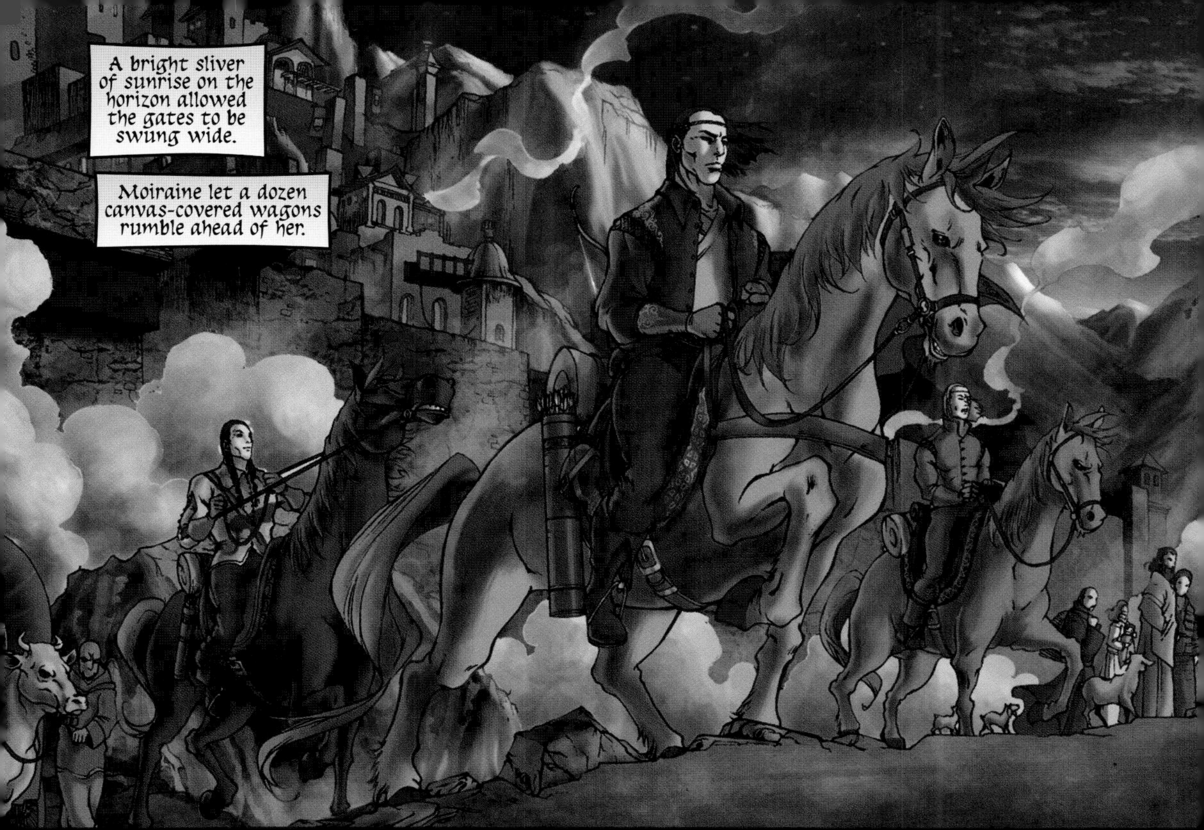
A bright sliver of sunrise on the horizon allowed the gates to be swung wide.
Moiraine let a dozen canvas-covered wagons rumble ahead of her.

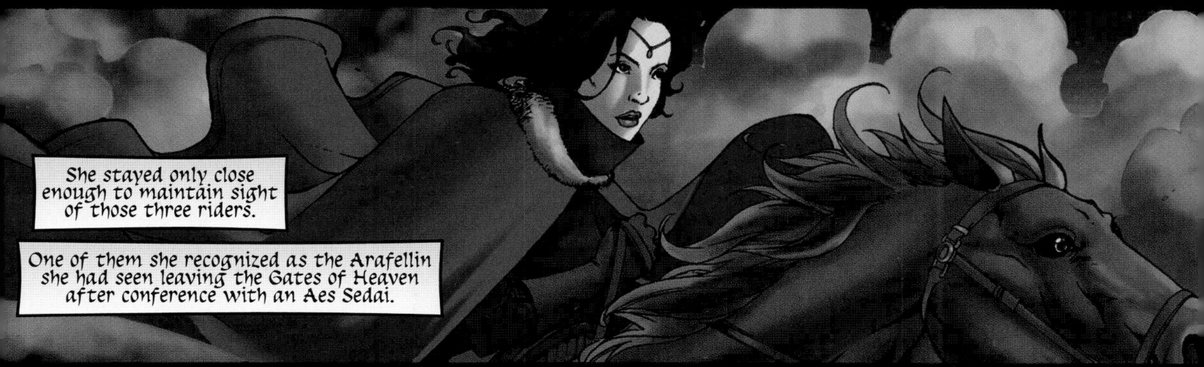
She stayed only close enough to maintain sight of those three riders.
One of them she recognized as the Arafellin she had seen leaving the Gates of Heaven after conference with an Aes Sedai.

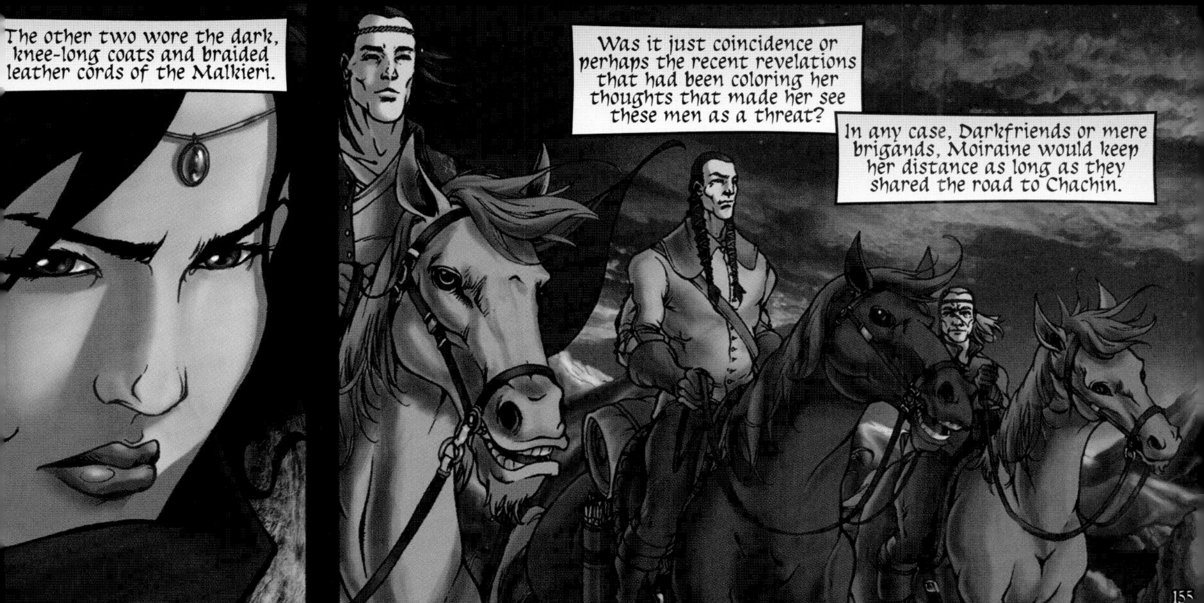
The other two wore the dark, knee-long coats and braided leather cords of the Malkieri.
Was it just coincidence or perhaps the recent revelations that had been coloring her thoughts that made her see these men as a threat?
In any case, Darkfriends or mere brigands, Moiraine would keep her distance as long as they shared the road to Chachin.

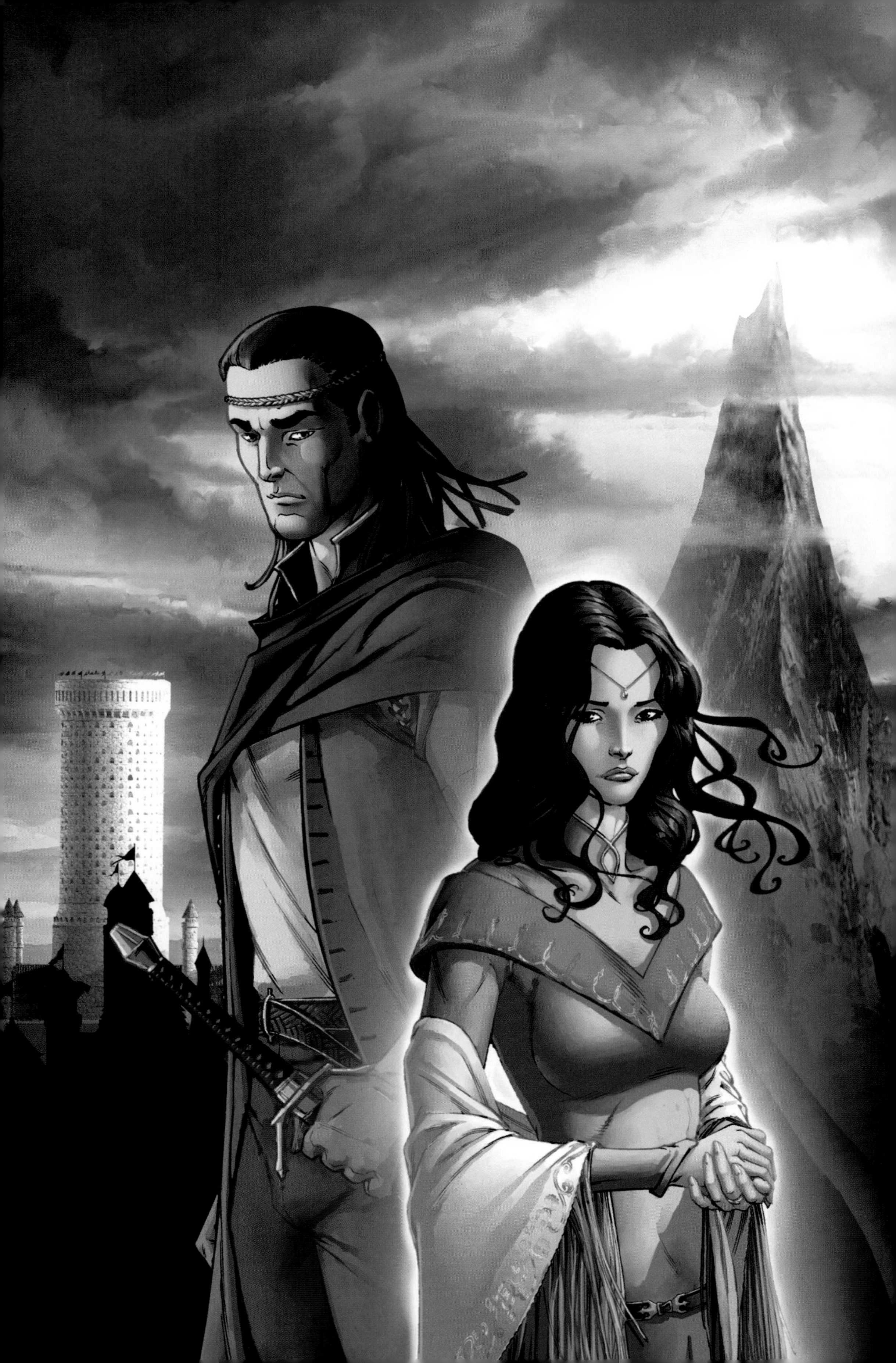

chapter seven

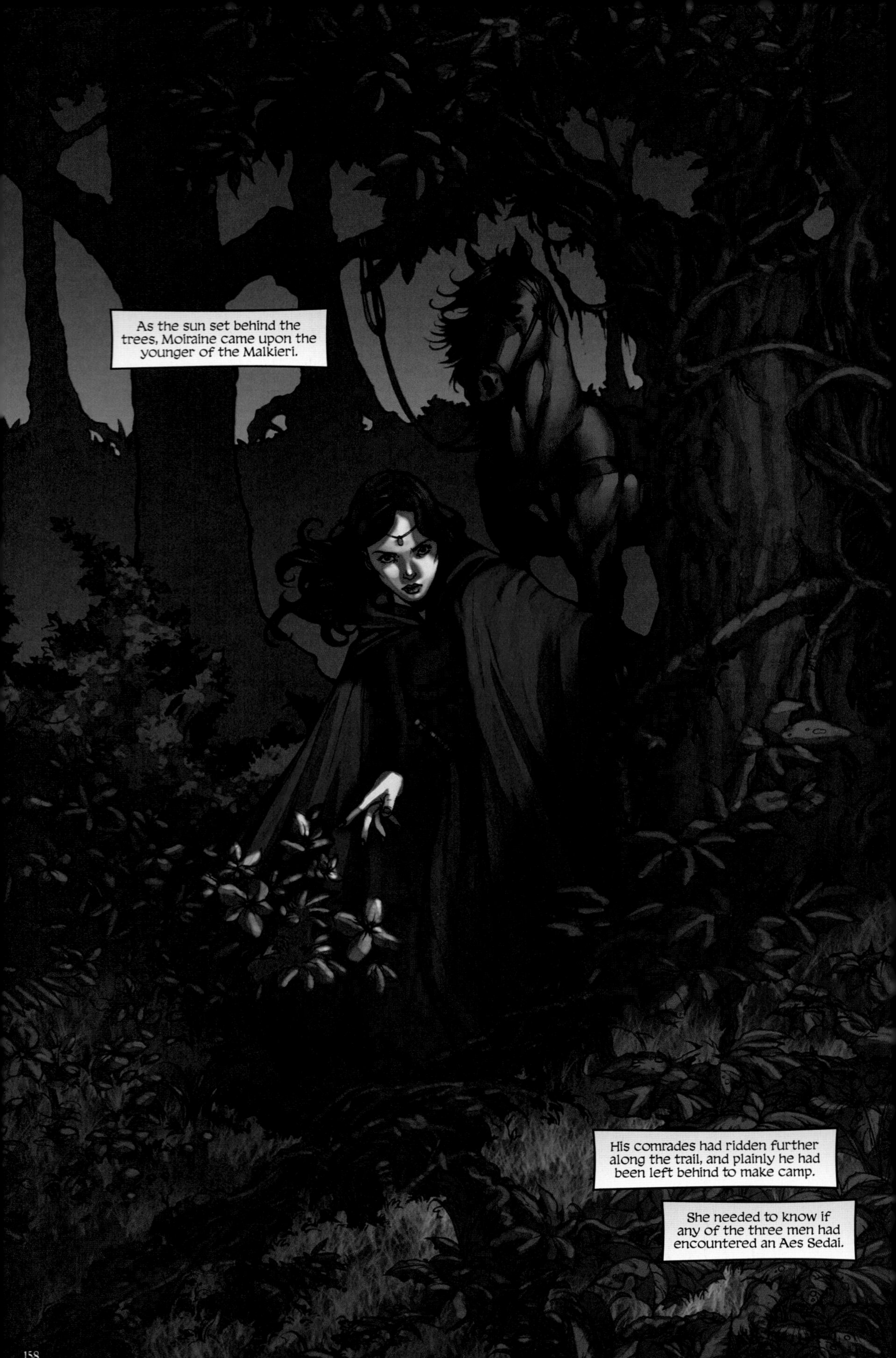
As the sun set behind the trees, Moiraine came upon the younger of the Malkieri.
His comrades had ridden further along the trail, and plainly he had been left behind to make camp.
She needed to know if any of the three men had encountered an Aes Sedai.

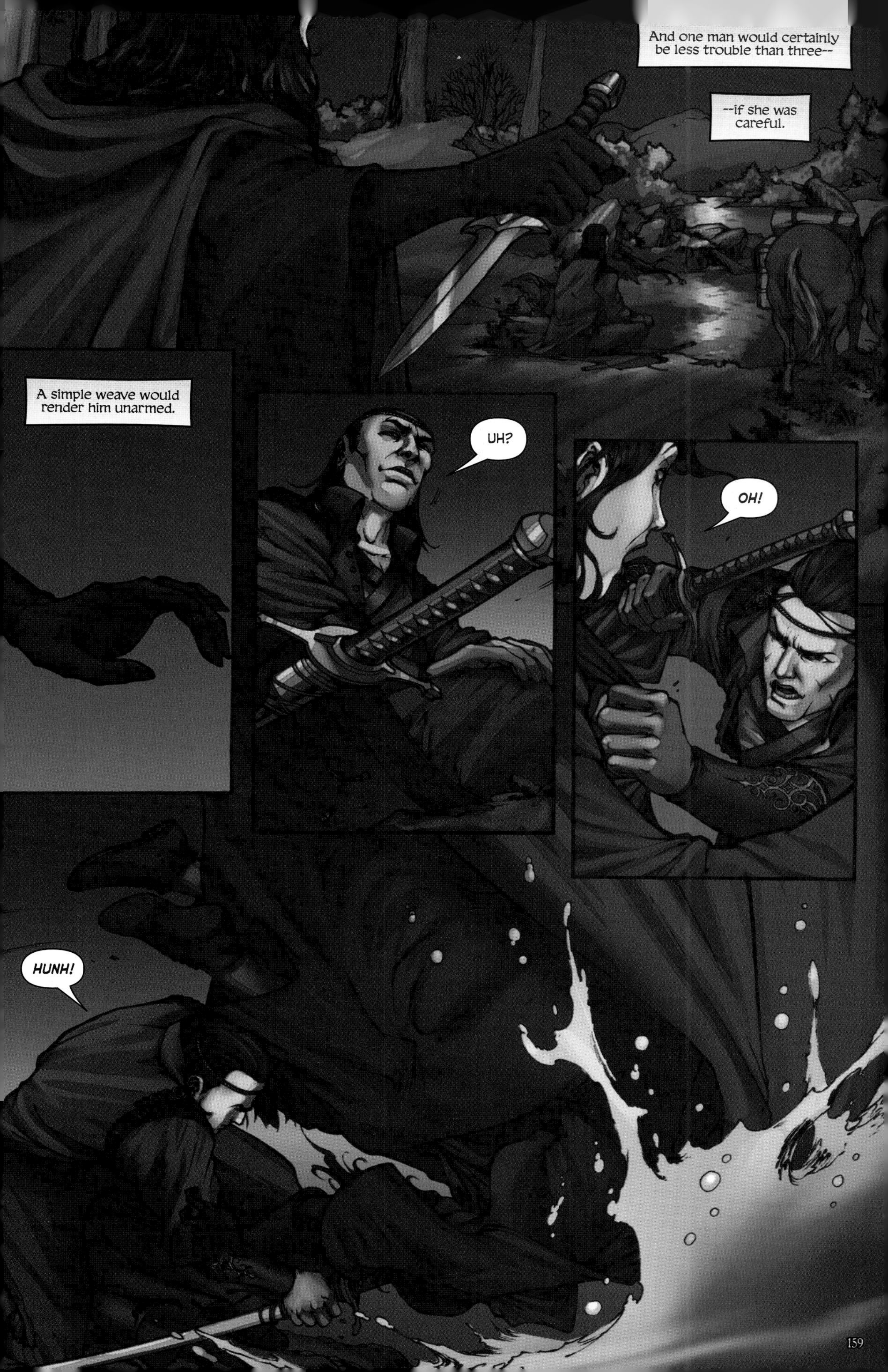
And one man would certainly be less trouble than three--
--if she was careful.
A simple weave would render him unarmed.
UH?
OH!
HUNH!

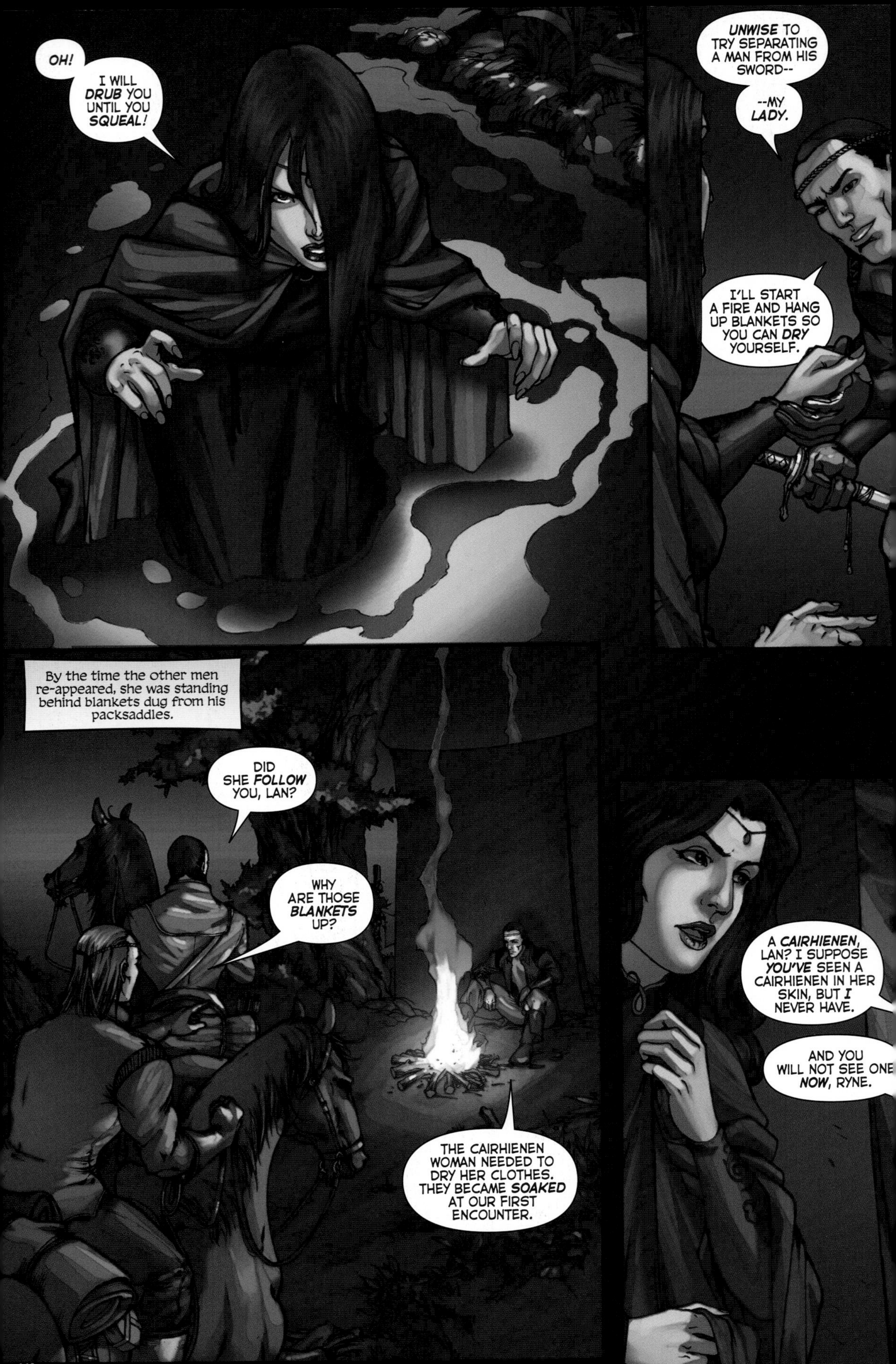
OH!
I WILL DRUB YOU UNTIL YOU SQUEAL!
UNWISE TO TRY SEPARATING A MAN FROM HIS SWORD--
--MY LADY.
I'LL START A FIRE AND HANG UP BLANKETS SO YOU CAN DRY YOURSELF.
By the time the other men re-appeared, she was standing behind blankets dug from his packsaddles.
DID SHE FOLLOW YOU, LAN?
WHY ARE THOSE BLANKETS UP?
THE CAIRHIENEN WOMAN NEEDED TO DRY HER CLOTHES. THEY BECAME SOAKED AT OUR FIRST ENCOUNTER.
A CAIRHIENEN, LAN? I SUPPOSE YOU'VE SEEN A CAIRHIENEN IN HER SKIN, BUT I NEVER HAVE.
AND YOU WILL NOT SEE ONE NOW, RYNE.

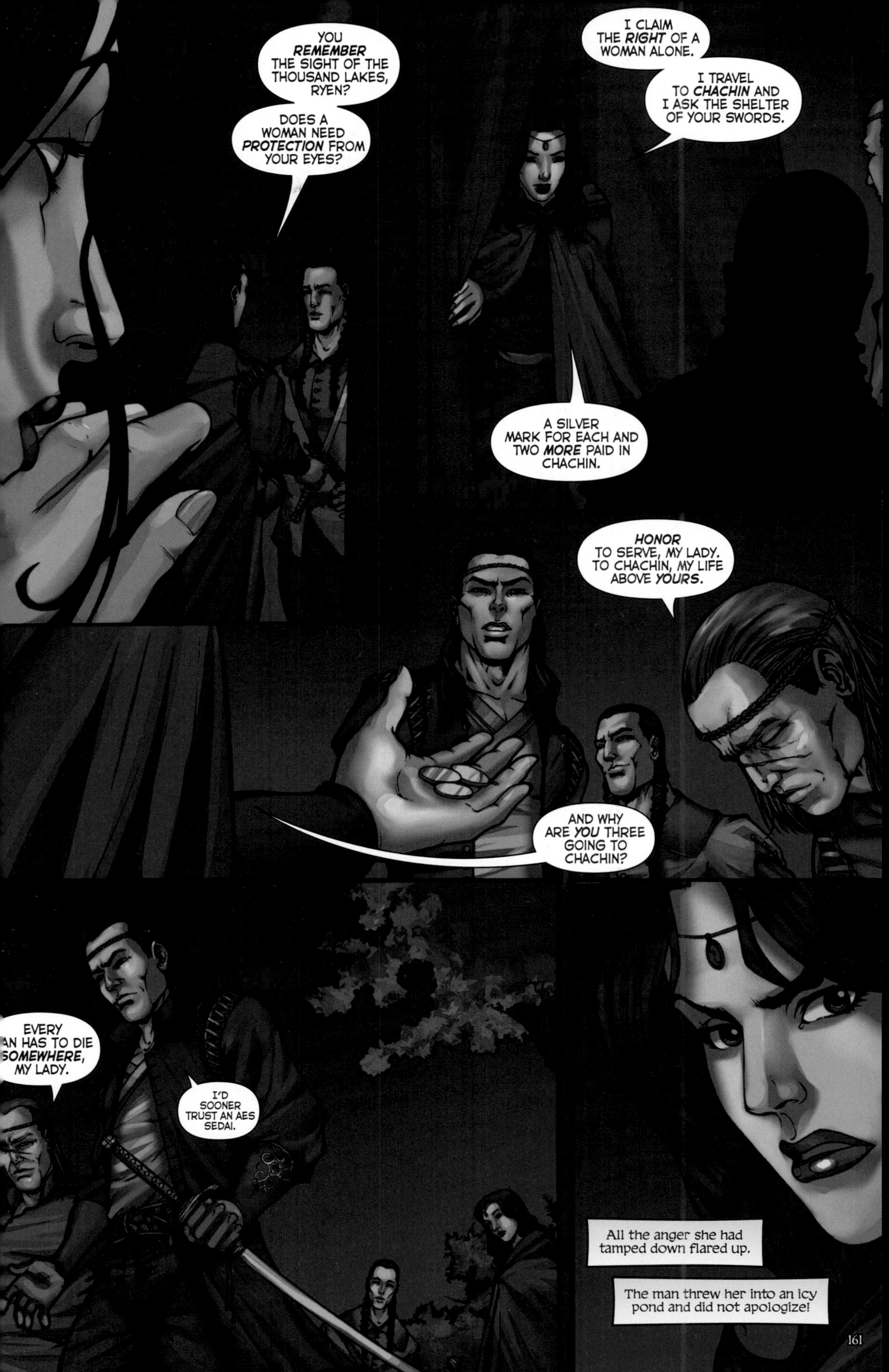
YOU *REMEMBER* THE SIGHT OF THE THOUSAND LAKES, RYEN?
DOES A WOMAN NEED *PROTECTION* FROM YOUR EYES?
I CLAIM THE *RIGHT* OF A WOMAN ALONE.
I TRAVEL TO *CHACHIN* AND I ASK THE SHELTER OF YOUR SWORDS.
A SILVER MARK FOR EACH AND TWO *MORE* PAID IN CHACHIN.
HONOR TO SERVE, MY LADY. TO CHACHIN, MY LIFE ABOVE *YOURS*.
AND WHY ARE *YOU* THREE GOING TO CHACHIN?
EVERY AN HAS TO DIE *SOMEWHERE*, MY LADY.
I'D SOONER TRUST AN AES SEDAI.
All the anger she had tamped down flared up.
The man threw her into an icy pond and did not apologize!

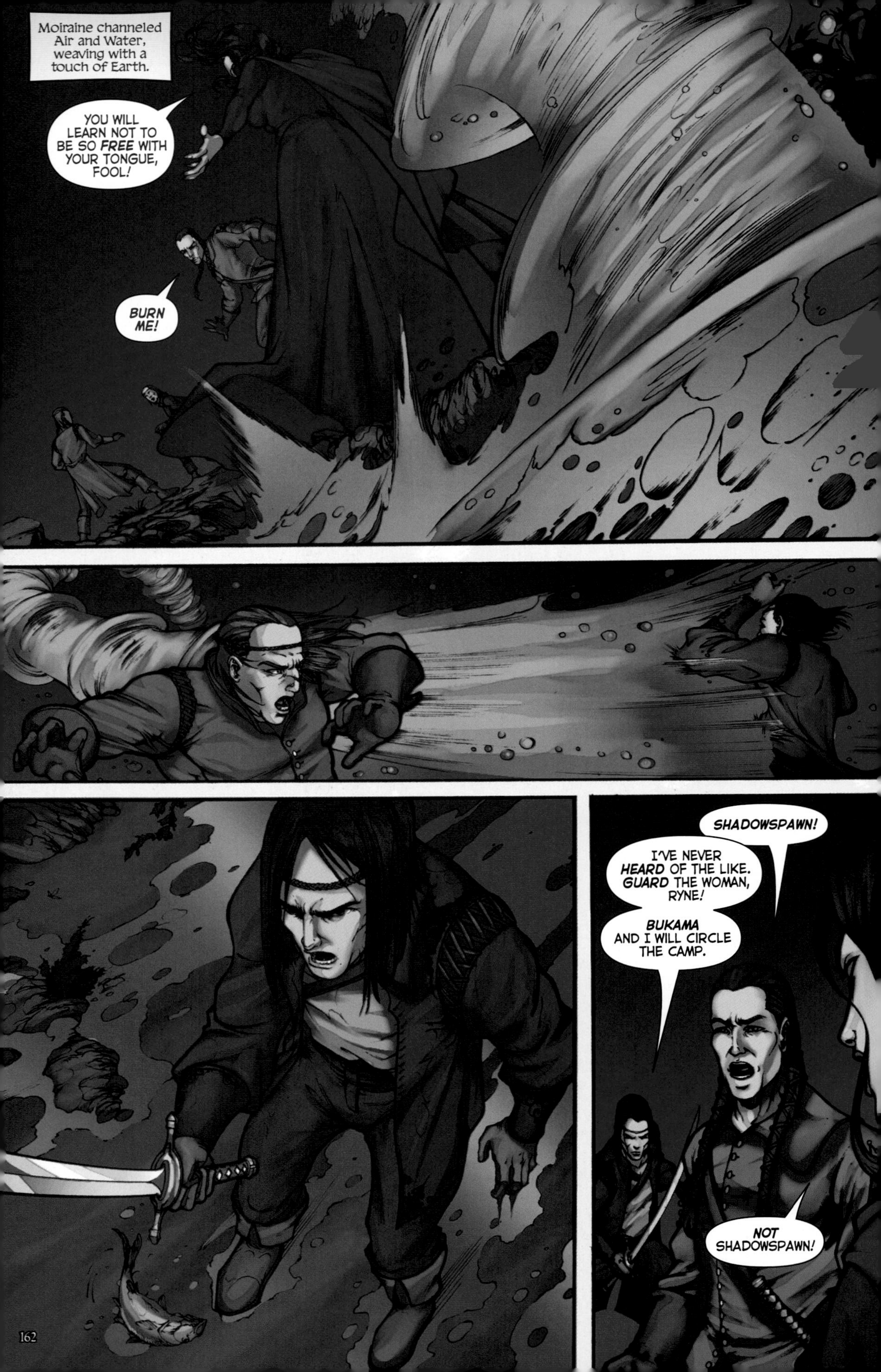

Moiraine channeled Air and Water, weaving with a touch of Earth.
YOU WILL LEARN NOT TO BE SO FREE WITH YOUR TONGUE, FOOL!
BURN ME!
SHADOWSPAWN!
I'VE NEVER HEARD OF THE LIKE. GUARD THE WOMAN, RYNE!
BUKAMA AND I WILL CIRCLE THE CAMP.
NOT SHADOWSPAWN!

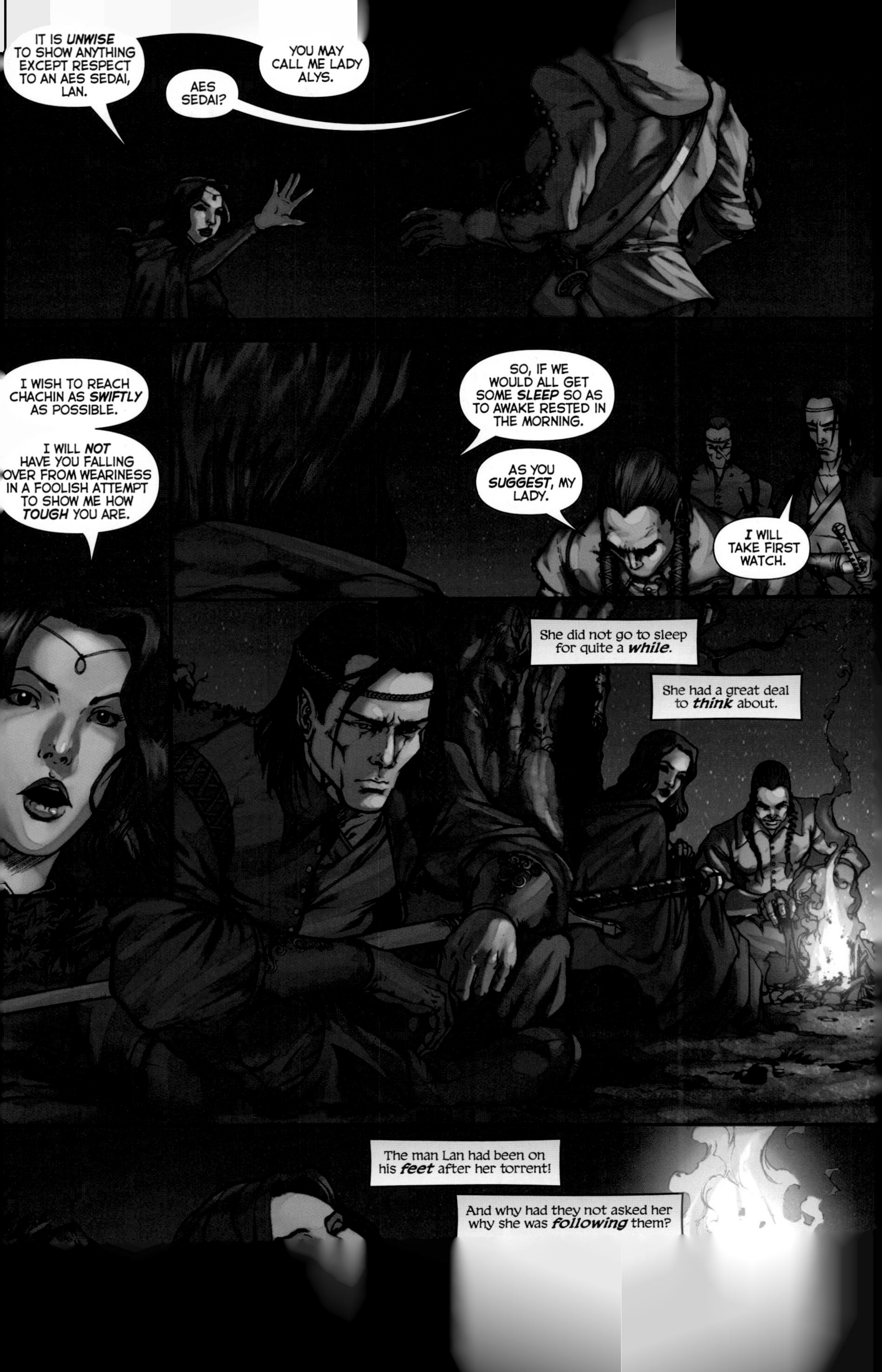
IT IS UNWISE TO SHOW ANYTHING EXCEPT RESPECT TO AN AES SEDAI, LAN.
AES SEDAI?
YOU MAY CALL ME LADY ALYS.
I WISH TO REACH CHACHIN AS SWIFTLY AS POSSIBLE.
I WILL NOT HAVE YOU FALLING OVER FROM WEARINESS IN A FOOLISH ATTEMPT TO SHOW ME HOW TOUGH YOU ARE.
SO, IF WE WOULD ALL GET SOME SLEEP SO AS TO AWAKE RESTED IN THE MORNING.
AS YOU SUGGEST, MY LADY.
I WILL TAKE FIRST WATCH.
She did not go to sleep for quite a while.
She had a great deal to think about.
The man Lan had been on his feet after her torrent!
And why had they not asked her why she was following them?

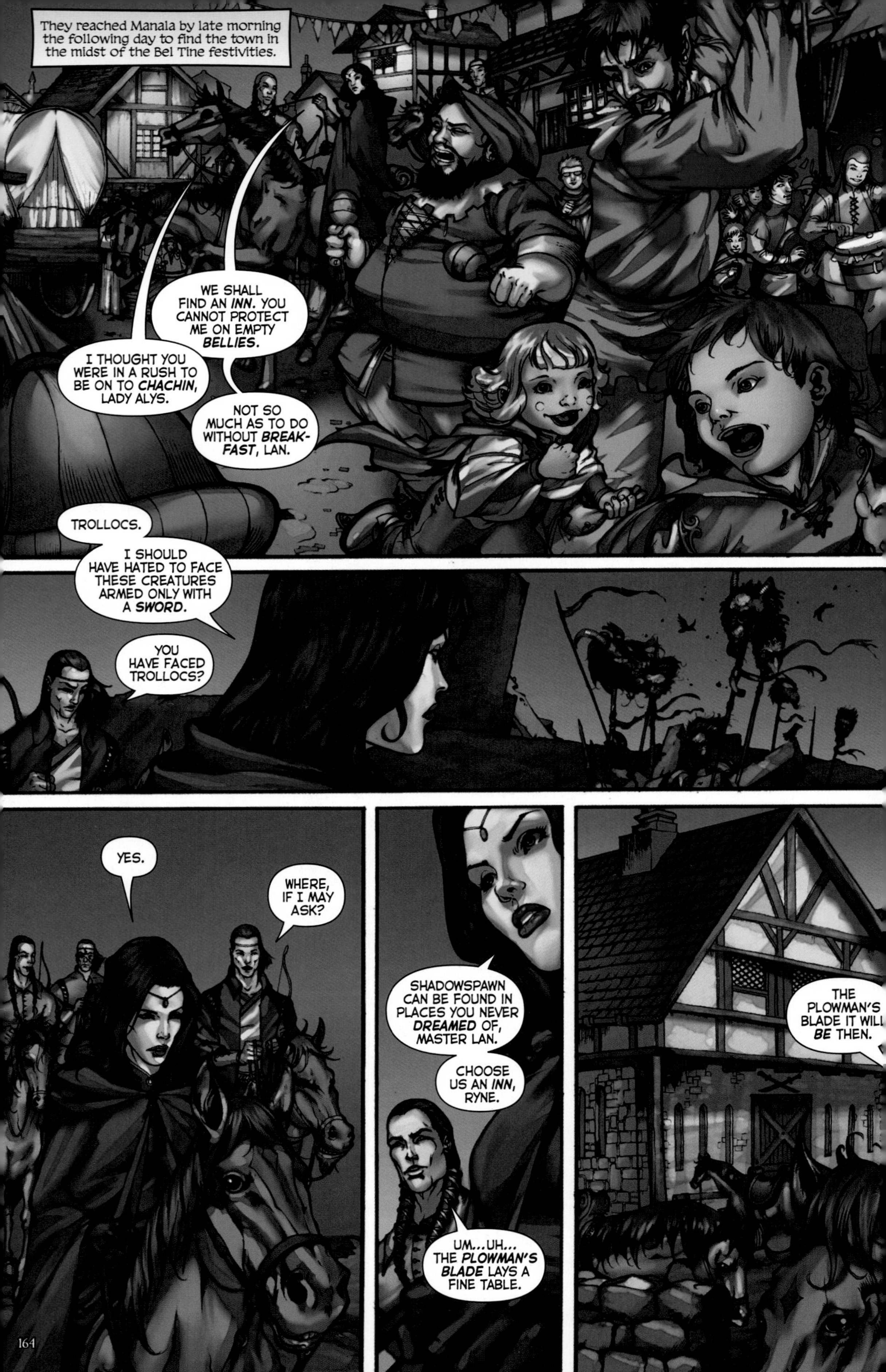
They reached Manala by late morning the following day to find the town in the midst of the Bel Tine festivities.
WE SHALL FIND AN INN. YOU CANNOT PROTECT ME ON EMPTY BELLIES.
I THOUGHT YOU WERE IN A RUSH TO BE ON TO CHACHIN, LADY ALYS.
NOT SO MUCH AS TO DO WITHOUT BREAKFAST, LAN.
TROLLOCS.
I SHOULD HAVE HATED TO FACE THESE CREATURES ARMED ONLY WITH A SWORD.
YOU HAVE FACED TROLLOCS?
YES.
WHERE, IF I MAY ASK?
SHADOWSPAWN CAN BE FOUND IN PLACES YOU NEVER DREAMED OF, MASTER LAN.
CHOOSE US AN INN, RYNE.
UM...UH... THE PLOWMAN'S BLADE LAYS A FINE TABLE.
THE PLOWMAN'S BLADE IT WILL BE THEN.

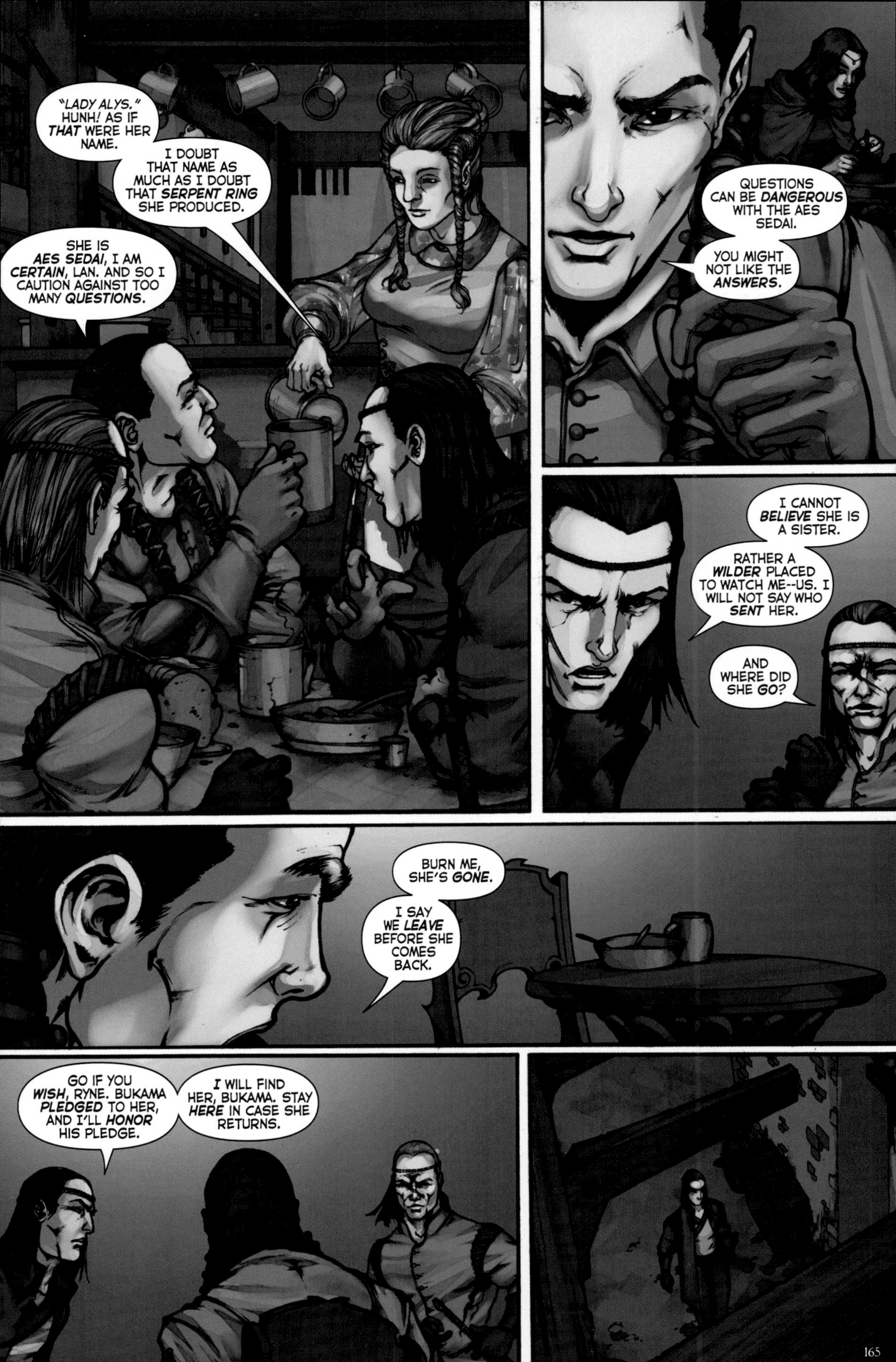
"LADY ALYS." HUNH! AS IF THAT WERE HER NAME.
I DOUBT THAT NAME AS MUCH AS I DOUBT THAT SERPENT RING SHE PRODUCED.
SHE IS AES SEDAI, I AM CERTAIN, LAN. AND SO I CAUTION AGAINST TOO MANY QUESTIONS.
QUESTIONS CAN BE DANGEROUS WITH THE AES SEDAI.
YOU MIGHT NOT LIKE THE ANSWERS.
I CANNOT BELIEVE SHE IS A SISTER.
RATHER A WILDER PLACED TO WATCH ME--US. I WILL NOT SAY WHO SENT HER.
AND WHERE DID SHE GO?
BURN ME, SHE'S GONE.
I SAY WE LEAVE BEFORE SHE COMES BACK.
GO IF YOU WISH, RYNE. BUKAMA PLEDGED TO HER, AND I'LL HONOR HIS PLEDGE.
I WILL FIND HER, BUKAMA. STAY HERE IN CASE SHE RETURNS.

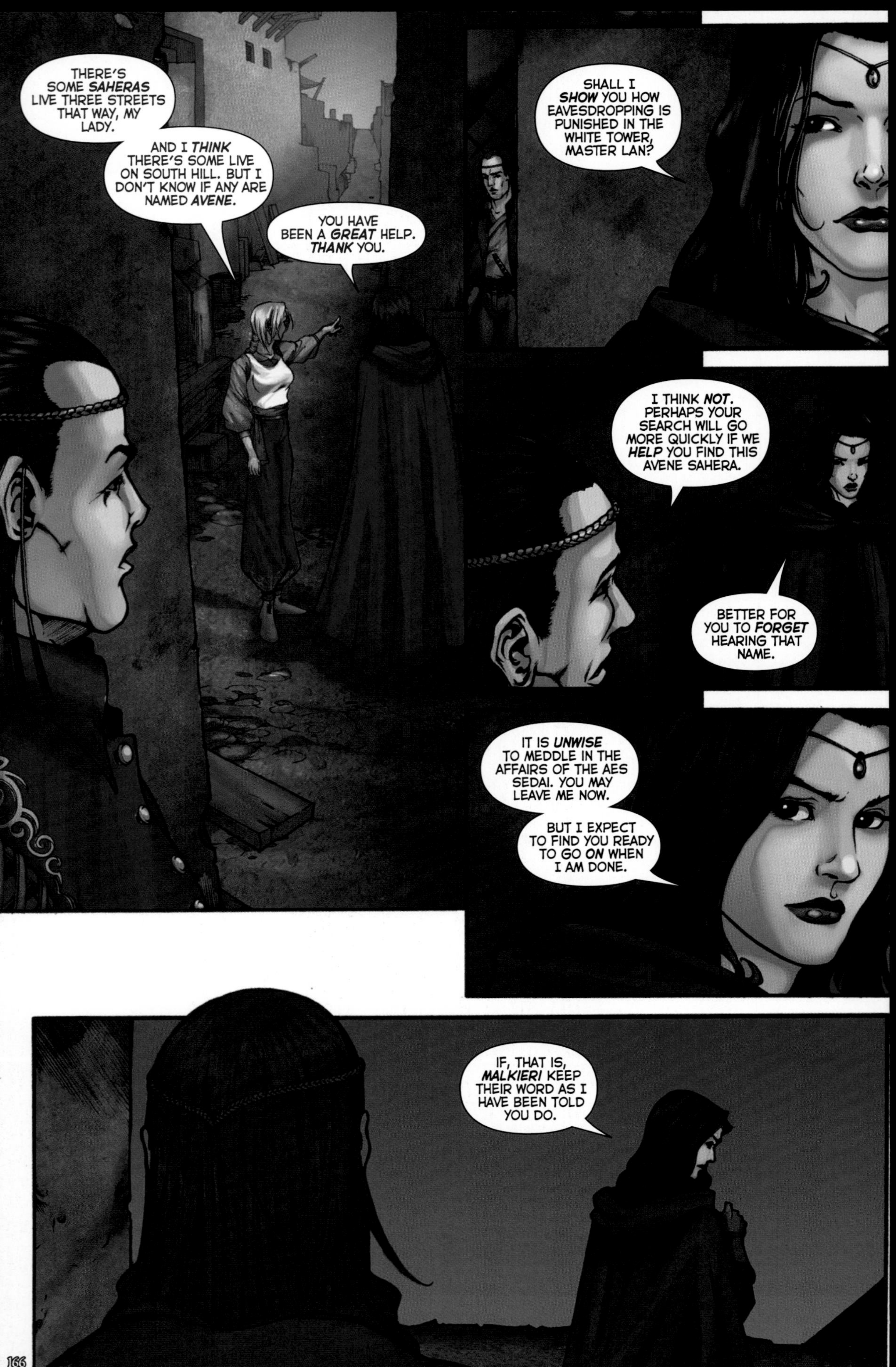
THERE'S SOME SAHERAS LIVE THREE STREETS THAT WAY, MY LADY.
AND I THINK THERE'S SOME LIVE ON SOUTH HILL. BUT I DON'T KNOW IF ANY ARE NAMED AVENE.
YOU HAVE BEEN A GREAT HELP. THANK YOU.
SHALL I SHOW YOU HOW EAVESDROPPING IS PUNISHED IN THE WHITE TOWER, MASTER LAN?
I THINK NOT. PERHAPS YOUR SEARCH WILL GO MORE QUICKLY IF WE HELP YOU FIND THIS AVENE SAHERA.
BETTER FOR YOU TO FORGET HEARING THAT NAME.
IT IS UNWISE TO MEDDLE IN THE AFFAIRS OF THE AES SEDAI. YOU MAY LEAVE ME NOW.
BUT I EXPECT TO FIND YOU READY TO GO ON WHEN I AM DONE.
IF, THAT IS, MALKIERI KEEP THEIR WORD AS I HAVE BEEN TOLD YOU DO.

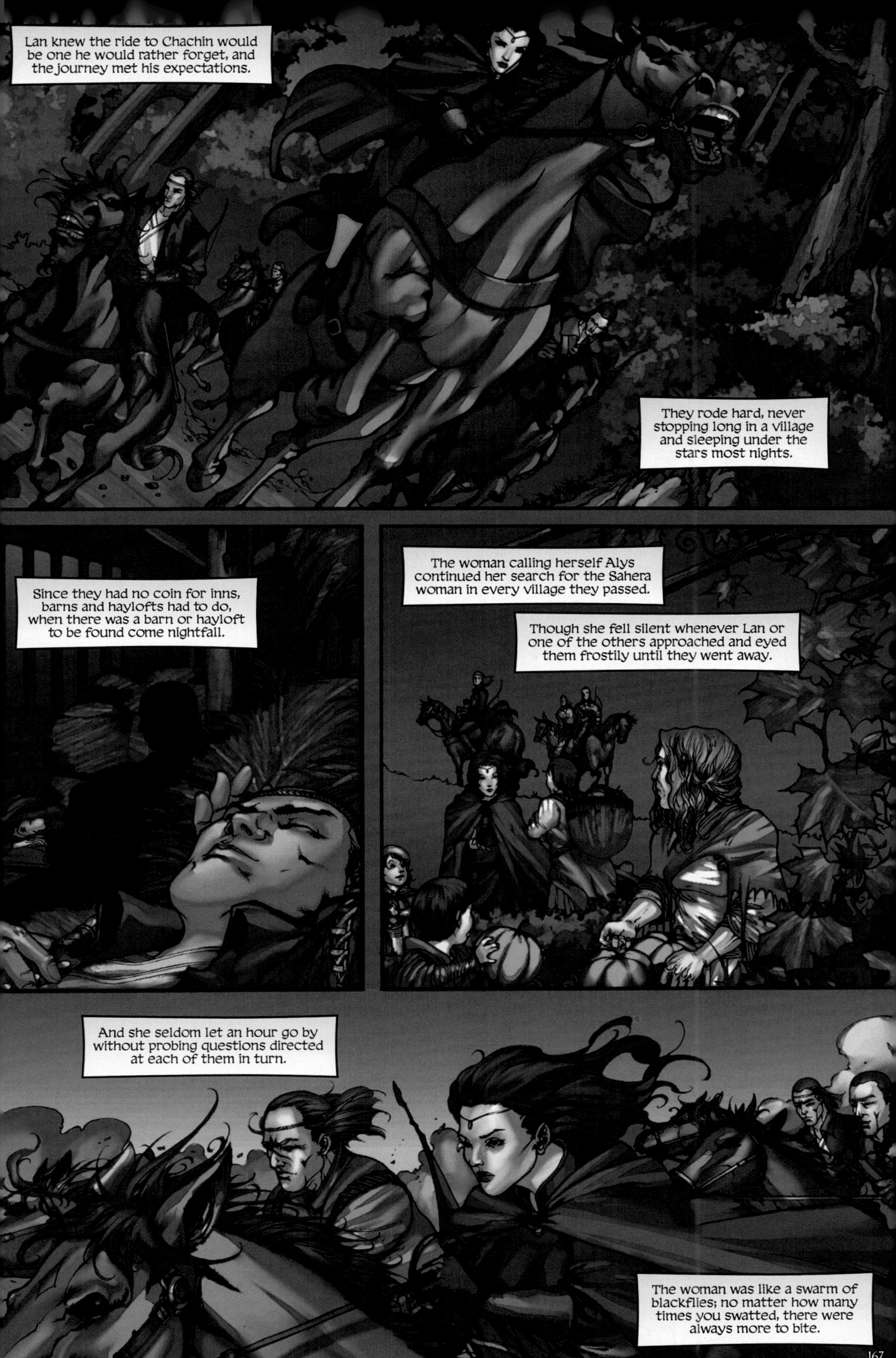
Lan knew the ride to Chachin would be one he would rather forget, and the journey met his expectations.
They rode hard, never stopping long in a village and sleeping under the stars most nights.
Since they had no coin for inns, barns and haylofts had to do, when there was a barn or hayloft to be found come nightfall.
The woman calling herself Alys continued her search for the Sahera woman in every village they passed.
Though she fell silent whenever Lan or one of the others approached and eyed them frostily until they went away.
And she seldom let an hour go by without probing questions directed at each of them in turn.
The woman was like a swarm of blackflies; no matter how many times you swatted, there were always more to bite.

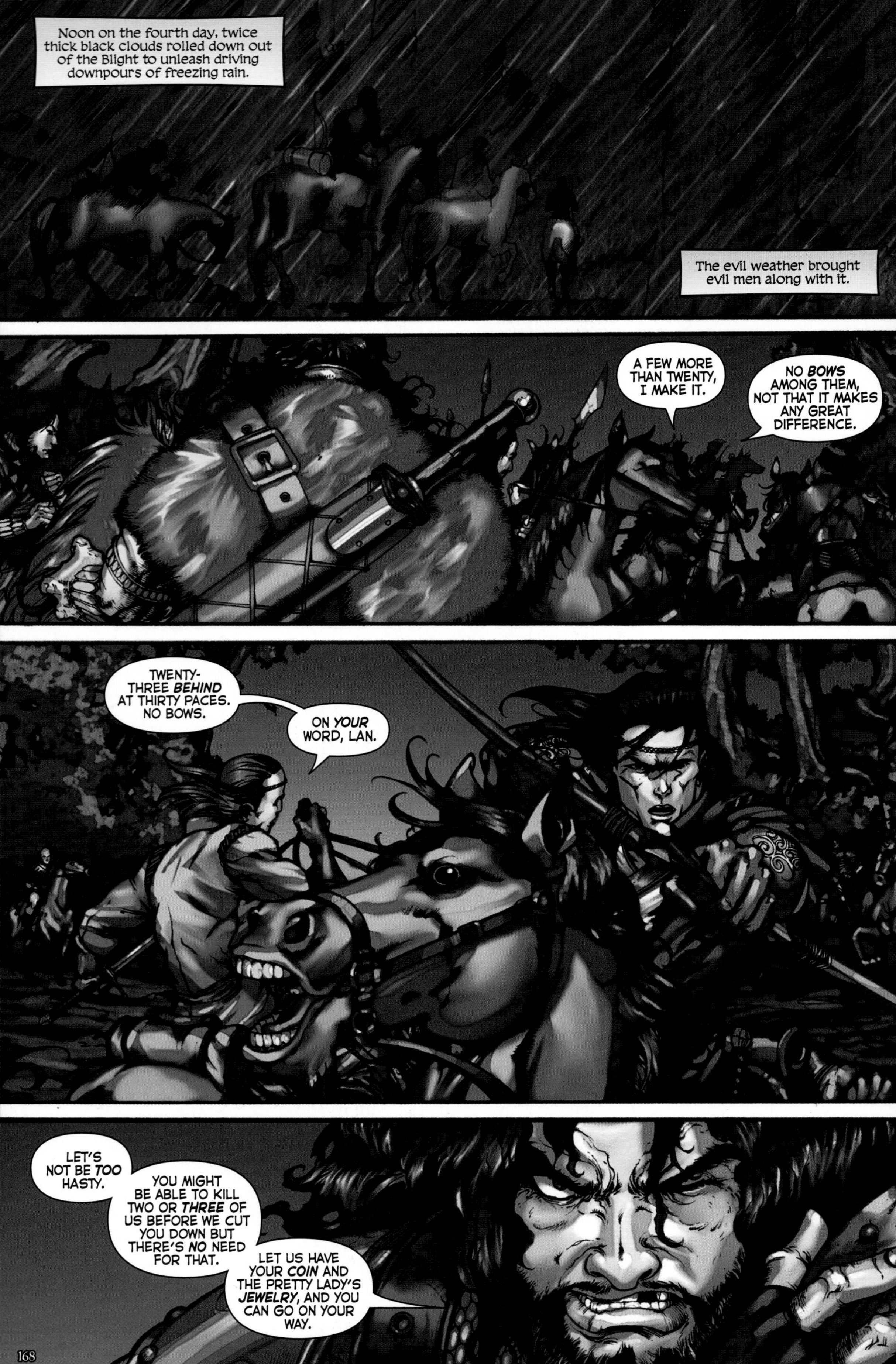
Noon on the fourth day, twice thick black clouds rolled down out of the Blight to unleash driving downpours of freezing rain.
The evil weather brought evil men along with it.
A FEW MORE THAN TWENTY, I MAKE IT.
NO BOWS AMONG THEM, NOT THAT IT MAKES ANY GREAT DIFFERENCE.
TWENTY-THREE BEHIND AT THIRTY PACES. NO BOWS.
ON YOUR WORD, LAN.
LET'S NOT BE TOO HASTY.
YOU MIGHT BE ABLE TO KILL TWO OR THREE OF US BEFORE WE CUT YOU DOWN BUT THERE'S NO NEED FOR THAT.
LET US HAVE YOUR COIN AND THE PRETTY LADY'S JEWELRY, AND YOU CAN GO ON YOUR WAY.

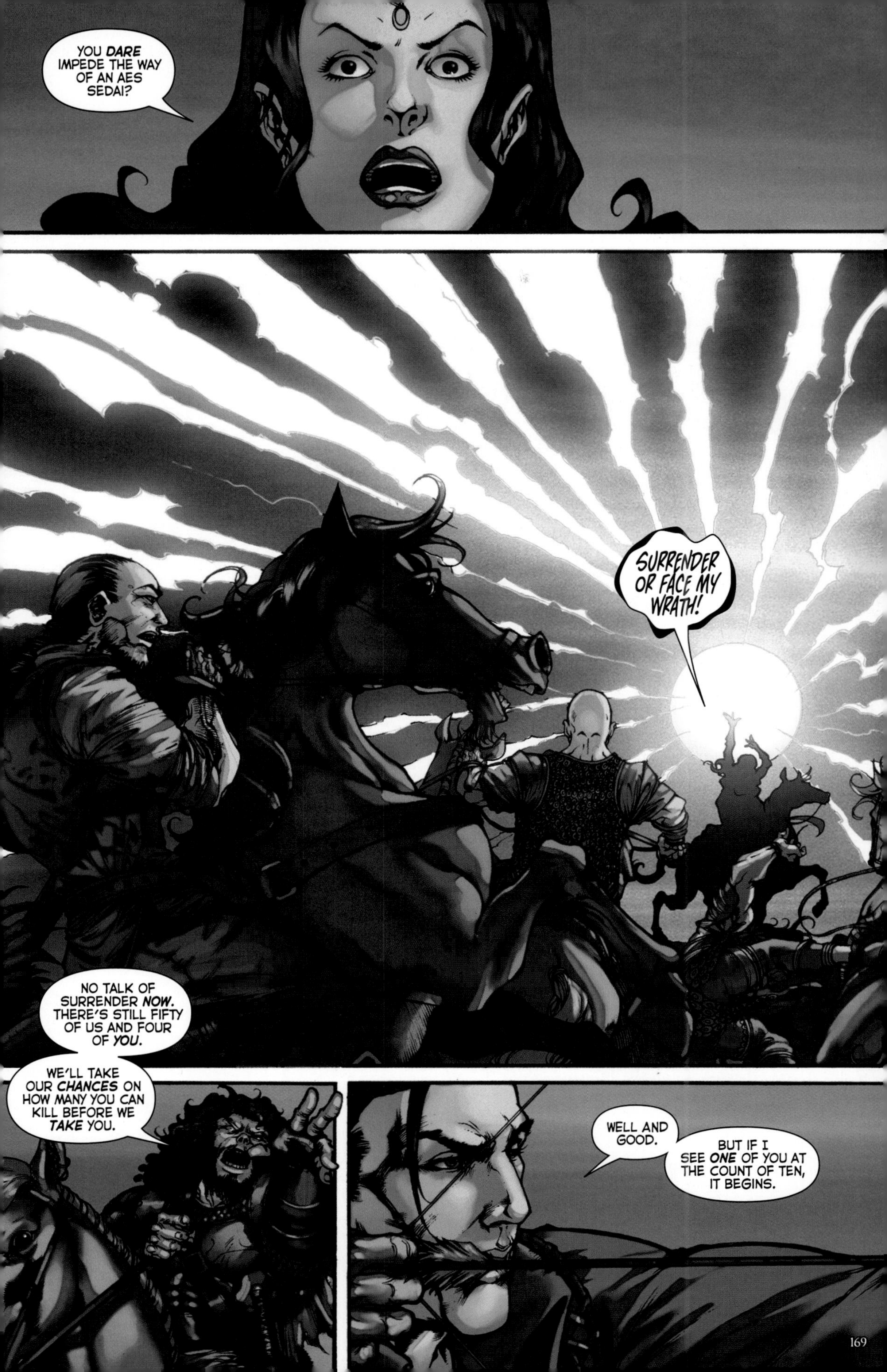
YOU DARE IMPEDE THE WAY OF AN AES SEDAI?
SURRENDER OR FACE MY WRATH!
NO TALK OF SURRENDER NOW. THERE'S STILL FIFTY OF US AND FOUR OF YOU.
WE'LL TAKE OUR CHANCES ON HOW MANY YOU CAN KILL BEFORE WE TAKE YOU.
WELL AND GOOD.
BUT IF I SEE ONE OF YOU AT THE COUNT OF TEN, IT BEGINS.

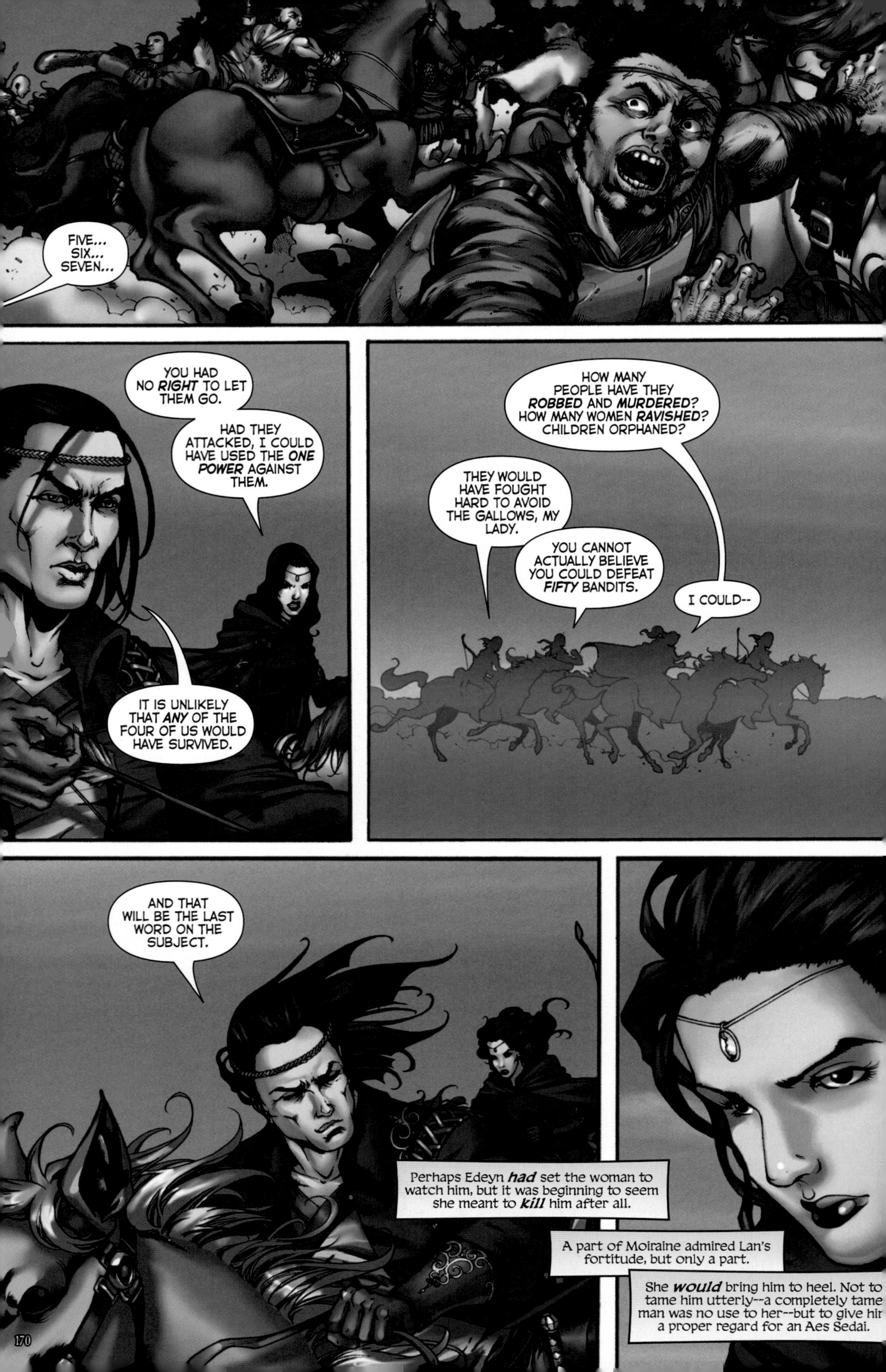
FIVE... SIX... SEVEN...
YOU HAD NO RIGHT TO LET THEM GO.
HAD THEY ATTACKED, I COULD HAVE USED THE ONE POWER AGAINST THEM.
IT IS UNLIKELY THAT ANY OF THE FOUR OF US WOULD HAVE SURVIVED.
HOW MANY PEOPLE HAVE THEY ROBBED AND MURDERED? HOW MANY WOMEN RAVISHED? CHILDREN ORPHANED?
THEY WOULD HAVE FOUGHT HARD TO AVOID THE GALLOWS, MY LADY.
YOU CANNOT ACTUALLY BELIEVE YOU COULD DEFEAT FIFTY BANDITS.
I COULD--
AND THAT WILL BE THE LAST WORD ON THE SUBJECT.
Perhaps Edeyn had set the woman to watch him, but it was beginning to seem she meant to kill him after all.
A part of Moiraine admired Lan's fortitude, but only a part.
She would bring him to heel. Not to tame him utterly--a completely tame man was no use to her--but to give hir a proper regard for an Aes Sedai.

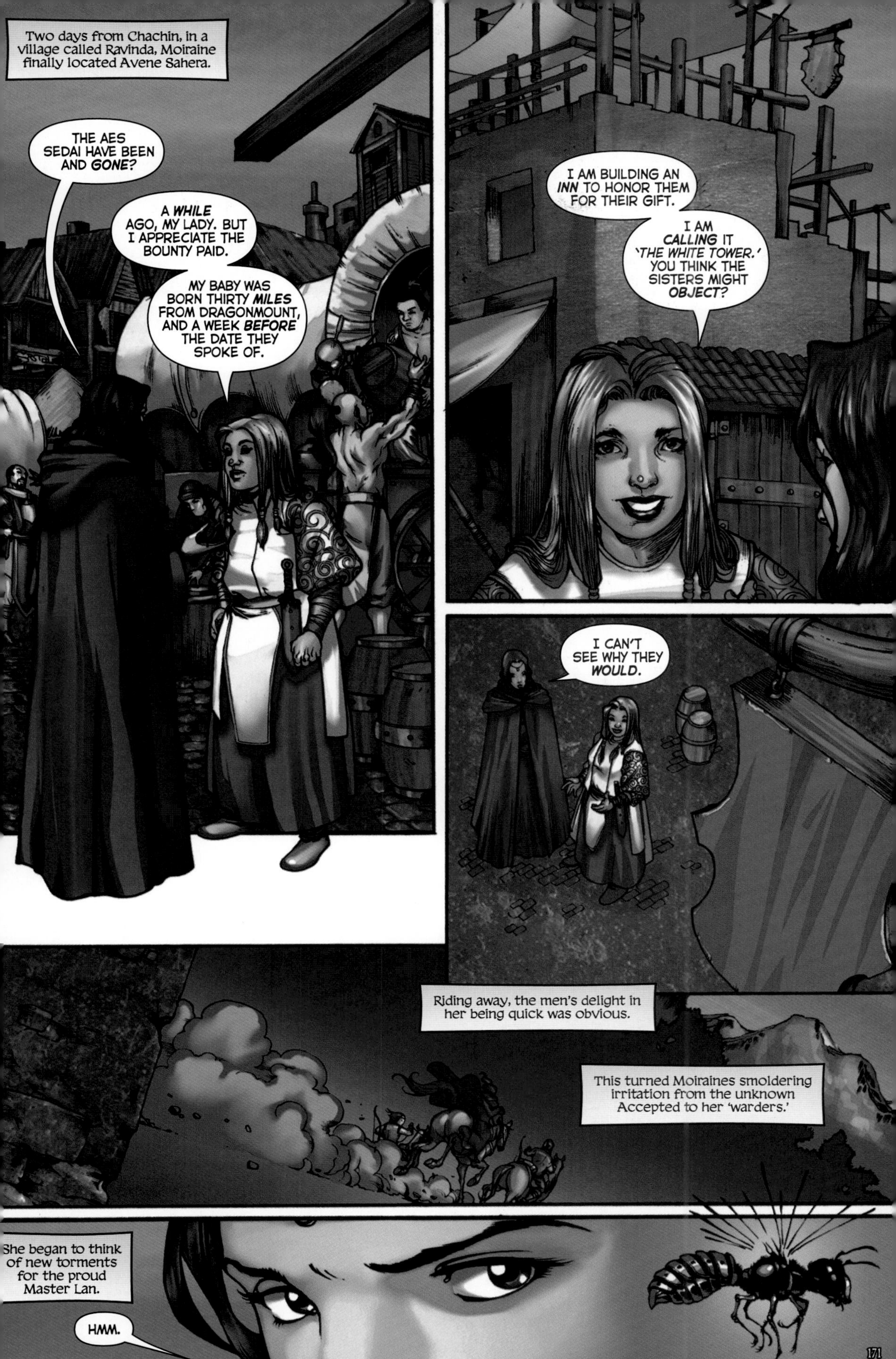
Two days from Chachin, in a village called Ravinda, Moiraine finally located Avene Sahera.
THE AES SEDAI HAVE BEEN AND GONE?
A WHILE AGO, MY LADY. BUT I APPRECIATE THE BOUNTY PAID.
MY BABY WAS BORN THIRTY MILES FROM DRAGONMOUNT, AND A WEEK BEFORE THE DATE THEY SPOKE OF.
I AM BUILDING AN INN TO HONOR THEM FOR THEIR GIFT.
I AM CALLING IT 'THE WHITE TOWER.' YOU THINK THE SISTERS MIGHT OBJECT?
I CAN'T SEE WHY THEY WOULD.
Riding away, the men's delight in her being quick was obvious.
This turned Moiraines smoldering irritation from the unknown Accepted to her 'warders.'
She began to think of new torments for the proud Master Lan.
HMM.

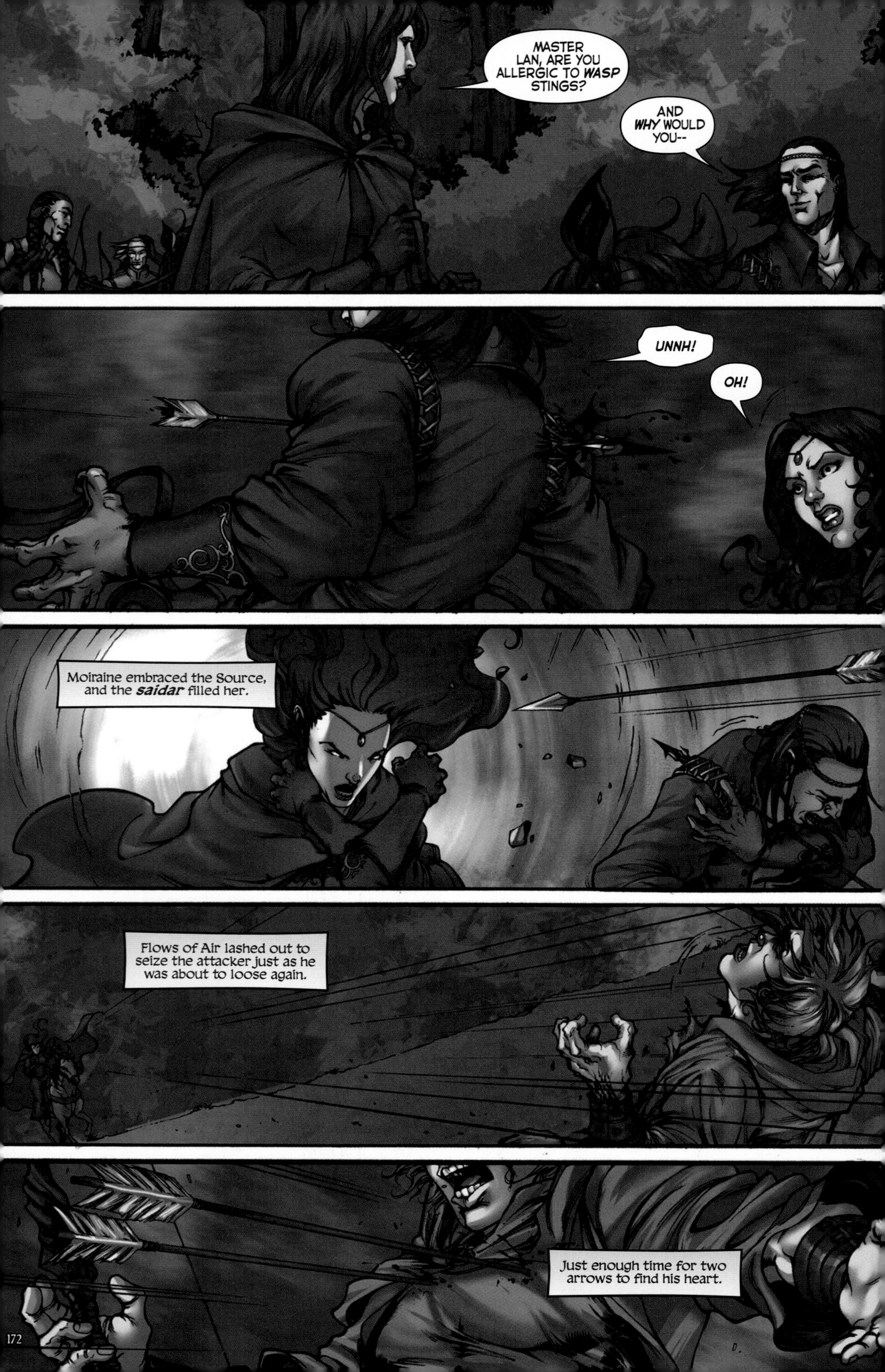
MASTER LAN, ARE YOU ALLERGIC TO WASP STINGS?
AND WHY WOULD YOU--
UNNH!
OH!
Moiraine embraced the Source, and the saidar filled her.
Flows of Air lashed out to seize the attacker just as he was about to loose again.
Just enough time for two arrows to find his heart.

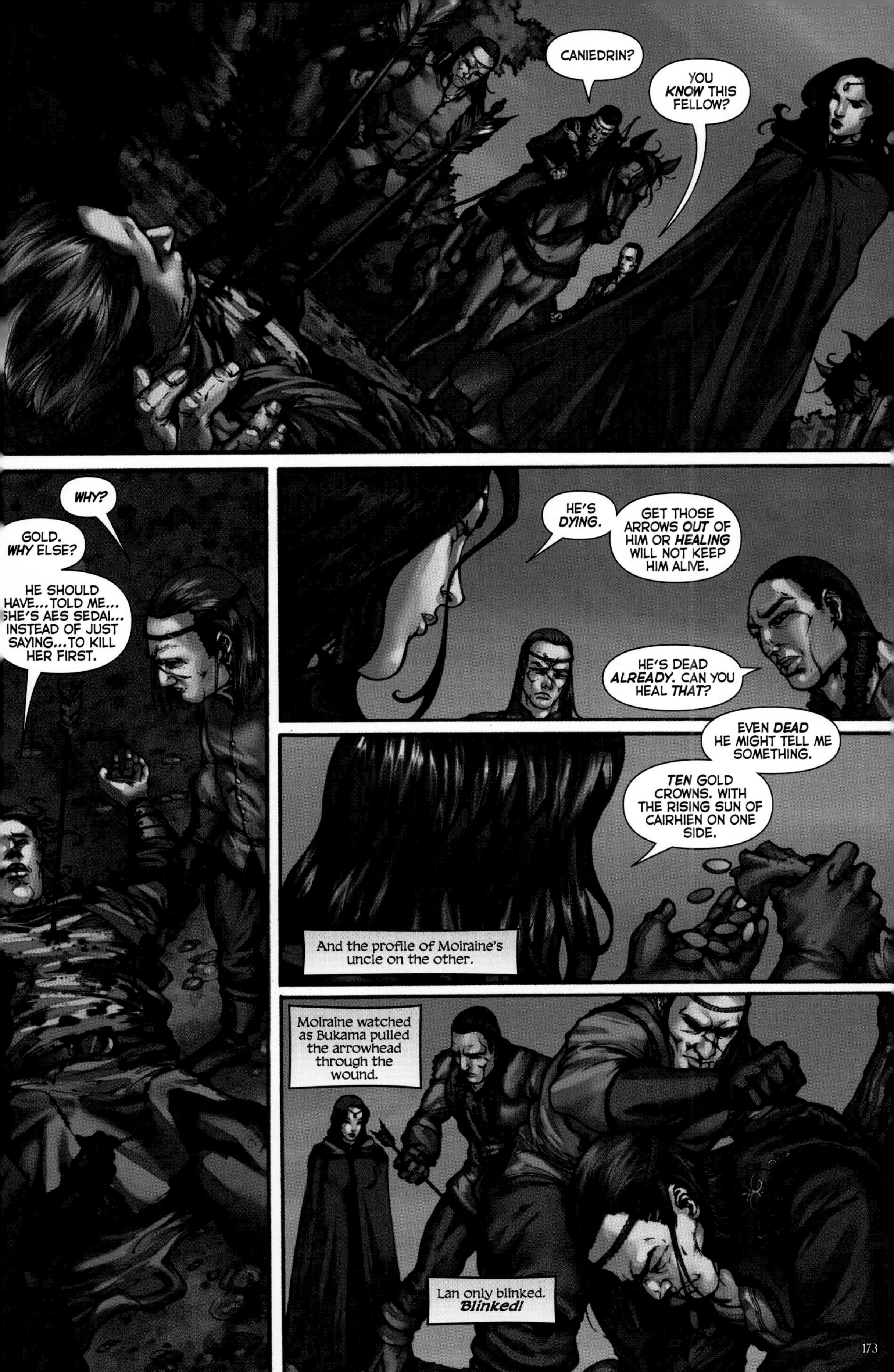
CANIEDRIN?
YOU KNOW THIS FELLOW?
WHY?
GOLD. WHY ELSE?
HE SHOULD HAVE...TOLD ME... SHE'S AES SEDAI... INSTEAD OF JUST SAYING...TO KILL HER FIRST.
HE'S DYING.
GET THOSE ARROWS OUT OF HIM OR HEALING WILL NOT KEEP HIM ALIVE.
HE'S DEAD ALREADY. CAN YOU HEAL THAT?
EVEN DEAD HE MIGHT TELL ME SOMETHING.
TEN GOLD CROWNS. WITH THE RISING SUN OF CAIRHIEN ON ONE SIDE.
And the profile of Moiraine's uncle on the other.
Moiraine watched as Bukama pulled the arrowhead through the wound.
Lan only blinked. Blinked!

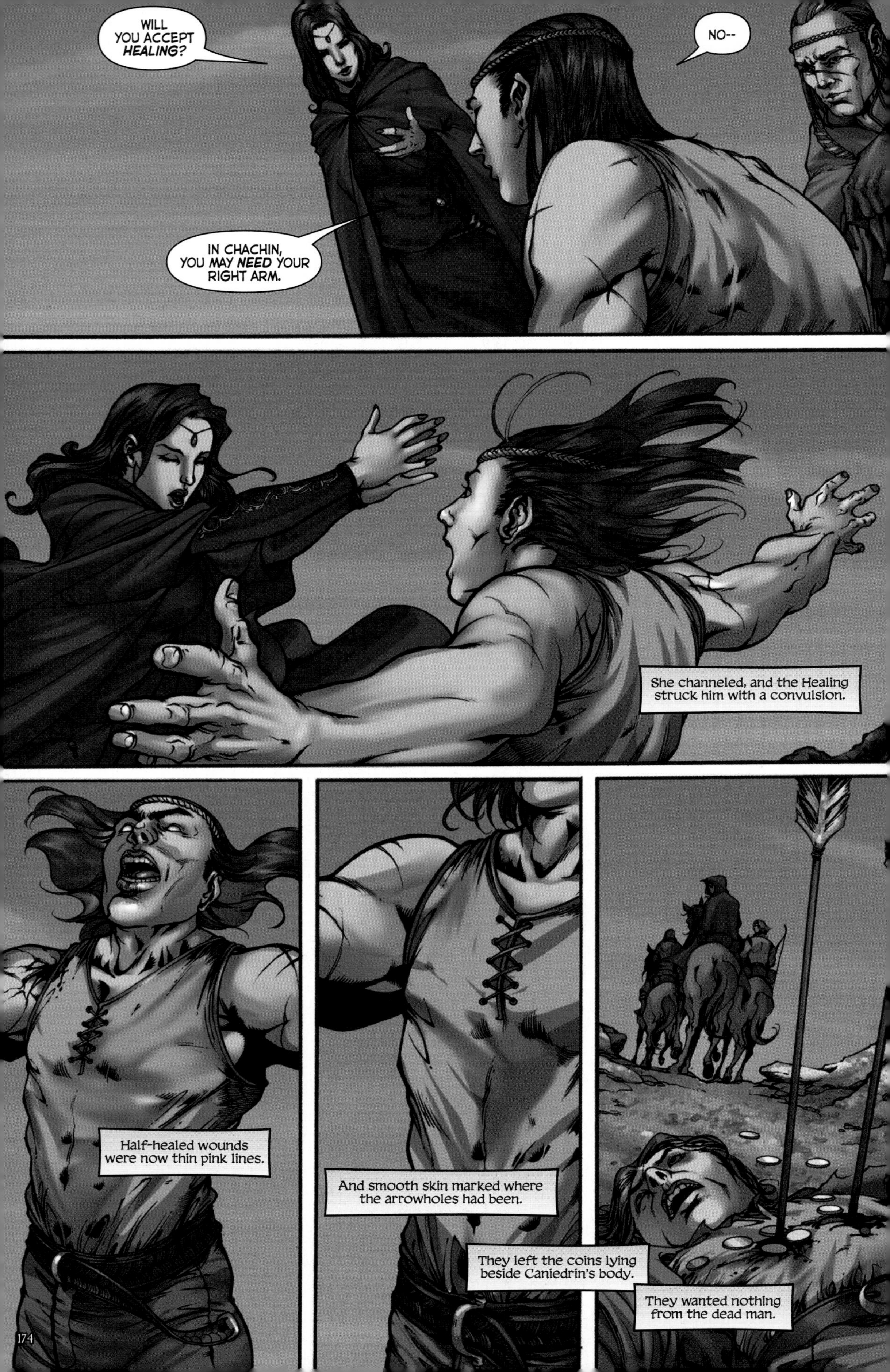
WILL YOU ACCEPT *HEALING?*
NO--
IN CHACHIN, YOU MAY ***NEED*** YOUR RIGHT ARM.
She channeled, and the Healing struck him with a convulsion.
Half-healed wounds were now thin pink lines.
And smooth skin marked where the arrowholes had been.
They left the coins lying beside Caniedrin's body.
They wanted nothing from the dead man.

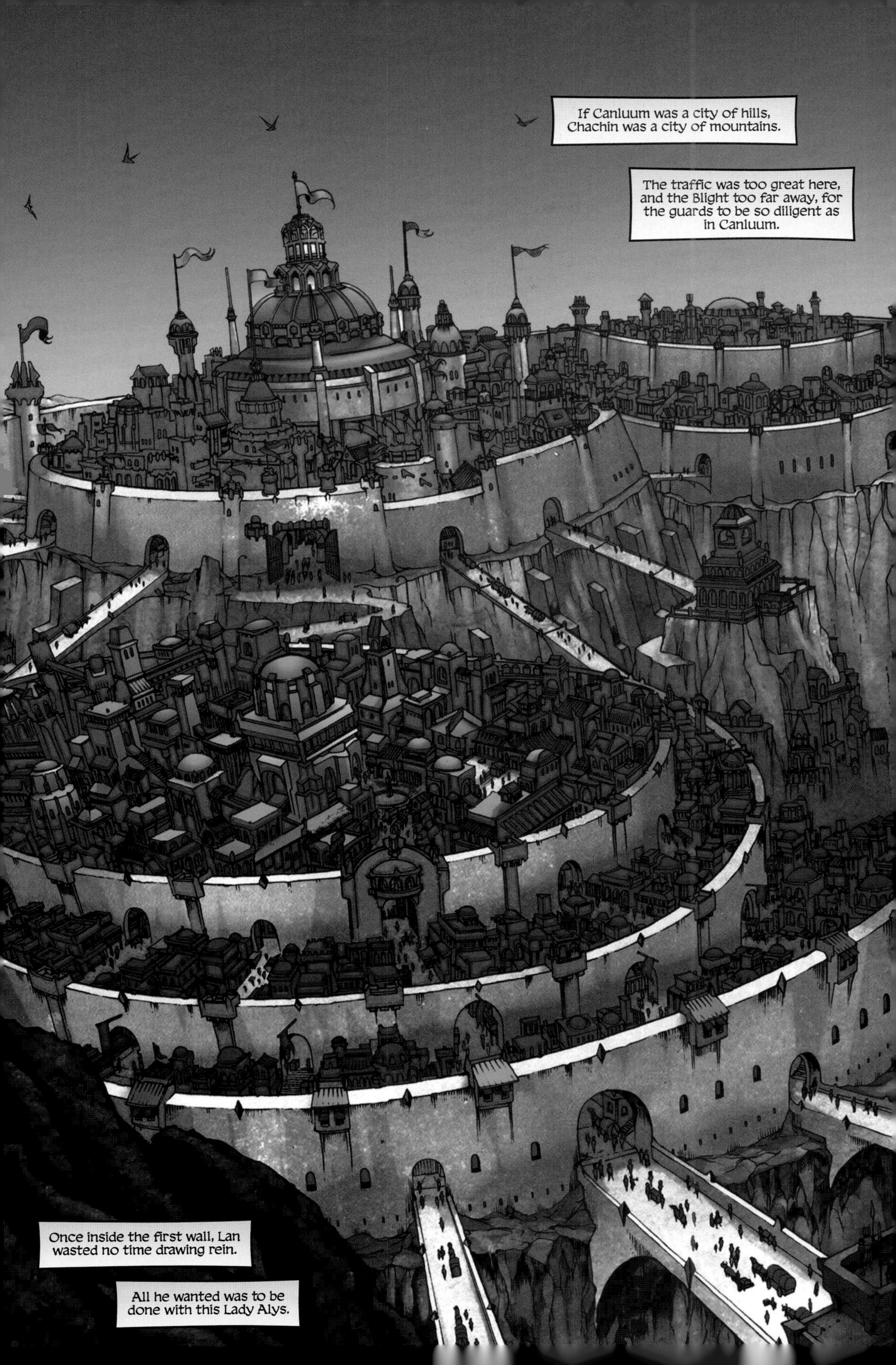
If Canluum was a city of hills, Chachin was a city of mountains.
The traffic was too great here, and the Blight too far away, for the guards to be so diligent as in Canluum.
Once inside the first wall, Lan wasted no time drawing rein.
All he wanted was to be done with this Lady Alys.

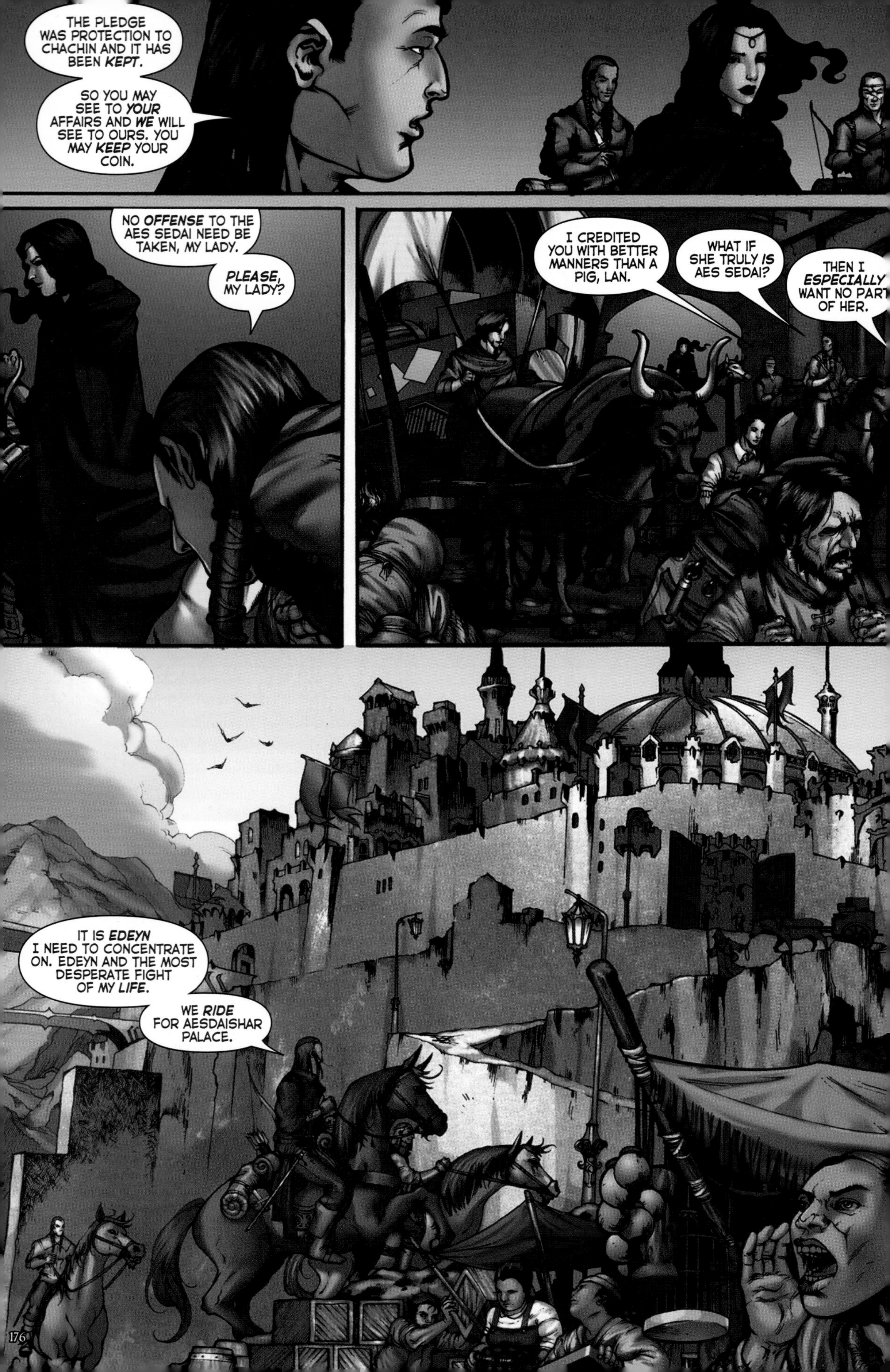
THE PLEDGE WAS PROTECTION TO CHACHIN AND IT HAS BEEN *KEPT.*
SO YOU MAY SEE TO *YOUR* AFFAIRS AND *WE* WILL SEE TO OURS. YOU MAY *KEEP* YOUR COIN.
NO *OFFENSE* TO THE AES SEDAI NEED BE TAKEN, MY LADY.
PLEASE, MY LADY?
I CREDITED YOU WITH BETTER MANNERS THAN A PIG, LAN.
WHAT IF SHE TRULY *IS* AES SEDAI?
THEN I *ESPECIALLY* WANT NO PART OF HER.
IT IS *EDEYN* I NEED TO CONCENTRATE ON. EDEYN AND THE MOST DESPERATE FIGHT OF MY *LIFE.*
WE *RIDE* FOR AESDAISHAR PALACE.

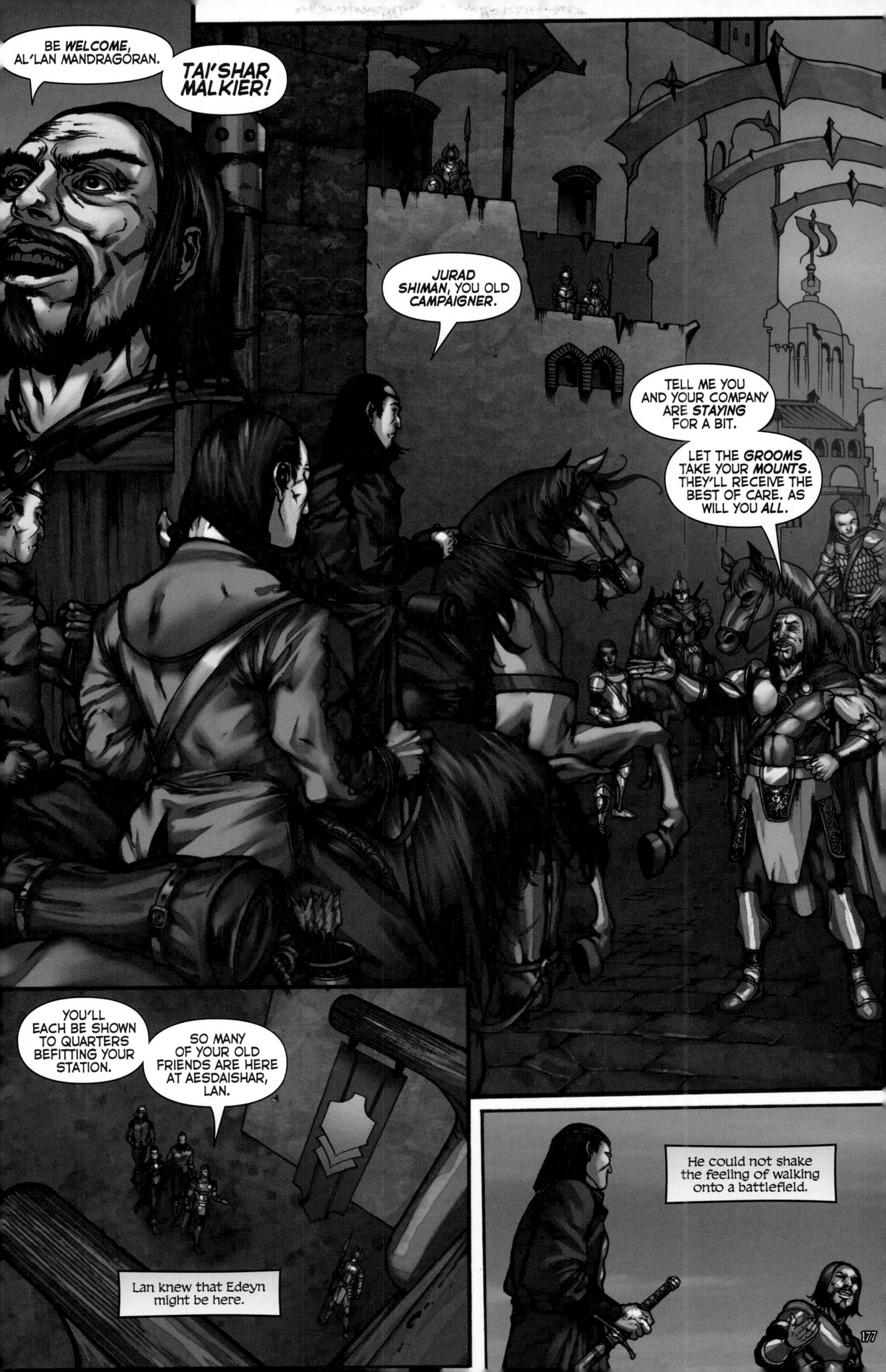

BE WELCOME, AL'LAN MANDRAGORAN.
TAI'SHAR MALKIER!
JURAD SHIMAN, YOU OLD CAMPAIGNER.
TELL ME YOU AND YOUR COMPANY ARE STAYING FOR A BIT.
LET THE GROOMS TAKE YOUR MOUNTS. THEY'LL RECEIVE THE BEST OF CARE. AS WILL YOU ALL.
YOU'LL EACH BE SHOWN TO QUARTERS BEFITTING YOUR STATION.
SO MANY OF YOUR OLD FRIENDS ARE HERE AT AESDAISHAR, LAN.
Lan knew that Edeyn might be here.
He could not shake the feeling of walking onto a battlefield.

Bukama settled in happily—well, happily for him—pleased to be assigned to a barracks with many of his old fighting comrades.

...room, a room all to himself, with a tiled stove built beneath the overstuffed bed.

To Lan's great relief, he was not given a visiting king's apartments.

It was all entirely suitable to his station.

THANK YOU, MISTRESS ROMERA, FOR LOOKING AFTER MYSELF AND MY MEN SO **GRACIOUSLY.**

YOU FAVOR ME TOO **MUCH,** MY LORD.

IT IS MY DUTY AND PLEASURE TO **SEE** TO YOUR NEEDS.

ANYA AND **ESNE** WILL TAKE CARE OF YOUR CLEANING AND SUCH TIDYING AS YOU NEED.

YOUNG **BULEN** WILL RUN ANY **ERRANDS** YOU WISH PERFORMED.

I TAKE MY **LEAVE,** WITH YOUR PERMISSION, MY LORD.

I HOPE YOU **ENJOY** YOUR TIME IN CHACHIN.

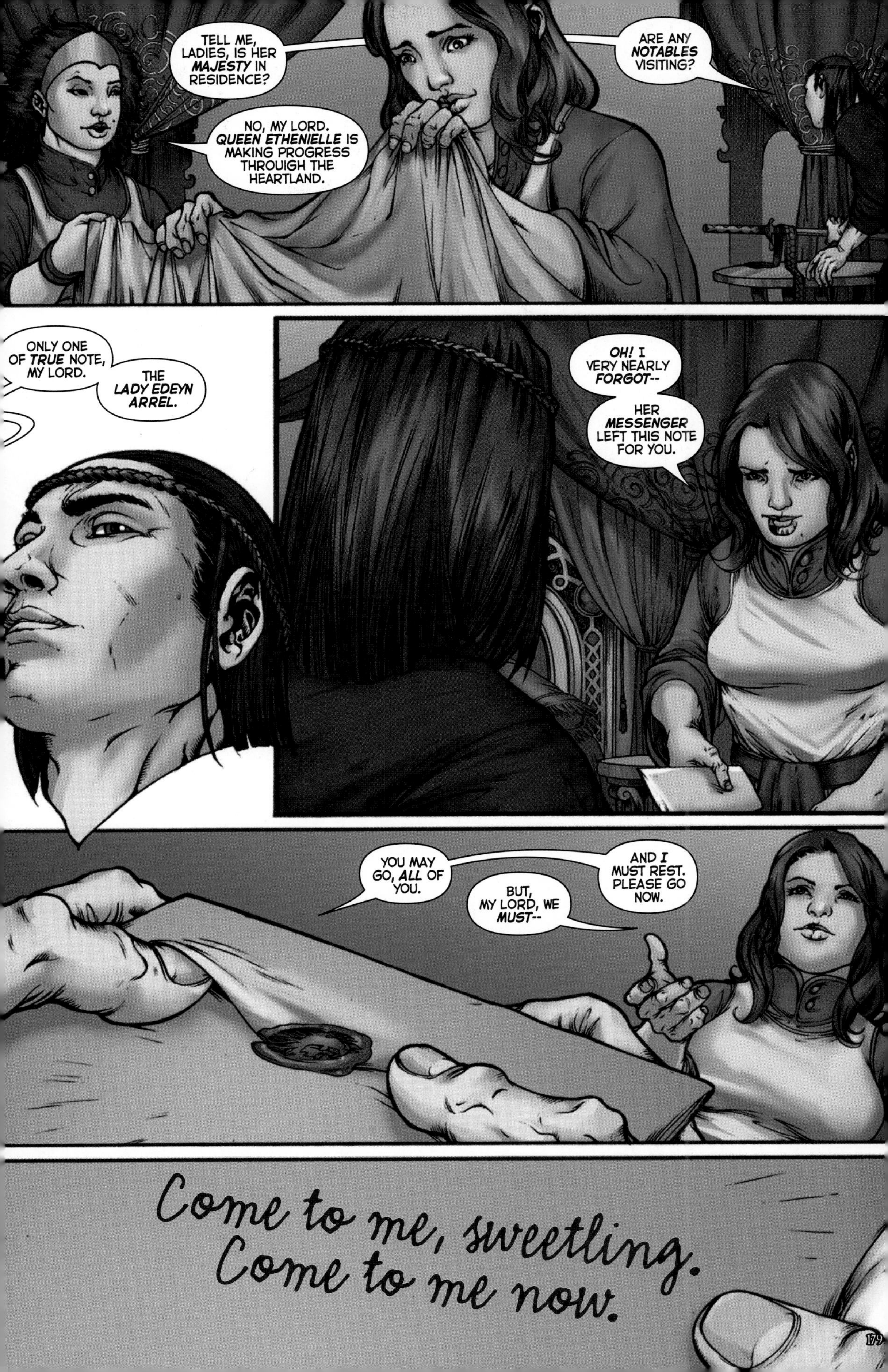
TELL ME, LADIES, IS HER MAJESTY IN RESIDENCE?
NO, MY LORD. QUEEN ETHENIELLE IS MAKING PROGRESS THROUGH THE HEARTLAND.
ARE ANY NOTABLES VISITING?
ONLY ONE OF TRUE NOTE, MY LORD.
THE LADY EDEYN ARREL.
OH! I VERY NEARLY FORGOT--
HER MESSENGER LEFT THIS NOTE FOR YOU.
YOU MAY GO, ALL OF YOU.
AND I MUST REST. PLEASE GO NOW.
BUT, MY LORD, WE MUST--
Come to me, sweetling. Come to me now.

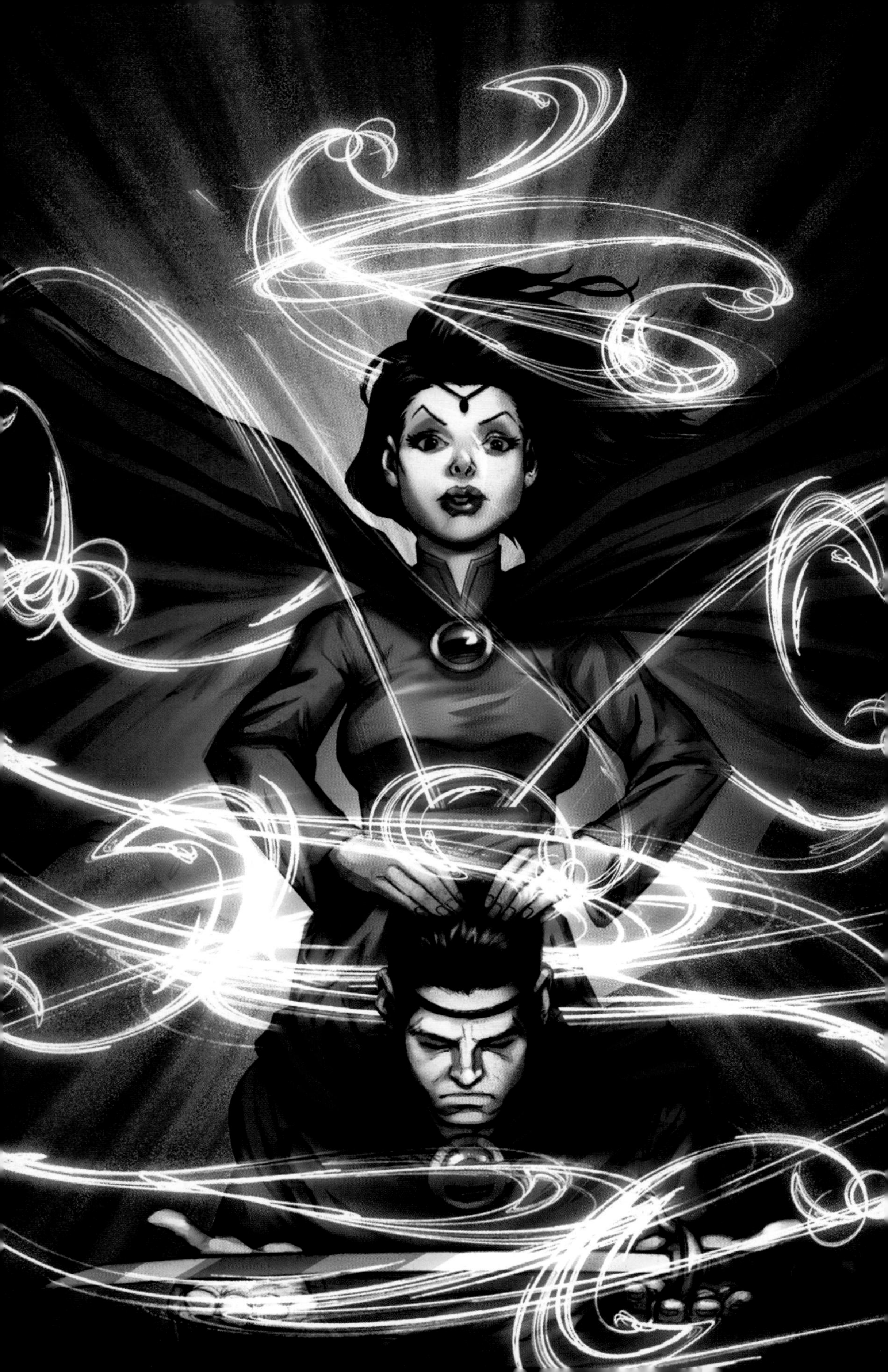

chapter eight

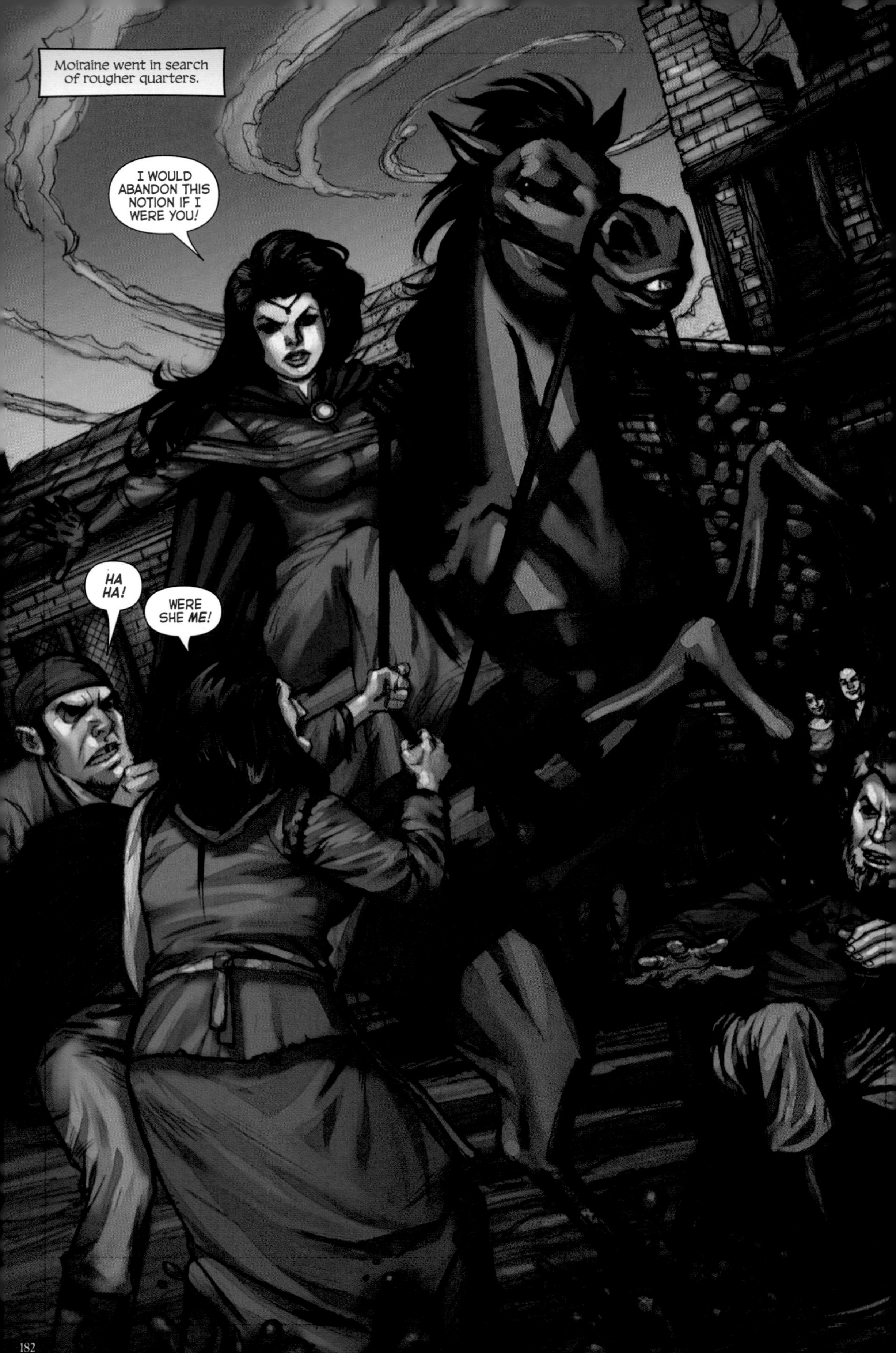
Moiraine went in search of rougher quarters.
I WOULD ABANDON THIS NOTION IF I WERE YOU!
HA HA!
WERE SHE ME!

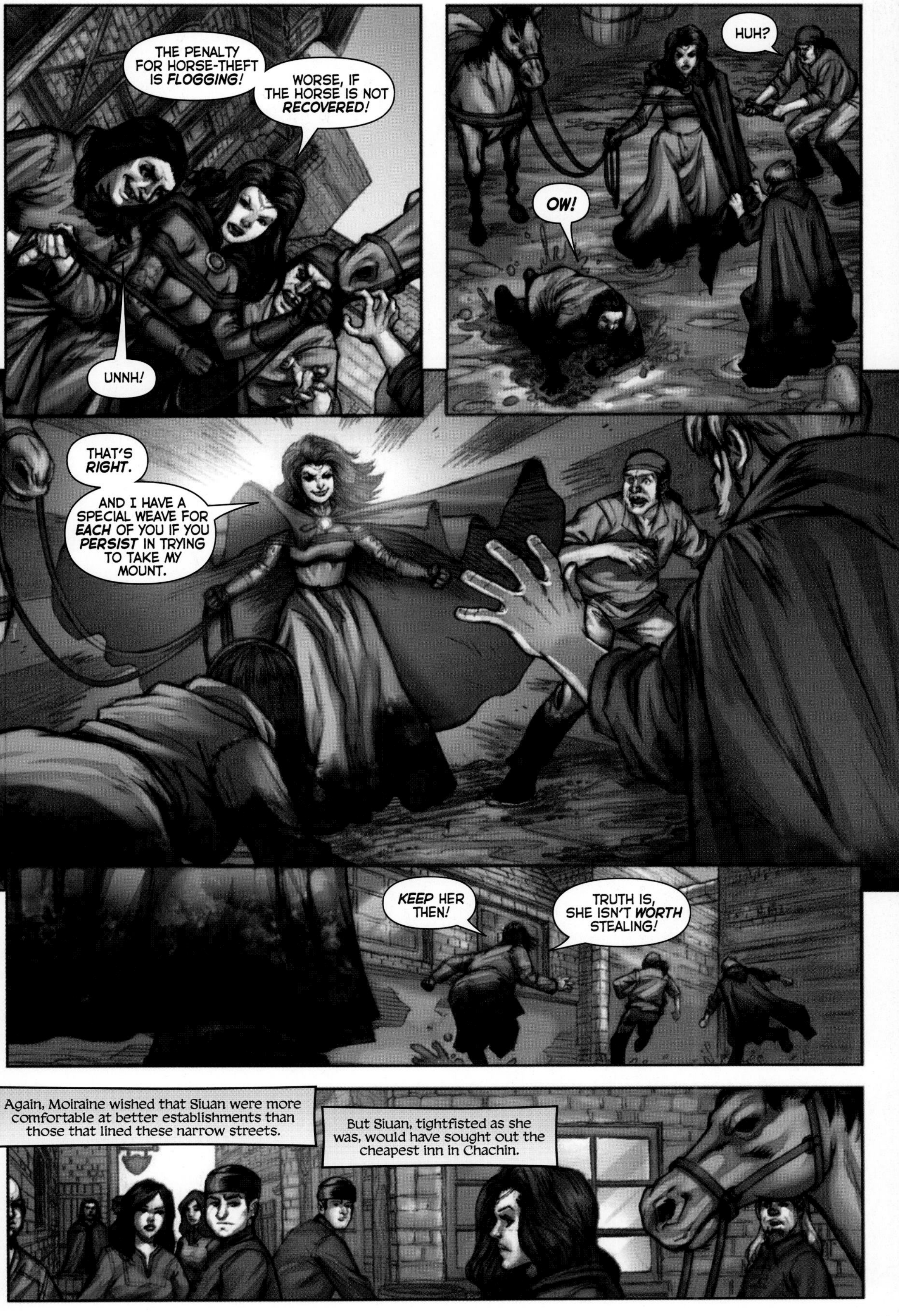
THE PENALTY FOR HORSE-THEFT IS FLOGGING!
WORSE, IF THE HORSE IS NOT RECOVERED!
UNNH!
HUH?
OW!
THAT'S RIGHT.
AND I HAVE A SPECIAL WEAVE FOR EACH OF YOU IF YOU PERSIST IN TRYING TO TAKE MY MOUNT.
KEEP HER THEN!
TRUTH IS, SHE ISN'T WORTH STEALING!
Again, Moiraine wished that Siuan were more comfortable at better establishments than those that lined these narrow streets.
But Siuan, tightfisted as she was, would have sought out the cheapest inn in Chachin.

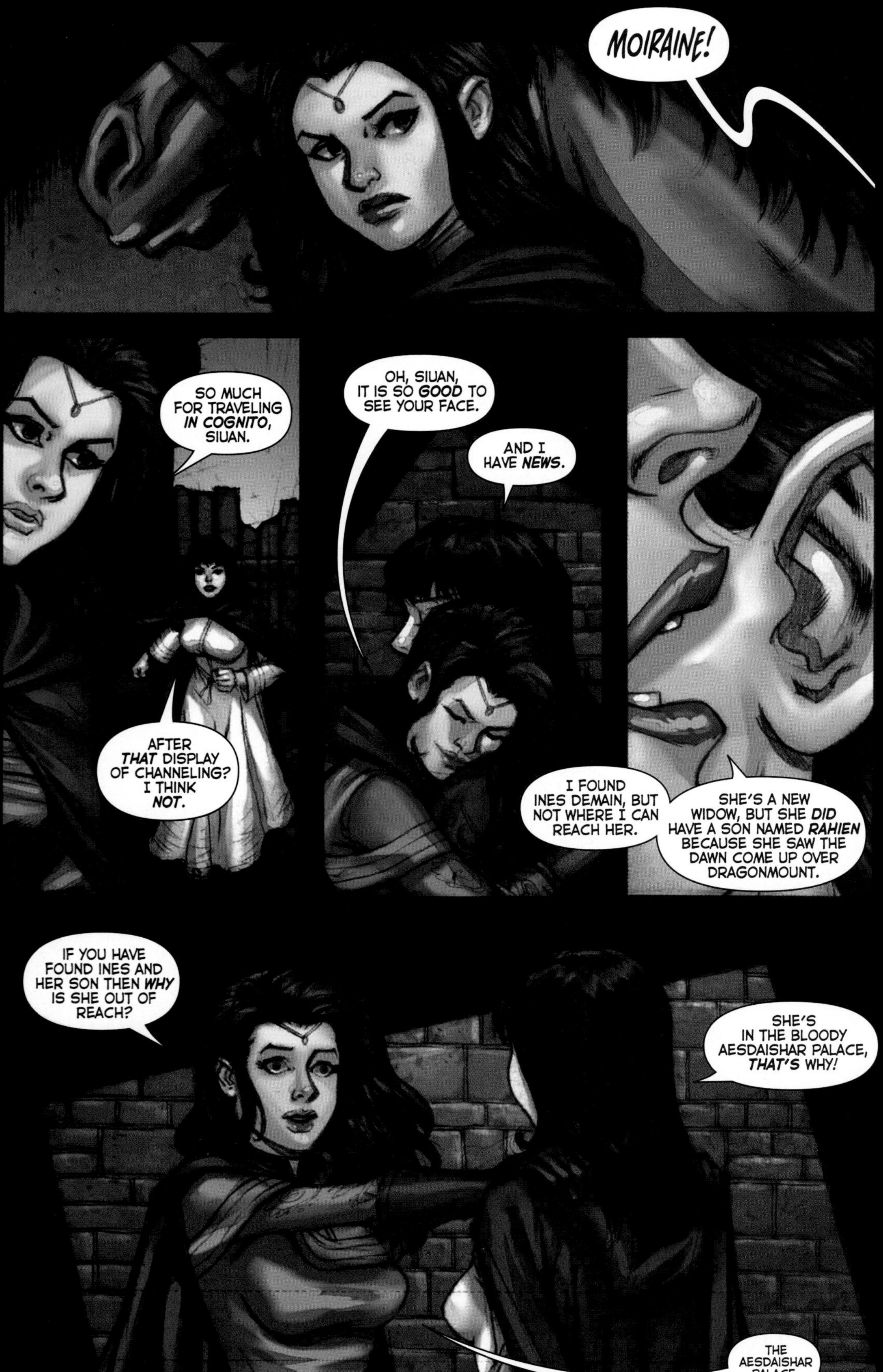
MOIRAINE!
SO MUCH FOR TRAVELING IN COGNITO, SIUAN.
AFTER THAT DISPLAY OF CHANNELING? I THINK NOT.
OH, SIUAN, IT IS SO GOOD TO SEE YOUR FACE.
AND I HAVE NEWS.
I FOUND INES DEMAIN, BUT NOT WHERE I CAN REACH HER.
SHE'S A NEW WIDOW, BUT SHE DID HAVE A SON NAMED RAHIEN BECAUSE SHE SAW THE DAWN COME UP OVER DRAGONMOUNT.
IF YOU HAVE FOUND INES AND HER SON THEN WHY IS SHE OUT OF REACH?
SHE'S IN THE BLOODY AESDAISHAR PALACE, THAT'S WHY!
THE AESDAISHAR PALACE.

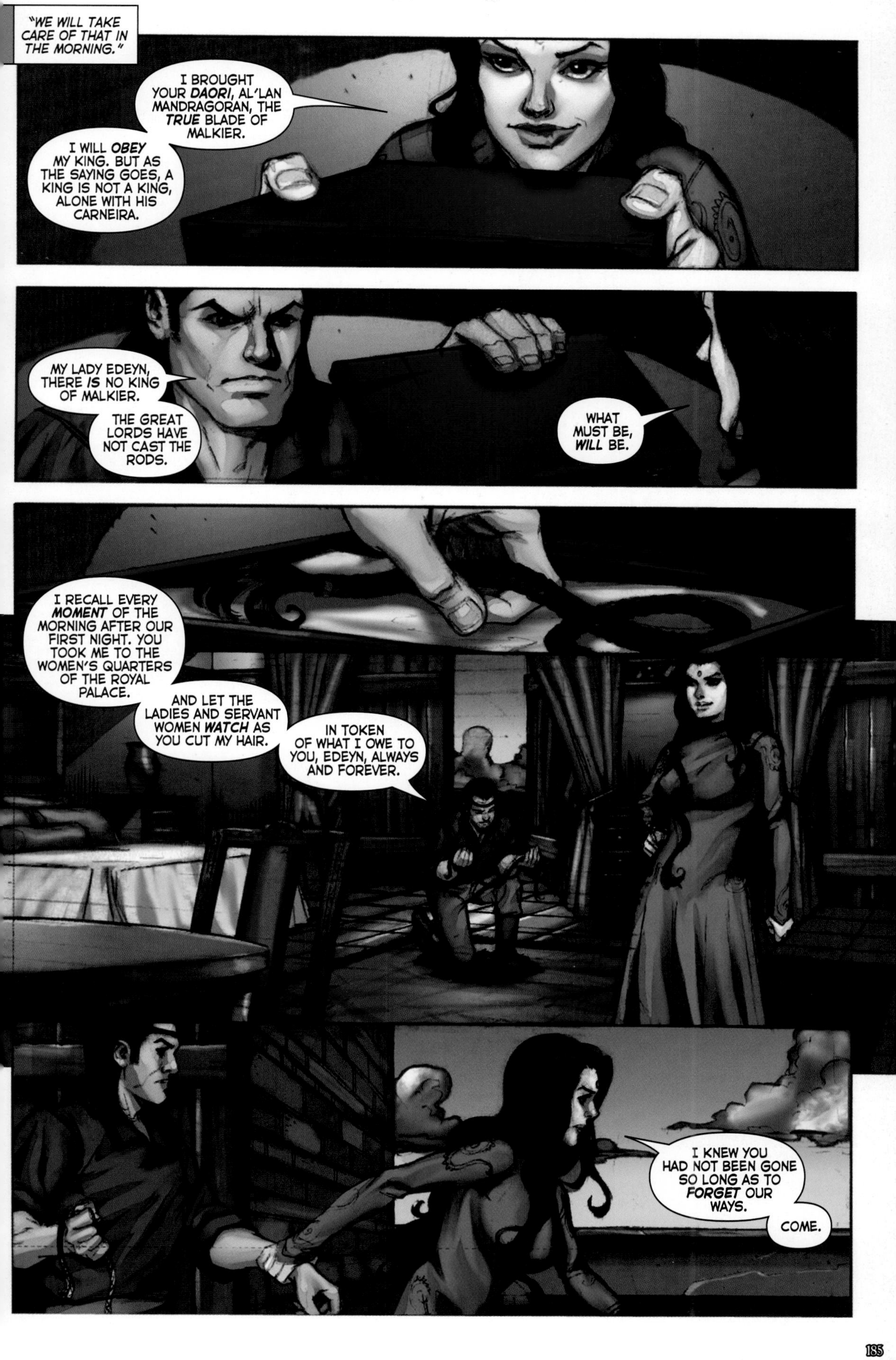
"WE WILL TAKE CARE OF THAT IN THE MORNING."
I BROUGHT YOUR *DAORI*, AL'LAN MANDRAGORAN, THE *TRUE* BLADE OF MALKIER.
I WILL *OBEY* MY KING. BUT AS THE SAYING GOES, A KING IS NOT A KING, ALONE WITH HIS CARNEIRA.
MY LADY EDEYN, THERE *IS* NO KING OF MALKIER.
THE GREAT LORDS HAVE NOT CAST THE RODS.
WHAT MUST BE, *WILL* BE.
I RECALL EVERY *MOMENT* OF THE MORNING AFTER OUR FIRST NIGHT. YOU TOOK ME TO THE WOMEN'S QUARTERS OF THE ROYAL PALACE.
AND LET THE LADIES AND SERVANT WOMEN *WATCH* AS YOU CUT MY HAIR.
IN TOKEN OF WHAT I OWE TO YOU, EDEYN, ALWAYS AND FOREVER.
I KNEW YOU HAD NOT BEEN GONE SO LONG AS TO *FORGET* OUR WAYS.
COME.

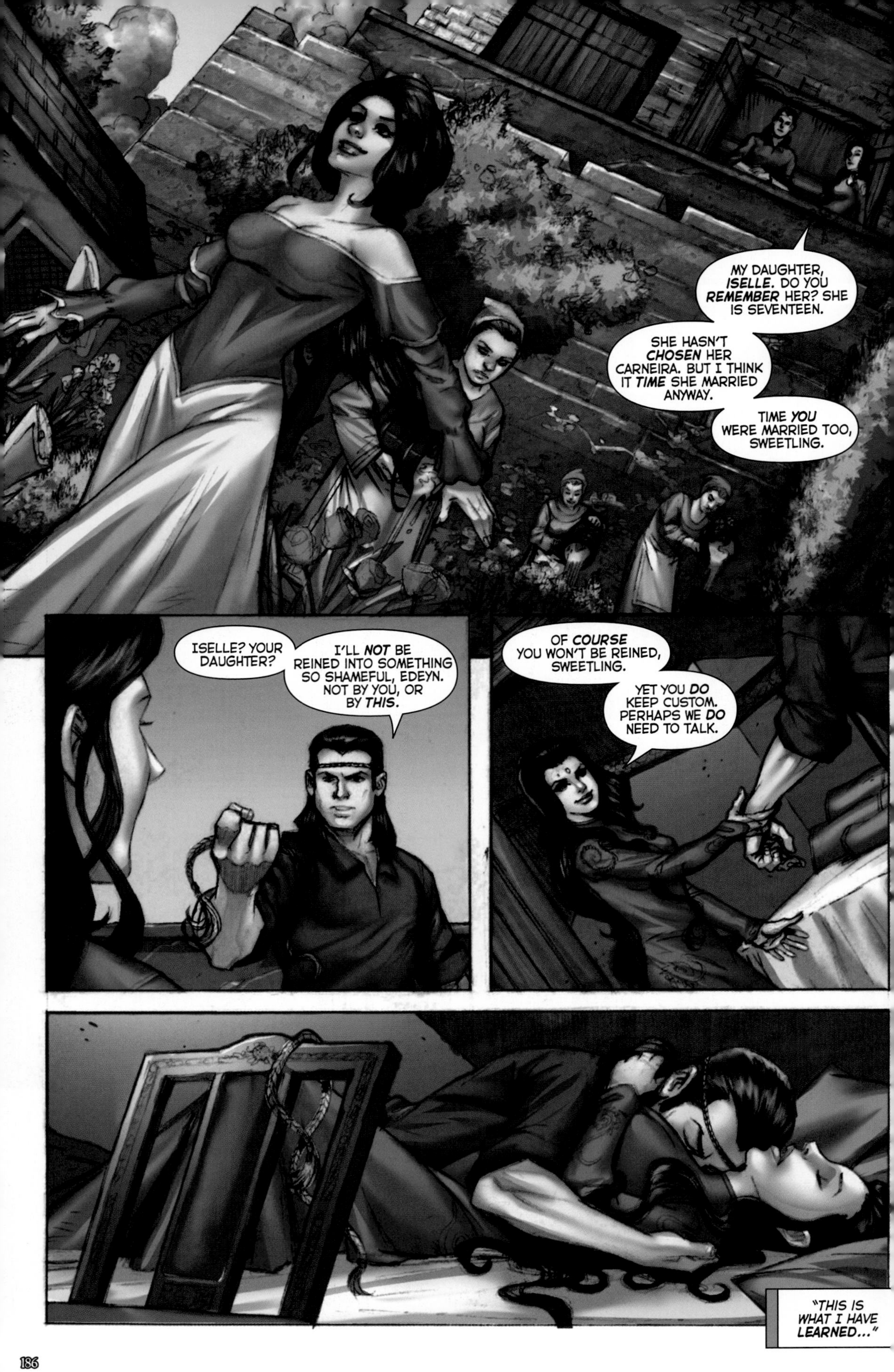
MY DAUGHTER, ISELLE. DO YOU REMEMBER HER? SHE IS SEVENTEEN.
SHE HASN'T CHOSEN HER CARNEIRA. BUT I THINK IT TIME SHE MARRIED ANYWAY.
TIME YOU WERE MARRIED TOO, SWEETLING.
ISELLE? YOUR DAUGHTER?
I'LL NOT BE REINED INTO SOMETHING SO SHAMEFUL, EDEYN. NOT BY YOU, OR BY THIS.
OF COURSE YOU WON'T BE REINED, SWEETLING.
YET YOU DO KEEP CUSTOM. PERHAPS WE DO NEED TO TALK.
"THIS IS WHAT I HAVE LEARNED..."

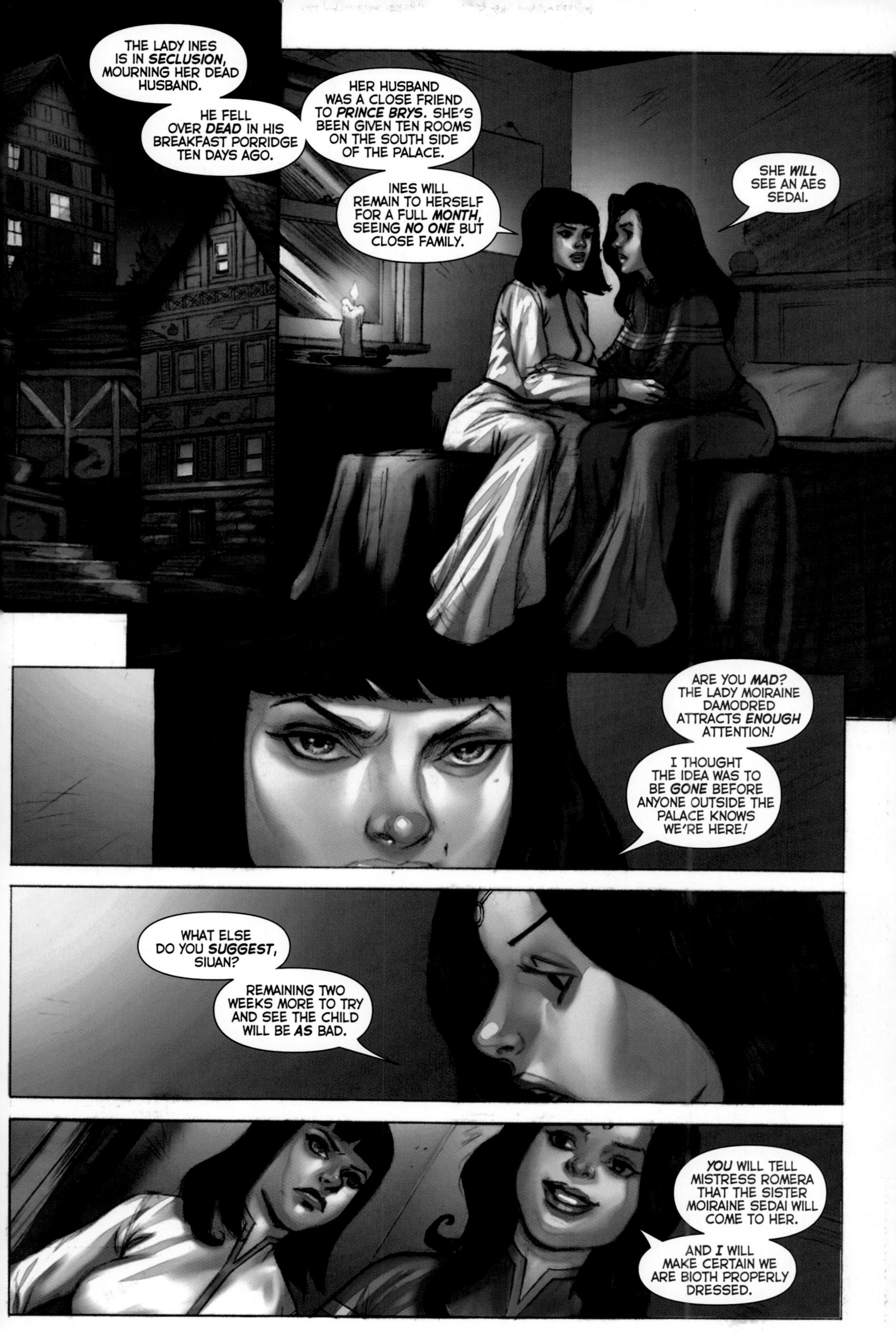
THE LADY INES IS IN SECLUSION, MOURNING HER DEAD HUSBAND.
HE FELL OVER DEAD IN HIS BREAKFAST PORRIDGE TEN DAYS AGO.
HER HUSBAND WAS A CLOSE FRIEND TO PRINCE BRYS. SHE'S BEEN GIVEN TEN ROOMS ON THE SOUTH SIDE OF THE PALACE.
INES WILL REMAIN TO HERSELF FOR A FULL MONTH, SEEING NO ONE BUT CLOSE FAMILY.
SHE WILL SEE AN AES SEDAI.
ARE YOU MAD? THE LADY MOIRAINE DAMODRED ATTRACTS ENOUGH ATTENTION!
I THOUGHT THE IDEA WAS TO BE GONE BEFORE ANYONE OUTSIDE THE PALACE KNOWS WE'RE HERE!
WHAT ELSE DO YOU SUGGEST, SIUAN?
REMAINING TWO WEEKS MORE TO TRY AND SEE THE CHILD WILL BE AS BAD.
YOU WILL TELL MISTRESS ROMERA THAT THE SISTER MOIRAINE SEDAI WILL COME TO HER.
AND I WILL MAKE CERTAIN WE ARE BIOTH PROPERLY DRESSED.

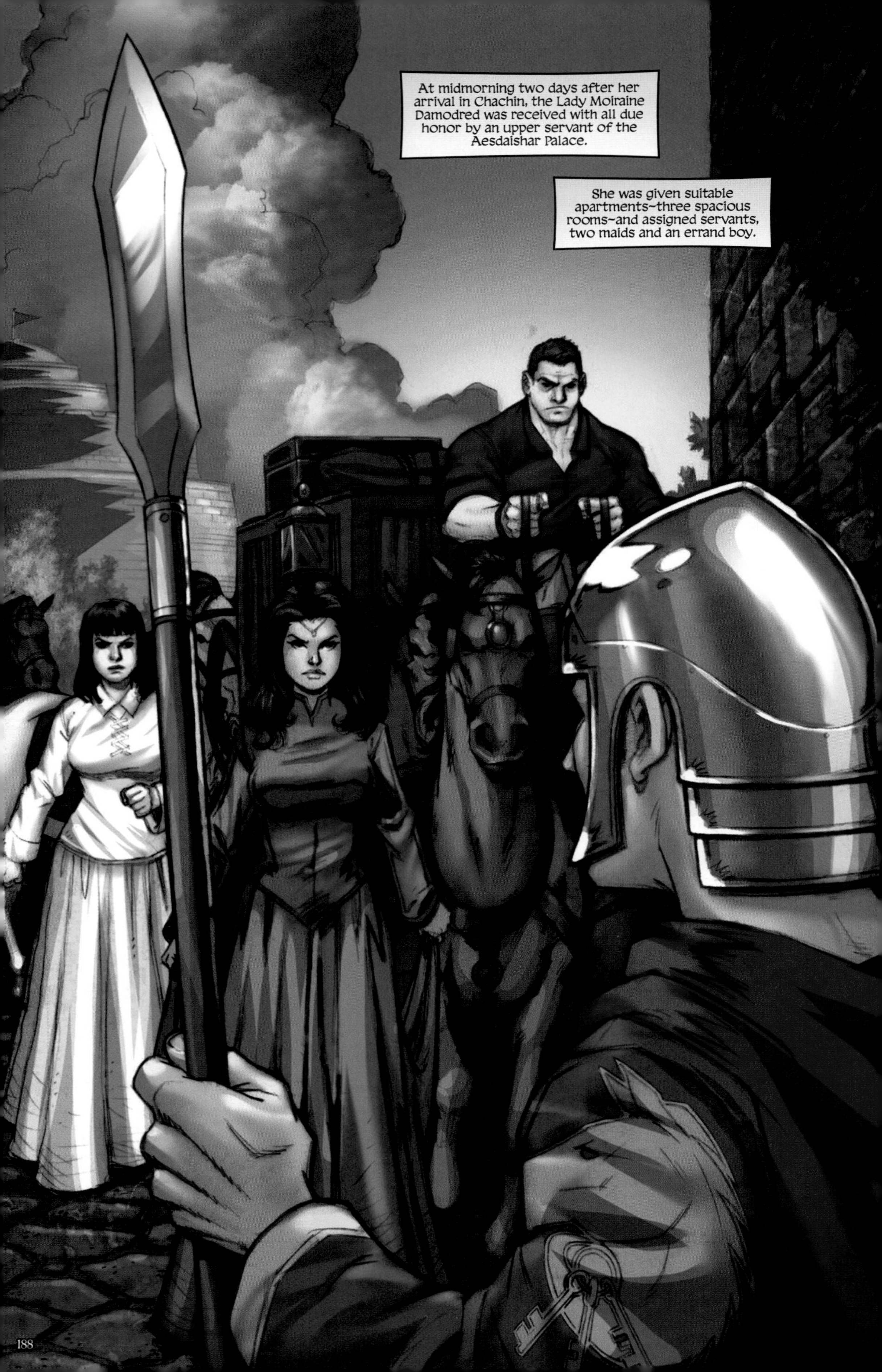
At midmorning two days after her arrival in Chachin, the Lady Moiraine Damodred was received with all due honor by an upper servant of the Aesdaishar Palace.
She was given suitable apartments~three spacious rooms~and assigned servants, two maids and an errand boy.

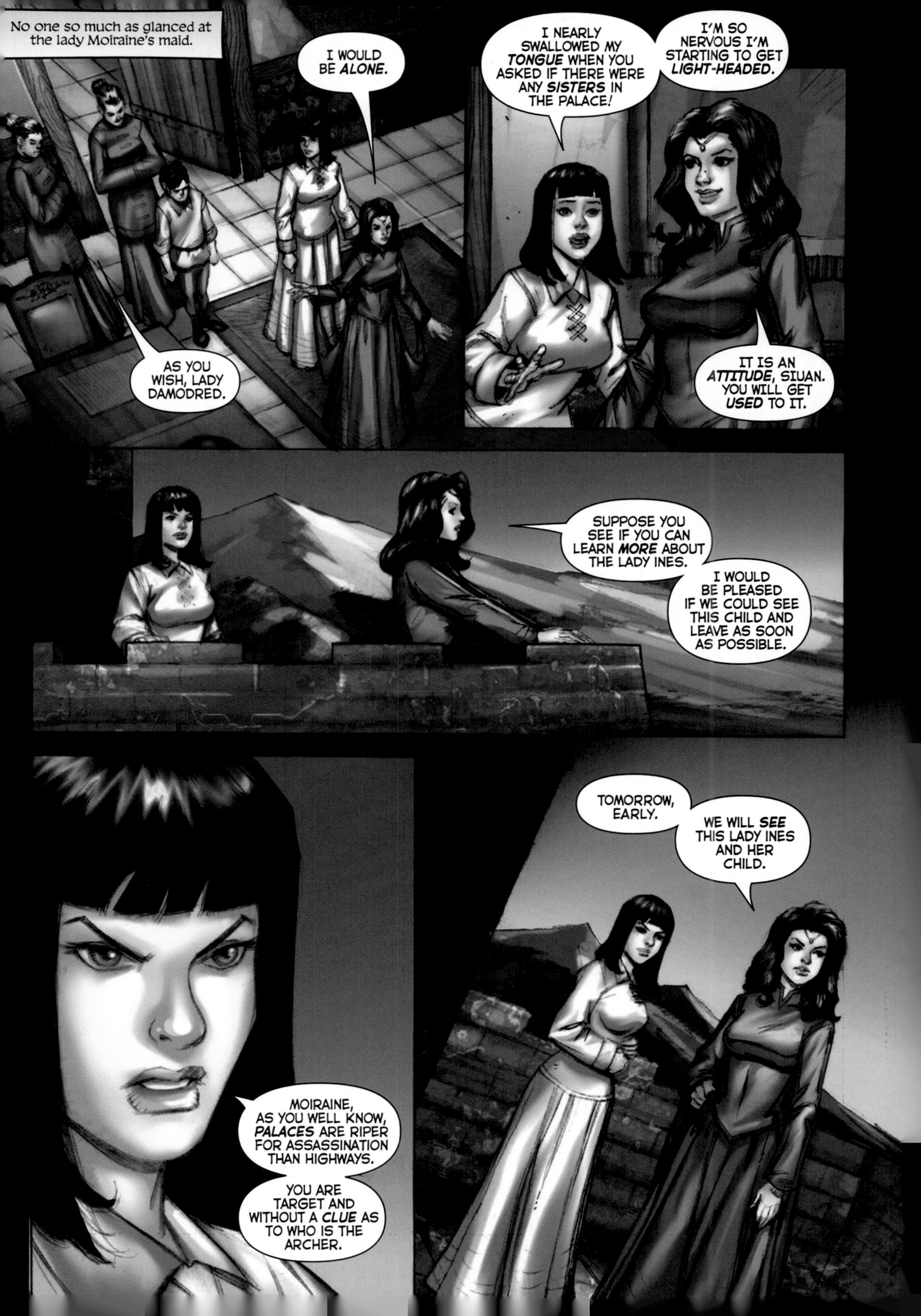
No one so much as glanced at the lady Moiraine's maid.
I WOULD BE ALONE.
AS YOU WISH, LADY DAMODRED.
I NEARLY SWALLOWED MY TONGUE WHEN YOU ASKED IF THERE WERE ANY SISTERS IN THE PALACE!
I'M SO NERVOUS I'M STARTING TO GET LIGHT-HEADED.
IT IS AN ATTITUDE, SIUAN. YOU WILL GET USED TO IT.
SUPPOSE YOU SEE IF YOU CAN LEARN MORE ABOUT THE LADY INES.
I WOULD BE PLEASED IF WE COULD SEE THIS CHILD AND LEAVE AS SOON AS POSSIBLE.
MOIRAINE, AS YOU WELL KNOW, PALACES ARE RIPER FOR ASSASSINATION THAN HIGHWAYS.
YOU ARE TARGET AND WITHOUT A CLUE AS TO WHO IS THE ARCHER.
TOMORROW, EARLY.
WE WILL SEE THIS LADY INES AND HER CHILD.

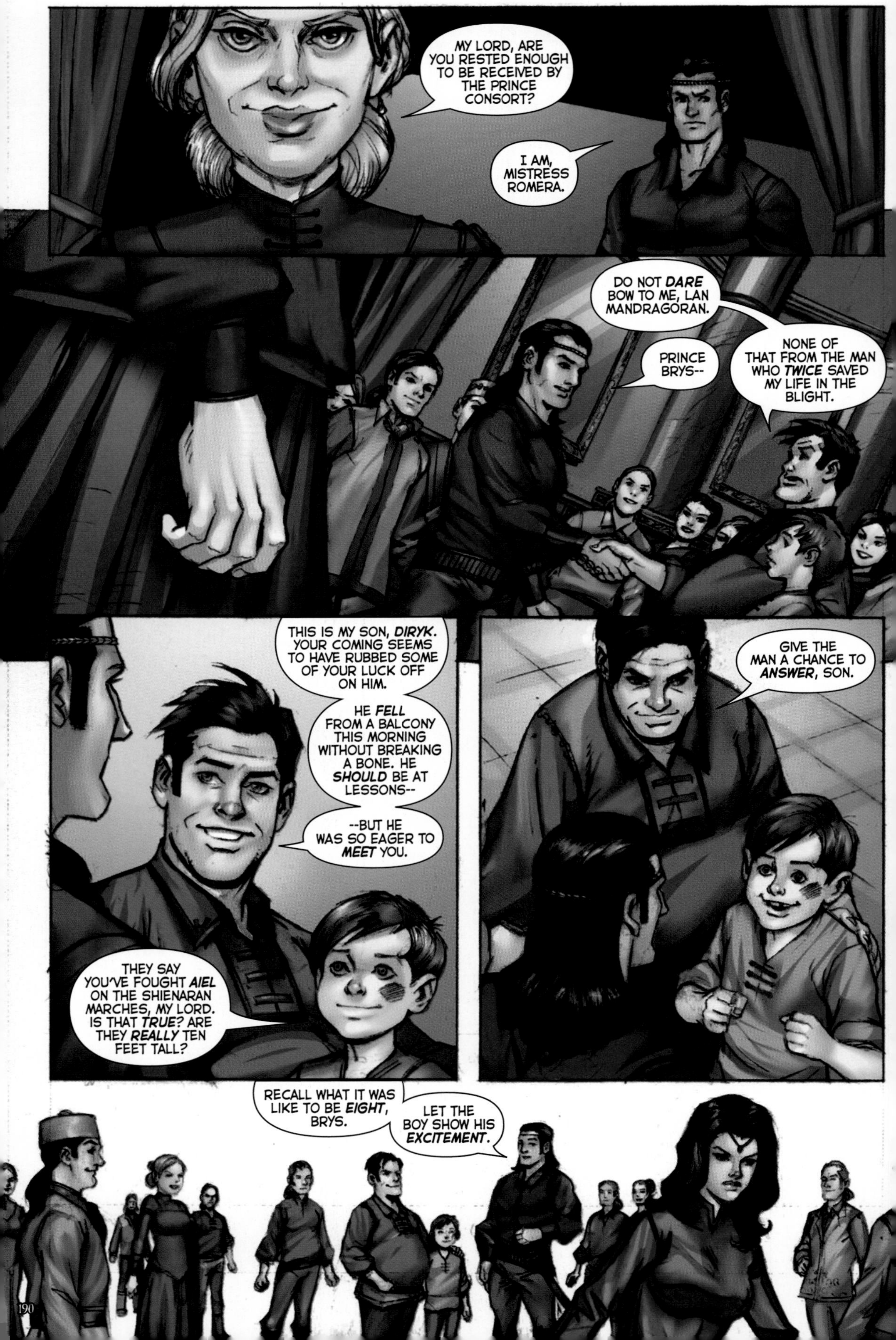
MY LORD, ARE YOU RESTED ENOUGH TO BE RECEIVED BY THE PRINCE CONSORT?
I AM, MISTRESS ROMERA.
DO NOT DARE BOW TO ME, LAN MANDRAGORAN.
PRINCE BRYS--
NONE OF THAT FROM THE MAN WHO TWICE SAVED MY LIFE IN THE BLIGHT.
THIS IS MY SON, DIRYK. YOUR COMING SEEMS TO HAVE RUBBED SOME OF YOUR LUCK OFF ON HIM.
HE FELL FROM A BALCONY THIS MORNING WITHOUT BREAKING A BONE. HE SHOULD BE AT LESSONS--
--BUT HE WAS SO EAGER TO MEET YOU.
THEY SAY YOU'VE FOUGHT AIEL ON THE SHIENARAN MARCHES, MY LORD. IS THAT TRUE? ARE THEY REALLY TEN FEET TALL?
GIVE THE MAN A CHANCE TO ANSWER, SON.
RECALL WHAT IT WAS LIKE TO BE EIGHT, BRYS.
LET THE BOY SHOW HIS EXCITEMENT.

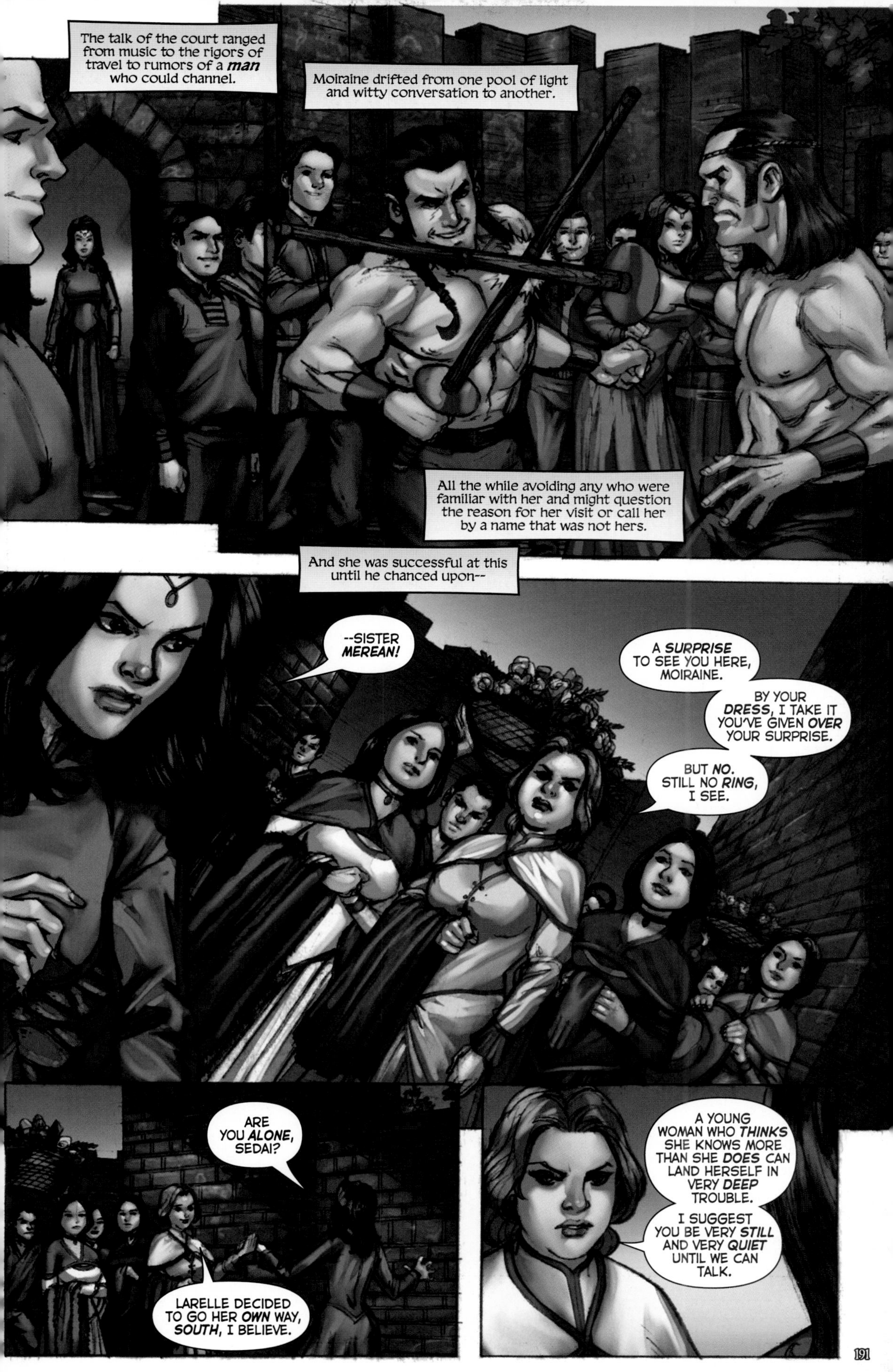

The talk of the court ranged from music to the rigors of travel to rumors of a *man* who could channel.
Moiraine drifted from one pool of light and witty conversation to another.
All the while avoiding any who were familiar with her and might question the reason for her visit or call her by a name that was not hers.
And she was successful at this until he chanced upon--
--SISTER *MEREAN!*
A *SURPRISE* TO SEE YOU HERE, MOIRAINE.
BY YOUR *DRESS*, I TAKE IT YOU'VE GIVEN *OVER* YOUR SURPRISE.
BUT *NO*. STILL NO *RING*, I SEE.
ARE YOU *ALONE*, SEDAI?
LARELLE DECIDED TO GO HER *OWN* WAY, *SOUTH*, I BELIEVE.
A YOUNG WOMAN WHO *THINKS* SHE KNOWS MORE THAN SHE *DOES* CAN LAND HERSELF IN VERY *DEEP* TROUBLE.
I SUGGEST YOU BE VERY *STILL* AND VERY *QUIET* UNTIL WE CAN TALK.

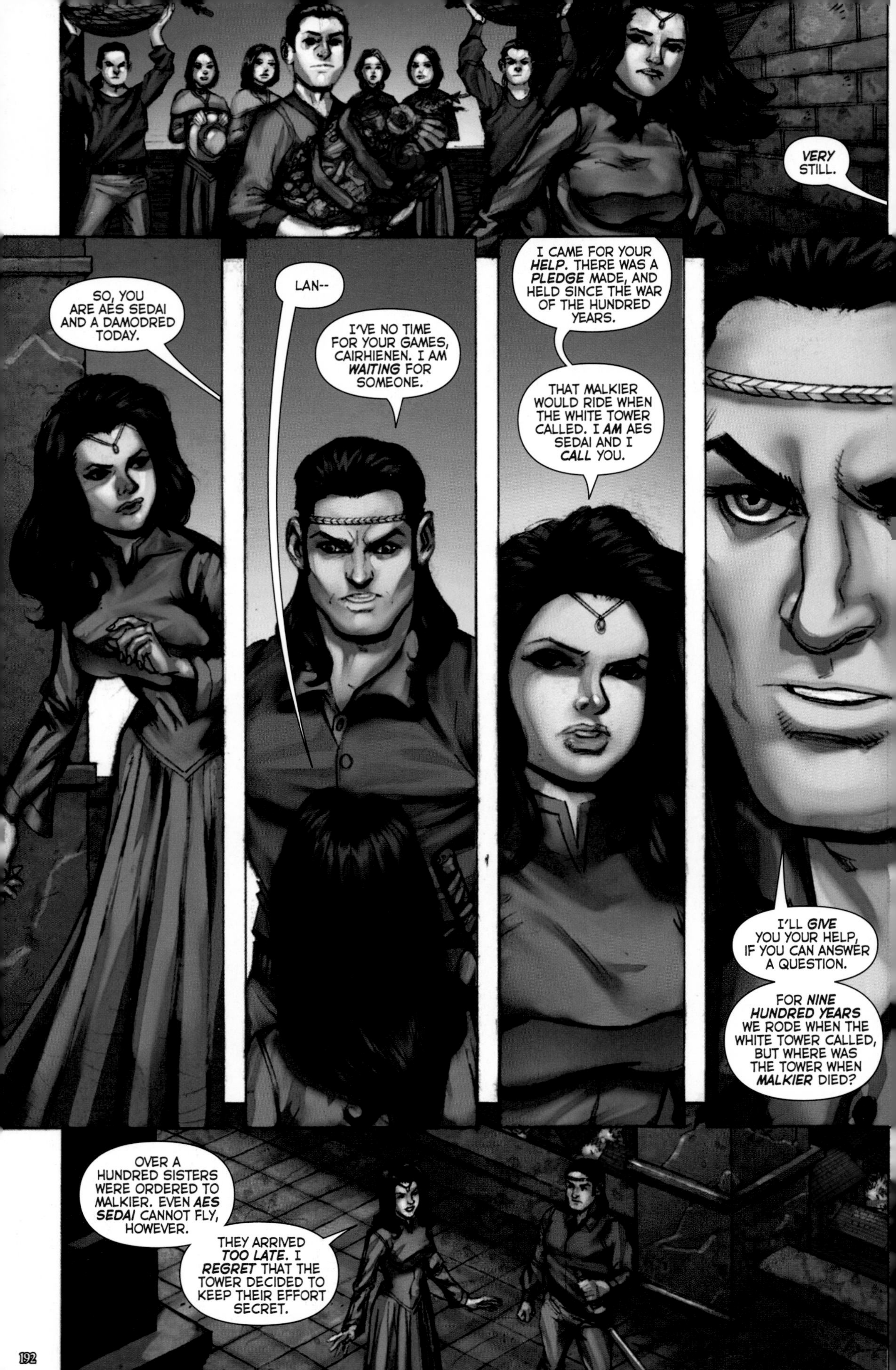
VERY STILL.
SO, YOU ARE AES SEDAI AND A DAMODRED TODAY.
LAN--
I'VE NO TIME FOR YOUR GAMES, CAIRHIENEN. I AM WAITING FOR SOMEONE.
I CAME FOR YOUR HELP. THERE WAS A PLEDGE MADE, AND HELD SINCE THE WAR OF THE HUNDRED YEARS.
THAT MALKIER WOULD RIDE WHEN THE WHITE TOWER CALLED. I AM AES SEDAI AND I CALL YOU.
I'LL GIVE YOU YOUR HELP, IF YOU CAN ANSWER A QUESTION.
FOR NINE HUNDRED YEARS WE RODE WHEN THE WHITE TOWER CALLED, BUT WHERE WAS THE TOWER WHEN MALKIER DIED?
OVER A HUNDRED SISTERS WERE ORDERED TO MALKIER. EVEN AES SEDAI CANNOT FLY, HOWEVER.
THEY ARRIVED TOO LATE. I REGRET THAT THE TOWER DECIDED TO KEEP THEIR EFFORT SECRET.

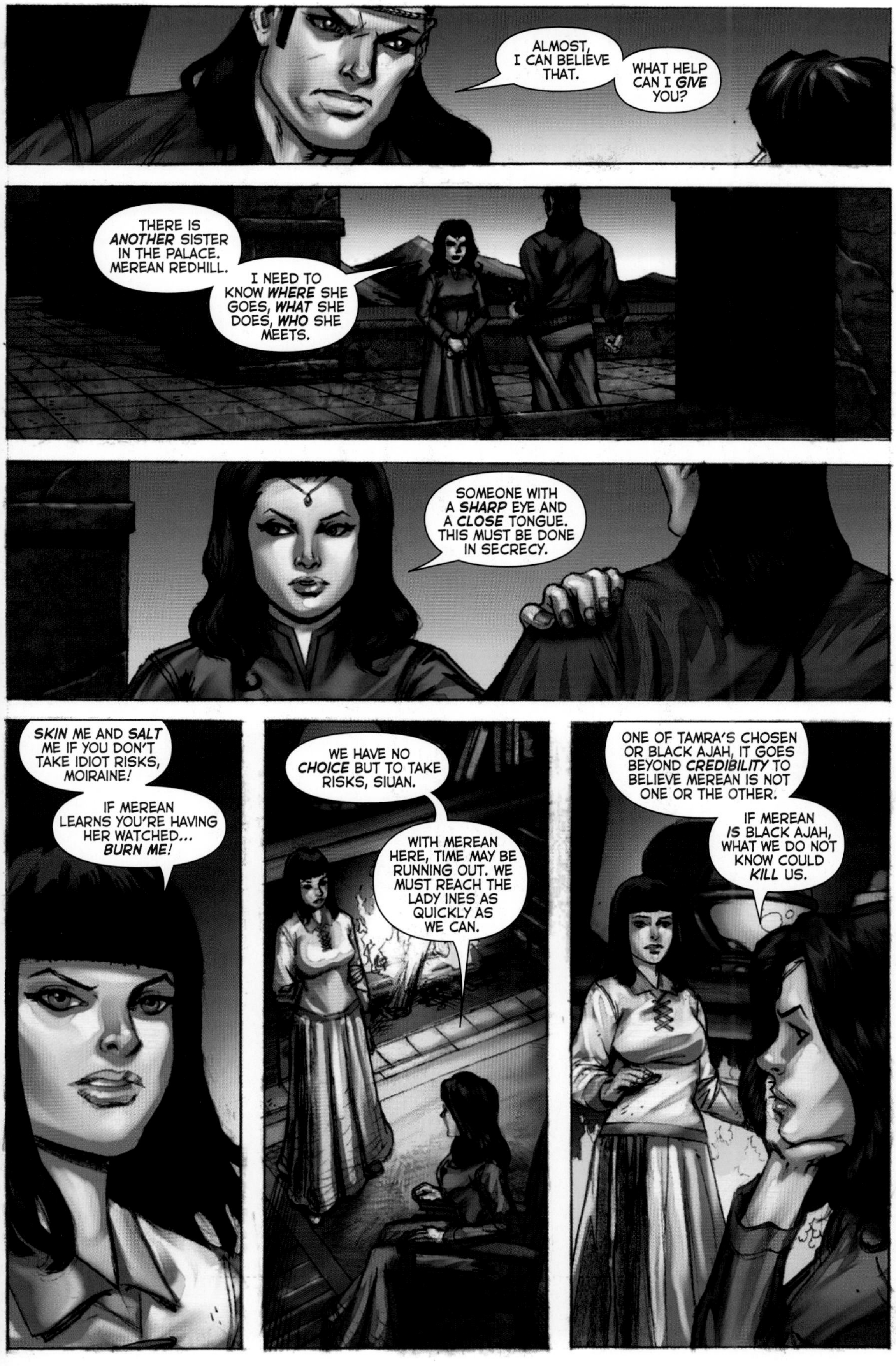
ALMOST, I CAN BELIEVE THAT.
WHAT HELP CAN I *GIVE* YOU?
THERE IS *ANOTHER* SISTER IN THE PALACE. MEREAN REDHILL.
I NEED TO KNOW *WHERE* SHE GOES, *WHAT* SHE DOES, *WHO* SHE MEETS.
SOMEONE WITH A *SHARP* EYE AND A *CLOSE* TONGUE. THIS MUST BE DONE IN SECRECY.
SKIN ME AND *SALT* ME IF YOU DON'T TAKE IDIOT RISKS, MOIRAINE!
IF MEREAN LEARNS YOU'RE HAVING HER WATCHED... *BURN ME!*
WE HAVE NO *CHOICE* BUT TO TAKE RISKS, SIUAN.
WITH MEREAN HERE, TIME MAY BE RUNNING OUT. WE MUST REACH THE LADY INES AS QUICKLY AS WE CAN.
ONE OF TAMRA'S CHOSEN OR BLACK AJAH, IT GOES BEYOND *CREDIBILITY* TO BELIEVE MEREAN IS NOT ONE OR THE OTHER.
IF MEREAN *IS* BLACK AJAH, WHAT WE DO NOT KNOW COULD *KILL* US.

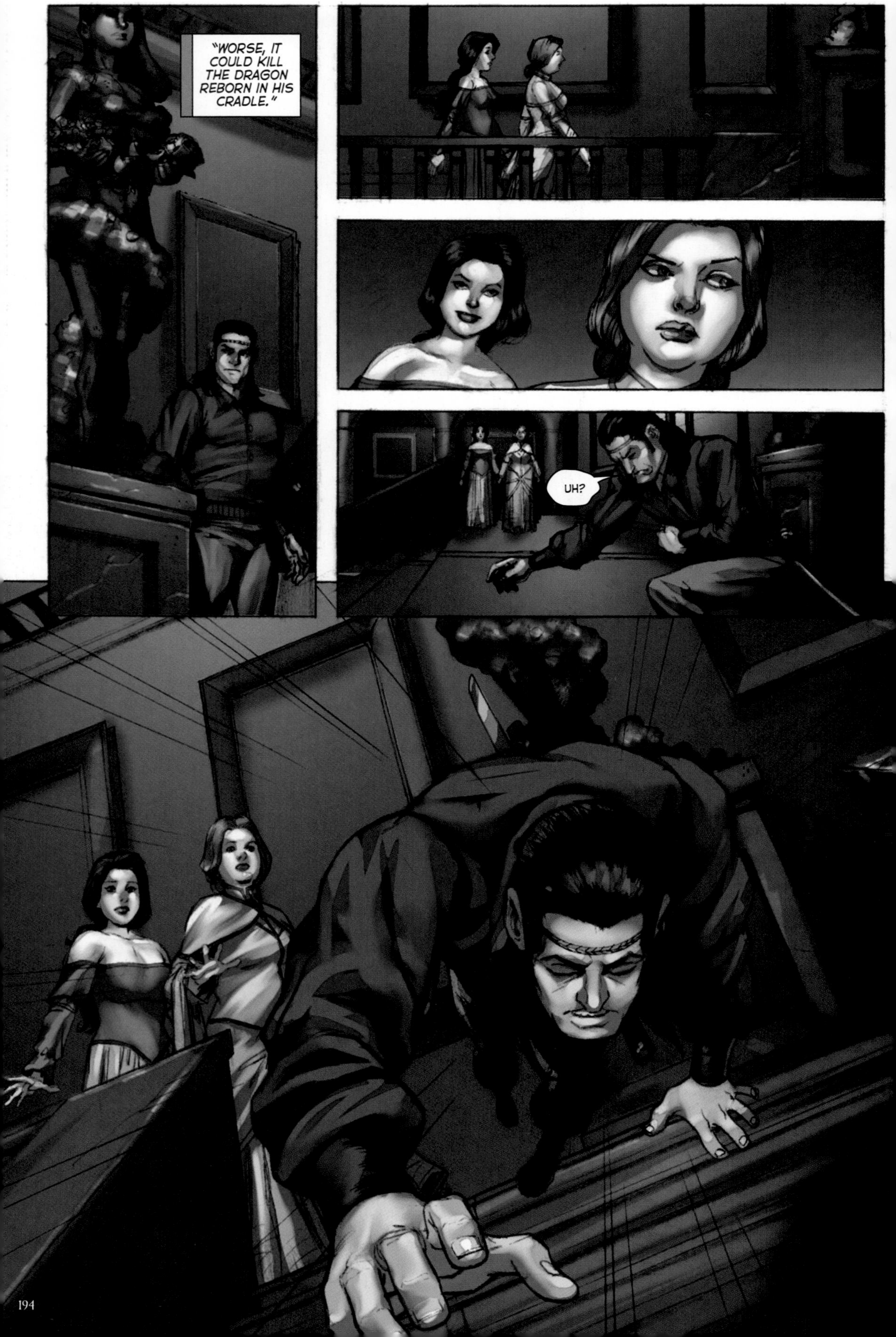
"WORSE, IT COULD KILL THE DRAGON REBORN IN HIS CRADLE."
UH?

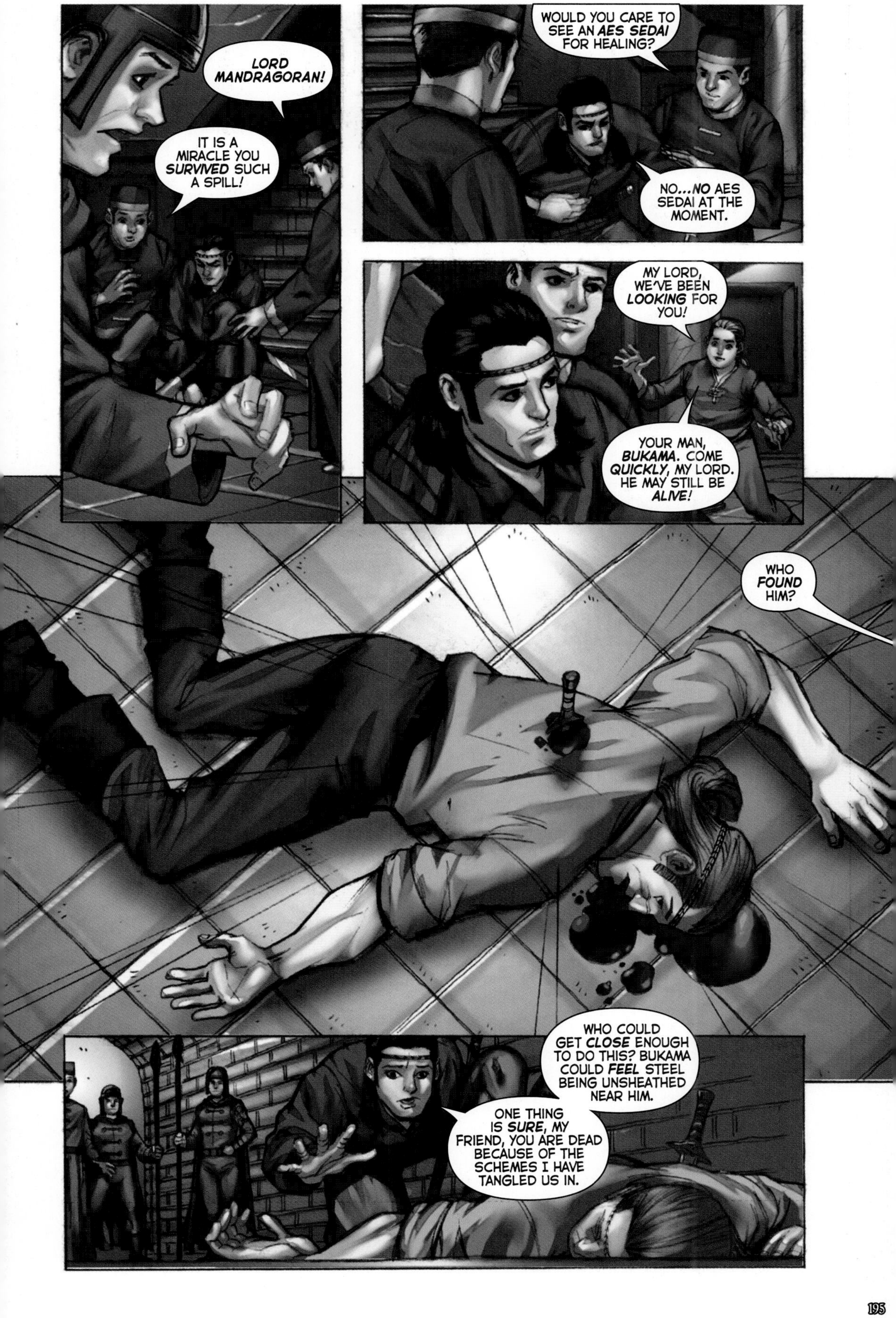
LORD MANDRAGORAN!
IT IS A MIRACLE YOU SURVIVED SUCH A SPILL!
WOULD YOU CARE TO SEE AN AES SEDAI FOR HEALING?
NO...NO AES SEDAI AT THE MOMENT.
MY LORD, WE'VE BEEN LOOKING FOR YOU!
YOUR MAN, BUKAMA. COME QUICKLY, MY LORD. HE MAY STILL BE ALIVE!
WHO FOUND HIM?
WHO COULD GET CLOSE ENOUGH TO DO THIS? BUKAMA COULD FEEL STEEL BEING UNSHEATHED NEAR HIM.
ONE THING IS SURE, MY FRIEND, YOU ARE DEAD BECAUSE OF THE SCHEMES I HAVE TANGLED US IN.

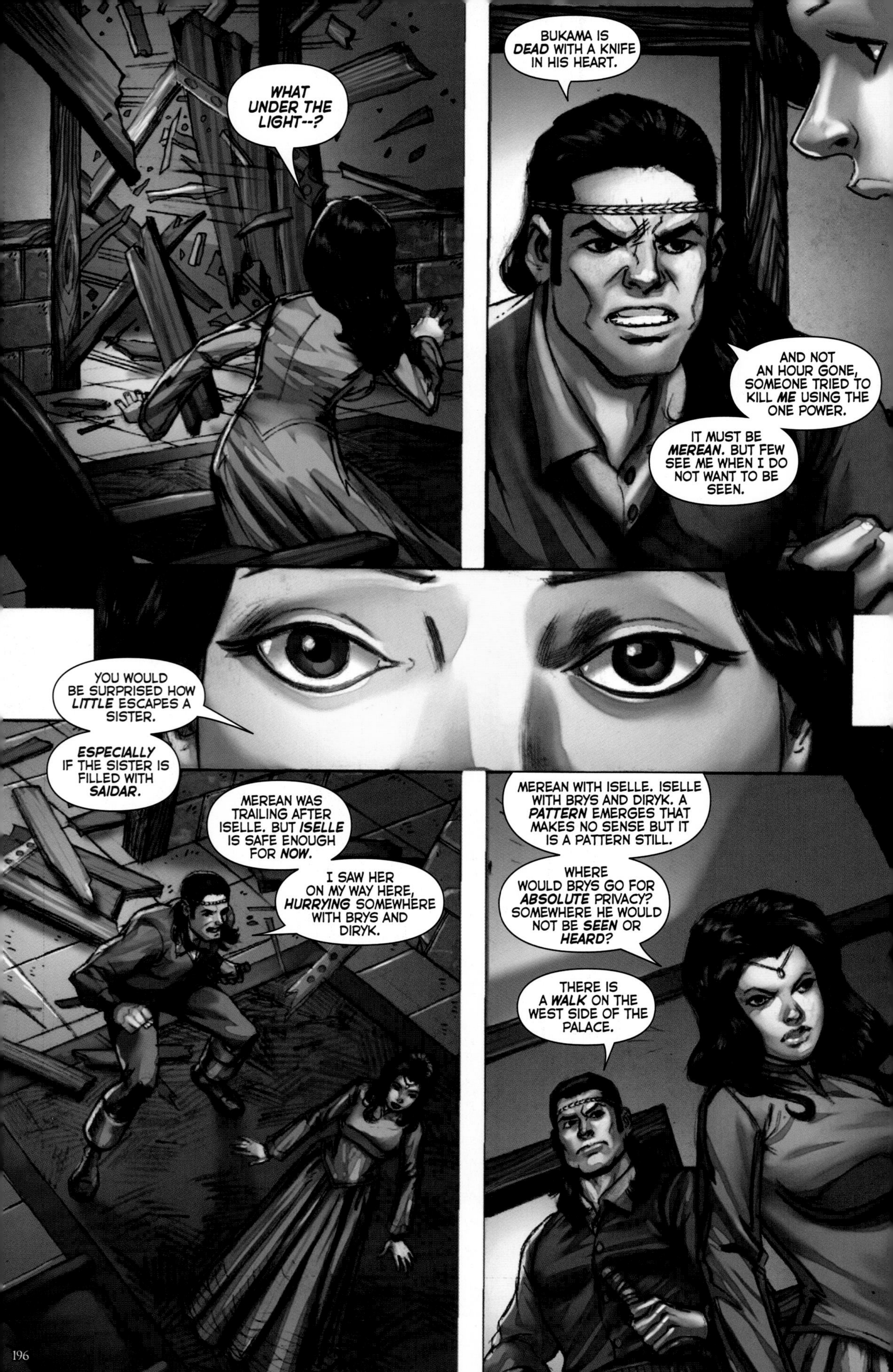
WHAT UNDER THE LIGHT--?
BUKAMA IS DEAD WITH A KNIFE IN HIS HEART.
AND NOT AN HOUR GONE, SOMEONE TRIED TO KILL ME USING THE ONE POWER.
IT MUST BE MEREAN. BUT FEW SEE ME WHEN I DO NOT WANT TO BE SEEN.
YOU WOULD BE SURPRISED HOW LITTLE ESCAPES A SISTER.
ESPECIALLY IF THE SISTER IS FILLED WITH SAIDAR.
MEREAN WAS TRAILING AFTER ISELLE. BUT ISELLE IS SAFE ENOUGH FOR NOW.
I SAW HER ON MY WAY HERE, HURRYING SOMEWHERE WITH BRYS AND DIRYK.
MEREAN WITH ISELLE. ISELLE WITH BRYS AND DIRYK. A PATTERN EMERGES THAT MAKES NO SENSE BUT IT IS A PATTERN STILL.
WHERE WOULD BRYS GO FOR ABSOLUTE PRIVACY? SOMEWHERE HE WOULD NOT BE SEEN OR HEARD?
THERE IS A WALK ON THE WEST SIDE OF THE PALACE.

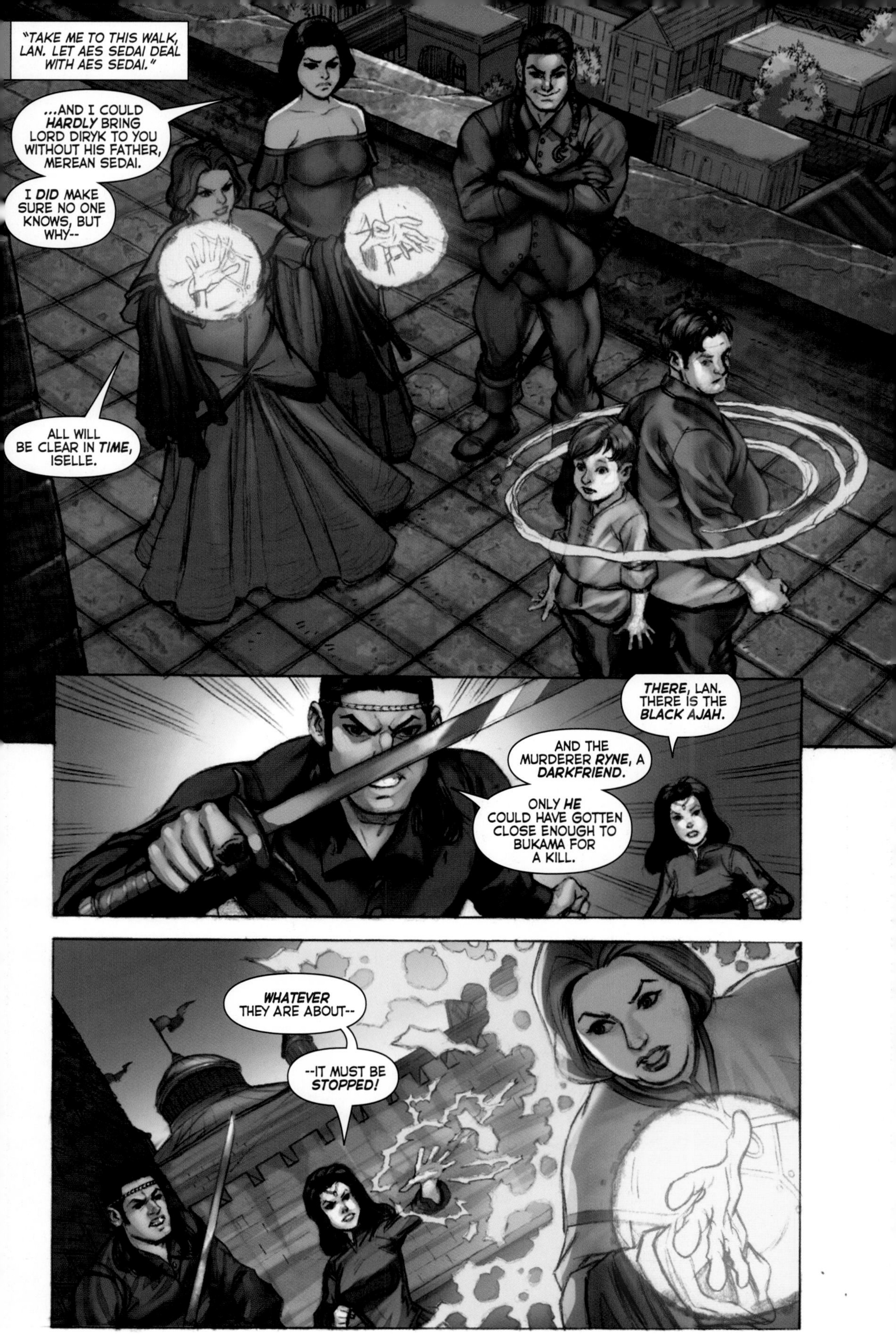
"TAKE ME TO THIS WALK, LAN. LET AES SEDAI DEAL WITH AES SEDAI."
...AND I COULD HARDLY BRING LORD DIRYK TO YOU WITHOUT HIS FATHER, MEREAN SEDAI.
I DID MAKE SURE NO ONE KNOWS, BUT WHY--
ALL WILL BE CLEAR IN TIME, ISELLE.
THERE, LAN. THERE IS THE BLACK AJAH.
AND THE MURDERER RYNE, A DARKFRIEND.
ONLY HE COULD HAVE GOTTEN CLOSE ENOUGH TO BUKAMA FOR A KILL.
WHATEVER THEY ARE ABOUT--
--IT MUST BE STOPPED!

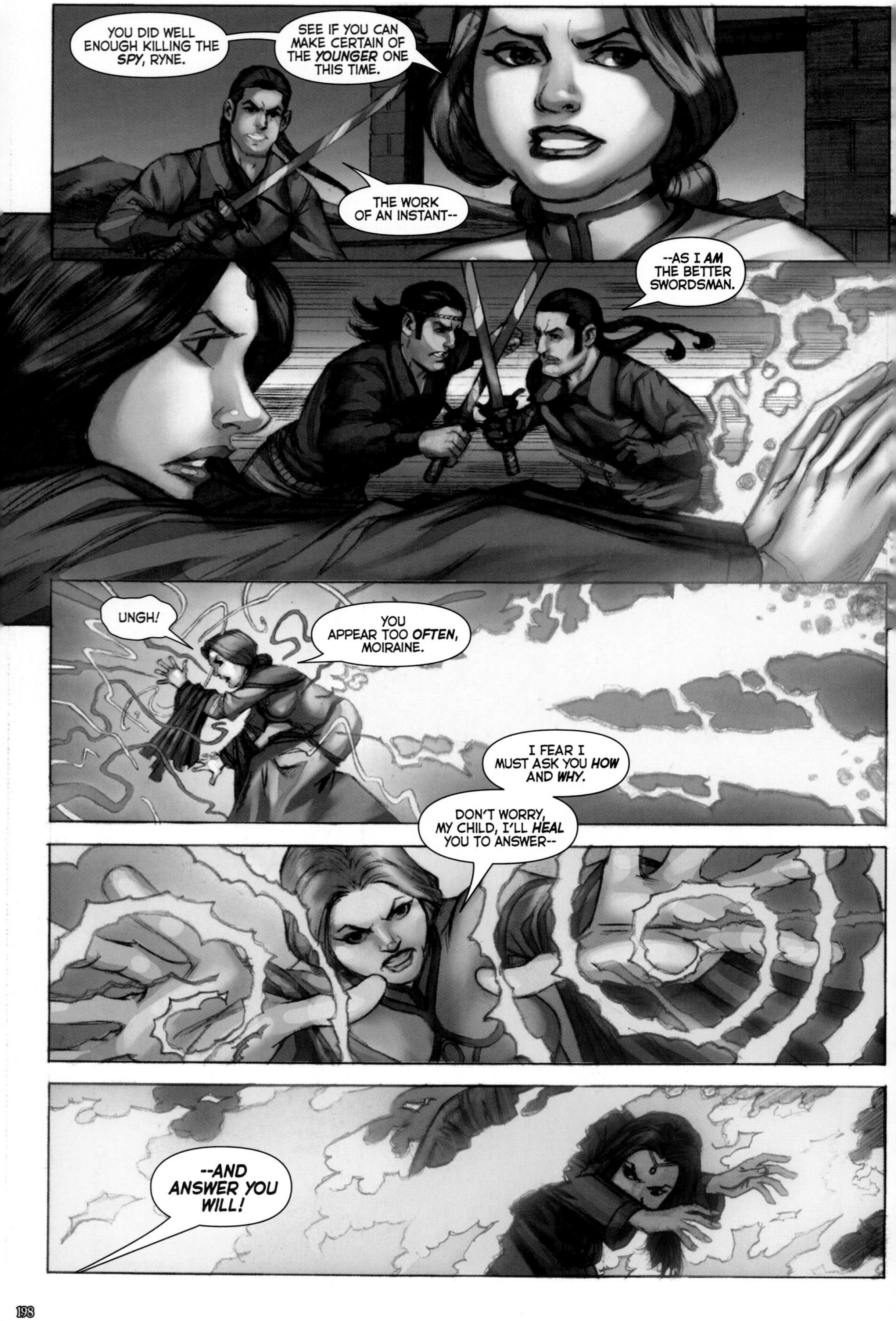
YOU DID WELL ENOUGH KILLING THE SPY, RYNE.
SEE IF YOU CAN MAKE CERTAIN OF THE YOUNGER ONE THIS TIME.
THE WORK OF AN INSTANT--
--AS I AM THE BETTER SWORDSMAN.
UNGH!
YOU APPEAR TOO OFTEN, MOIRAINE.
I FEAR I MUST ASK YOU HOW AND WHY.
DON'T WORRY, MY CHILD, I'LL HEAL YOU TO ANSWER--
--AND ANSWER YOU WILL!

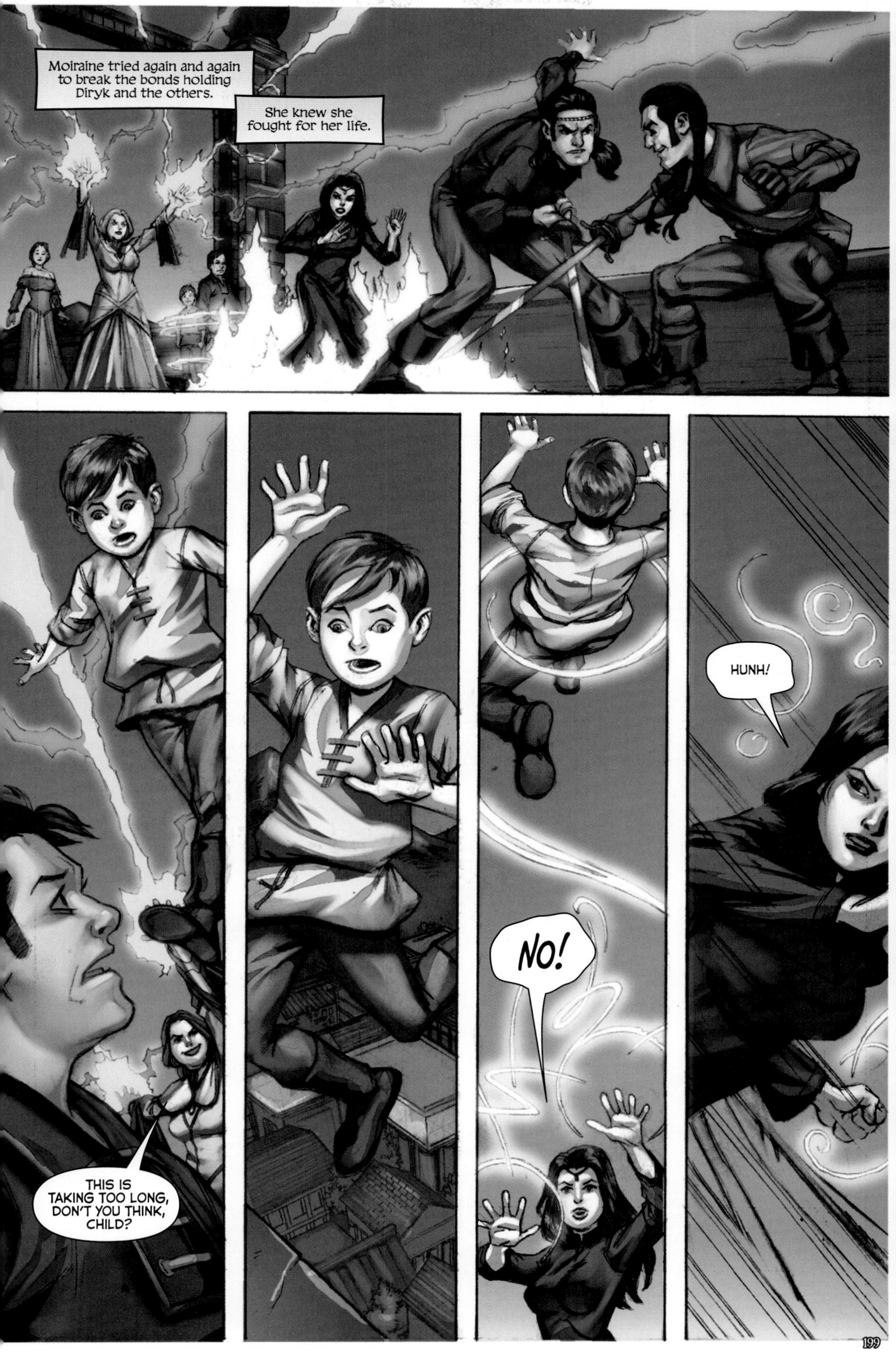

Moiraine tried again and again to break the bonds holding Diryk and the others.
She knew she fought for her life.
THIS IS TAKING TOO LONG, DON'T YOU THINK, CHILD?
NO!
HUNH!

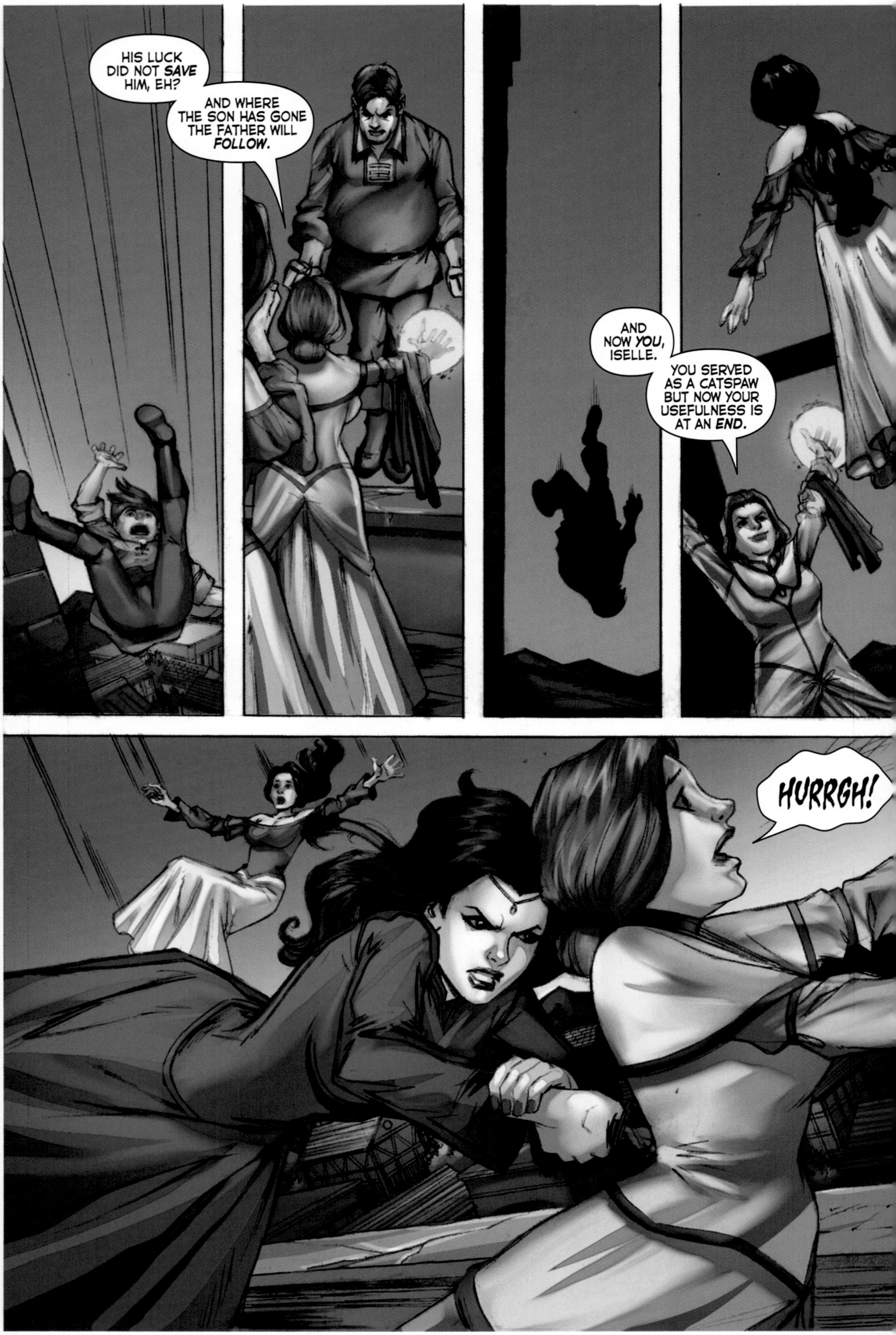
HIS LUCK DID NOT SAVE HIM, EH?
AND WHERE THE SON HAS GONE THE FATHER WILL FOLLOW.
AND NOW YOU, ISELLE.
YOU SERVED AS A CATSPAW BUT NOW YOUR USEFULNESS IS AT AN END.
HURRGH!

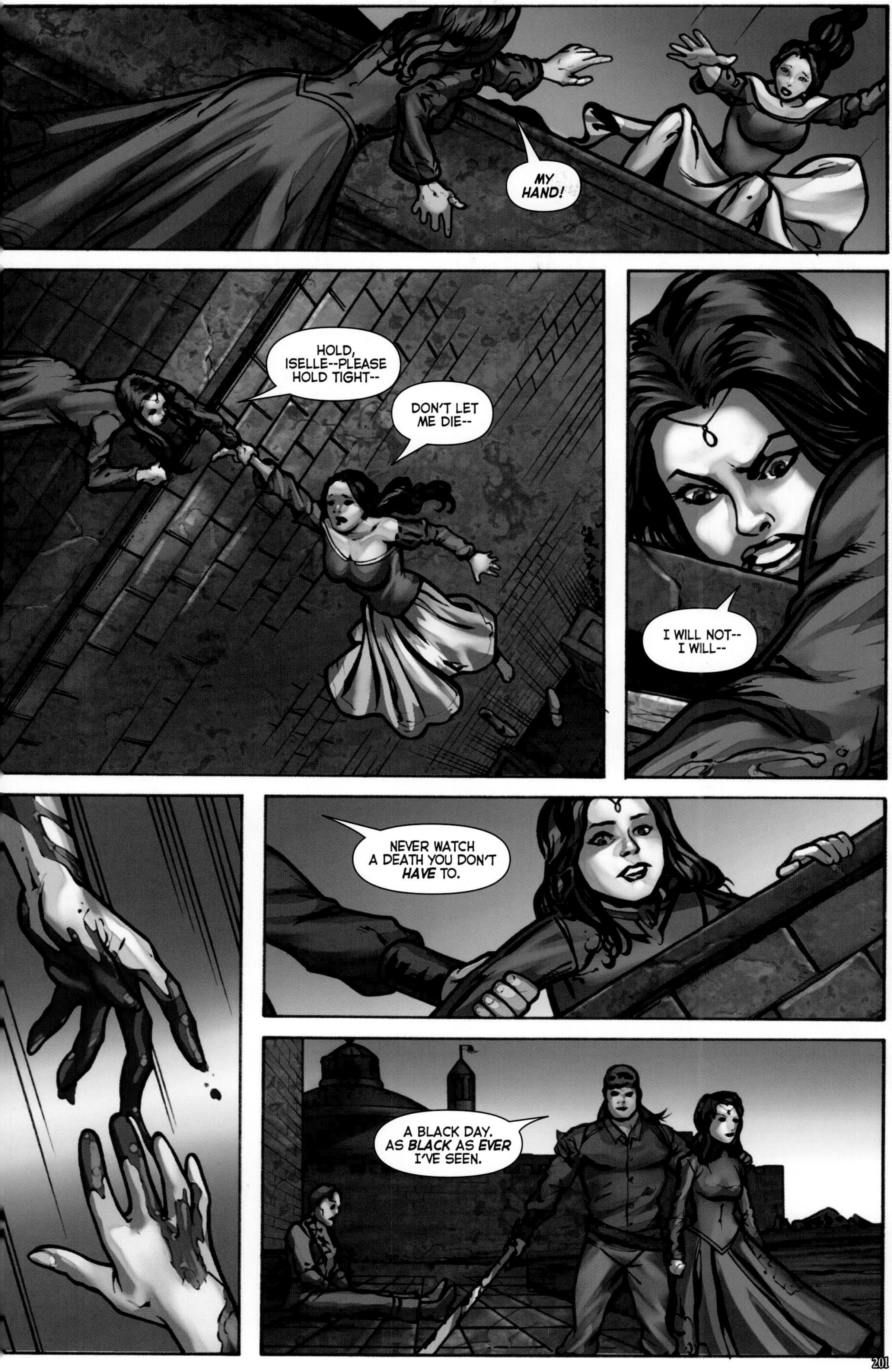
MY HAND!
HOLD, ISELLE--PLEASE HOLD TIGHT--
DON'T LET ME DIE--
I WILL NOT-- I WILL--
NEVER WATCH A DEATH YOU DON'T *HAVE* TO.
A BLACK DAY. AS *BLACK* AS *EVER* I'VE SEEN.

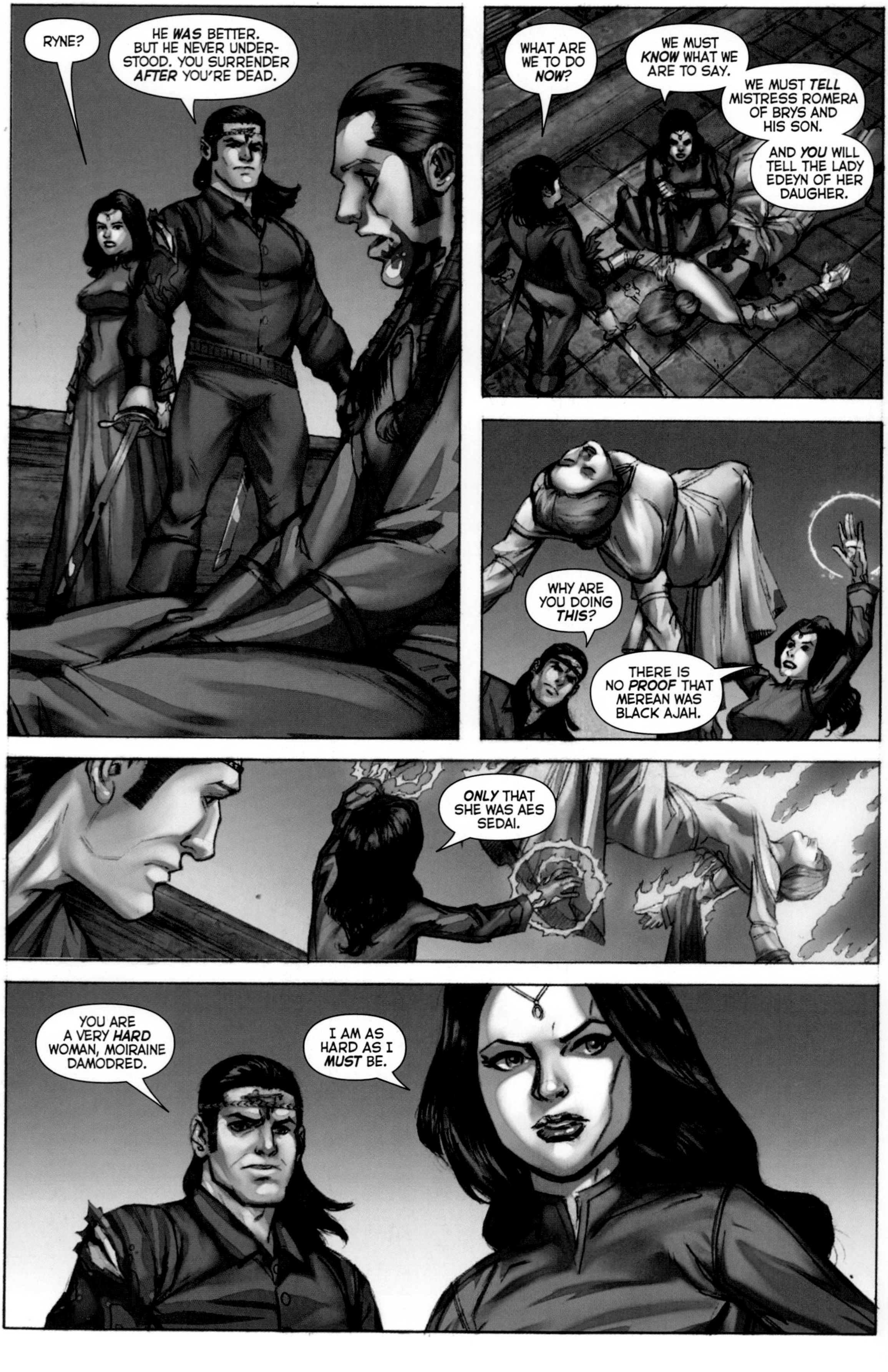
RYNE?
HE WAS BETTER. BUT HE NEVER UNDER-STOOD. YOU SURRENDER AFTER YOU'RE DEAD.
WHAT ARE WE TO DO NOW?
WE MUST KNOW WHAT WE ARE TO SAY.
WE MUST TELL MISTRESS ROMERA OF BRYS AND HIS SON.
AND YOU WILL TELL THE LADY EDEYN OF HER DAUGHER.
WHY ARE YOU DOING THIS?
THERE IS NO PROOF THAT MEREAN WAS BLACK AJAH.
ONLY THAT SHE WAS AES SEDAI.
YOU ARE A VERY HARD WOMAN, MOIRAINE DAMODRED.
I AM AS HARD AS I MUST BE.

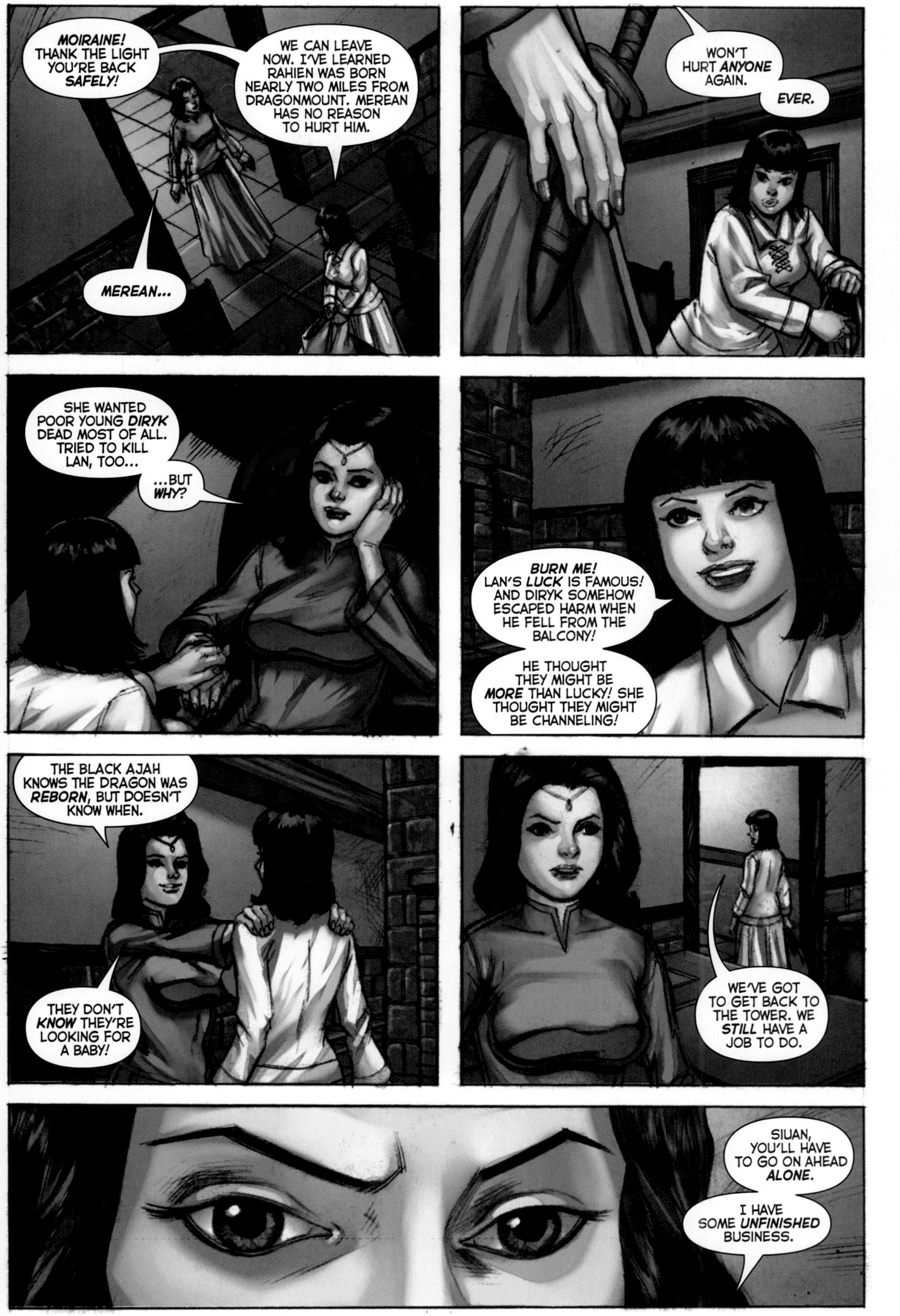
MOIRAINE! THANK THE LIGHT YOU'RE BACK SAFELY!
MEREAN...
WE CAN LEAVE NOW. I'VE LEARNED RAHIEN WAS BORN NEARLY TWO MILES FROM DRAGONMOUNT. MEREAN HAS NO REASON TO HURT HIM.
WON'T HURT ANYONE AGAIN.
EVER.
SHE WANTED POOR YOUNG DIRYK DEAD MOST OF ALL. TRIED TO KILL LAN, TOO...
...BUT WHY?
BURN ME! LAN'S LUCK IS FAMOUS! AND DIRYK SOMEHOW ESCAPED HARM WHEN HE FELL FROM THE BALCONY!
HE THOUGHT THEY MIGHT BE MORE THAN LUCKY! SHE THOUGHT THEY MIGHT BE CHANNELING!
THE BLACK AJAH KNOWS THE DRAGON WAS REBORN, BUT DOESN'T KNOW WHEN.
THEY DON'T KNOW THEY'RE LOOKING FOR A BABY!
WE'VE GOT TO GET BACK TO THE TOWER. WE STILL HAVE A JOB TO DO.
SIUAN, YOU'LL HAVE TO GO ON AHEAD ALONE.
I HAVE SOME UNFINISHED BUSINESS.

Epilogue

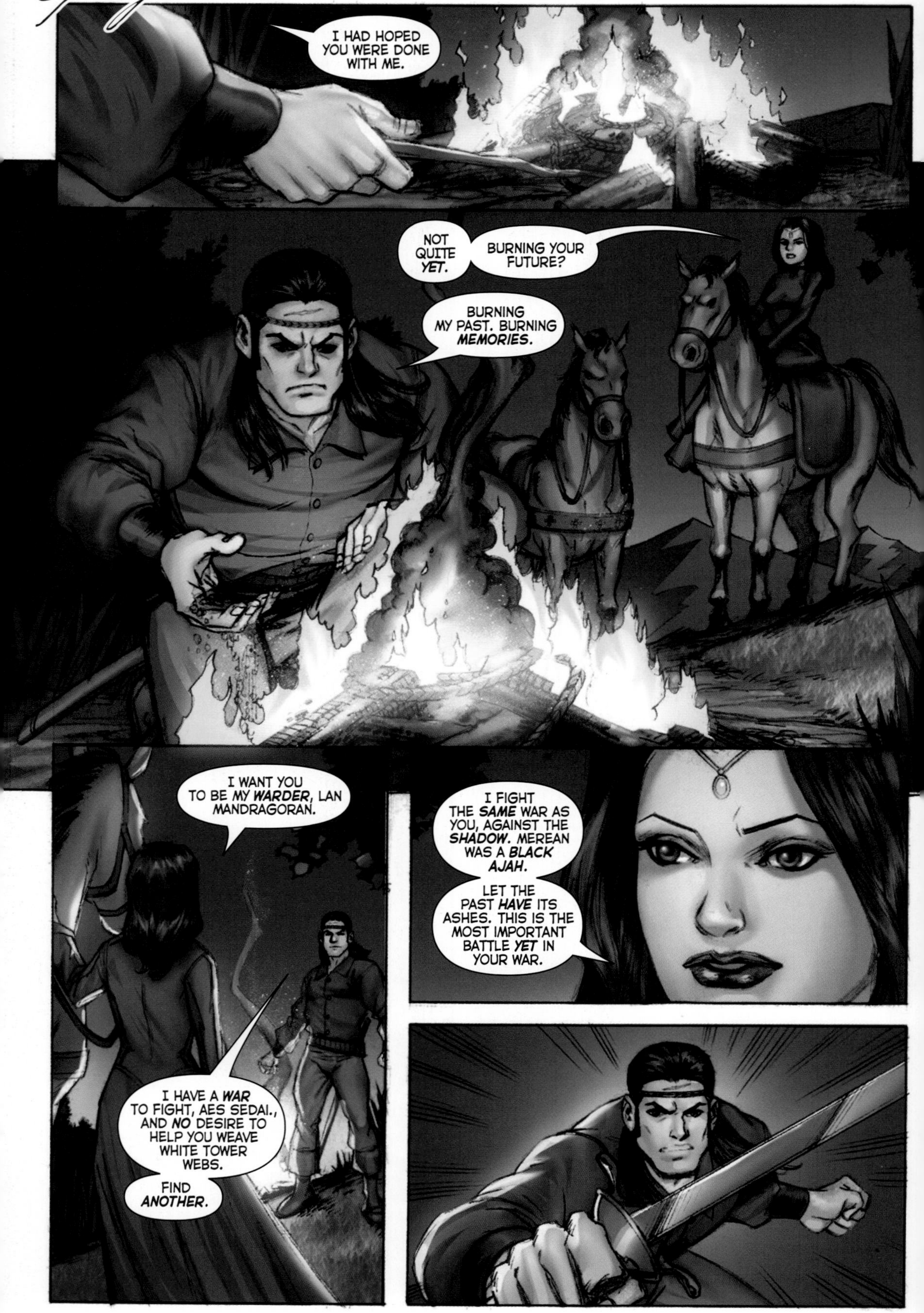

I HAD HOPED YOU WERE DONE WITH ME.
BURNING YOUR FUTURE?
NOT QUITE YET.
BURNING MY PAST. BURNING MEMORIES.
I WANT YOU TO BE MY WARDER, LAN MANDRAGORAN.
I HAVE A WAR TO FIGHT, AES SEDAI., AND NO DESIRE TO HELP YOU WEAVE WHITE TOWER WEBS.
FIND ANOTHER.
I FIGHT THE SAME WAR AS YOU, AGAINST THE SHADOW. MEREAN WAS A BLACK AJAH.
LET THE PAST HAVE ITS ASHES. THIS IS THE MOST IMPORTANT BATTLE YET IN YOUR WAR.

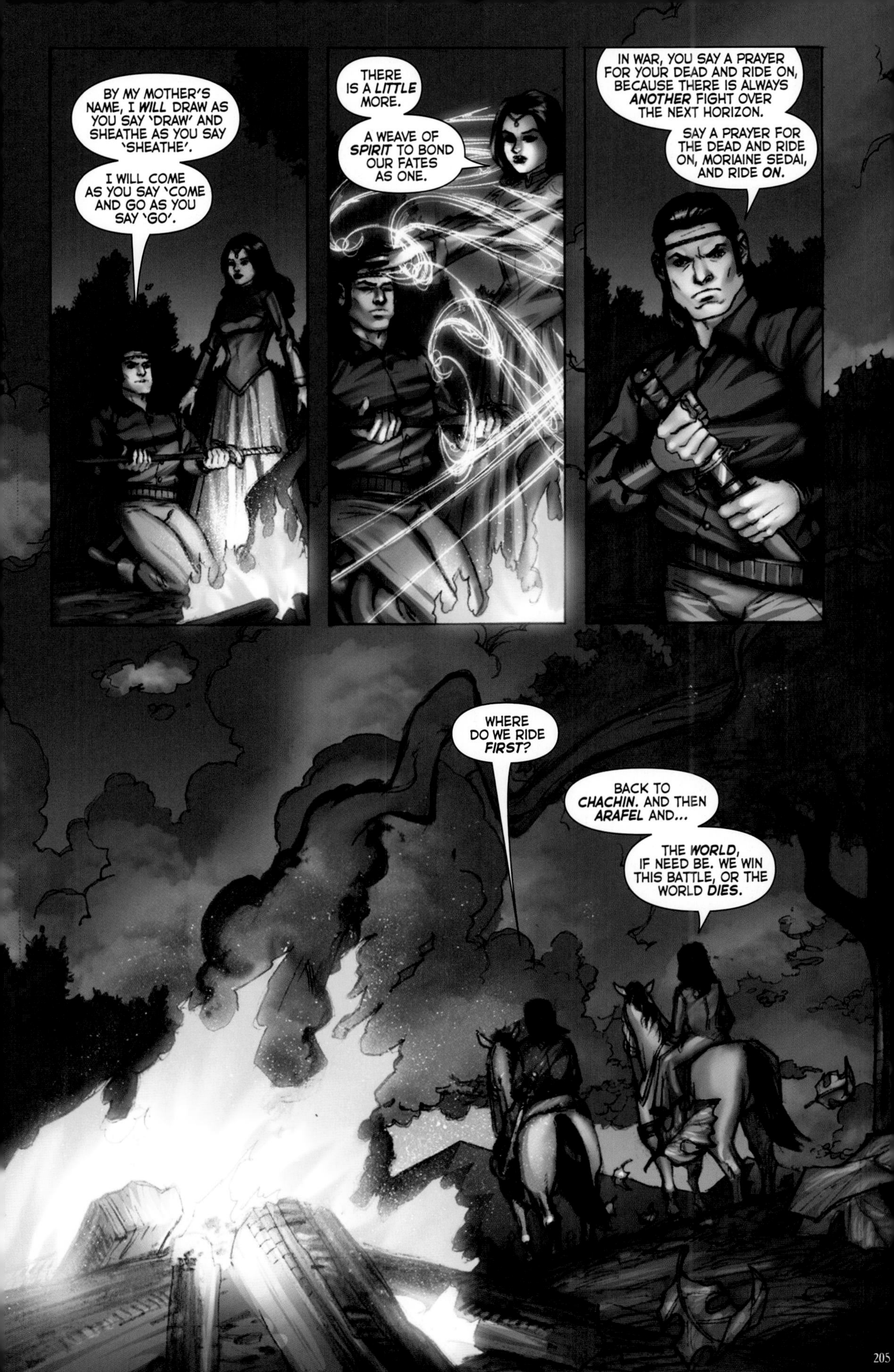

BY MY MOTHER'S NAME, I *WILL* DRAW AS YOU SAY 'DRAW' AND SHEATHE AS YOU SAY 'SHEATHE'.
I WILL COME AS YOU SAY 'COME AND GO AS YOU SAY 'GO'.
THERE IS A *LITTLE* MORE.
A WEAVE OF *SPIRIT* TO BOND OUR FATES AS ONE.
IN WAR, YOU SAY A PRAYER FOR YOUR DEAD AND RIDE ON, BECAUSE THERE IS ALWAYS *ANOTHER* FIGHT OVER THE NEXT HORIZON.
SAY A PRAYER FOR THE DEAD AND RIDE ON, MORIAINE SEDAI, AND RIDE *ON*.
WHERE DO WE RIDE *FIRST*?
BACK TO *CHACHIN*. AND THEN *ARAFEL* AND...
THE *WORLD*, IF NEED BE. WE WIN THIS BATTLE, OR THE WORLD *DIES*.

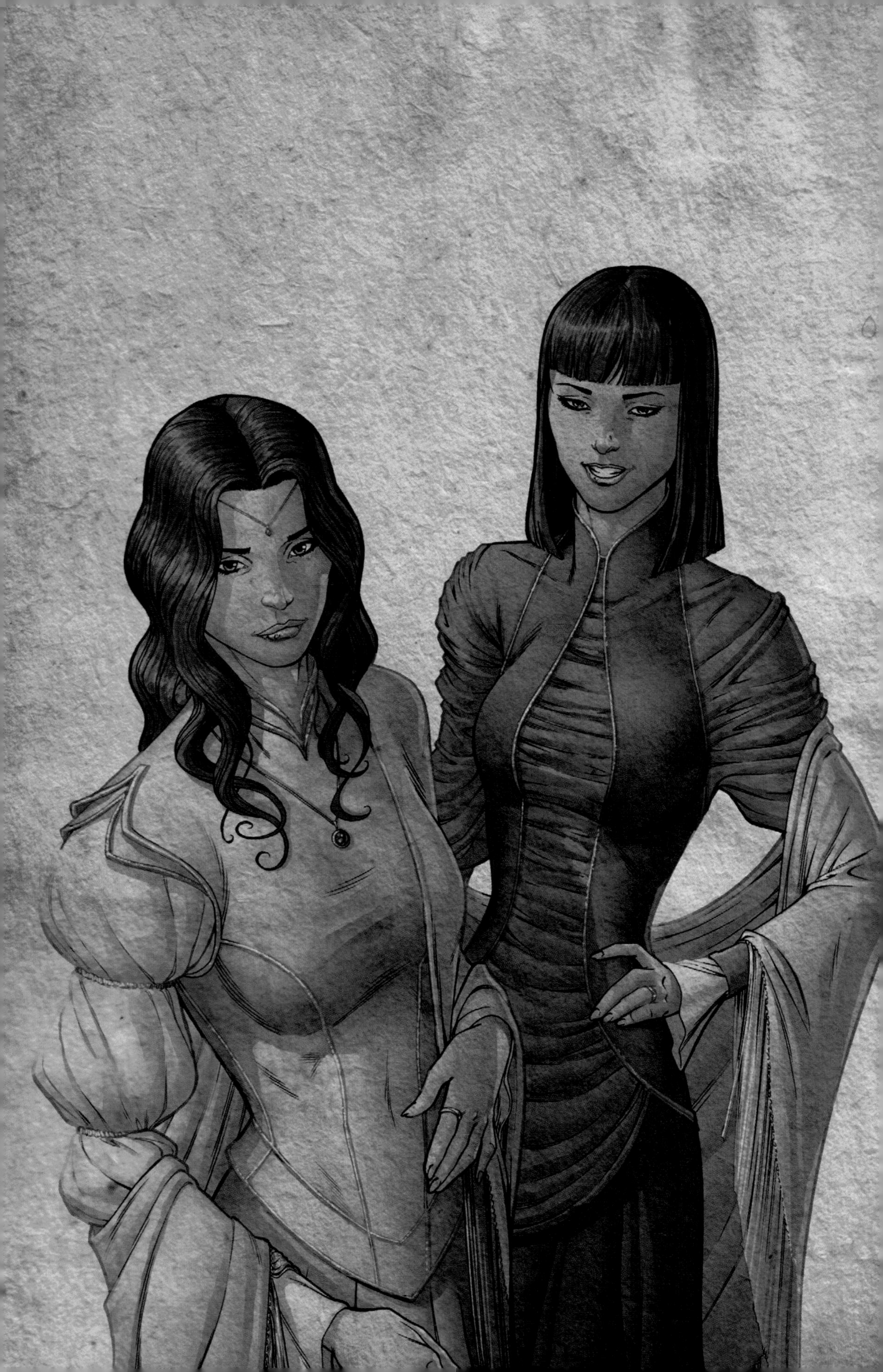

bonus material

Robert Jordan was very much
involved in the development of
New Spring: The Graphic Novel.

On the following pages,
you will read emails that include his detailed
instructions to the production team and the
artists who created this book.

Taking the time to explain the things
that lived within his mind, Robert Jordan
helped guide the artists to a true
representation of the worlds he
had created.

From: Robert Jordan
To: Les Dabel
Sent: Wednesday, March 24, 2004 2:55 PM
Subject: Re: Fw: New Spring Script

Dear Les,

I decided to look beyond the first few pages and found that this is indeed a new script. I'm sending you a copy of it with my comments. Chuck took my comments to heart in many places and occasionally bettered them, but in others, which are very important, he seemed to ignore them altogether. There are mentions of Aiel riding horses, wearing armor, carrying pikes, all of these things that the Aiel don't do. And he still has Moiraine, Siuan, Tamra and Gitara wearing robes instead of dresses. I hope he will take to heart the comments I have put into the script.

Take care, Les. All my best,
Jim

From: Robert Jordan
To: Les Dabel
Sent: Thursday, March 25, 2004 12:12 PM
Subject: Re: Fw: New Spring

Dear Les,

Very good! Please tell Chuck that he did an excellent job. There is only one point that I need to raise. Tamra and Gitara would not be wearing robes. The descriptions of their dresses and jewelry can be found in the book. I appended a note to that effect in the note on the relevant panel, and I'm sending you this version back. Once that change is made, I'm good to go with this script.

Thanks. All my best,
Jim

From: Robert Jordan
To: Les Dabel
Sent: Friday, March 26, 2004 11:57 AM
Subject: Re: Final Corrections

Dear Les,

Very good! I added a note, for the Trollocs at the end, and corrected a few typos -- he where it said eh, changing would to what in one place where it was plain that what was needed and would made no sense, adding or removing the occasional s to a word, such as horses for horse, where appropriate -- but that was all minor stuff. Go with it.

As for the ageless look, I have always imagined it as being a difficulty in setting an age to the woman. You glance at her the first time and think she's 40, but the next instant, you think she can't be more than 20, and you just can't settle on where she belongs in age bracket. If you try the idea about combining the two faces, I suggest using 20 and 40, not 50. But do you then end up with a face that simply looks 30? I wish I could give you more guidance or a good suggestion. It's a lot easier when I only have to envisage the image in my head.

Take care, Les. All my best,
Jim

From: Robert Jordan
To: Les Dabel
Sent: Wednesday, March 31, 2004 3:03 PM
Subject: Re: Characters

Dear Les,

I'll get onto the additional characters ASAP.

Here are my comments on the new images.

The Aiel is very good except for the boots, which still need to look more like Apache moccasins. That is how they are described in the main sequence books, a soft, laced boots. The coat is much better. As a note, remember that the Aiel average about 6'2" for a man, about the same as the Masai. There are plenty of them as tall as Lan and Bukama, and a few taller. An Aiel man who is 5'10" tall would be considered short by himself and by other Aiel.

The eagle-beak Trolloc is very good. It was a small thing, but the devil is in the details, and Trollocs just don't get ornamentation on their weapons. Plain -- so to speak, despite all the hooks etc -- functional, and not a lot of effort into making them look good. They aren't exactly crude -- crudely made weapons just don't usually function as well as well-made ones -- but they are never fancy.

Cadsuane. This is not so good. She looks too old and too thin, almost gaunt. Her dress is way too frilly for Cadsuane, and it shows way too much cleavage. Her garments are silk, but cut simply. When she has lace, it's just a touch, perhaps at the neck and cuffs, but she more likely doesn't have any lace at all. She's a woman who does a lot of traveling, and she wants clothes that are easy to care for and can be tended by a poorly trained maid at some country inn. The cross-lacing is off. Dresses in this world almost always button up the back. And Cadsuane is more likely to have a high neckline than not. She makes no efforts to appear in the highest or latest fashion, nor does she try to impress other women with her clothes or jewelry, or to attract men; she's too busy for such foolishness, as she sees it. She is quite impressive enough being who she is, thank you very much. The hair ornaments also appear to be attached to one another, which they aren't. Each of the ten ornaments hangs from its own individual hairpin. The bun should be right on top of her head, not toward the back.

As a note on her character, Cadsuane was born in the city-state of Far Madding, which is an out-and-out matriarchy. Far Madding has no hereditary nobility, but its politicians and wealthy merchants are all women. There are men who are craftsmen, but a wealthy man in Far Madding is one whose wife or mother gives him an over-generous allowance. The only men allowed to carry weapons of the usual sort are the Wall Guard, and then only when on duty. The Street Guard is limited to truncheons, sword-breakers and catchpoles. Men visiting from other places must either leave their weapons at checkpoints coming into the city or have them peace-bonded, with severe punishments for being found with the wires of the peace-bond broken. Very few of the city's men seem to be unhappy with the way things are. Far Madding is a prosperous trade center. The usual form of address by a woman to man whose name she doesn't know, or sometimes to one whose name she does, is "boy." None of this has any bearing on NEW SPRING, but it gives some insight into Cadsuane, because the city shaped her early years. Quite aside from being the most powerful Aes Sedai living at the time of NEW SPRING, Cadsuane is a formidable woman.

Gitara Moroso. I like this very much, though the dress would not be off-the-shoulder. That strapless look isn't used in this world. Most Aes Sedai wouldn't show that much bosom, but Gitara would. And I like the face, too. Very good!

Moiraine. The dress is excellent, though the sleeves are a bit too wide, I think -- remember, Accepted's dresses are described as "simply cut" -- but the face seems to have shifted again. I've attached the faces that I approved for Moiraine and Siuan. Also, she wouldn't have her hair in a bun. It would be worn loose. Her left hand also seems way too big; it's nearly half the width of her waist.

Ryne. This is very good except that his expression here seems on the sour side. That would be okay at the end, when he is unmasked as a Darkfriend, but the continuous view of Ryne until then is that he is charming and personable. He's much more likely to be smiling, especially if there is a pretty woman around. As a note, the dagger he is holding is too elaborate in the blade shape. I know there are a lot of fancy blade shapes out there today -- Gil Hibben has much to answer for -- but knives and daggers that are, or were historically, used by actual people had practical reasons for their blade shapes, even the yatagan and the falcata.

Tamra. Overall she looks very good. The only things I don't like are the off-the-shoulder dress, too much cleavage showing for her -- her dresses would have high necklines, much like what you show on the Accepted's dress on the Moiraine image, or at least a neckline that showed no cleavage -- and her hands both look much too large. The left hand is also oddly shaped.

Bukama. Yes. I like this one much better. Whatever Andrea did to the chin works just fine. And I like the armor. I hope this helps.

Take care, Les. All my best,
Jim

From: Robert Jordan
To: Les Dabel, Ernst Dabel
Sent: Tuesday, September 28, 2004 9:53 AM
Subject: SCRIPT #2

Dear Les and Ernst,

Here is Script #2 with my comments added in. There aren't many, this time, and they all have to do with dialogue. Some of that is too stilted, now, especially for Siuan. Moiraine speaks without nay contractions, but Siuan is much more casual in her speech. And there is at least one place where someone says something that isn't needed, and in Bannerman Steler's case, is actually wrong.

Sorry to have been so long with this.

Mike Miller has shown me his artwork for the spread showing all of Tar Valon, and I must say that it is beautiful. I'm talking to him about getting my hands on it after you guys are done with it.

Take care, guys. All my best,
Jim

From: Robert Jordan
To: Les Dabel
Sent: Thursday, February 03, 2005 12:09 PM
Subject: Re: Update

Dear Les,

Things are going pretty well for me. I'm hard at work on Knife of Dreams, closing in on the finish. It will be good to get regular updates again. It would be good to get together during Dragon-Con, but as yet, I don't know what they will be having me do or when, so I can't make any commitments. Once I find out my schedule, things will shake out.

Take care, Les. Good to hear from you again.
All my best, Jim

From: Robert Jordan
To: Les Dabel, Ernst Dabel
Sent: Thursday, April 28, 2005 12:52 PM
Subject: NUMERALS

I'm sending this to both of you to make sure it gets through to one of you. Here are the numerals I came up with. I think they fit well with Elisa's alphabet. I am considering that maybe the zero should be made a mirror image so it doesn't resemble a d so much. What do you think?

Jim

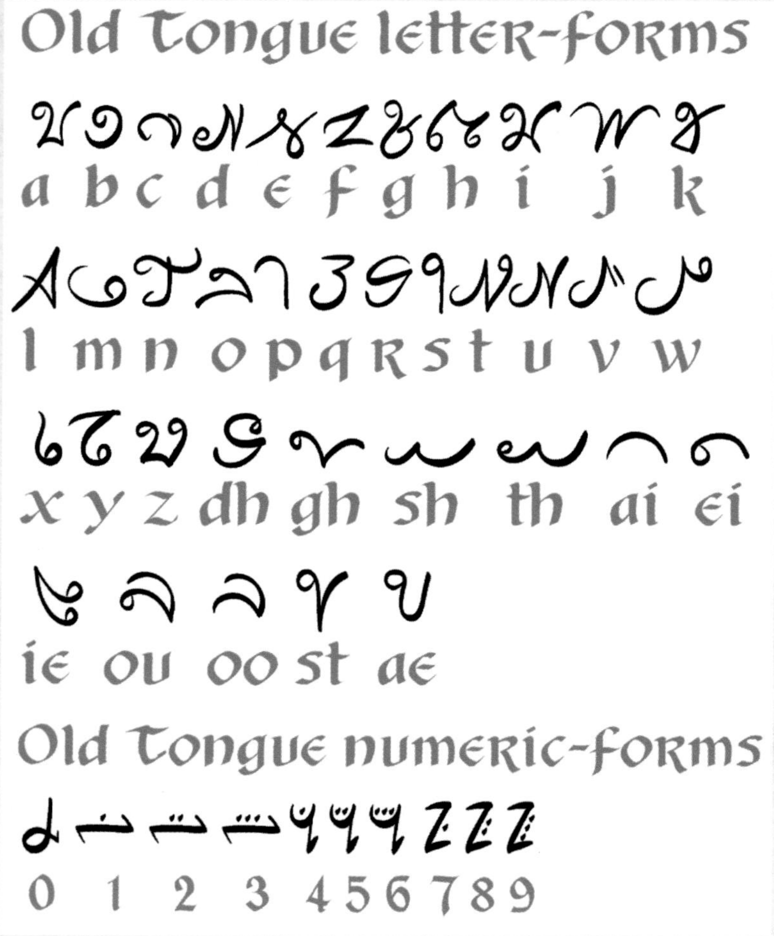
Old Tongue letter-forms
a b c d e f g h i j k
l m n o p q r s t u v w
x y z dh gh sh th ai ei
ie ou oo st ae
Old Tongue numeric-forms
0 1 2 3 4 5 6 7 8 9

From: Robert Jordan
To: Les Dabel, Ernst Dabel
Sent: Wednesday, November 16, 2005 5:16 PM
Subject: Re: Seruko and Canluum Guard revised sketches/ Page layouts 4, 5, 6

The layouts look good, and I look forward to seeing the inks. I do have some corrections for the script, though.

A correction for the wording on page 7, panel 1. It should read, "Lan floated in the ko'di, one with his sword." And in panel 2, it should read, "Lan danced the forms; time flowed like cool honey." Also, on page 12, panel 1, Merean should be saying, "She's undisciplined, Larelle, and too old, I'd say."

Jim

From: Robert Jordan
To: Ernst Dabel
Sent: Wednesday, November 16, 2005 5:35 PM
Subject: Re: layouts 14 - 18

Dear Ernst,

I agree with most of the Consultants' suggestions. I know these are layouts and thus rough, but in
the finals, the women really need to be wearing dresses. Even in the first image, they wouldn't be
wandering about in just their shifts, especially since they have come all the way from their rooms
in the Blue Ajah quarter down to the Accepted's Quarters. Both would be wearing something
fairly plain, in wool most likely, though Moiraine may have silk. Each has a white ribbon of
mourning tied to her hair on either side of her face like forelocks, while Moiraine also has long,
lace-edged kerchiefs tied around her upper arms so that the ends dangle to her wrists.

Page 15, panel 2 and panel 4. Here Tamra is shown in a coffin. She would be wrapped in a shroud
and laid atop a bier of wood. No coffin. A correction for the script. The panel 3 caption should
read: "According to Tamra's wishes, her body was to be consumed by fire and her ashes scattered
across the grounds of the Tower by the sisters." Fire should not be capped here.

Regarding Sierin Vayu on pages 16 and 17, please heed to the Consultants' comments. She is as
they describe, not as drawn.

Page 18, panel 4. You can shift Moiraine's ring to another finger, but in fact, an Aes Sedai can wear
her ring on any finger she chooses or not at all.

Take care, Ernst. All my best,
Jim

From: Robert Jordan
To: Ernst Dabel
Sent: Monday, November 28, 2005 4:54 PM
Subject: Re: NS6 Pg 2 & Pg 1

Dear Ernst,

Page 1 looks terrific, but while Seroku is properly shown with two swords on his back there, on
page 2 he is shown with only one sword on his back. The Thematic Consultants' comments are, as
always, good.

Jim

From: Robert Jordan
To: Ernst Dabel
Sent: Monday, November 28, 2005 4:59 PM
Subject: Re: Kandori women & Kondori men

Dear Ernst,

Regarding the women, there are all right, but remember that the baggy trousers are garb of country
women, not city women, who would wear dresses. For that matter, some country women will.
Also, some of these women should have a short coat rather than a shawl.

The Kandori men are all right by and large, but the peasant looks too Medieval. Tell him to think more 1690-1700 AD.

By the way, Racelle looks just fine.

All my best,
Jim

From: Robert Jordan
To: Ernst Dabel
Sent: Monday, November 28, 2005 5:11 PM
Subject: Re: Thematic Consultants

Dear Ernst,

The image of Eadyth is spectacular, although, as noted elsewhere, she must have a Great Serpent ring. As for pages 15, 17 and 18, I haven't seen those, yet.

I have seen pages 12, 13, 14 &16.

On page 12, Siuan seems to have a Great Serpent ring on her left hand in panel 2, but not in panel 4.

On page 13, Moiraine doesn't seem to be wearing a Great Serpent ring.

For the others, they are fine.

All my best,
Jim

From: Robert Jordan
To: Ernst Dabel
Sent: Tuesday, November 29, 2005 12:38 PM
Subject: Re: Thematic Consultants -- pg 14, 15, 16, 17 & 18

Okay, Ernst, here are my comments on 15, 17 & 18, plus some additional comments on 14 & 16.

Pg 14, panel five: we should be able to see the vines and leaves on Siuan and Moiraine's shawls.

Pg 15, panels 2 & 3: the sisters should all have white ribbons in their hair as a sign of mourning. These are long ribbons fastened to the temples so that they dangle on either side of the face. Moiraine also should have a long white lace scarf tied around each upper arm, dangling so that if her arms were at her sides, the ends of the scarves would reach her wrists.

Pg 15, panel 3. Moiraine's dress is wrong here. For one thing, it shows folds where it should fit quite snugly. For another, it displays cleavage where it should have a high neck. The titillation factor for this dress comes entirely from the embroidery, which is done so as to emphasize the body's curves.

Pg 16, panel 1. Sierin needs a seven-striped stole, and also a Great Serpent ring on her right hand.

Pg 16, panel 3. Sierin needs the Amyrlin's stole here, too.

Pg 16, panel 4. The woman doing the birching should have her hair in "long, beaded braids" that flail about as she works the birch. This woman's hair is gathered atop her head.

Pg 17, panels 2 & 3. Sierin needs a Great Serpent ring (right hand) and the Amyrlin's stole. Remember that Sierin's stole is only half as wide as Duhara's. (Duhara being the woman seated behind her. Her stole, remember, is red.)

Pg 17, panel 4. Moiraine's shawl needs the vines and leaves. Part of Sierin's stole would be visible here, too.

Pg 18, panel 3. Moiraine is galloping as though being pursued here, but in fact she is supposed to be riding away very quietly so as to attract no attention.

pg 18, panel 5. The banker looks too tall, as if she would be taller than Moiraine if she stood. Remember, she is markedly shorter than Moiraine.

All my best,
Jim

From: Robert Jordan
To: Ernst Dabel
Sent: Tuesday, November 29, 2005 12:47 PM
Subject: Re: Swordsmen

First off, Ernst, let's go over the five (out of six) who were actually described.

1) "A lean heron of a fellow."

2) a "fat man."

3) a "ginger-haired young splinter."

4) a "bald man."

5) a "fork-bearded fellow with shoulders like a blacksmith's." He wore a "too-fine coat," i.e. one clearly above his station.

None of the six men is bare-chested. The are described as "six ordinary men with swords at their belts, like any man on any street in the city."

These guys look like extras from a Conan the Barbarian movie. Remember, Ernst, for these guys AND for the Kandori men, their clothing should reflect about 1690-1700 but with Japanese influences. They would not be carrying multiple swords, but rather one each.

Let's see what he can come up with on another try.

All my best,
Jim

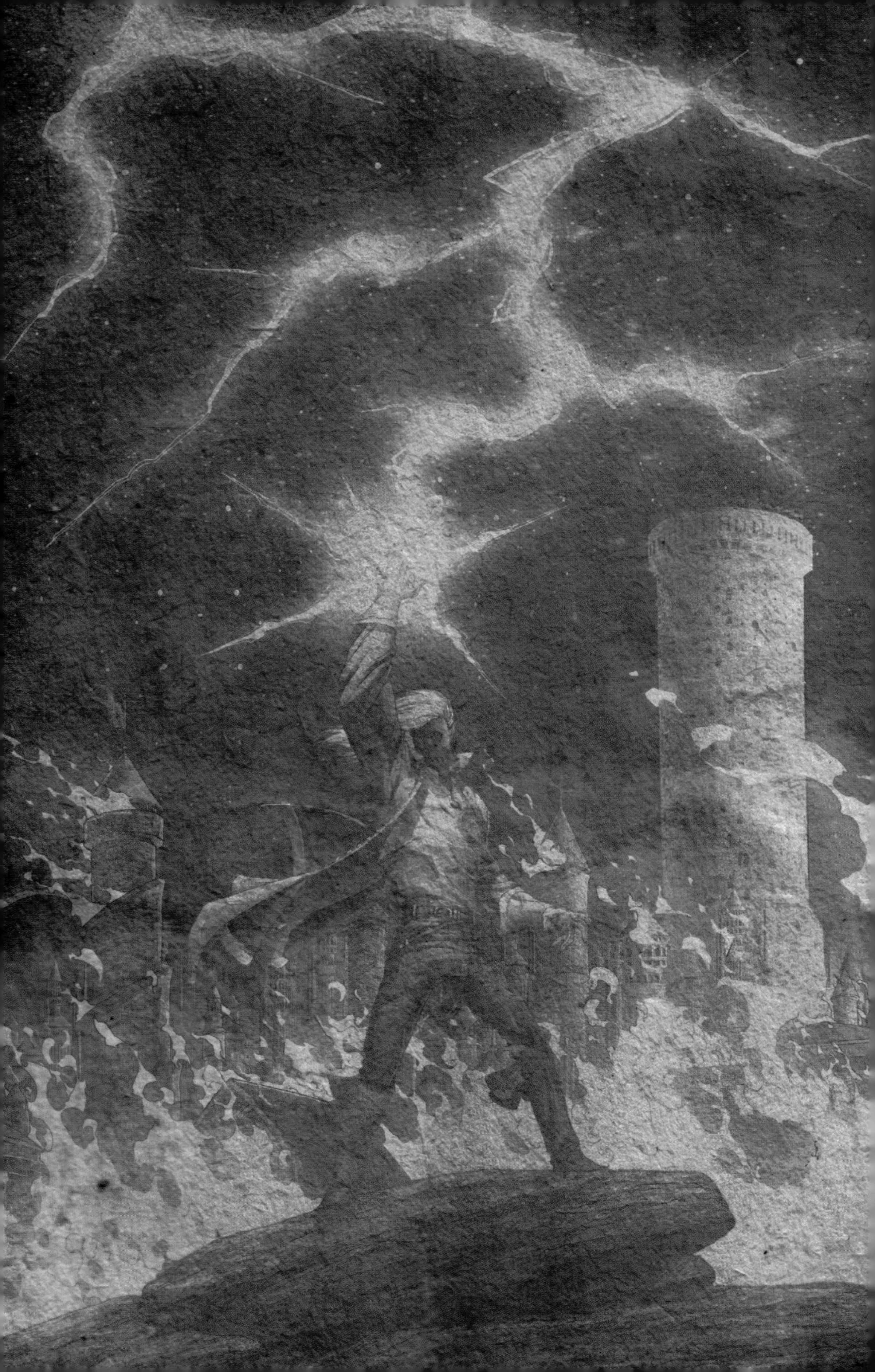

illustrated glossary

Accepted Dress

Novices in the White Tower wear all white, even their shoes and hair ribbons. When they are raised to Accepted their dresses are altered with bands of color at the hem and cuff. These bands of color represent the seven Ajahs of the White Tower. In order from top to bottom, Blue, Green, Yellow, Red, White, Gray and Brown.

Aeldra Najaf: AIL-drah nah-JAHF

An Aes Sedai of the Blue Ajah and Keeper of the Chronicles for Tamra Ospenya following the death of Gitara Moroso. She has the coppery skin of Arad Doman. She wears her white hair cut short.

Aes Sedai: EYEZ seh-DEYE

Channelers of the One Power. Both men and women in the Age of Legends, since the Breaking of the World all Aes Sedai are female. The Aes Sedai of the White Tower are organized in seven Ajahs with differing missions and goals. The Ajahs are Blue, Green, Yellow, Red, White, Gray and Brown.

Aes Sedai Shawl

When an Accepted passes the final test for Aes Sedai, she is awarded a shawl. The Aes Sedai shawl is embroidered with vines, leaves or flowers: every shawl is different. In the center of the back is a large teardrop, the Flame of Tar Valon. Each shawl has a long fringe in the color of the wearer's Ajah.

Aiel: eye-EEL

The people who inhabit the Aiel Waste, the vast desert east of the great mountain range, the Spine of the World. They are a tall people and fair-skinned (though sun darkened) with light eyes and hair. They are widely regarded as barbarians and savages by westerners and, indeed, they are fierce warriors. But they actually have a sophisticated culture and complex system of honor and obligation, *ji'e'toh*. They are skilled fighters with weapons or with bare hands but they will not touch a sword. They veil their faces in battle, which they call the Dance. After three thousand years of isolation, three years ago they invaded the lands of the west. Their true purpose is known only to a few.

al'Lan Mandragoran: AHL'LAN man-dra-GOR-an

A commander of the Grand Coalition. He is very tall, with broad shoulders and shoulder-length hair held by a Malkieri leather headband or *hadori*. His face is hard and angular and he has piercing blue eyes. Lan was the son of the King and Queen of Malkier. When he was still an infant, Trollocs and Myrddraal from the Blight overran the land and destroyed it. All of his family died but twenty of the King's Bodyguards carried Lan to safety in nearby Shienar, where he was raised in Malkieri tradition. Lan denies his birthright, refusing to use the royal al' with his name and even refusing to lead Malkieri troops in battle. When he came of age he began a one-man war with the Blight to avenge the destruction of his homeland. Three years ago he honored a debt and became a commander in the Grand Coalition in the Aiel War, but afterwards he intends to return to the Blight to fight to his death. The Aiel, knowing his history and respecting his skill in battle, call him "Aan'allein" or one man who is a nation.

Alindaer: AL-ihn-dayr

Surrounding Tar Valon there are six large villages at the ends of
the great bridges. Clockwise from the south these villages are
Alindaer, Darein, Jualdhe, Luagde, Daghain and Osenrein. While
Tar Valon has never been conquered, the same does not hold true
for the villages, which have been sacked and burned many times
over the centuries, most recently during the Aiel War.
Despite repeated attacks, the villages are always rebuilt and
during peacetime, they thrive.

Anaiya: ah-NEYE-yuh

An Aes Sedai of the Blue Ajah. She looks like a farmer's wife
but she has a wonderful smile. She is relatively strong in the
One Power. She has unfortunate taste in laces and frills.

Bittern

A stringed instrument similar to a sitar.

Blue Ajah

The Blue Ajah of the Aes Sedai is dedicated to noble causes and justice. The Blue Ajah is the second smallest Ajah but has the largest network of eyes-and-ears, informants and information gatherers.

The Breaking of the World

The War of the Shadow, where the forces of the Light battled the Dark One and his minions, ended when the hold in his prison was sealed. The true devastation began then, for the back blast from the sealing tainted saidin and drove all male Aes Sedai insane. These men of good heart became random destroyers. For two hundred years they ravaged the world until the last male channeler died. The face of the world was changed. All that remained of the wonders of the Age of Legends were memories and scattered artifacts.

Brown Ajah

The Brown Ajah of the Aes Sedai forsakes the mundane world and dedicates itself to seeking knowledge. Their dress and style tends to be plain. Sisters of the Brown Ajah are often known for being lost in their own thoughts, unaware of events around them.

Bukama Marenellin: boo-KAH-mah

A Malkieri soldier sworn to Lan. He is bluff and broad, almost as tall as Lan. His gray hair is shoulder length and he has blue eyes. Bukama is the last survivor of the twenty King's Bodyguards who carried infant Lan to safety when the Blight overran Malkier. He is a dour man who always sees the dark side of life. He is fiercely loyal to Lan and to Malkieri traditions. The latter often causes him trouble as many Malkieri expatriates have adopted the ways of their new homes.

Cairhien

One of the western lands, and also the name of the capital city. It lies north of Tear and Andor and south of Tar Valon. The sign of Cairhien is the Rising Sun on a field of sky blue. Cairhienin tend to be short in stature with dark hair and eyes and pale skin. They are known for their manipulation and political intrigue, *Daes Dae'mar* or the Game of Houses.

Caniedrin: cah-NIE-drihn

A Kandori soldier and a member of Lan's company in the Aiel War. Though young, he is a skilled archer. He is usually happy, especially when he is killing.

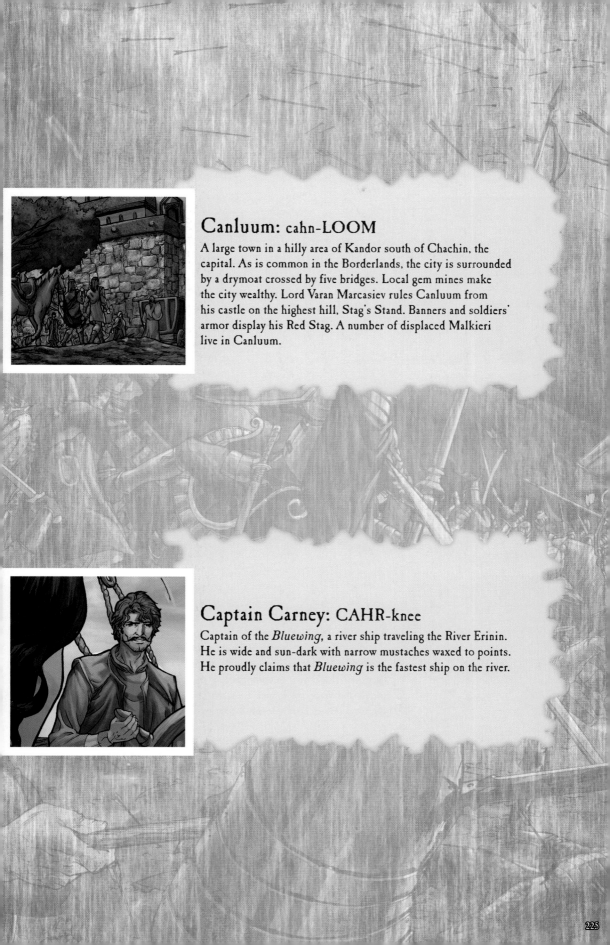

Canluum: cahn-LOOM

A large town in a hilly area of Kandor south of Chachin, the capital. As is common in the Borderlands, the city is surrounded by a drymoat crossed by five bridges. Local gem mines make the city wealthy. Lord Varan Marcasiev rules Canluum from his castle on the highest hill, Stag's Stand. Banners and soldiers' armor display his Red Stag. A number of displaced Malkieri live in Canluum.

Captain Carney: CAHR-knee

Captain of the *Bluewing*, a river ship traveling the River Erinin. He is wide and sun-dark with narrow mustaches waxed to points. He proudly claims that *Bluewing* is the fastest ship on the river.

Cetalia Delarme: seh-TAHL-ee-ah deh-LAHR-may

An Aes Sedai of the Blue Ajah and head of the Blue Ajah eyes-and-ears organization. Originally from Tarabon, she is tall and square-faced. Moiraine and Siuan will eventually be stronger than Cetalia in the One Power, but for now she is the stronger and so requires deference.

Channeling the One Power

The ability to tap into the True Source and wield the One Power. The One Power is, in reality, Five Powers, Air, Earth, Fire, Water and Spirit. A channeler can grasp threads of these Powers and weave them individually or in combination. In general, women are stronger in Air and Water while men are stronger in Earth and Fire. Weaving the One Power, channelers can accomplish wondrous deeds.

Children of the Light

Also known disparagingly as Whitecloaks. The order of the Children of the Light was founded centuries ago to fight the Shadow and defend the Light. Their sigil is a golden sunburst. Their headquarters are in Amador, the capital of Amadicia. Nowadays they are more feared than respected. Their rigid code leads them to identify, question and hang Darkfriends whether or not there are truly any to be found. In particular Whitecloaks consider channeling the One Power to be blasphemy. Aes Sedai are, therefore, all Darkfriends in their eyes. The Children of the Light sent four thousand troops led by Lord Captain Commander Pedron Niall to fight with the Grand Coalition.

Coalition Camps

Many of the soldiers in the Grand Coalition are conscripts, farmers and villagers who were forced to take up weapons to fight alongside professional soldiers. Many of these conscripts brought their families with them instead of leaving them to starve. The women and children live in poorly kept camps that follow the fighting: there are now many such camps in the vicinity of Tar Valon. They spend every day hoping that their loved ones will return to them alive and unharmed.

Dalresin Damodred

A Cairhienin noble and father of Moiraine Damodred. He died while Moiraine was at the White Tower. He was a kind and gentle scholar, and his ambitious Damodred relatives despised him.

The Dark One and the Creator

At the moment of Creation the Creator made the Wheel of Time, the world and all that is in it. The True Source from the Creator turns the Wheel of Time. At the same time, he sealed the Dark One in a prison outside the Pattern of the world. The Creator takes no active role in the turning of the Wheel, but the Dark One constantly strives to free himself from his prison so that he may touch the world and remake it in his own image.

Death's-Head Spider

A poisonous spider from the Aiel Waste. The gray marking on its back resembles a human skull. One bite from a death's-head spider can sicken a strong man and two can kill.

The Dragon Reborn

In the Age of Legends Lews Therin Telamon, the leader of the
Aes Sedai, was known as the Dragon. Three thousand years later
mankind remembers that the Dragon sealed the hole in the
Dark One's prison, ending the War of the Shadow, but subsequently
he and the other male Aes Sedai destroyed the world in their madness.
For three thousand years mankind has lived in fear, for prophecy
says that the seals will weaken and the Dark One will touch the
world again. The Dragon will be reborn to once more save the world.
And to break it.

Dragonmount

A gigantic mountain near the River Erinin. After slaying all whom
he loved, Lews Therin Telamon was given a moment of sanity. In
his grief he destroyed himself with a great blast of the One Power.
This blast raised a huge volcanic mountain many miles high. It also
created a large island in a nearby river. Today this mountain is known
as Dragonmount and the island is the city of Tar Valon.

Eadyth: ee-DITH

An Aes Sedai and a Sitter for the Blue Ajah. She is also First Selector, the leader of the Blue Ajah, though this is strictly confidential within the Ajah. She is stout and round-faced with waist-length white hair.

Elaida do Avriny a'Roihan

An Aes Sedai of the Red Ajah recently raised to the shawl. She will do anything in her power to see Moiraine and Siuan succeed as Aes Sedai even though she despises them.

Elyas Machera: ee-LY-ahs mah-CHEER-ah

A Warder to Rina Hafden.

Feast of Lights

The Feast of Lights is a two-day celebration of the winter solstice, starting on the last and shortest day of the year and lasting through the first day of the new year. Every window in the White Tower is lit, creating a glorious image. In Cairhien, the Feast of Lights is a party of wild abandon and expatriate Cairhienin everywhere hold lavish parties. In many localities the second day of the Feast of Lights is called First Day and is considered a time for charitable giving.

Funeral of Tamra Ospenya

The funeral of an Aes Sedai is a solemn occasion. Her body is sewn into a simple shroud the color of her Ajah and she is laid on a bier. As a sign of mourning, the Aes Sedai wear white ribbons tied in their hair and to their arms, except for sisters of the White Ajah, who wear black ribbons.

Gitara Moroso: gih-TAH-rah moh-ROH-soh

An Aes Sedai of the Blue Ajah and Keeper of the Chronicles to Tamra Ospenya. She is tall, voluptuous and beautiful, with snow-white hair. She accentuates her looks with flamboyant dress and jewelry. She is rumored to be over three hundred years old. Gitara served as counselor to Queen Mordrellen of Andor until she was called back to the White Tower to serve as Keeper of the Chronicles. She is one of the few Aes Sedai in recent history to have the Foretelling—at unpredictable times powerful visions of the future strike her.

Grand Coalition

In response to the invasion of the Aiel, many nations of the west pledged troops to fight in the war. These pledges varied from many thousands from Shienar and Andor to a few thousand from Murandy and Altara. This army is known as the Grand Coalition or Great Coalition. Though they numbered in excess of a hundred thousand the majority of the troops were poorly trained conscripts, so they were not particularly effective as a fighting force. Command of the Coalition rotates among the commanders of the individual forces.

Great Oval Ring Ter'angreal: tear-ANH-gree-all

In the lowest level of the White Tower is a chamber containing a great oval ring a pace wide and over a span tall. It is a *ter'angreal*, an object of the One Power made in the Age of Legends. When a woman who can channel the One Power passes through the ring, she enters a place of alternate reality. Other channelers around the ring control the reality and can create a broad range of environments. The Aes Sedai use this device in the test for the shawl, creating dangerous and distracting situations for the candidate while she performs difficult weaves.

Great Serpent Ring

All Accepted and Aes Sedai wear a gold Great Serpent ring.
The ring, in the form of a snake eating its own tail, symbolizes the
eternity of the Wheel of Time. Accepted are required to wear the ring
on the third finger of the left hand. Aes Sedai may wear the ring on
any finger or not at all if they so choose.

Green Ajah

Also known as the Battle Ajah. The Green Ajah holds itself in
readiness to fight the Shadow at Tarmon Gai'don, the Last Battle.
As such, the Green is the only Ajah whose sisters may bond more
than one Warder.

Ilain Dormaile: ee-LAIN dohr-MILE

A banker in Tar Valon. She is slim and graying, even shorter than Moiraine. She is from Cairhien and her family has done business with House Damodred for many years.

Jarna Malari: JAHR-nah MAL-ah-ree

An Aes Sedai and Sitter of the Hall for the Gray Ajah.

Karile: Kah-REEL
A Warder to Kerene Nagashi.

Katerine Alruddin: KAH-ter-een ahl-RUD-dihn
An Accepted of the White Tower. She has a sharp face and a sharp tongue.

King Laman Damodred: LAH-man DAH-moh-drehd
King of Cairhien and uncle to Moiraine Damodred. He cares more for his personal power than for the welfare of his people. His death coincides with the cessation of aggression from the Aiel.

Language

The peoples of the western lands speak and write a common language. This is a holdover from the Age of Legends, when there was a true global society. The Old Tongue, the language of the Age of Legends, degraded and changed during the Breaking so that now only scholars can understand and speak it. Ogier have their own language, though they all speak and read the human language fluently. Trollocs and Myrddraal also have their own language.

Leane Sharif: lee-AHN shah-REEF

An Aes Sedai of the Blue Ajah, recently raised to the shawl. She is tall and willowy with the coppery skin of Arad Doman. While she was still Accepted she was close friends with Siuan and Moiraine. Though Domani women are trained in charm and seduction she has an abrupt, matter-of-fact manner.

Merean Redhill: MEH-ree-an red-hill

An Aes Sedai of the Blue Ajah and Mistress of Novices at the White Tower. She is kind and motherly but she is a strict disciplinarian.

Moiraine Damodred: mwah-RAIN DAHM-oh-drehd

An Accepted of the White Tower. She has large, dark eyes, pale skin and dark hair hanging in ringlets. She is slim and quite short, barely over five feet tall. Lady Moiraine of House Damodred is a Cairhienin noble of high rank and niece to King Laman of Cairhien. She was raised in the Sun Palace, the royal palace in the city of Cairhien, where she learned political intrigue known as *Daes Dae'mar*, the Game of Houses. She began to channel the One Power at an early age and went to the White Tower for training when she was sixteen. She and Siuan are exceptionally strong and talented. They were raised from novice to Accepted after only three years and were ready for the test for the Aes Sedai in only three more.

Murandy: MEW-ran-dee

A nation of the western lands. It lies south of Andor and north of Illian and Altara. The sigil of Murandy is the Red Bull. While it is nominally a nation, the nobles hold only loose fealty to the king in the capital of Lugard. Some three to four thousand Murandian soldiers are fighting in the Grand Coalition while their wives, women as varied as Lady Meri do Ahlan a'Conlin and Susa Wynn, wait in the camps near Tar Valon.

Myrelle Berengari: my-REHL beh-renh-GAH-ree

An Accepted in the White Tower. Myrelle is from Ebou Dar in southern Altara and is known for her fiery temper.

Northharbor and Southharbor

The north and south ends of the island of Tar Valon are sculpted into great circular harbors. There is a steady stream of river traffic, large ships and small, carrying cargo and passengers to and from the city.

Novice

An initiate of the White Tower. Novices spend much of their time at chores, but they also receive schooling and basic training in the use of the One Power. Novices must wear all white, even their shoes and hair bows. After extensive training, usually five or more years, they are allowed to take the test to be raised to Accepted.

Oath Rod

The Oath Rod is a *ter'angreal* from the Age of Legends. It is used to bind Aes Sedai to the three oaths they swear. When one speaks an oath while holding the Oath Rod and the rod is touched with Spirit, it becomes physically impossible to the swearer to break the oath. Swearing on the Oath Rod also causes a tightening of the skin that gives Aes Sedai an unusual, "ageless" appearance.

Ogier: OH-gehr

A race of sentient beings. They resemble humans but are much larger, averaging nine to ten feet in height. They are quite long-lived and rarely venture out of the *stedding*, their homes, before they are a hundred years old. They devote their lives to learning and to the care and raising of the Great Trees, but their main contact with humans comes through their extraordinary skill as stone masons. Most of Tar Valon was built by Ogier, hence its great variety and beauty.

Rafela Cindal: rah-FELL-ah sin-DAHL

An Aes Sedai of the Blue Ajah, recently raised to the shawl. She is Tairen with dark skin and hair; she is pretty and slim. She is a stickler for rules.

Red Ajah

The Red Ajah of the Aes Sedai is the largest. Sisters of the Red Ajah devote their efforts to locating and gentling men who can channel. The Red Ajah is the only one that does not bond Warders.

Saidin and Saidar: seye-DEEN / seye-DAHR

Gifted men and women can tap into the True Source and channel the One Power. The True Source is divided into two parts, *saidin*, which can be channeled by men, and *saidar*, which can be channeled by women. The techniques of channeling *saidin* and *saidar* are completely different. When Lews Therin Telamon and his Companions sealed the hole in the Dark One's prison, the back blast tainted *saidin* so that all male channelers are now doomed to go insane.

Sedan Chairs

A common mode of transportation for the wealthy in large cities. A sedan chair is a small, enclosed seat with handles. Porters carry the sedan chair smoothly through the crowded streets.

Shadowspawn

Shadowspawn were the creation of the Forsaken Aginor during the War of the Shadow. They include Trollocs, Myrddraal, Draghkar, Darkhounds and many other creatures. Tainted by the Dark One, all Shadowspawn are inherently evil and lust to kill.

Sheriam Bayanar: SHEH-ree-ahm bay-ah-NAHR

An Accepted of the White Tower. She is from Saldaea. She is something of a gossip.

Shienar: shy-NAHR

The easternmost of the Borderlands bordering the Great Blight.
Shienaran lancers are the finest heavy cavalry in the westernlands.
Warriors shave their heads except for a topknot. The banner of
Shienar is a swooping black hawk on a field of three blue and
two white stripes.

Shining Walls

The great walls surrounding the city of Tar Valon and also a term for
the city itself. The walls are constructed of white stone streaked with
silver so they gleam in the sun.

Sierin Vayu: see-EH-rihn VEYE-oo

An Aes Sedai of the Gray Ajah, though she seems to have more affinity for the red. She is raised to the Amyrlin Seat upon the death of Tamra Ospenya. Sierin is very plump, but her round face is stern. She is a no-nonsense authoritarian and strict disciplinarian.

Siuan Sanche: SWAHN SAHN-chay

An Accepted of the White Tower. She is handsome, pretty when she smiles. She is of medium height, a hand taller than Moiraine, with fair skin and blue eyes. She has a delicate mouth and dark glossy hair to her shoulders. The daughter of a poor Tairen fisherman, Siuan led a life of hardship until she began to channel at age sixteen. When this was discovered she was put on a ship to Tar Valon before sunset of the next day. She and Moiraine are exceptionally strong and talented. They were raised from novice to Accepted after only three years and were ready for the Aes Sedai in only three more.

Stepin: STEH-pihn

A Warder to Kerene Nagashi.

Tamra Ospenya: TAHM-rah oh-SPEHN-yah

The Amyrlin Seat of the White Tower. She has long dark hair that is lightly streaked with gray. She has a square, determined face. Tamra has been the Amyrlin Seat, the Leader of the Aes Sedai, for six years. She was raised from the Blue Ajah. Despite her power as Amyrlin Seat she is considered fair, just and often kind.

Tar Valon: TAHR VAH-lon

The first city built after the Breaking of the World. It was built by Ogier to be the new center of power for the Aes Sedai. Three thousand years later Tar Valon remains one of the largest, most prosperous and most cosmopolitan cities in the western lands. The Ogier stonework, fluid, flowing and colorful, makes the city a breathtaking spectacle both near and far. The city sits on an island in the River Erinin, almost in the shadow of the gigantic mountain Dragonmount. Six great bridges span the river, three to each side, and there are large villages at the foot of each. Tar Valon is a natural center of trade with large, circular harbors at either end of the island. The city walls are known as the Shining Walls, built of silver-streaked white stone so they glisten in the sun. Tar Valon is governed by a council of Aes Sedai. The heart of Tar Valon is the White Tower.

Tarna Feir: TAHR-nah feer

An Accepted in the White Tower. Tarna is from northern Altara. She is arrogant and humorless.

Tear: TEER

The most southeasterly country in the western lands. It lies south of Cairhien on the Sea of Storms between Illian and the great mountain range, the Spine of the World. Tairens are average in stature and tend to be dark complexioned, but some are fair-skinned and blue eyed and a few even have light hair. Men wear beards trimmed to a point and oiled. Tear is ruled by the council of High Lords. The High Lords are ruthless rulers and guard their power so jealously that the city of Tear, on the delta of the River Erinin, is the only major population center in the country. The High Lords and many other nobles reside in the greatest fortress in the western lands, the Stone of Tear built by Aes Sedai shortly after the Breaking of the World. Despite its heritage, channeling the One Power is outlawed in Tear. The banner of Tear is three white crescent moons slanting across a field half red, half gold.

Trollocs: TROL-ocks

Trollocs are a form of Shadowspawn, a cross-breed between animals and humans. They appear as enormously large men, eight feet tall and bulky, with animal faces—wolves, eagles, boars, goats and such. Trollocs were created by Aginor as warriors for the Shadow. They are strong, fast and bloodthirsty, so they are fearsome and dangerous. They are also stupid, lazy, cowardly and unreliable, so they make poor soldiers.

Verin Mathwin: VEH-rihn MATH-wihn

An Aes Sedai of the Brown Ajah. She is short and plump with a square face and dark eyes. The gray in her brown hair indicates that she is quite old. Like many sisters of the Brown Ajah she often appears to be lost in her own thoughts, but occasional moments of sharp perception my indicate that there is more to Verin than meets the eye.

Weaves of the One Power

To the channeler, the flows seem to originate in his or her very immediate vicinity, not to emanate from themselves, although to another channeler, those flows do seem to be emanating from the channeler. The latter is the actual case, as the One Power is passing through the channeler, one of the reasons for individual limits on how much of the Power a particular person can handle. A channeler sees the flows as very faintly colored according to which of the Five powers is involved (red = Fire, blue = Water, green = Earth, yellow = Air, white = Spirit). That is how someone can tell that somebody else has channeled Fire and Earth in their vicinity without seeing the flows.

The White Tower

The center of power of the Aes Sedai. It was built by Ogier, aided by Aes Sedai and the One Power, shortly after the Breaking of the World. At a height of six hundred feet it dwarfs the other buildings of Tar Valon and can be seen for miles in any direction. It shines in the sun like polished bone. The "White Tower" is actually a complex of buildings including the Tower itself, the Great Library and many ancillary structures. The extensive basements and subbasements of the Tower hold the most closely guarded secrets of the Aes Sedai. The order's most powerful ceremonies are held on these levels, concealed from any outsiders. At any given time roughly half the Aes Sedai are in residence at the Tower, while the other half are out in the world serving the causes of the seven Ajahs. Accepted and novices are not allowed out of the Tower grounds except under strict supervision.

White Tower Guard

The army of the White Tower in Tar Valon, they bear the Flame of Tar Valon emblazoned on their banners and tabards. Some twelve thousand of the Tower Guard led by Captain Azil Mareed are fighting with the Grand Coalition.

Yellow Ajah

The Yellow Ajah of the Aes Sedai is dedicated to the art of Healing. Sisters of the Yellow Ajah see Healing as the only worthwhile use of the One Power. They tend to be arrogant and flamboyant.

Yuan: you-AHN

An Aes Sedai of the Yellow Ajah. She is slim with gray eyes.

biograp

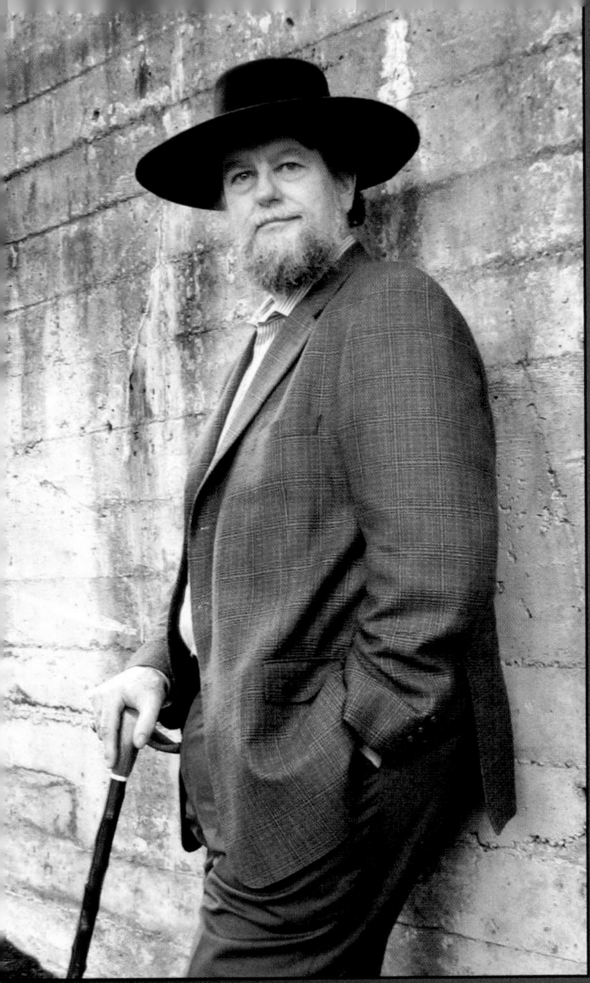
HOTO CREDIT: LIZA GROEN TROMBI/LOCUS

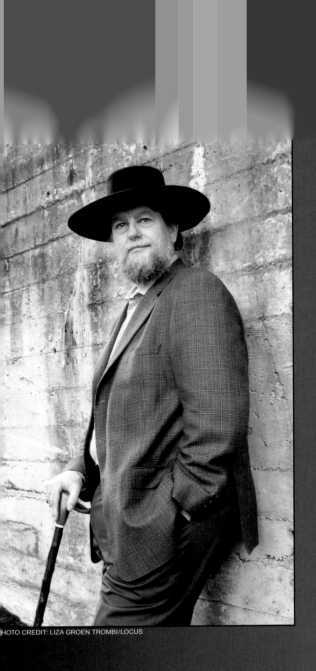

ROBERT JORDAN

Mr. Jordan was born in 1948 in Charleston, South Carolina. He taught himself to read when he was four with the incidental aid of a twelve-years-older brother, and was tackling Mark Twain and Jules Verne by five. He was a graduate of The Citadel, The Military College of South Carolina, with a degree in physics. He served two tours in Vietnam with the U.S. Army; among his decorations are the Distinguished Flying Cross with bronze oak leaf cluster, the Bronze Star with "V" and bronze oak leaf cluster, and two Vietnamese Gallantry Crosses with palm. A history buff, he also wrote dance and theater criticism and enjoyed the outdoor sports of hunting, fishing, and sailing, and the indoor sports of poker, chess, pool, and pipe collecting. He began writing in 1977 and went on to write The Wheel of Time®, one of the most important and bestselling series in the history of fantasy publishing with over 14 million copies sold in North America, and countless more sold abroad. Robert Jordan died on September 16, 2007, after a courageous battle with the rare blood disease amyloidosis.

CHUCK DIXON

Mr. Dixon has worked for every major comic book publisher as a professional comic book writer. His credits include *The Hobbit* graphic novel, *The Punisher, Birds of Prey, Batman, Catwoman, Green Arrow, Green Lantern, Star Wars*, and *Simpson* comics and the Dabels' comic adaptation of *Dean Koontz's Frankenstein*. Chuck currently resides in Florida.

MIKE MILLER

Mr. Miller began his career in comic books at Malibu as an inker in 1992, and moved quickly up to being a penciler at both Marvel and DC comics, working on titles such as *Superman, X-Men*, and many others. In 2004 he was contacted by the Dabel Brothers and joined the company as art director, helping the Dabels develop several titles at the time, including illustrating George R. R. Martin's *The Hedge Knight* and Robert Jordan's *New Spring*. Mike currently lives in California with his family and operates under the studio name of Abacus Comics.

JOE COOPER

Mr. Cooper is a professional artist with more than fifteen years of experience in illustration, storyboards, character development, sequential art, and painting. Joe attended the School of Visual Arts, where he graduated with honors and received a BFA in illustration in 2000. His past clients include DC, Marvel, Image, Simon & Schuster, McCann Erickson, and Powell Skateboards, among others. He currently lives and works in Santa Barbara, California.

HARVEY TOLIBAO

Mr. Tolibao is a professional artist who started out in the industry working on projects such as Top Cow's *Mith*, Marvel's *Unlimited X-Men*, and Dynamite's *Red Sonja*, assisting other artists or handling backgrounds. Harvey has also worked as solo artist on Dark Horse's *Star Wars: Knights of the Old Republic*. He currently lives and works in the Philippines.

TOR®